T0193226

RIDE THE SEA

An Attempt to Placate the Implacable

Samantha Narelle Kirkland

Order this book online at www.trafford.com
or email orders@trafford.com

Most Trafford titles are also available at major online book retailers.

Print information available on the last page.

ISBN: 978-1-4907-7534-0 (sc)
ISBN: 978-1-4907-7533-3 (e)

Trafford rev.   08/28/2019

 www.trafford.com

North America & international
toll-free: 1 888 232 4444 (USA & Canada)
fax: 812 355 4082

DEDICATION

To Judith Barbara Smith
for her many years of laughter, insight, and faithful support

CONTENTS

PREFACE

There have been many books, articles, and several movies detailing the terrors and errors on the night of April 14-15, 1912 when the stunning new passenger liner, *H.M.S. Titanic*, met with disaster on the open waters of the Atlantic Ocean. The discovery of the wreck site in 1987, by Dr. Robert Ballard, led to an entirely new round of speculation regarding the whys and wherefores of the demise of this wondrous achievement by Mankind. The book you hold in your hand, *Ride the Sea*, goes in a different direction, but is inspired by that tragic event.

Human beings believe what they want to believe. Their prejudices and rationales are formed by growing up around adults, attending school, competing with their contemporaries, and undergoing personal experiences. Most important among these are, of course, one's contemporaries. Watching how someone is treated by those you respect or emulate, or simply enjoy being around, solidifies behavior before a person even realizes beliefs are being molded.

The same can be said regarding one's environment. If arrogance guides one's behavior toward others, it will similarly lead a person astray when confronted with the challenges of Nature. A careless attitude can leave a man exposed to wrath from natural forces even if the day is sunny and calm.

In the early 20th Century, making a ship competitive, rather than 100% secure, guided the behavior of their wealthy owners. With the demise of the luxurious, ebullient *Titanic,* the world would never be quite the same again.[1] Controversies surrounding her sinking remain with us even today. The cold, dark ocean depths retain answers to questions which we are not yet wise enough to ask. Can some of these answers be found today amid the cavorting, chilled waves of the Atlantic Ocean?

If you are one of the many devoted students of the *Titanic's* sinking and therefore need answers at once, please consult the Appendix. If my dear reader prefers to plunge directly into the suspenseful drama of *Ride the Sea*, then please turn the page.

---

1 Dr. Robert D. Ballard and Rick Archbold. *The Discovery of the Titanic*. New York: Warner Books, Inc., 1987; p. 195.

CHAPTER ONE

WALLACE MATTHEWS

I was born in June of 1880, but my life began in earnest the day I met Jim Stahl. We served together as junior officers aboard the passenger steamer *Jason*. That was some time ago, around 1910 if I recall.

Working aboard a steamer was a tough way to earn a buck back then, especially if you were assigned to the engine room. It wasn't just the constant, deafening noise that got to you. What really made it a living hell was the fuel. Burning coal was the dominant power source. True, the exhaust stacks were intended to spew out choking smoke, but those funnels were too tall for all the cinders to escape. Thus, working in the engine room meant you would get downright filthy.

The air was thick with coal dust; this meant an explosion was an ever-present threat. You simply took that in stride. For the stokers and trimmers, they'd really have it bad. What got to them was the contrast between beads of sweat running down their chest from the furnace fires, yet simultaneously they'd be shivering from the cold air blowing down on them from the air intakes.

I always seemed to bag assignments routing across the North Atlantic. During the freezing winter runs, I'd try and check up on the engine room crews regularly. I've always been right comfortable around people, so the various captains whom I served under typically assigned me personnel duty. In 1910, I had been assigned as the 6th officer aboard a pleasure vessel, as we referred to passenger steamers back then.

One day, a trimmer got badly fried by a blow-back when he opened the fire grate. Second Officer Jim Stahl was the first person to come down from the Bridge and assist my getting the sailor to the first aid station. We took a few minutes to relax after the crisis and found ourselves sharing personal problems each of us had faced in the past. It wasn't long before we realized that we had a lot in common: we both liked to speak our mind. That started a friendship that remained valued and strong throughout his life, so now is as good a time as any to relate how my real adventure with him began.

* * *

Around Christmas of 1928, the steamer I was serving on ran aground. Once we were back on shore, our company dismissed all us officers. As 2nd officer on that ship, I was fourth in line for command, but blame couldn't be pinned on any single man, so we all got the boot. At that time of year, it was very difficult to find a new position. Even though I had genuine experience to offer, I still couldn't find a posting. Several months later, I had suffered several rebuffs. That is why, after my fourth rejection, my story found me down at Milligan's Restaurant. At the time, Prohibition under the Volstead Act had been in effect for eight years. As a consequence, I am not permitted to reveal the address of said "restaurant" but you can bank on the fact that it was a place of refuge and solace for someone like me.

The beefy barman looked over at my figure slumped across the table in the darkest corner of his place.

"OK, Buddy, it's time you went home to the missus."

"No, no, bring me another whiskey, tall like the last one." I was barely able to raise my head to make a protest, my hair was disheveled, and my bleary eyes were bulging from strain. I stood up to make my point, almost fell over, and then tried to repeat myself. All I was able to do was lean both hands forward, supporting myself against the tabletop. There I remained, steady as a statue, without quite knowing why I was standing.

The owner of the speakeasy came from behind his bottle-lined fortress of pleasures and leaned onto the table himself.

"Look, fella, you've had more than enough. It's not that I'm limiting your drinking. In fact, I want to see you back again tomorrow, and the next night. I'm protecting my investment here. There must be some woman who is aching for your company, yet here you are, denying her the happiness she deserves. Come on, let me find you a cab."

"Naw, I don't wanna go anywhere. Right here is fine with me!" Clearly, I didn't know what I was about.

"Come along, that's a good man. There ya go. We can't have you mooning about the streets in this condition; people would start asking questions."

The barman finally had me up and lurching toward the door; he wasn't about to lose me now that I was underway. "Ben, get out on the street wit' ya and flag down a cabbie, will ya? But be quiet about it!"

My teetering exit must have been anticipated for, even as the tavern's door opened and Ben appeared, a driver leaned from his vehicle and inquired, "Anyone need a ride?"

Together, Ben and the barman unrolled my sodden form across the back seat and said simply, "Take this man home!"

"Well now, right you are, me boys. Whereabouts might that home be?" the cabbie inquired.

I raised my arm and used my index finger to point out straight. "Go along there, my good man," and with that, I was out cold.

Ben and the barman pawed through my pockets. Working together, they soon found my wallet. This revealed my name to be "Wallace Matthews" and my address listed as: 22 Wimpole Street, Providence, Rhode Island. Removing an amount sufficient to cover his services to me, the barman replaced my wallet and urged the cabbie to proceed.

The driver waved as he said, "Thanks, I'll get him there, rest assured. I'll keep my eye out; this same guy will probably be right back here tomorrow!"

That said, the door was closed, the cabbie pressed the accelerator, and soon his car completed the journey and stopped opposite the address shown on my identity card. As a former seaman during the Great War, the driver showed respect for me; indeed, my identification stated I was an officer of the Merchant Marine.

Opening his door and removing the ignition keys, the cabbie went up to the house, climbing its front steps quickly, and rang the chime mounted on the frame. The door opened, revealing warm lamplight from a pleasantly decorated living room, imported floor rug on the vestibule floor, and delicious aromas from a meal being prepared from a nearby room.

A decorous, middle-aged woman with elegant bearing addressed the cabbie.

"Good evening, what may I do for you?" she inquired.

"Ma'am, hello, I'm Alfred from down at the cab company. I believe my fare belongs to you, but he's in no condition to find his way up those steps. If truth be told, he'll need help simply extricating himself, as you can see." The cabbie turned, pointing his finger at a dark, huddled lump immobilized in the back seat.

The pleasant woman turned toward the stairwell. "William, come help get your father up to bed. He must have had another refusal; he's around the bend again!"

There was a loud clumping along the 2nd floor hall and a strong-looking lad of seventeen appeared at the head of the stairs, sighed as he looked the cabbie over, and then trundled down the steps to his mother's side.

"Dear, help this man with your father. Whatever the fare is, give him this as a tip," Mary said as she handed her son some silvery coins.

Then, turning toward the patient cabbie, she said, "Thank you, my good man. I hope my husband was not too much trouble."

"No, ma'am, we made out just fine. We're both men of the sea. Thank you for the fare. Now let's roust him out of that back seat!"

It required all three of them to extract me from the comfortable leather seat, lug me up the entrance stairs, and finally lay me on my back across the red velvet couch in front of the living room fireplace.

"Thank you so much, Alfred. You were a dear to provide such attention. Good night."

As the cabbie descended the steps, he briefly reflected, "Geesh, my business sure lets me see people at their worst!" Then, starting the engine, he put the car in gear and went off into the night, looking for yet another sad sack.

Thereupon, Mary Matthews closed the front door and, setting her hands on her hips, went over to study my prostrate form.

"Ma, he's really put on a bender this time."

"Honey-child, I believe the correct term is 'he's really tied one on!' Take note of what liquor does to you. I hope you limit yourself to wine and never end up like this!"

"Shall I get some water?" William looked expectant.

"No, dear, I don't think that's a good idea. Wally doesn't look like he'd be able to swallow it."

"Ma! I wasn't going to give it to him to drink. I wanted to splash it on his face to see if it would bring him around!"

"Oh." Mary hadn't thought of that.

Regaining her composure, she directed: "William, wet a towel and dampen his face with it. Maybe that will be enough."

"Ah, Ma, that's no fun," sighed William, but he trudged out to the kitchen anyway.

Kneeling bedside her husband of nearly 25 years, Mary stroked my forehead while holding one of my hands.

"Oh, my dearest, what happened this time? It has really affected you badly. Tell me, my darling. You're safe at home now; come on, talk to me."

My face must have looked gruesome, being all puffed out from illegal liquor, while my eyes were glassy and bloodshot. Slowly, I rolled my face toward my wife as I opened one lid. Gradually, her gentle smile and concerned expression came into focus, I felt the pressure of her hand in mine. It took a bit for me to comprehend: I was at home!

"Oh-my-gosh, Mary. I'm so sorry. It was just too much. I was in the office of the famous Arthur H. Rostron, asking to crew for him on the *Berengaria,* but he ushered me out without even conducting an interview. He was polite and all, but his rejection was so belittling. I've got more than two decades of solid, obedient service, but this great man would not even listen to my roster of assignments. I'm beaten down, Mary. This is my fourth rejection this month. I can't muster pride in my profession; it's making me lose faith in myself. What can I do?"

"Well, perhaps this will help."

With that being said, my wife took a white envelope from the side table and placed it in my hand. "This arrived today," she affirmed while looking at my face for a reaction.

"Who is this from? It's not an invoice, is it?"

"Come on Wally, you can't be that far gone! Can't you recognize your good friend's handwriting?"

My wife shoved the letter underneath my nose. There it was, in clear, bold script:

James Stahl, Captain
American Transatlantic Company
128 Catamount Street, Providence, Rhode Island

"Mary, you open it. I'm too shaky to be able to see straight."

Stahl was one of my oldest, and indeed closest, friends. Mary's fingers excitedly tore at the flap and summarized the contents to me as I remained prostrate.

"Wallace, this is very exciting! Jim has been given his first command and he's invited you to join him as his Chief Officer. What do you think of that?"

"What's that you say?" My cheeks began to show a rosy glow. "He's got a command and wants me to crew with him, is that right?"

As I sat up, my head cleared and I read the letter through, growing more excited by the minute. American Transatlantic Company was the premier passenger line in New England.

"William, come here, lad, your dad's got an assignment. You're going to have to be the man of the house for a while. His ship, the *Reliance,* is going to Europe transporting both vacationers and cargo. We'll be gone, let me think, I bet we'll be gone for three weeks what with the various ports of call and the cargo deliveries. Can you behave yourself and set a good example in front of your mother for that long, William?"

"Good golly, Dad, you know me," stated my son sheepishly.

"That's right, I do know you! That's why I'm asking for your commitment to honor your mother as well as behave yourself. Is that girl of yours—what's her name, 'Jenny?' Does Jenny know that I rely on you to be the man of the house when I'm away crewing?"

"Golly, Dad, we really don't talk about you much when I'm with her." My son hung his head with embarrassment as he said this.

I immediately understood what my son was implying. This, however, was not the time for any sort of father-son talk about the facts of life, as my friends with older children would have put it. William would simply have to control himself and act like the gentlemen his parents had raised him to be.

"Mary, get me upstairs and into bed. After a good night's sleep, I'll telegraph Jim and tell him I'm coming. When did he say the *Reliance* is sailing? On Thursday? Okay, we've got two days to get everything in order here. You'll have to call your sister and extend my apologies for my not making her dinner party on Saturday. And William, keep your eyes clear and field a lot of fly balls during Friday's game against Merton High. Aren't they last year's league champs?"

"Ah, Dad, you don't have to worry about me on the ball field. I may not hit like Babe Ruth, but I can field as well as that new guy on the Yankees, Joe DiMaggio!"

It was enjoyable to hear my son boast like that, even if we both knew the lad's ideas of grandeur were mostly hot air.

As we wended our way up the stairs and into the bedroom, I looked deeply into Mary's eyes. They were a dark brown. When I'd gaze into them, her eyes had the power to make me feel like a wandering minstrel who has found his way back to happiness.

"Honey, will you be all right if I go?" I probed. "Did you get the doctor's report back yet; does he know why your stomach is painful?"

Her eyes seemed to absorb me, taking me all the way into her soul as she smiled and replied, "It's just a short-term thing, Wally, cramps or something. Doctor Abrams said it should clear up in no time soon."

At this moment of affectionate sharing, Mary Matthews was not about to burden me with the knowledge that her doctor strongly suspected she was developing cancer. Her goal was to simply hang on and be alive to welcome me home when I returned from this sail aboard the *Reliance*. That would have to suffice. Doing so would require all her energies.

CHAPTER TWO

JAMES STAHL'S COMMAND

James Stahl leaned confidently against the rounded, white metal of the Bridge railing as he looked over the starboard side of his new assignment, the *S.S. Reliance*. He had worked toward the status of being captain of a ship for some twenty-four years. While in the employ of the American Transatlantic Company, his tenure had been characterized by an ever present eagerness to learn every facet of running a great ocean liner. As the dock hands and cranes feverishly loaded cargo, he felt great pride as he observed the orderly stacks of tires and bales of cotton that soon would be taking up space in the holds below. Everything he saw appeared to be, as they say, "shipshape."

The *Reliance* was designed by naval architect Scott Terry, a protégé of James when they had both worked as draftsmen for Cummins & Company back in 1905. Nowadays, if you sought solid construction technique, you chose Newport News Shipbuilding & Dry Dock Company in Virginia. To assure her launch in 1927, her financing had been assisted by the U.S. Government to bolster the Atlantic trade between the United States, England, and the coasts of France. She was thus consigned to ply the cold waters off Greenland at the start of a voyage. Icebergs would calve off the Petterman Glacier during the summer months, and then these would float down on the Labrador Current through Baffin Bay and wind up in the shipping lanes during winter.

No matter their size, these ice formations could always be a danger to shipping.

Reliance was not intended to be spectacular or superior in any way. The superlatives and records established by the famous *Mauretania* or *Berengaria* were not for her. Her owners made no boasts about her seaworthiness or about her being the "biggest" something or other. Being 670 feet long by 74 feet at her beam and weighing 30,500 gross register tons (GRT), she was considered simply "average" for ships of her time. Counting the weight of the equipment on board and a full complement of passengers, she would boast a Displacement Tonnage of 38,300.

Because of this, once she was fully loaded, she would require more than a mile in which to come to a complete stop should she encounter a dangerous obstacle in her course.

Perhaps more significant than the foregoing, her depth was 25 feet below the waterline, making her total height over 60 feet. Even a bergy bit submerged below the level of the waves could be an inconvenient hindrance.

To move all this bulk, she had been fitted with twin shafts boasting outward turning four-bladed bronze screws. The hull enclosed four oil-fired furnaces to heat the Scotch-type high pressure boilers. These provided the steam required to power the

General Electric turbo generators. These modern power sources had finally displaced the old workhorse, steam turbines fired by coal, which had been so successfully perfected by Sir Charles Algernon Parsons early in the century. The *Titanic* herself had employed that very same system.

The GE generators in turn powered the electric propulsion motors geared down to 100rpm. This rate had proven to be optimal for ocean liner propeller shafts. There was an additional boiler dedicated to cabin heating. If a passenger remained inside, even a winter crossing could feel most pleasant. Watertight bulkheads could be closed to encapsulate each of these three adjacent rooms in the event of fire or, at worst, flooding.

Black gold had been the fuel of choice for decades, but coal was dirty, heavy, back breaking to load, and subject to spontaneous combustion should moisture get in a storage bin. As a result, shipping had—at almost a single stroke—converted over from coal to the use of fluid fuel once oil supplies became plentiful following the Armistice for the Great War. Unlike coal, strikes in the drilling fields seemed of little importance given the varied sources for supply. Indeed, recognition by producers, even a giant cartel such as Standard Oil, that there was enough to go around for everyone ensured that rig workers and transporters earned a living wage. This approach went a long way to forestalling wildcat strikes in the seemingly prosperous 1920's.

By the time *Reliance* put to sea that chilly April in 1929, fuel oil was decidedly the reliable way to fire her boilers.

The owners wanted an attractive, dependable and—above all—safe vessel. Nothing on her was touted as, nor intended to be, extravagant. Only two objectives were uppermost in the minds of her owners when they designed and built the *Reliance*: to earn her keep, and to do so for a minimum of two decades. Ships during this era seemed to last about that long, give or take a war or two, before expensive major overhauling and fixture replacement might consign a vessel to the scrap yard.

James Stahl had walked into, through, or over every inch of her in the week after being assigned as Captain of the *Reliance*. With some 29 years' experience behind him, including 5 designing ships and over two decades sailing them, he felt confident that he had "been there, done that." He adhered to the standard that a ship's captain should be so qualified that, if asked, he could figuratively hold the ship's operations, as well as everything on board, in the palm of his hand. Should any malfunction or adverse event occur, everyone would look to him for the solution; a good captain must know immediately how to respond.

"Well, what do you think of her?" he asked, turning toward Henry Hoskins, his Chief Engineer for this voyage.

"I've got to say, Captain, she looks tight to me. I've been all over her, fore to aft, and nothing appears amiss. How long has she been afloat, did you say?" Henry looked over at his captain. They both sported a height close to six feet, but Captain Stahl was some ten years older and boasted considerably more girth than did the engineer.

"She was constructed at Newport News and launched during 1927. She was fully fitted out and tested as she steamed up from Virginia, but this is her first trip under my command, so I'm determined to make it a good one! As we get underway, stay below and listen for any unexpected leakage in her hull while you're checking the turbines, will you?"

"Aye, aye, sir!" said Henry, nodding toward his superior as he raised his right arm in salute. When he reached the ladder (stairway), he extended his elbows atop each rail and actually slid downward without touching the steps. In an instant, he had disappeared below.

The Captain turned to the other man who was standing at his shoulder.

"What do you think, Wallace? Glad to be aboard?"

I was leaning over the railing staring into the deep cavern of the forward-most cargo hold. I turned to face Captain Stahl while displaying a broad grin of pleasure on my mouth.

"Jim, I've got to say, I was grateful when I received your invitation to crew with you, but looking her over, being here is better than I had imagined. Nothing appears overdone, there's little leeway for cargo shift that could heel us over in a gale, and from what you've said about her power plant, we've got plenty of thrust which should make for smooth sailing when our passengers get loaded aboard. I'm happy to be in my element again, Captain, that's for certain!"

"I thought you would appreciate crewing on her, Wally. Let's take a tour aft to look over the safety measures. You know how I feel about lifeboats—useless clutter that impedes sleek progress and efficiency."

"True enough, sir, but we've got to follow the Board of Trade guidelines." I winked Jim's way, but Captain Stahl was not about to be amused.

"The beastly things will surely malfunction or get tangled in the davit lines should we be heeled over and flooding. Their sole value is as transport for passengers when we dock offshore at some Mediterranean port. In such a situation, everyone wants to disembark to go shopping. Honestly, if we run this ship properly, we'll use only a half dozen for transshipment of fresh vegetables or tourist excursions. Mark my words!"

Jim Stahl was not immune to danger. He'd known fear and suffering in his career. Lifeboats or not, he thrived when sailing on the sea. Ashore, he had once been in love and married, but his dear wife Alice had perished in a fiery accident more than two decades ago. Now that he had reached his fifties, Jim's primary joy was being aboard an ocean-going vessel. An unattached bachelor without children, he now preferred to maintain a girl in every port, as the saying goes. He could be assigned to and remain comfortable on a ship for two or even three years without complaint, but the very thought of being tied down to any woman other than his departed wife made his legs itch to start walking.

In this regard, while it was fact that his ship incorporated the latest in stabilizers, including Frahm anti-roll tanks amidships, roll and pitch had become such a part of his psyche that he could not sit for long on shore unless he was provided with a rocking chair. Being underway aboard the biggest vessel he had yet commanded was exactly what he had been born for. His bearing and demeanor reflected this assurance. His subordinates respected him all the more for it.

Now that he had full responsibility for a ship carrying many hundreds of paid fares, Captain Stahl decided to familiarize himself with what were considered, by him at least, to be eye candy for the passengers. As a very conscious decision, following current international rules of the sea, the builders had installed 10 lifeboats along the port as well as the starboard sides of A Deck. These were slung from highly regarded

Welin swing davits. These thirty-five person boats were covered by a tarpaulin to keep out the weather, but were otherwise ready for loading and lowering on short notice. They provided more than sufficient capacity for the entire complement of crew (including seamen, officers, stewards, kitchen staff, and specialists such as medical, massage, and beauty parlor staff, plus the ship's sergeant-at-arms amounting to 238) and passenger capacity of 460.

In addition, there were two smaller motorized launches located astern of No. 10 and No. 20 lifeboats. Adapted for fast deployment in the event of overboard rescue, these 30 person boats provided a safety valve in case launching all the prepared lifeboats was impeded.

Captain Stahl's prescribed duties required that sufficient drills were carried out in port so that every sailor aboard knew his assigned station in the event the lifeboats were needed. Once at sea, lifeboat drills would include the passengers as well as the crewmen assigned to them. The captain believed that repetition instilled familiarity and thus confidence.

As for today, he would direct the stewards to explain how the lifeboats functioned, but he would delay holding an actual passenger drill until tomorrow. Following the well publicized 1912 hearings conducted by Senator William Alden Smith in America, and that chaired by Lord Mersey in Britain, on the subject of the *Titanic* disaster, efforts had been made by high-minded, international governing bodies to assign each passenger to not just a lifeboat, but a particular seat in each such conveyance.

In Captain Stahl's experience, this was folly. If truth be told, he and his contemporaries considered lifeboats to be a public relations ploy. Painted a gleaming white and hung from formidable-looking davits, the presence of lifeboats would lure ticket holders to believe that, were anything to happen to the ship itself, these little crafts could provide safe exit.

Stahl knew that in the majority of cases, these tubs of safety were figments of some bureaucrat's imagination. In a real emergency, all sorts of factors—darkness, smoke, dazed minds, noise, terror, slanting decks, chilled temperatures or winds, forgotten seat assignments, panicked movement blocking routes of access, even disorientation—convinced him that a captain who relies on rational behavior regarding lifeboat assignments in times of crisis will be sorely disappointed.

His crew, of course, was expected to perform their duty because he would have trained them in this regard.

Every ship had a right and a left side; to keep them oriented, passengers needed to be taught that port is the left side as one faces toward the bow. The onboard stewards were told to patiently explain that the words <u>port</u> and <u>left</u> each had four letters, while <u>starboard</u> and <u>right</u> went together since each word had more than four letters. Which was which, the captain steadfastly believed, would be the first thing forgotten by passengers in the event of an emergency. He subscribed to the theory that the simpler, the better. On *Reliance,* he eschewed actual seat assignments.

"Simply head for the one nearest to your location at the time the 'abandon ship' alarm sounds." That was what he would advise tomorrow. His approach was simple and easy.

If an emergency arose, conditions would doubtless be such that confusion would reign. People pushing to try and reach a particular seat or boat would only create chaos. He would follow the famous motto of the United States Marines— leave no one behind—but lifeboat seats on *his* ship would be loaded on a first-to-show basis, with a sailor posted at each rescue craft to direct its loading.

The sole standing order regarding lifeboats which Captain Stahl issued was that all seats were to be filled prior to a boat being lowered over the side.

He was pleased with the way his crew had handled themselves while executing dry runs in port these past few days, drilling repeatedly for fire or damage emergencies. Nevertheless, he had made a pledge to himself that his crew would never have to display such skills. He would monitor every operation in such detail that nothing would be allowed to fail.

Fate, of course, has no regard for human resolutions.

* * *

A major convenience offered passengers by booking a cabin aboard the *Reliance* was the presence of a wash basin and toilet in each room. A few select cabins on A Deck provided a bathtub but, in general, showers for men and bathtubs for ladies were in separate changing facilities located in the center of each deck. Additionally, the exercise/weight room set up in the aft section of B Deck had its own set of showers. The stewards made sure fresh towels, soap, and washcloths were always available in these facilities. The ship's designer felt these would be amenities that were highly valued by the passengers without adding undue burdens on the ships structure or convoluted piping.

As a consequence of the design and outfitting of the cabins, *Reliance* enjoyed a competitive position relative to her British, Italian, French, and particularly the German trans-Atlantic rivals. Her furnishings, decor, and epicurean offerings were looked down upon, even disparaged, by the owners of the longtime great European luxury liners such as *Olympic* and *Mauretania* but, significantly, they couldn't match her pricing. Along with her desirable ports of call, the affordable cost of one of her comfortable cabins had made this voyage 95% booked. That was high for this time of year.

Ships plying the Atlantic Ocean could not be counted on, like a train, to make frequent regular stops according to some specified timetable. One never knew when the weather would intervene. Rather, boarding her was more like sailing off into the sunrise for a major adventure to new, even exotic, experiences.

The owners had capitalized on this as the tagline for their advertising appeal: *"Come sail aboard the Reliance for adventure in exotic ports of call!"* This unusual approach seemed to be working: nearly every cabin for this voyage had been booked some three months in advance by travelers eager to experience unusual get-a-ways.

A rule of purchase disallowed cancellation within two weeks of departure date. Though the British companies scoffed, its introduction eliminated hectic uncertainties in the company's operations and was diligently adhered to. This approach made them money.

There was one source of revenue—immigrants—that her owners had decided during the design phase to forego. These were, on the one hand, reliably served by competing lines such as White Star and Cunard, as well as French and Scandinavian liners. On the other hand, such a decision would be well-timed due to the restrictions on immigration which the United States had imposed following the aftermath of the Great War and—possibly worse—the introduction of Prohibition in January 1920.

Today was Thursday, April 19, 1929. The sun was shining overhead in a pale blue sky devoid of clouds. The pleasures of springtime were being enjoyed on land, but it was still too cold for passengers to walk the decks of the *Reliance* without heavy outer coats.

CHAPTER THREE

HIGH SCHOOL DREAMS

While looking over the ship that was now totally in his charge, Captain Stahl reflected on the steps he had taken, and the roads he had chosen to eschew, that had led him to this huge responsibility. He'd been born fifty years earlier into a family living on the Main Line, a string of suburbs heading west from Philadelphia. They were so named because they sat astride the Pennsylvania Railroad's trunk line that strung out to Chicago and points west. In the 1800's, the gentlemen who ran the city's banks, brokerage houses, and law firms had built summer homes on the cool and tree-shaded lanes such as Morris Avenue or Spring Mill Road. Just as the well-endowed structures on Long Island or the coast of Maine were called "cottages" despite they're being three story rambling mansions with multiple car garages and quarters full of servants, these summer get-a-ways were very elaborate. The wealthy would spare no expense to get away from the searing heat of summer in a city.

Time sputtered along. By the 1900's, changed economic conditions had converted many of these cottages into full-time residences. The owners now commuted to their places of work.

The main thoroughfare, Lancaster Pike, was ostensibly named after the Amish town through which it ran. Route 30 increased its significance by connecting the state's capital, Harrisburg, with the steel town of Pittsburgh and on into the Ohio valley industrial areas. Along this well-traveled highway, various kinds of shops had strategically located to serve and support the rich residents. They began springing up after the Civil War, nesting close together in order to provide convenience—a sort of symbiotic existence.

Usually, the icehouse was the first to appear because people needed ice cream and food preservation year round. A doctor's office or an apothecary, then a butcher, and very soon that most American of emporiums—the hardware store—followed. Now there was an item for every imaginable household repair, from sharp tacks to saddles and stoves, to be purchased locally. When automobiles became reliable, and priced at $300 so ubiquitous, these stores adapted to stock spare car parts. This new branch of business thrived until some enterprising individual or group took a chance and opened a certified dealership.

With summer residents becoming permanent, boarding schools began to take notice and locate their campuses within these communities: the environment was genteel and safe. Colleges for men, and even women, set up shop in these towns. Locating a hospital nearby would inspire building meeting places such as a Masonic lodge for the town leaders and soda shoppes for the young. To oversee the behavior of all these souls, churches were built. Even a one room box furnished with plain benches would suffice: folks seem to demand that forgiveness be readily available.

Gradually, these collections of people and buildings found that they would be better off incorporating as a town that would be deserving of some name on a map. Places sited along the main rail line running west from Philadelphia grew rapidly. Once towns such as Paoli, Ardmore, and Merion had grown sufficiently in importance to attract a tailor and dressmaker to open a shop, their residents would begin hosting and attending fancy parties. Thus, by 1920, these villages had become known collectively, and rather snobbishly, as "the Main Line." If you were born here, your future well-placed marriage or business success was guaranteed.

In 1879, James had been born into a middle class family in just such a town. Haverford was more or less centrally located between the nether region of Paoli and the well regarded metropolis of Philadelphia. His dad, Samuel, was not rich, but he was employed by a life insurance company and could, through sales commissions, earn over $12,000 a year. He could thus support a family life that was comfortable and steadfast. To prepare his son for the rigors of society, his dad had involved James in the Boy Scouts, sent him to summer camp in the lakes region of New Hampshire, and required that he work every Saturday at the local hardware store to, as he eloquently put it, "be exposed to the rigors of life."

As a result, the young Stahl learned not only how to tie a bowline knot, steer a sailboat, and handle tools such as drills and planes, but also developed a self-reliance for solving problems. If a customer was in a bad mood and short with him, he learned how to soothingly turn the man's ire into a sale. If a person appeared at the hardware shop with obvious frustration at not having the right tool, the solution was quickly, even expertly, placed in his thankful hand.

Without knowing he was doing it, young James was developing a knack for guiding and leading without offending. Few have this skill. He became invaluable to the storeowner, Tom Sills. This man even pleaded with Samuel to let young James work full time and forget about the fall term at school. But the boy's father would not be swayed; he had long ago set a goal that his son was going to be a college man.

Alas, the best laid plans and big dreams of parents for their children are almost always derailed. In his senior year at the Haverford School, James enrolled in a course on drafting. The teacher was not held in high regard by the students because he also taught a mathematics course and was very hard on grading his students. He had, as a result, earned the acronym of "Bitchie Ritchie." However, once James had sat at the tilted drawing board for a week, experienced the strict rules for cleanliness of his materials and neatness in execution of his drawings, and seen his black and white renderings take shape in recognizable objects, he could have cared less what the teacher did. He was absolutely enthralled with learning perspective, shading and, especially, scale. In short, seeing objects become "real" as his hand flowed over the drawing paper gave him a satisfaction and pride that far exceeded any trophies or awards he had previously won for athletic prowess. He found himself drawn to doing something constructive with his life as soon as he was able. Putting off the future by attendance at college may have been the dream of his father, but it was not his.

During the long light that persisted in the summertime, he would finish his afternoon work at the hardware store, borrow the family car or hitch a ride with his high school buddy Peter North, and then beeline for the Philadelphia Naval Yard. Standing on the docks, with the seemingly ever-present tang of sea salt breezing around his cheeks, he'd stare for hours at the sleek gray hulls of the warships and admire their fully functional decks.

"A device for every challenge, and everything in its place," he would muse in admiration.

One day, on a whim, Peter proposed they ask about boarding one of the destroyers for a tour. The guards at the vehicle gate had been lax about letting them onto the yard (the Navy could always use young recruits), but getting aboard a ship itself seemed like a forbidding task. The boys had appeared so often that their faces were well known to the shore patrol guards, especially Ensign Franks, so they asked him how to obtain permission for a tour. The year was 1896 and the United States was not fighting in the Philippines or invading Cuba, so it was a simple matter to holler up to Lieutenant Jenkins aboard the Curtis Class ship. When the lieutenant spied these clean-cut young men in the company of his buddy Jordan Franks, he did not stand on ceremony. Rather, he eagerly welcomed these future inductees aboard and, to ensure they would not injure themselves or anyone on the boat, proceeded to conduct their guided tour himself.

Pete North was impressed by the gunnery and wanted a turn up in the wheelhouse, but James was drawn to the ship's innards. He wanted to know all about the boilers that fired on coal and then heated water into steam that powered the reciprocating piston engines down in the bowels of the vessel. The steel struts and cross bracing that made up the ship's skeleton drew him as though he was magnetized. A look at the propeller shafts and the steering mechanism for the rudder was also high on his list. When he learned this ship could approach 19 knots (over 20 mph), he gulped; he could only make 12 miles an hour on his bicycle, and even that had to be on level roadway.

Since this boat was tied up at dock, neither boy had the chance to test his sea legs, but they left amidst sincere thanks and vivid imaginings of voyaging to exotically distant lands. When they reached home, Peter said this day had been special, but for James it was much more than that. It had been definitive. He had made up his mind. He would become a designer of ships: a naval architect. Before he could do that, he had to experience life aboard an ocean going vessel so he'd have perspective. Reading manuals was important, he figured, but only after a man had actually felt the sea rolling beneath wooden planking could he truly understand what the designation "seaworthy" meant.

He finished out his senior year, graduating with acceptable marks in all his subjects except drafting; in that, he proudly earned an "A." He had held his father at arm's length long enough. In early summer of 1897, it was time he pursued his own life's dream.

The next day, his father proposed that his newly graduated son should visit some prospective colleges. James, thinking fast, jumped at this chance. Concocting a story that he was going to go up to Providence, Rhode Island to look over Brown University as a possible prospect, he hopped the train into Philadelphia, changed to a north-bound headed to New York and, with just a suitcase containing his toiletries and two changes of clothes, stepped off in Rhode Island headed to the highly regarded professional training academy, the Providence Maritime Institute. He could not foresee then that fate would divert him from the design of ocean-going vessels to their management.

CHAPTER FOUR

THIN ICE

At the close of the century, prosperity was so strong that the benefits of employment and wealth accumulation were affecting every maritime nation. The gradual improvement in the reliability of using coal to generate steam for powering turbines not only permitted the use of larger capacity vessels, but also made adherence to schedules an accepted way of doing business. Commerce by ocean-going transport thrived. With seagoing trade flourishing, the need for educated men to design, or to command, the large vessels plying the waters of the world was at a peak. The Providence Maritime Institute had, for some decades, catered to this growing demand.

When young James Stahl stood in front of the large oaken door of the academy's administration building, he took a deep breath and reached forward to open it. As he did so, he stepped into a world completely unfamiliar to him. The men studying there were not called students, but rather "cadets," and each strutted the hallways (soon to be known to him as passageways) attired in a dark blue wool jacket and trousers over an always spotless white shirt with four-in-hand tie, or lightweight linen trousers and white cotton shirt with a blue kerchief looped around the cadet's neck during the warmer months.

What struck James instantly, before he'd even shaken hands with an admissions counselor, was the pride that these cadets exuded. Their erect postures, tidy attire, and books or papers hidden in neat attaché cases showed they were studying to be professionals, and they therefore took their studies seriously. Indeed, whether seated at a tilted drafting table, or standing straight and tall while piloting a ship, the thoughts and actions of these future graduates would influence, directly or indirectly, thousands of people. Whether the people in their charge lived or perished on the cold, unforgiving seas was going to be in their educated hands.

Young Stahl recognized the difference with the atmosphere of his high school immediately: these cadets **wanted** to be here. Each one had, like himself, accepted the responsibility and was daily preparing for his life's work.

The young runaway—for he knew that was what his father would label him—knew instantly that he had made the correct career choice. He headed straight for the office of the man in charge: Director Bertram Hathaway. After identifying himself to the clerk posted outside Hathaway's door, he was directed to sit on the wooden bench placed along some wainscoting. From here, he surveyed the interior of the reception area. Painted a pale blue, the walls boasted large paintings of ships at sea; some under sail, others obviously steam powered with tall stacks billowing smoke. For only an instant, a feeling of jealousy pained his face; he wished he'd had any one of these pictures adorning his bedroom as he grew up.

His musing was interrupted by the clerk motioning toward the closed door and announcing: "Mr. Hathaway will see you now." With that as his clarion call, James Stahl stood and strode into the Director's office.

Entrance to this institution was immediate in his case. When James—as a prospective student—displayed his mechanical drawings to Director Hathaway, explained his familiarity with modern ships of every kind, and evidenced his obviously sincere motivation to succeed in this profession, the Director approved his admission on the spot.

The new cadet was sent to the supply room to be fitted with the appropriate uniforms, bed linens, and sundry personal items such as soap. The Institute permitted the growing of beards by its students, so long as they were neatly trimmed. One's hair had to conform to the current standards, but sideburns were deemed a mark of maturity. However, personal jewelry was not tolerated, so such preferences as an earring in one's ear were eschewed. Black shoes maintained at a high polish were standard. These rules of personal grooming were already followed by James, so he adapted readily.

The only thing the lad needed now was a bed and, most likely, roommates. These were to be assigned to him by Mr. Roberts, the bookkeeper ensconced in some cubbyhole of a room down the passageway from the Director.

With his quarters squared away as best he could (how to prepare for occasional inspections would be learned from his bunkmates later), James slipped into an empty seat in the lecture hall where engine dynamics were being discussed. He'd have a lot of catching up to do, but the Director had assured him that his roommates would help him get up to speed.

He had let that slide for the moment. He'd have to meet them and, most importantly, gain their trust before they'd offer any help. It wasn't competition for scores that would make them initially reticent. Exams here were not administered for the purpose of racking up points to earn a high grade. None of these boys were going to apply for some graduate school. They were going to go right to work. Indeed, that was how their schooling was paid for. The Institute took one-third of each graduate's earnings over a five year period to compensate its professors and cover its overhead expenses.

The number of exam questions a student answered correctly enabled the proctors—in accordance with the rules of the school—to gauge a cadet's comprehension and absorption of the information being imparted. There was no point whatsoever in cramming for a test, passing it, and then moving on to the next challenge while forgetting about what had just been tested. Cadets here had to learn the information, make it a part of their daily lives, and then carry around in their head everything that they had mastered up to that point.

They would need to draw on such knowledge, possibly in an instant, during their professional lives. "Cram and then forget," so normal in civilian school, was replaced by "absorb and retain" at the Institute. Thereby, a cadet could be examined not only on what he had studied last week, but last year as well. Knowledge that was built up block-by-block was thus cemented into place by the likelihood of being tested on any such block at any time.

James would have to apply himself more diligently than he ever had in high school, but when you are doing something that you like, having chosen it to the exclusion of all else, such diligence comes easily. He studied hard, often by small lamp deep into the night, but he loved what he was doing. Most importantly, he was retaining the material. Even trigonometry and mastering the use of the sextant came to him readily, especially with such good help at hand.

There was one lesson he learned without any instruction whatsoever: an individual officer can't know everything, so the wise commander surrounds himself with people who can complement his knowledge. As a synergistic team, they would be far abler than any one of them acting alone.

As it turned out, the Director had been right; his roommates did indeed come to his aid. Matt Johnson was a tall drink of water from Texas who spoke with a slow drawl and easygoing manner that made him likeable. More assertive and thus less likeable was Art Dillon. He hailed from a small village along the Maine coast and had grown up with seafaring roots in his blood, but he stood only five feet tall; consequently, he endlessly needed to prove that he belonged with the grown-ups. His forte was book learning. Almost every day, he could be seen leaning over the shoulder of some taller cadet who was slumped morosely in a chair while trying to comprehend how to size a hull for design load capacities, etc. Simply bigger and wider was not enough—she had to float, so displacement was the key calculation.

Art's voice patiently explaining esoteric rules of hull design could be heard droning down the hallways like a honeybee continually at work constructing the hive.

For James, the best roommate was Peter North, his longtime buddy from high school, who showed up out of the blue with just the sort of limited knowledge that James had but boasting the same drive to learn his chosen field. Their bond of friendship would endure for as long as they lived.

In 1898, the fall colors faded and winter winds began howling about the grounds, the cadets found themselves indoors and studying more often, but competing outside at touch football less. Cooped up with other men at a school, a cadet gets antsy pretty quickly. Around Thanksgiving, the temperature dropped below freezing and would remain so through February. As this was their second year at P.M.I., the cadets' study habits had become ingrained; nevertheless, diversion would always be an appealing option.

Only a few months later, with the last clutches of winter battling with the first taste of spring in the air, James was taking a stroll some distance from campus "to clear the cobwebs from my soul," as he'd put it to his friend Peter. It was late March 1899 and James was feeling a fresh excitement course through his veins. The hint of renewal borne along the frigid springtime air seeped into bones which were too long fatigued from sitting still. After about a mile of walking, he thought he saw something glinting beyond a copse of bare tree trunks. As he drew near, he realized it was a pond, probably belonging to a local farm. He could see a barn atop a small hill nearby overlooking the peaceful, but still snow-covered, valley. As soon as he reached the frozen surface, he tentatively put a foot on the ice, shifted his weight, slid for a bit, and then tested its sturdiness with all his weight. No cracking appeared, no groans sounded in the clear, still air.

"Where are my skates!" he suddenly exclaimed out loud.

Taking his glove off, he ran his palm along the surface.

"Not bad for an outdoor pond," he thought. There were tiny burbles and deformities in the surface caused by small twigs and air bubbles, but the ice was definitely good enough to skate on.

He rushed back to his quarters, rummaged through his foot locker, and then proudly held up the hockey skates his parents had sent him just that Christmas.

"Time to test you boys out!" he exclaimed eagerly as he bundled them and an extra pair of socks under his arm. He was striding toward the door when he was hailed.

"Hey, where do ya think you're going all bright and cheery?" asked Matt idly looking up from the heavy tome, *Principles of Seamanship.*

"There's a pond off of Emerson Road; you know where I mean, don't ya?" volunteered James.

His buddy North chipped in, "Going skating, are ya? It's sure cold enough! Be sure you test the surface, anyway. Want one of us to go with you, just in case?"

"In case of what? Hey, I've been skating since I was nine; I know what I'm doing!"

With that having been said, he turned in a rush of eagerness and trooped down the stairs and out the door. His mates rose from their chairs and watched him seemingly fly across the quadrangle and disappear into the rolling white hills.

"Look, we don't have an exam for another three days. We've got nothing else on; let's follow him and see what kind of fix he's about to get into!" North challenged them. He had been friends with Jim Stahl long enough to know that blind excitement such as this could lead to trouble.

"Good idea. Take gloves and a hat for your ears. We may be lying in wait longer than we anticipate." said Matt Johnson. As the tallest of the three, he'd be the most easily spotted on a surreptitious mission such as this. He didn't yet know what sort of trick they'd play on their roommate, but he knew the answer would come to him once they arrived at the pond.

As the other two arose from the comfort of their study chairs, Art Dillon watched them with disdain. He'd been deep in the theory of modern bulkhead design when the studious calm of the suite had been shattered by Jim's whirlwind arrival and subsequent departure. On the other hand, he did not want to be left hanging about all alone, especially when there might be real tricks to play on a roommate. With luck, maybe they'd even see some deer or foxes. With an audible sigh, he donned his thick, fur-lined alpaca jacket. For good measure, he raised the warm hood over his ears as the threesome forayed out into the afternoon chill.

Jim was by now far ahead of them, having quickened his pace as he anticipated what was coming. At the sight of the gleaming, seemingly smooth ice on the pond, he whooped for joy and leapt into the air with a high heel kick. Conditions for a solo skate seemed perfect, with barely a whisper from the breeze and nary a soul in sight. He could practice, and even try new moves, to his heart's content without worrying about some out-of-control youngster careening into his path. He picked out a good resting spot, sat down next to a strong-looking young tree about four inches thick, left his cap atop his coat, and laced up his skates. He held the extra sox in reserve in case he got overheated while enjoying this experience. Then, with his excitement building at the coming pleasures, he pulled on his gloves and moved out onto the ice.

What a feeling of exhilarating freedom! Unlike land, a very simple thrust from a blade canted against a frozen surface could send a person effortlessly across ten, even twenty yards of ice. He carefully eased along the entire perimeter, checking for protruding chucks or twigs that could catch a blade. Almost smack dab in the center of the pond was his only area of concern: the ice looked rather thin there. He wasn't sure, but he thought he could see dark water resting beneath the white surface. If a skater could spot circles with white outer rings flitting about, like small flying saucers scooting haphazardly beneath the surface, that ice was thin, and therefore dangerous!

Being alone, he decided to stay away from the center and stick to the perimeter today.

At first, he didn't think about his breathing. He simply began making wide circles around the perimeter, using a basic maneuver where one foot crosses over the other and then the trailing leg lifts forward to cross over again with a repetitive rhythm. After two circuits, he reversed himself and repeated the process clockwise. This warmed up his entire body. Rhythmically push off, step over, push off, glide, and step over. As he gained a feel for the surface, he did a 180 degree turn and began to skate backward using reverse crossovers, leaning inward slightly as he increased his speed.

His course was defined by the borders of the pond where it met hard pack snow. Otherwise, there was neither object nor person to inhibit his ongoing circling. He began hanging his arms out away from his sides, about even with his waist, thereby increasing his balance and providing a secure platform for more speed. He always kept his head turned forward in this maneuver and looked some yards ahead to spot the safest course. After a few minutes, he couldn't resist making some ice hockey moves. He began turning backward, quickly reversing to skate forward, but then quickly changing to a backward crossover again.

"Keep your knees flexing and supple," he reminded himself.

If only he had a hockey stick, then he could really put on some speed!

He spotted a fairly straight branch about five feet long lying a few feet up on the bank, skated over to it, knelt onto his knees against the snow, and was just able to clutch it and then stand back up on the ice. Now he could deeply bend his knees, thus lowering his center of gravity, and gain more speed against the wind resistance. A huge smile crept across his mouth, his eyes sparkled, and his cheeks reddened with the wind-chill he was generating. Completely absorbed in the pleasures of this day, he never saw his friends creep down and secret themselves in some nearby holly bushes.

His confidence rising as he became ever more familiar with the layout of the pond, he began increasing his speed until he could feel his tear ducts welling up from the chill of the wind. Using the stick as a guide, he could almost reach the speed he used to generate when breaking away to close on an opposing goalie. He had made the varsity Third Forward Line as a sophomore, had scored or assisted fairly consistently, and then for the next two years was on the Varsity Wing position. Nothing spectacular, perhaps, but he produced a very steady performance. His good friend Peter North had been elected co-captain with him when they were high-school juniors. The two played right and left wings in their senior year, always competing for the highest centering pass count. An effectively centered pass to an open forward was almost as good as shooting the goal yourself.

"Teamwork! Teamwork! Teamwork!" was what their coach Tom Branson had drilled into, as he was fond of saying, "their puckin' noggins." Besides, a player always got credit for an assist, so there was no need to be a frigging hero and hog the puck. He could still hear the strident calls of Coach Branson ringing in his ears as he dodged and wove around the pond today.

The sun dipped a little lower in the western sky and began to shine just a bit into his eyes as he completed a turn around the eastern perimeter. As he started another circuit, James decided it was time to call it quits. He was absolutely filled with joy. To keep the setting sun from blinding him, he turned to face the southern edge of the pond and, dropping lower to compress his knees, reared up backwards and executed a flip.

As he reached the apex of his leap and arched his back, he imagined—just for an instant—that he spotted some girl standing on the bank looking his way. It was just for a moment, and then he was catapulting his legs over his head and downward, ready to flex his knees and raise his arms in a whoop of triumph. He'd done this often after his team had vanquished some rival school's hockey squad.

As his skates came down, they plunged right through the thin center section of ice. He raised his arms all right, but it was to utter an amazed yelp of shock!

His blades went straight down and touched bottom in the thick, gooey mud. His chest and respiratory system were so instantly stunned into paralysis that he couldn't move his mouth, couldn't even flail his arms for his stick. Thick, tight bands around his chest prevented his being able to breathe. He remained upright, exclaiming desperate, unintelligible "huugh, huugh" sounds, but otherwise lacking any self-control. His lungs seemed paralyzed and he couldn't get any air into either them or his throat. He'd been in a brawl once when he'd had the wind knocked out of him by a sucker punch, but this was far worse.

"This can't be happening, not after the sheer joy I've felt!" was all he could think as he looked around wildly for help, any help at all. His body was too paralyzed by the chill to have room for fear.

"We see you, you dumb fool. Hold tight, we're coming!" shouted Johnson as the three would-be pranksters transformed into life-savers. Seeing Jim's predicament, Dillon, being the shortest, grabbed onto the nearest tree like an anchor. This was where Stahl had sat so expectantly only forty minutes earlier. Art extended his hand to North who locked on and extended his other hand to hold onto Johnson's trouser leg; the tallest of these roommates then promptly extended his body lengthwise across the ice, reaching for Stahl.

Their body chain was stretched as far as possible across the ice, but they were three feet short.

Desperately seeking some form of extension, Johnson moved to retrieve the stick Jim had been using. As he did so, he saw the girl. Standing on the bank, seemingly riveted by the calamity unfolding before her, this person made no move to assist. She was obviously warmly dressed, with her feet in furry boots and a knitted cap on her head; nevertheless, she seemed to be frozen stock-still by the drama.

Matt screamed at her to come and help. Suddenly, she awoke from her dazed state. Alice Kenny scampered across to Johnson, lay flat between him and the distressed skater and removed her mittens. Matt clamped both his hands on her calves above her boots. The girl slid forward, yelling as loud as she could at this imperiled man to penetrate the frozen inaction of his mind. He did not seem to hear her.

Keeping her body on firm ice, she extended her arm across the now gaping hole Jim's plunge had created, inched toward his flailing hands, just a little more, then she grabbed one of Jim's wrists and, wrapping her fingers around it as tightly as she had ever gripped anything, yelled at the others to start pulling them in.

The going was slow. Jim was made all the heavier by the water that had now penetrated his clothes; moreover, he was so chilled as to be virtually immobile.

Alice was straining so hard to hang onto this almost lifeless wrist that her eyes started filling with tears. The thought flashed across her mind, "How could this be? A moment ago, this person was so heroic and manly, but now he is dying right in front of my eyes!"

She got her other hand on Jim's wrist. His glove slipped off, but that didn't matter. All she had to do was hold on and not let his wrist slip from her grasp.

"Keep pulling!" Alice screamed as she felt Jim begin to inch forward onto his chest. The edges of the thin ice gave way, causing Alice to almost pitch forward herself, but now she had Jim at a flatter angle. She wriggled backward onto more solid ice. She could feel the man holding onto her legs pulling her backward.

As soon as she could, she grabbed the sweater material covering the skater's shoulders and commanded: "Now, now! Pull for all you're worth!"

Art had wrapped one arm crooked around the tree trunk and then grabbed onto his coat; he focused all his energy on keeping those fingers closed on the material. His other hand stayed locked in a curled-finger grip with Peter's, and that lad kept his hand closed on Matt's trouser cuff. Nevertheless, in this position, neither of them had any leverage. It would have to be up to Matt, the largest and strongest of the roommates.

Twisting his torso and shoulders, Matt was able to pull the girl backward just enough that he could see Jim's skates emerge from the icy water. Then he slid Jim's inert body as well as the girl across to strong solid ice. North immediately rose to his feet and rushed forward to drag his friend over to the bank.

For a moment, the four rescuers huddled over the body that was curled up like some immobile fawn abandoned by its frightened doe. As they brushed the ice chaff from their clothes, each of them simply stood there, practically stunned into disbelief.

Matt wondered aloud, "What should we do?"

The girl responded first: "Carry him toward that barn up the hill," she directed. "I'll tell my father to start a fire in the kitchen stove. We'll get him into my house and warm him up!"

The three cadets tried lifting the sodden, inert frame that had once been their studious, stalwart roommate. Two on the torso, one carrying both legs, was simply insufficient. When Alice looked over and saw the struggle, she placed her hands under Jim's drooping head. Now all four of them made their way up the snow-covered slope as quickly as the slippery surface and their burden would permit.

As they neared the porch of the farmhouse adjoining the barn, Alice dropped her burden and raced for the door, yelling, "Daddy, Daddy, come now! A man has fallen through the ice and his lips are already turning blue. Help, come now!"

Jim's head now hung down toward the porch floorboards. His eyes were closed and his tongue lolled to the side of his mouth. He wasn't an attractive sight. The door opened and a slightly balding head stuck its face out, took one look at the young people struggling toward him, and disappeared back into the kitchen.

"Martha, Martha, get cracking! Put on some water to heat while I stoke the stove and get the fire up. We need dry blankets, and get my wool sox. Move, woman, get along with you!"

Martha Kenny was actually way ahead of her husband Deal. She had heard her daughter's entreaties and was already rummaging the closet for blankets, opening the bureau drawer and fishing out some of Deal's hunting socks, and then bustling into the kitchen. She spread two blankets in front of the stove as her husband forced more wood into the open cover and blew on the embers to fan them into flame. As the kitchen filled with the rescuers and the family members, Deal asked them to lay Jim on the nest of blankets. Then he took a kitchen knife and with two deft swipes released the boot laces. He immediately proceeded to strip off the lad's soaking trousers.

"You, there, get his sweater and shirt off. Is he breathing?"

Matt confirmed that he could just feel shallow breathing as he laid his ear against the mouth of his inert friend.

As the fire began to take hold and spread heat into its iron belly, Deal directed Johnson to strip and lie astride the now naked James Stahl and warm his backside, while he himself lay astride Jim's chest. Holding the young man so their chests touched, he closed his mouth over the blue lips and exhaled warm air into the cold lungs, then pressed against the solar plexus with the heel of his free hand to help expel air from the lungs. While he did so, he looked at Peter and Art and, after introductions, told them to prepare to serve as warming relief in about two minutes. They readied themselves while Alice and her mother Martha did their best to restrain themselves in the face of all this male nudity. The situation was far too serious for any levity.

When Deal felt the cold of James' torso begin to sap his own warmth, he said, "Okay, boys, it's time for you to jump in here."

With some embarrassed maneuvering, Peter replaced Deal and Matt was replaced by Art. The difference in their height was too much of a stretch for Martha. She ran into the bedroom to fetch slippers and additional wool socks. These she promptly slipped over Jim's feet, but his toes felt icy cold to her touch, so she removed the socks and directed her daughter to kneel like an Indian fakir and hold Jim's feet to her bare stomach beneath her hands.

She grabbed an extra quilt with which to restore body temperatures during respites. As things stood, another go round would definitely be necessary.

After a subsequent turn at close-body warming, James' lips began to turn from a bluish tinge to a pink, even ruddy color, and he began quivering and shaking. This meant blood was circulating into his limbs. When he began crying out in agony, they continued the warm body shifts, but everyone knew this meant he was going to live.

When frostbitten, limbs always hurt like hell as circulation is restored. Jim's agony simply had to be endured until full function returned.

The pot-bellied stove continued to warm the entire kitchen. Gradually, the tense emergency eased and so, even before Jim opened his glazed eyes and gasped, "Where am I?" introductions had been made all around.

Martha took the water off the stove and, after adding a nip of cream, made cocoa. "Would anyone care for a marshmallow?"

Her light query made everyone chuckle. Soon, what could have been a tragedy began to turn into an impromptu gab fest with everyone talking at once about who had done what and how it had all happened. Jim raised himself up, but he was still so dazed that he simply sat silently watching. His breathing began to restore color to his features. As the pain in his limbs coming back to life gradually eased, he trotted out a rather obvious question.

"Who are these people, Peter? Where am I?"

Peter was quick to the mark. "You just relax, stay still, and warm yourself up, got that? There's plenty of time to fill you in." Then, turning his head and nodding to everyone there in the kitchen, he added, "You're very lucky to be alive, my boy. If it hadn't been for Matt wanting to play some trick on you, you'd be frozen solid in the water down there. Even if someone had seen you in the pond, no one would have had the lightest clue as to your identity until the Institute reported you missing.

"By the way, you owe Alice here a very large 'thank you.' We'd never have gotten you warmed up in time if it hadn't been for her and her folks here." He sat back, satisfied with himself. Looking her way, Peter wondered—just for a moment—whether Alice Kenny was dating anyone.

At this point, James was sufficiently recovered to be fully embarrassed by the trouble he'd caused. Looking around the warm kitchen, he sheepishly mumbled a slurred "thank-you."

"What was that? Cat got your tongue or something, hey there, Jimbo!" His buddy Peter could be downright derisive, but everyone knew he was joking. Humor. It is a gift that the animals don't have; in a tense situation, it can relieve the strain so well!

Thus goaded, Jim smiled briefly and made as if to rise and shake everyone's hand, but he was promptly forced back into his seat.

"No, no, we'll have none of that. There'll be plenty of time for gratitude later on. Can you feel your feet yet?" asked Peter solicitously.

Jim nodded as he acknowledged to himself, and the others, that they did indeed hurt like thunder. This allowed everyone to breathe a little easier. He was going to recover. Deal fetched some trousers and a sweater from the bedroom and offered them to Jim.

"Use these until your own gear dries out," suggested Deal. Jim donned them straightaway. There was no sense in retiring to the privacy of a room; everyone had already become quite familiar with what his body looked like.

"Would anyone like a serving of some hot vegetable soup?" Martha offered. The chorus of agreement released everyone to a task, such as setting the table or getting wood from the barn, and they were soon sitting down together and exchanging stories about the harshness of this winter, fishing in the now infamous pond during sultry summer days, or the importance of timing spring planting with the new moon.

As the conversation ebbed and flowed, it finally came round to Alice. She began to relate one of her favorite summer adventure stories about discovering a young male beaver that was intent on building a house in a large lake about ½ mile from the farm. As she described its search for, and subsequent harvesting of, willow saplings, their transport to the lake, and then applying mud to construct them into a sunken home, everyone sat back enjoying her tale.

Everyone, that is, except James. Even the storied arrival of a female beaver intent on making a home with the industrious male did not divert him.

He found himself transfixed. He heard her voice but paid no attention to what she said. He had first been attracted by her eyes as they sparkled with excitement while she regaled everyone with her tale. He then became riveted by the shape of her mouth as it moved, how it framed her words to provide inflexion and tone, and he suddenly found himself imagining what those lips would feel like if pressed against his.

When the meal was done and the cadets extended their hands in goodbyes, Martha and Deal invited them to come around anytime: there was always work to be done in the barn or fields. As James came to Alice, he took one of her hands and, holding it so gently, looked deeply into her blue eyes and said, "I wouldn't be enjoying looking at you now if it hadn't been for you. You saved my life. May I stop by and thank you properly sometime?"

"Please make it soon!" Alice's eyes were shining with an eagerness of their own. She had seen this young man at his worst and not been repelled. In fact, she found herself wanting to see him again—next time dry and fully clothed, perhaps—and at his best.

CHAPTER FIVE

PROPOSING

"Good god, man, what were you thinking, doing a flip like that!"

Now warmly ensconced back in their dorm room, Art was berating the hell out of his stupid showoff of a roommate.

"It just felt so good, as though I was attending a religious conclave rejoicing in the mercy of our Lord. He must have been there, looking on, or I wouldn't be here taking grief from you dolts!"

At that, all three of them—Peter, Matt, and Art—put their hands on his shoulders, forcing James to take a seat.

"Now listen, and listen real sharp, James," commanded Peter, ignoring his use of incorrect syntax. "I've known you for nearly a decade and these other guys have had to put up with you for nearly two years. It pains us to admit this, but you're the best cadet here. We've discussed this amongst ourselves, and we're not talking about General Robert E. Lee stuff like demerits and decorum. We're talking about the gut instincts and breadth of knowledge it takes to run a properly organized and safe ocean-going vessel. Probably the others at this academy would concur: you're the best that's come along for some time. You've got what it takes, man. Don't blow it on some wild goose-chase around a pond, you hear? We'll kill you if you pull some stunt like this again. We mean it!"

His roommates were dead serious, united as one front to guide him to greatness. He had no argument. He simply turned his head away and looked at the floor.

"Got it?" repeated Matt.

"I got it. Gees, you guys can really lay it on thick. Now you listen! I most definitely am going back there, but I will promise you this: it won't be the pond I'm after." He let these rather portentous remarks hang in the air for a bit, then added: "That Alice has got to be the cutest gal I've ever laid eyes on! She'll be what I'm after, you goons."

At that, the other three guffawed and slapped him hard about the shoulders. "You are a horny bastard! You had us going there, for a bit. So that's to be the prize, hey? Go for her, if you want, but I call Best Man at your wedding!" Peter snorted, just for emphasis.

At a stroke, he knew he had been beaten even before he'd put up a fight. If Jim wanted Alice, the competition was over. He took his drubbing like a man and put on his best face. After all, no one but he knew that Alice had so appealed to him. Peter had the whole affair sewn up even before his friend Jim had given romance and marriage an ounce of thought.

For some time thereafter, the young men got on with the business of learning their craft. March slipped into April, lending the air the sweet scent of freshly blooming flowers. An exam on the bracing and struts required for futuristic double-hull designs of ocean liners came up, but as soon as he finished it, Jim was out the door and headed over to the Kenny farm. Mrs. Kenny was in the kitchen chopping some carrots when she looked up and saw the cadet striding purposely up the hill to the farmhouse.

"Better put some ribbons in your hair, Alice. I think you've got a beau who's come a-calling."

"What was that, momma?" the athletic-looking girl inquired from upstairs. "You need a bow and arrow? For what?"

"No, honey child. You've got a young man who is about to knock down our door, and I'm pretty sure he hasn't come around for my beef stew. Go on and make yourself ready!"

Now Alice also looked out a window. From her bedroom, she spotted James Stahl striding purposefully across the fast-melting snow.

She gulped, but also thought, "I've never seen a man looking so determined. On the other hand, if I'm what he wants, I'll not disappoint him!" and with that said, she flew into a flurry of brushing her hair, applying some lipstick, and slipping into a daring red sweater that showed off her budding form.

Now eighteen, this girl would never be beautiful in a "bowl-me-over" sort of way, but she possessed comely looks that would endure and be very satisfying to James Stahl until the day she died.

After letting him in, Martha said something about checking on the beans cooking in the kitchen and left her daughter to do the entertaining of this swain. Living out in the country and tilling farmland didn't provide her teen-aged daughter with a bevy of suitors, so her mother wanted to give this man plenty of maneuver room.

"Besides," Martha reasoned, "he's already shown us how stupid he can be; hopefully, we've seen the worst and his behavior will be better from here on."

"Gosh, what a pleasant surprise! How are you feeling? All thawed out?" Alice playfully teased.

"I am at that! I've come to thank you and your parents properly. Here, take this," proffered Jim, extending his hand.

Alice looked at the rather roughly wrapped package. Obviously, this man was not born to work in a gift or sundries shop.

She mused, "I wonder what this could be."

She accepted the present as though it was some delicate, ancient treasure, and called: "Mummy, Daddy: Jim has brought us a thank-you present. Come and see!"

They turned as her father entered the hallway.

"Hello, Jim, it's good to see you," he stated. "It's been some time. Won't you join us here in the den?"

As everyone trooped after him, Deal asked, "Any trouble finding us, Jim? I wasn't sure whether you'd remember how, after the excitement and all."

This made the four of them laugh. It was easy for everyone to feel at ease in the presence of this young man; after all, they had all seen him fully naked. Deal invited everyone to sit down. Hefting the package, he wondered what could be inside. It felt round and smooth beneath the brown paper, but with a longish thin neck. The man of the house sat back in his cushioned chair and, monarch-like, looked over at the obviously virile and fully-restored gentleman before him.

Deciding to cut short any misunderstandings about how he ran his home, Mr. Kenny announced, "Jim, just so you know, we're not much for liquor in this house. A little wine, now and then, to celebrate and such, but we've no hard spirits what with the hullabaloo about liquor being so evil to family life. You know there are well-meaning temperance groups that are advocating its prohibition all-together. That may come to pass in your lifetime; they're very motivated, but at present it's largely the womenfolk who are all riled up about it, and of course they can't vote. But mind you, it may come to pass if the legislators get on board."

Then, covering his mouth, he said to Martha as an aside: "As if that could ever happen!"

"Don't worry, sir. You won't have a problem with this bottle, I assure you!"

Now curious without restraint, they crowded around as Deal Kenny removed the wrapping, revealing a replica of the famous U.*S.S. Constitution.*

"A fully rigged ship-in-a-bottle: good gracious, son, I'm impressed!" His eyes were wide with delighted surprise. "I'm pretty handy around farm and field tools, but I never could figure how you artists pull this magic off. Do you somehow split the bottle in half and then glue it back together?"

"No sir. In fact, I leave the bottle quite alone. You see the three masts; well, they're flexible at the bottom. I tie in all the rigging and then pull the masts down flat by looping a string through the top there, see? Then I slide the ship inside, pull out my string, and then the masts rise up straight when I tamp the base down."

There ensued awed silence as the ship-in-a-bottle was passed over to the women-folk. Their "oohs" and "aahs" of admiration were reward enough for Stahl; he knew his present was a hit.

Later, when he got a chance, he took Alice aside and said smoothly, "I've got a present just for you; here it is."

With that, he extended his hand holding a gold chain with a replica of a hockey stick suspended from its master link. "This is to remember the day you saved my life."

She held it gently, feeling the links of chain and admiring the luster of the trinket. "Jim, this is just beautiful. Here, please put it on me."

She twirled and presented the back of her neck, lifting up her radiant blond hair so he could maneuver the clasp. Then she turned and studied his face; his reaction was delightful. She had made sure the pendant hung down low enough to press her sweater in, just enough to heighten the appeal of her own assets. Jim took it all in and his eyes glowed with approval.

"Mom's got a ham baking. Would you like to stay for supper?" she asked, knowing full well the answer. In fact, Jim came by the Kenny household many times over the ensuing two years. He visited so often, in fact, that one day in May of 1901, Deal turned to his wife somewhat exasperated, and asked, "Damn it, Martha, when is that young man going to come to me and ask for Alice's hand in marriage? What's he waiting for, anyway!"

Martha calmly turned to him and said, "Don't worry, dear, he's way ahead of you. He has already asked, and she has accepted, so I wouldn't be surprised if you get a formal visit from him this very week. He graduates next month and he's probably trying to make sure all his coursework is completed before approaching you."

With a loud "harrumph!" Alice's father exclaimed, "You don't say! Well, I'll be doggone. So that lad really wants her, huh? You know I will agree, should he ask for my permission, don't you, Martha?"

"Good golly, Deal Kenny! I've known you wanted him as your son-in-law ever since that day he gave you the replica of the *Constitution*! Any kid who would take that much trouble to please an adult is going to be reliable and motivated; he'll be just the sort of son-in-law that we want. We'll be lucky to have him!"

That was that, so when Jim finally got up the nerve to pay a call on "the old man" and ask for Alice's hand in marriage, Deal readied his plan. No harm in having a little fun with this prospective son-in-law, he impishly figured.

Thus, when it came to pass that James Stahl, recent graduate of the Providence Maritime Institute, had notified his bride-to-be that he intended on calling upon her father that very evening to ask for her hand in marriage, Deal Kenny was prepared. Young Stahl appeared at the doorstep wearing a suit and four-in-hand tie and polished shoes; however, unbeknownst to him, his arrival had set the stage for some fun.

When Deal heard the confident knock on his front door, he opened it and said, "Hi, Jim! Come on in. We've been expecting you."

At this greeting, Jim's confidence, which he'd carried with him all the way over, suddenly evaporated. What did the elder Kenny mean by that? Alice knew he was coming but he doubted she would have mentioned it to her dad. With some trepidation, he entered the home of Martha and Deal Kenny. As he shook hands with Alice's father, he noticed that this man—whom he had known for almost three years—for some strange reason appeared to be noticeably taller tonight. Was that because he was wearing tall-heeled riding boots? Was that a whip he had in his hand? No, but it was a riding crop.

Additionally, there were two very ominously large men sitting on the couch; each one had a cap pulled low so their expressions were obscured. Nevertheless, they looked to be brooding, as though some youngster had done their family a terrible wrong and they were there to mete out punishment. Each man had a walking stick sporting a brass knob laid next to him on the couch. They rose, glowering his way as he crept in.

"Have a seat, young man," Mr. Kenny invited, or rather commanded. "Now, what was it you came to see me about tonight?"

As he asked this, the three men stepped forward to form an erect semi-circle around his seated position. Jim felt not only dominated, but cornered. He felt like the biblical David, but now with three Goliaths to deal with.

Nevertheless, he came here tonight on a mission from which he was not about to be dissuaded. He pressed his position.

"Sir, I will soon have credentials as a graduate of P.M.I., and my goal will be to design ships from the ground up, primarily directed at the passenger trade. I hope to pursue this goal at the shipbuilding yards of Newport News, Virginia. At some point, in five or so years, I will seek assignment by my company for shipboard duty. With that experience in hand, I will know a great deal about how to manage a ship at sea together with all her limitations. My goal will be to obtain a captain's license for command of an oceanic passenger ship. That is my career path, sir."

There was a moment of silence. Jim could hear the three men standing over him breathing heavily down on him. Or was that, in fact, his heart pounding? The three giants waited on the graduate in silence; there was nothing they needed to be nervous about.

Eventually, Deal asked," Is that it? Is there anything else?"

"Yes sir, there is. In fact, this is the most important thing. I've come to ask for permission to marry your daughter, Alice. She has accepted my proposal and, with your blessing, we will marry this coming June."

He held his breath, waiting for the beating that seemed imminent. He was soon to realize that all this had been a skit to test his mettle.

"Congratulations, Jim!" confirmed Mr. Kenny. "Yes, you have my permission as well as my blessing. In fact, these are my brothers, Harold and Jason, and they are here to offer you and your bride the chance to stay at their inn at White Sulphur Springs. You'll have hikes and horseback riding in the rolling hills of West Virginia. You might even catch a glimpse of some famous golfers; Harry Vardon has competed there as well as several famous American professionals. If you want to lie in bed and simply relax, their cottages are as comfortable as they come. It'll be their wedding gift to you. Stand up, my boy, and welcome to the family!"

With surprise and relief etching his face, Jim Stahl stood up and was accepted into the Kenny household as a fully-fledged member. Alice and her mother joined the happy throng. Dinner at their house that night was a very happy occasion.

CHAPTER SIX

INSPIRATION

"Well, honey, here's to us!" exclaimed Jim to his bride of five years. The year was 1906, and while the newlyweds had enjoyed their time at Newport News, James had been so successful in his goal of mastering the art of hull design and efficient propulsion that he had been lured into a new position up north near his former training academy. Living on the coast of Rhode Island, as they were, had made him want to get on board a ship. There, he could feel the tang of the salt air sting his lips and almost revel in the congenial swish of a prow as it slipped through the rocking ocean swells.

"Darling, does that mean you want to be traipsing all about the world, going hither and yon with no regard for me and our home? You may want to delay this gallivanting all about for a while. It could be that you're needed here at home."

Alice's face was demure, but her eyes sparkled with mischief.

"Now you know my desire to be aboard some ship, and eventually rise to the level of captain, has been in my heart from the time I entered the Institute. I was honest with you right from the start; I told you about my plan the day I gave you that hockey stick chain."

His wife's eyes continued shining as she clasped her hands behind his neck and gently nuzzled him under his ear. "But dear, back then there were only two of us to worry about. Our twosome is soon to become a threesome!"

James pulled back and looked hard at his wife's face. She was serene and all aglow with the pinkish hue of health coloring her cheeks. She looked the happiest he had ever seen her. Moreover, damned if she didn't look proud, too! He'd have to add that to the mix, as well. What in the world was she up to? Some ten seconds ticked by while he stood staring into her beatific face. Then slowly, oh so slowly, his expression began to soften from hard resistance at being outmaneuvered to one of wide-eyed realization. His eyebrows, always thick and furry eyebrows arched like two caterpillars about to do battle; the corners of his mouth began to tilt up and his cheeks to plump into a wide smile. He began to feel rather full of himself.

"Are you telling me…?" He paused, letting this weighty realization sink in. "Are we going to have a baby? Holy shark fins, Alice, this is amazing! How did it happen?"

"Oh ricketypoo, you loveable man! How do you think it happened? Don't you remember how we celebrated my 25th birthday four months ago?"

He reflected back, happily recalling how the two of them had gone for a "roll in the hay" following the Halloween festivities at the Kenny's house. Her parents had invited the young couple to stay for a long weekend in order to celebrate Alice's birthday. It had been one heck of a rollicking good three days. His in-laws had provided a brief time away from responsibilities. Alice and Jim had acted like two teenagers not only in love, but hot-to-trot, as the saying goes.

As she pressed right up against him, Jim understood there was a dividend from that marvelous weekend: the product of their devotion to one another.

"Now you just sit down right here, honey," gently intoned Jim as he removed his wife's arms from around his neck. "Let me get you a glass of root beer, or would you rather have some juice, or milk? There; do you need a pillow? I'll volunteer to make dinner, tonight, if you'd like."

"Jim, Jim, calm down. I'm not going to fall apart or anything; we women are made for this! As a matter of fact, being pregnant has made me feel as though I've been given a brand new chance at life."

She was still playful and happy at sharing this news with her husband, but a hint of seriousness had crept into Alice's tone.

"I've been extraordinarily lucky. There's been very little discomfort and just slight morning sickness. I feel like this is the purpose for which I was born. It's as though I can stand outside my body and look myself over and announce, 'Alice, you've really accomplished something here!' In fact, let me get that juice; I'm not going to break by exerting myself. Besides, you're beginning to look like you need that drink more than I do!"

Jim indeed was turning somewhat pale as the full impact sank in: he was going to be a daddy! In all his dreaming and planning out his career path, such an addition to his life had never been figured in. Having a child was going to be a major change. He'd have to stay home. He wanted to be involved in the care of his son—yes, his first born was going to be a boy—because this baby was the product of their sincere affection for one another. He was damned if he was going to let some outsider, even if she were a professional nanny type, take charge of raising his boy. Even if he had to, *ugh*, help with changing the tyke's linen, he was going to be involved every step of the way.

"Look here, and I mean this very seriously, Alice. I am overjoyed! You have honored me, as well. When this child comes, I pledge that I will stand side-by-side with you and assist in whatever you need doing. Yes, yes, that includes getting up what, every six hours—no, every three—okay, every few hours to clean him. What about feedings? When does he go on a bottle?"

"Sometime after two to three months, honey."

"Okay, fine, I'll do whatever is required. But, and you must mind me on this, you cannot ever let on to any of your friends, least of all your father, that I'm being fully involved. Can you understand? The boys down at the drafting office would never let me live it down. 'That's a woman's job!' they would say, and then laugh in my face. After three years with Cummins & Company, everyone means too much to me. Plus, if I get promoted, I want to be the sort of leader that my men look up to. I couldn't stand being the butt of their jokes. Can you promise to keep my being involved in his care a secret just between us? I'd surely appreciate it."

"Oh, James. You can be so silly! Don't fret yourself, I won't let on. But you're not to worry. You'll see. It'll be more fun than work. Yes, there'll be wailing and bleary eyes and all sorts of helpful contraptions, such as a bassinet, that we don't yet have, but the pleasure and reward of seeing something that we created grow up before our eyes will provide fulfillment that not everyone gets to experience. Now, let's sit down and write my folks right away; they're going to love this news!"

She took out some writing paper, then paused and looked over at her husband. Her eyes had narrowed.

"Just what do you mean by referring to 'him' or 'his?' What makes you think this baby won't be a girl?"

"Because he's *my* child! Of course he'll be a boy!" James couldn't have been more sure of himself.

Alice smiled at her husband's naiveté. For all his smarts, he could be very provincial. She loved him for it.

The couple sat down to write Deal and Martha their happy news. Jim thought he'd wait to write his own folks. He had some thinking to do first. Most importantly, he decided on the spot to forgo his plans to begin serving aboard a ship. He would stick with his office work designing, and then testing, models at the company's mock-up facility. After all, he had responsibility for three other draftsmen there. Life at sea would have to take a back seat now that his family was about to become three. Moreover, he was in line for promotion to sub-manager at the office. This position involved supervisory duties, not just over people, but also responsibility for a project itself: staging, accumulating inventories of the very parts which he had most likely designed, and shepherding construction through to launch.

"Yes," he reasoned, "I can make a very satisfying life for myself by staying right here. Going to sea will have to take a back seat."

Or so he thought.

During the next week, the house filled with activity. Each of their friends stopped by to wish them well and, for the men, this occasioned some serious toasting which, fortunately, was still easy to do in 1906. Then Deal and Martha showed up in late February to stay for a few days. If Jim had thought he was pleased as punch, it was nothing compared to Deal's pride: he was about to be a grandfather! In his eyes, such status made him just about equal to a king of England.

While her folks were out sightseeing on Saturday, Alice turned to Jim and said, "I've never let on to you because, when we first met, you were in such dire straits that I didn't want you to associate my skating with bad memories. However, the temperature is in the upper 20's today, the wind is calm, and it would be great to take a turn around some good ice before I get too big to even move. What do you think; want to come watch me?"

"I most certainly do, if you think it'll be safe!"

He'd been taken off guard. The subject had never come up since that day back in 1899 when he'd almost died and his future wife had helped save him. Now here she was, standing before him and saying, "Surprise! I can skate!" To himself, he wondered how many other secret skills his wife harbored.

As if she had read his thoughts, she said, "Don't worry. You'll be safe today. There are a lot of things I know how to do that you have not yet discovered."

Intrigued, he agreed to go, but only to watch. As far as he was concerned, he wanted another decade to pass before he put skates on again. The fearsome memory of how the icy water had chilled him almost instantly to a helpless, moaning stiff was, even today, still fresh in his mind.

He bundled up in sweater and thick jacket and cap while Alice slipped into warm leggings, sweater with a high neck, knitted hat, and mittens. They trooped together to the formal ice rink that the local navy families maintained for the school kids to practice on. As this was the weekend, the place was crowded with people. Most of the parents were seated atop folded blankets along the bank, but a few were brave enough to venture onto the ice and try to survive the throngs of kids rocketing around the surface. Jim spotted Harry and Barbara Bryant, and so he nudged Alice over to their blanket.

"Hi, Alice, Jim! Going to take a spin or two, are you?"

"Hey you-all. No, just Alice will. She says she's pretty good, though a bit rusty."

"Rusty, you say? Well, we'll see about that. Skating is like bike riding; once you know how, it comes back very quickly. Just watch," Alice said confidently as she tightened the laces on her high white boots.

She stood up and moved tentatively out on to the ice, gradually found her footing, and was soon speeding around the perimeter, weaving in and out amongst the teeming kids. After a couple of circuits, she came back to where Jim was parked and stopped with a hard side-braking of her blades. Jim was showered with a curtain of cold particles, but he only laughed and smiled her way.

"Think you're pretty tough, huh? You just let me go back to the house and get my hockey skates, and then you'll see some real snow curtains!" Of course, he was just joshing. His skates would remain stored in the closet for some time to come. Perhaps when his son was old enough, then he might spruce them up for another go, but not today, for sure.

His wife interrupted his reverie to say, "Let's see if I still have it. Just watch, you three, you'll see."

With that, she gracefully headed toward the center of the pond where only a few skaters were focused on doing more than simply trying to remain upright. Stopping, Alice bent over and touched her toes, stretching her hamstrings and quadriceps muscles. Then she flexed her knees so low that Jim momentarily began to rise and assist her getting back up, but Alice quickly straightened her legs, getting ready. She twisted her hips and then rotated each knee several times, balancing on one blade as she did so. Then she smiled over to her man and waved.

In a flash, she got going. As he watched, she seemed to move with a grace that was even more exquisite than the light sway she used when walking. Keeping her knees supple and flexing, she let each foot trail gracefully, pointing its toe as she began leaning into a continuous circling, when suddenly he saw her lift her trailing leg high into the air. With her arms planning out to the side and her back arching, a wide smile lighting up her face, she held her free leg so elevated it seemed to rise even higher than the cute contour of her fanny. Jim had tried just this sort of "flying camel" in his youth, but his toes always pointed down toward the ice and his leg got no higher than his other thigh. Alice's foot was gracefully turned both out and her toes pointing above the horizontal, when suddenly she straightened and pulled her free foot in close, resting it astride the foot on the ice.

Jim was a left hander and he could remember how he was startled to find that his right foot was the stronger of his legs. His wife was right-handed, so today he was surprised when she began to bring her arms in close and spin on her right foot. He briefly wondered whether humans are "right-footed" or "left-footed" just like they are right or left-handed, or right or left eye dominant. Was there some sort of relationship or predetermined pattern there? But his wife's next move so transfixed him and both of their friends that all conversation ceased as they watched grace and balance come together in a spin of overwhelming speed.

Alice had pushed her arms upward so her hands intertwined over her head, then she brought her knees close together, and in an instant she was turning in one spot so fast that Jim thought she might be drilling down toward China. He stood up and found himself applauding. She suddenly ended her spin by putting her arms out to the side, bending her right knee lower, and then planting the toe of her free skate out to the side. Most everyone there erupted into cheers and applauding.

"She's a really good figure skater!" Jim thought. She gracefully coasted over to their blanket and lay back against her elbows. She was panting some, but Jim had never seen such fire in her eyes. Her smile was as broad as her parent's barn door.

"I'll bet you didn't know I had that in me, did you?" she kidded her husband.

"You were just absolutely terrific! Wow, you could be in a traveling show, Alice." The jealousy in Barbara's face was obvious, but so was her admiration.

"Well, we have more important things on the way, don't we Jim?" said Alice, looking affectionately at him.

Barbara picked up on the wavelength immediately. "Wow, you guys are expecting?" she queried.

"That's right. I figured today would be my last fling before I become a roly-poly butterball!" replied Alice.

"When are you due?" inquired Barbara.

"Late July, probably." Alice sounded thrilled at the prospect.

"Honey, how on earth can you spin like that? You were dramatic, like an Olympian!" Her husband's eyes shone with admiration.

"Well, the important thing is this." Alice took off one of her skates and turned it upside down. "Here, Jim, sight along the length of the blade and then mentally compare it to your own skates."

"My god, I see what you mean. Your blade has a groove, like it's been milled down the centerline so there are actually two edges with a hollow separation. My hockey blade is more like a solid piece with the edges sharpened."

"Now hold the shoe perpendicular to your line of sight." His wife could be remorseless when it came to complete comparisons. That gave her an advantage when dealing with the local butcher.

"I've never paid attention. I merely thought white skates were for the girls and brown leather for men. I never thought about the shape of the steel until today. I'm used to my blade being almost straight across, but yours has a bend, or bow out here toward the toe. I always thought these teeth were what let a skater spin."

"Good grief, no. They're used for stopping," explained Alice. "The male figure skaters also use them to propel themselves into the air when they do a spread eagle or jumping twirl, which I've never tried. Do you see that forward part of my blade, right behind the teeth? That's what I spin on; it's a bit curved up from the main blade."

Jim took the shoe and held it reverently in his hand, as though it were some new-found object from an Egyptian tomb that was about to open up new realms of understanding.

"Is your other boot made the same way?" he inquired.

"Yes, they're identical; only the foot sole is made to conform to a right or left foot size. You could interchange the blades, but you could never exchange my blade for one on your boot. You'd fall on your face the first time you stole the puck and raced toward the goalie!"

Jim laughed. "Indeed, I would not want to do that! I've trouble enough staying upright on my own shoes. But I'm just fascinated by your blades. Turning is so much more responsive, and your ability to work them simply beautiful."

On the spot, he drew some paper sheets from his pocket, produced a pencil, and sketched the blades fore and aft. Then he rendered a full-on perpendicular view. With these aspects preserved and safely in his pocket, he escorted his wife home.

Harry Bryant called after him, "You better have new-found respect for her, Jim. Your wife is a very talented woman!"

"You don't have to tell me!" he replied with pride. "See you, Harry, 'bye Barb." He took his wife by the elbow and guided her along the path. She let him; after all, she was going to have a baby in about five months. But, what a day of freely spinning she had enjoyed!

"The two of them are so in love," noted Barbara as they disappeared down the path. "Lucky stiffs!" she ruefully opined to herself as she looked over at her own husband sitting there like a fat brown toad. "I wouldn't be surprised if he opened his mouth and croaked!" she thought surreptitiously.

Then she called out to her own children, "Come on kids, it's time to go in and get warm!" Her children were her life now. She focused her love on them.

CHAPTER SEVEN

REVOLUTIONARY DESIGN

When Jim arrived at the Cummins & Co. building where he maintained his design table in one of the draftsman's cubicles, he rubbed his hands together. He was excited to begin work for the new week; however, at his desk he found Harry Harley already standing astride a roll of drawings.

"Jim, we've got a rush on that Stapleton job. The owner has apparently been given a completion option that would mean a big bonus for the men who worked on it if we bring it in early. I know you submitted your plans two weeks ago, but they have to be altered. Here they are with all the modifications suggested by Stapleton himself. Can you put everything aside and get right on these for us?"

In a twinkling, all of James' plans for this day went by-the-bye. He'd have to delay playing around with the unusual ideas that Alice had given him until later.

"I'll get right on them, Harry. Let's see, some five pages, right?"

"Right! Thanks, Jim. I'm down the hall all day if you need me." With that, Vice-President Harley and a dutiful aide pattered their way down the hall, leaving much of what Jim had so diligently worked on for the last few weeks lying like so much tattered trash on his desk.

"Boy, you can win some but then lose some in a flash, all due to some rich fellow's whim," he sighed. Then he put on his green eye shade, took up his planimeter, weights, straight edges, and splines, and got to work reconfiguring what he'd already designed.

By 3:00 PM, or 1500 in seaman's parlance, he had completed the requested alterations and he strode down the hall triumphantly.

"Here you go, Harry. This should satisfy even Stapleton!" he declared triumphantly.

Having made this pronouncement, he returned to his tilted table and, taking a clean sheet, began idly free-handing some sketches. To an outsider, they looked like bridge arches atop abutments, but to James they were mere translations to aid him in computing and adjusting for load capacities as these related to hull displacements. After some eight sketches had accumulated on his paper, he started to reach for a fresh sheet when Bill Walker walked by, glanced Jim's way, and found himself pausing astride the draftsman's work table. As Harley's boss, Bill was the final link to the company's president himself. Thus, when Jim became aware of someone standing over his shoulder and looked up to see the senior vice-president there, he promptly leaned back in order to provide the man with a good look.

"What the hell are those things, Jim? Are you moonlighting and building a bridge or something?"

"Sir, it's really too early for me to explain. These are some concept ideas running through my head. I'm just fiddling with parameters."

"Hmm," murmured Walker as he thoughtfully stroked his chin. "What have you got in the hopper at present?"

"Mr. Walker, I just handed the do-over to Harry that Mr. Stapleton had demanded. He's probably inspecting them as we speak. I had a few moments to myself, so I started kicking these ideas around."

"Keep me abreast of what you get, if you come up with something, will you, Jim? And by that, I mean bring them directly to me; don't bother with the chain-of-command."

Mr. Walker had no idea what Jim was dreaming up, but what he had seen on the drafting paper that day had so riveted his imagination that he didn't want office politics interfering with the genius of this draftsman.

Jim promptly responded, "Yes, sir! Indeed I shall."

"Wow!" he rejoiced. He hadn't been ordered to toss out these projections; indeed, he'd been encouraged to develop and then to share them! Perhaps God had sent this baby that Alice was carrying to be a sign that he should, indeed, remain chained to a desk, although he'd never thought of himself as being enslaved. The management at Cummins & Co. was ahead of its time, he believed. They encouraged a man to think, imagine, even to go outside the accepted norms.

Look at how the invention of the concept of steam powering a device to increase man's strength had revolutionized industry, travel, construction, and even excavation techniques; why, the list was endless. Perhaps Jim could transform water travel with these "water-pods" as he light-heartedly had dubbed his experimental renderings.

Humming serenely as he bent over the new sheet he had tacked up, he formed a broad, relatively shallow arch that connected to a sort of bathtub affixed at each terminus. Above each tub he extended a straight line, then changed his mind and placed the vertical lines further in toward the middle of the arch; a ratio of one-to-five, he estimated. Then he positioned additional verticals in parallel rows, each with cross bracing supporting the adjacent members. Atop the vertical lines he drew a parallel set of girders reinforced with cross bracing between the higher and lower levels.

He made an overhead rendering and fore/aft diagram to complement his stern-on view. At this point in his sketching, what the bow looked like didn't matter yet. He'd work that out in the future. For the moment, though, it was time to take this drawing downstairs. That was where the wizard whom everybody called "The Man" worked.

Opening the double-swing doors that provided access to the company's test tank, James passed through as though on a mission. He carried his drawings safely rolled up under his arm. He soon located Frank Jones. This fellow had earned the nickname of "The Man" because everyone in the company, including President Clyde Cummins himself, would come down to the water tank for a complete evaluation of all new concepts that were developed.

To his delight, James found The Man in a good mood; the Boston Americans Baseball Team had just won a game, for once, and he'd made ten dollars on his bets. A goodly sum in those days, for sure; Frank didn't mind sharing the news of his good luck with James.

"Hey there, James, what say you? Can I take you and your lovely bride to dinner, tonight?" In addition to being shrewd at betting, The Man was usually generous with his winnings. This meant he was very popular with the men upstairs, as well.

"Listen, Frank, I've got an idea here that may just revolutionize shipping, whether along rivers or across oceans. Do you have time to take a look-see?"

"For you, my son, I will make time if I have to. Show me what you've got."

Frank Jones was only seven years older, but Jim appreciated the appellation. The two of them were about to become intimates sharing hitherto undiscovered secrets of Nature.

The draftsman unfurled what he thought might change the design of ocean-going vessels around the world forever. Lying on The Man's slanted table beneath perfect lighting that eliminated shadowing of any sort, the straightforward black lines he had drawn on simple white paper caused even the experienced, thirty-four year old Frank Jones to catch his breath.

"Jesus Christ, James. These concepts are stupendous! I've never ever seen anything that comes close to this. Now that you've put it on paper, it seems so obvious, like an Aristotelian theorem that describes a mathematical relationship which we busy humans simply failed to notice. Can you leave these drawings with me overnight? We'll make some mockups and then get the sheets right back up to you."

Then, without waiting for an answer, The Man yelled over his shoulder: "Peterman, get here on the double!"

Turning back to Stahl with a huge smile on his face, he said, "Thanks, James, for bringing these to me. If they prove out like you've made them look, you will have given ocean transport a shot in the arm that's at least as potent as the steel rail is to railroads. I mean that. Now get along with you so I can get to work. Peterman, where in the hell are you? Cooper, I need you now!"

As Jim turned and exited through the famous twin doors, he could hear, "Coming, boss, I'm coming! What do you have? I was lifting the prototype we'd made to compete with the *Mauretania* class ships out of the tank and had my hands full…"

His voice trailed off as The Man moved the new drawings under his face. "Wow!" was all that Peterman could utter. "These are amazing!"

"You're darn right!" Get that band saw started and let's get these mockups made as fast as possible to see if these concepts have value."

The two men labored, along with their assistant Cecil Cooper, right through the dinner hour and had wooden scale models ready to try out by 8:00 PM.

Carefully, the men placed these in the water tank. Spreading his hands securely on the wave generation controls, Jones directed Cooper, "Okay, now push it, then Peterman, you pull on that drawstring. Let's see how she rides when I create different conditions."

The results had never been seen before in the world of shipping. This experimental device initially used two relatively miniature hulls astride a wide platform that allowed it to ride the "swells" that Frank Jones created. The degree of yaw and roll so typical of single hulled ships of the day, even pitching, seemed more controlled. They placed weights on the central platform to simulate cargo, and then the new concept really performed. So long as the central portion was structured high enough so the waves could pass beneath it, it rode better than any vessel these men had ever seen or tested.

And fast! Their experimental pontoons seemed short, but were wide in the beam, so they offered far less resistance as they skimmed lightly across, rather than submerged within, the water. Full scale models would have a rudder to steer with, but tonight these were guided by the strings which Peterman maneuvered. Each sported a thin piece of wood which penetrated downward about two inches while its width had been estimated by James at one-tenth of the length of the pod. Extending much deeper, proportionately, than any heretofore keel, even on this small model, this upside down shark fin, as Cooper called it, kept the pontoon from bobbing erratically about.

All these pieces added up to so many variables that the draftsman upstairs had simply guessed at the initial dimensions in order to get the tests started.

It was immediately obvious that a perfectly balanced relationship existed. The correct proportional formulas would have to be deduced before they could build ships based on this low friction design. If the platform was too high, a crosswind or heaving swell might act on only one of the outrigger pontoons, as the men dubbed the pods, thereby causing the craft to tip over across its beam. Current hull designs were subject to a ship rolling over onto its sides, but usually they righted themselves prior to reaching the critical heel point and capsizing. In direct head or tail winds, Stahl's concept seemed to offer greater stability. If the central platform had a connecting underside that was too shallow, of course, forward progress would be badly impeded by friction with passing swells.

Much study would have to be conducted to understand the relationship of these variables if an ocean-going vessel were ever to come off their design boards, but the concepts which James Stahl had brought down to the tank that day were, indeed, revolutionary.

When James reported for work the next day, there was a message from Bill Walker.

"Come up to my office as soon as you get in. The Man says you are really on to something." Cryptic summons from Walker were the norm; he liked being direct.

The draftsman reported as summoned and the senior vice-president wasted no time: "Come on, Stahl; let's get down to the tank," he stated abruptly.

This time, Mr. Walker stood aside and respectfully held the double doors to the tank room open for his young draftsman. Cooper and Peterman were busy straightening the facility up. The Man was just getting in, having stayed late the night before, and he set about placing the demonstration models in the tank and drawing them around the water to show off their stability.

After a few minutes of this, Walker said, "Let me get Clyde down here!"

Unhooking a short black cylinder hanging on the wall, he pushed a buzzer and soon President Cummins picked up.

As usual, Walker was direct: "Clyde, how soon can you get down to the tank? Our man Stahl has come up with something that you ought to see right away!"

Then he turned to the employees in the room.

"Men, we're about to revolutionize shipping as we have known it! Tell your wives and families they may have to put up with you're spending a lot more time here than they are used to. If these ideas pan out, all of us will be earning money the like of which we have never imagined!"

With a loud bang, the double doors suddenly swung open simultaneously. The company president had stiff-armed both at once. Clyde Cummins was not impressive of stature, but everything about the man's demeanor exuded authority and determination. He was a natural-born, visionary leader, despite his bushy white eyebrows and clearly visible receding hairline.

"All right, Walker, you're got me here. What do you have?" As he bellowed this, he looked sharply at Jim, his eyebrows arching as if to demand an answer quickly from him as well.

The Man proceeded to demonstrate what his mockups could do; afterward, he escorted Clyde over to the tilt table displaying Stahl's drawings. It was so quiet in the tank room that even their assistant Cooper, standing off to the side, could hear the president's breathing.

"There's some powerful thinking going on in that head of his," he mused.

After studying the drawings for a bit, President Cummins motioned to Stahl and Walker. "Follow me," he commanded, and the three of them went upstairs to relax in the spacious office boasting stuffed easy chairs. Cummins removed a cigar from the humidor on his desk and offered one to the others. He didn't smoke, but James Stahl knew full well that, at august moments such as this one, you bluffed your way as a fellow smoker. He took one and rolled it between his fingers, acting as if he knew all about the merits of fine Cuban cigars.

Without further delay, the company president launched into his spiel.

"Well, gentlemen, you seem to have stumbled onto a principle of seafaring that has lain hidden these many centuries. I once was in the South Pacific, visiting an island called Samoa, where I swear the natives were using a principle of support roughly similar in their outrigger canoes, but these concepts as you have portrayed them James are, I believe, unknown to ship builders at the present time."

Leaning forward, he dropped some ashes into the bowl on his desk and looked James right in the eyes.

"Stahl, my man, I am promoting you, effectively immediately, to head up this project. What shall we call it? You know, my wife has pet cats at home. I've always admired the agility, balance and light touch of these animals. Let's call this craft, designed as it around pods, a pod-cat. Is that acceptable to you, James Stahl, Vice-President of Pod-cat Development?"

The newly promoted draftsman was, of course, all smiles. The three men stood up and shook hands.

"James, you'll have whatever funding it takes to prove your concepts. Work hand-in-hand with The Man, and add whomever you wish to augment your design and development staff as necessary. Best of luck!"

With that, the meeting in the president's office was concluded. As the former designer loped down the hall to his low-walled cubicle, the senior vice-president brought him up short and offered him an office of his own.

"No thank you, sir" James responded. "I work best where there is plenty of natural light and when I'm in the midst of others against whom I can test ideas. I'll remain right where I am, if that is acceptable."

Bill Walker thought for a moment, then proffered, "Well, now, James, we can't have a vice-president working elbow-to-elbow with staff members. What about this?" and Walker outlined a concept where Jim was provided quarters in an office having three walls, with the south-facing outer wall being largely windowed, and the open end fanning outward toward drafting tables that were arrayed like ice tongs. James jumped at the arrangement, thinking it would be conducive to the exchange of ideas without any single person becoming an annoying hindrance to his adjacent worker.

"That's an excellent idea, sir!" and with that said, Vice-President James Stahl returned to his drafting table.

After further thought, James realized that he would need to split this concept in two, with a port and a starboard single propeller pod as the rear support points, and another two smaller ones positioned forward. Steering was yet to be worked out. However, he had his initial concept on paper, made possible by using fuel oil stored in a feeder capsule toward the bow, rather than coal, to fire boilers which would generate steam to turn turbines. The stern pods would carry the engines while the fuel would be contained on the flat platform supported by the pods.

He was on his way to becoming noteworthy at his company.

N.B.: As the subsequent drawings are revealed, be aware that initial naval perspectives are nearly always heavily altered as refinements are made.

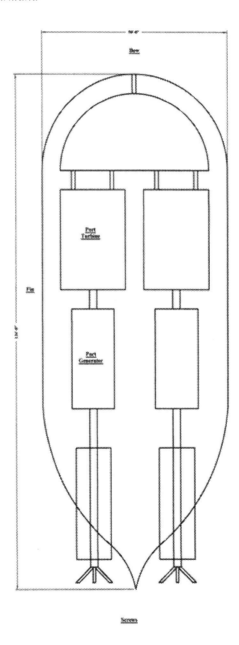

The top two perspectives are alternative front views, with the right hand view preferable. The pods would be attached to the outer portion of a bowed platform upon which the superstructure would rest. The stern pods would be three times or so the length of the bow pods and around 50 feet in breadth. These would house the propulsion mechanisms and provide working space for the engineers and stokers.

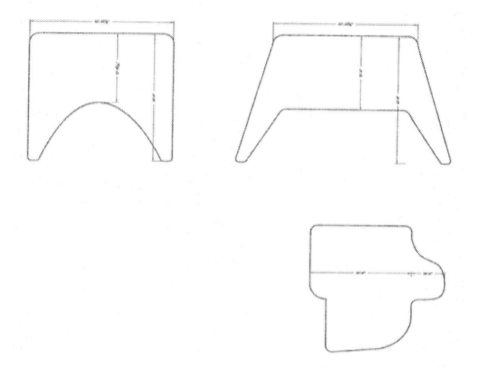

A bulbous bow is used to reduce pitch. Such a bow would be eliminated in the final versions since the intent of this craft would be to generate sufficient propulsive force that the four pods supporting the hull would actually rise upward until they rode just below the surface of the water. A single keel is replaced by fins astride the outboards, employing one on the right and one on the left supporting a rectangular air-filled space. Possibly, these would be designed to flare outward below the waterline. The two forward or bow pods are about 40 feet long, 43 feet from base to top, and 34 feet wide across their breadth. A superstructure with crew and passenger and command cabins for 1000 occupants would sit atop the four pods connected side-to-side by a shallow arched support.

CHAPTER EIGHT

EVERYTHING LOST

When he arrived home that evening, his wife knew immediately that something was up. He kissed her longer, and more firmly, for one thing, and he forgot to take his hat off for another. In fact, he fairly swaggered about the living room until she forced him to sit down. Taking his hat off for him and holding it across her ample belly, she admired her husband for a few moments and then challenged him.

"I think you have something to tell me. You're practically bursting at the seams! Come on, what is it? If you don't tell me, you won't get any of that delicious pot roast I've prepared tonight."

James knew he was licked. Pot roast was one of his favorites—after Thanksgiving turkey, perhaps. He didn't want to miss a bite.

"I've been promoted to Vice-President, honey, and given an office." As her face began to light up with smiles which seemed to radiate through her body, he added, "Now don't get all excited; this means I may have to go in on Saturdays, and most assuredly my regular hours will increase. What with the baby coming soon, I wasn't sure that you'd be pleased with these additional demands on my time."

"Don't you worry about us. You just take care of business; I've got support coming."

Two thoughts crossed Jim's mind. His wife was surprisingly well organized for an event that was brand new to them both. Second, she was already referring to herself in the plural. Clearly, she was ready for what was coming. She was an amazing woman; he was so very lucky to have her at his side!

For her part, Alice thought how smart she had been cultivating Jim's mom and preparing her own mother, Martha, for the big change that was drawing near in their lives. As a matter of fact, that big day better hurry up and come, she mused. Doing everyday tasks was becoming increasingly difficult. Nowadays, she felt less agile than those Antarctic penguins which she'd seen at the zoo, and they didn't even have fingers!

About eight weeks later, the town was in the full grip of summertime warmth. The air was filled with pleasantly fresh aromas from the myriad flowerbeds maintained by the local garden club. A constant drone from hundreds of bumblebees relishing all the available nectar filled the daylight hours. Being near the sea helped the flowers and trees bloom. Even though it took some time for the ocean waters to warm, the breeze wafting across the sea carried plenty of moisture to help young shoots grow and thrive.

Alice was in the midst of getting the house ready for company over the July 4th holiday. Jim's parents were due to arrive any hour for a visit. She knew them from her wedding reception, of course, but they kept pretty much to themselves and so their week-long stay now would be a pleasant chance to solidify her relationship with them. Jim's mom, Estelle, or "Stella!" as her husband liked to call her, had written that she wanted to learn the house inside and out. With this knowledge, she thought she could be helpful when her grandchild first arrived. If she had the ability to maintain her daughter-in-law's house without having to ask for instructions, she could take a huge load off Alice's shoulders.

"If there's anything I can do to make it easier for you, dear, please let me do it!" had been her explanation when they had corresponded regarding the visit.

At the time, Alice had not appreciated the difference that a mother-in-law could make to ease her daily chores. Now that she was, indeed, growing as big as a house, Alice had asked for time away from her job. She had explained that, since this would be her first baby, everything would be a new challenge and the burden of working in an office would simply be too much to handle. Her boss, and in turn his boss, had both agreed, but they had insisted that she provide them with some assurance she would return to work within three months. That she had promised to do. As she thought the matter thorough, she realized her mother-in-law would become a much needed ally if she returned to work in late fall; hence, their current visit.

The more she bustled about, the more Jim realized his parents were really coming to stay with them. His dad, so firm in his belief that Jim should have attended college, would see that his son had become successful in his chosen field. His mother, who had always thrust her second cousin's daughter at Jim, would see that he had made the right choice regarding a spouse, too. If he'd had suspenders on, he would have snapped them with pride. His folks were going to be proud of their son, for sure! He turned to his wife and tenderly wrapped his arms around her expanding stomach.

"I love you very much, Alice."

There was such endearing and heartfelt tenderness in this simple sentence that her knees gave way for a bit, but his embrace held her next to him. Her eyes were as blue as the summer sky and her hair sparkled with youthful luster. She was the very picture of health. Pregnancy provided this benefit to *les femmes enceintes* as a kind of consolation for the sore back, headaches, swollen hands, and other inconveniences that accompanied having a baby, Jim reasoned. Regardless, he couldn't have been more satisfied at this time in his life. It is at just such peaks of happiness when Fate plays its vilest tricks.

When she checked the mail delivery that day, there was a sealed invitation from Jim's workplace. Opening it, Alice discovered a surprise invitation to a party at the company's office. The date was convenient—being two days before the fireworks that would surely be set off on the Fourth—so she sat right down and wrote a gracious acceptance on behalf of Jim, herself, and then added that she would be bringing Jim's parents as well. Everyone would be excited to see Jim's new office arrangements, she added. Affixing the penny stamp, she posted her family's reply.

That afternoon, she heard a knock on her front door. When Alice opened it, there stood Estelle and Samuel Stahl, both sporting exuberant, wide smiles. It was obvious to them that not only was their daughter-in-law pregnant, but also that she was blooming with health. Clearly, they were soon to be happy grandparents! If ever there was an occasion to give thanks, the senior Stahls figured now was the time.

She welcomed them into her and Jim's home and quickly got them settled. Samuel opened windows in the living room, Alice brought out cool lemonade, and they were still there when James arrived a little after 7:00 PM. The reunion was warm and heartfelt. The members of this family reveled in the joy of being together.

Over dinner, Alice told them about the invitation to the company party to be held five days hence. "That should give us time to recover and get prepared for the fireworks and all that barbecuing!" she added.

"Get prepared? You mean get hungry again, right?" chimed in Samuel. "It looks like you have everything around here all set for the holidays! Your daisies and petunias really add to the pleasant ambiance, as well."

"Well, thank you, Sam. What with Jim's new responsibilities, he's gone long hours and that gives me plenty of time to fiddle and create decorations. Having time on my hands will surely end in a few weeks when the baby comes, though."

"Don't worry, dear. We'll come back and help out in whatever way you need. Don't fret yourself about that." Estelle's tone was reassuringly confident.

"Thank you, Mom. I've no doubt I will take you up on that offer!"

Indeed, despite her glowing appearance and the outward calm she showed her husband, Alice was beginning to get a little nervous now that her baby's time was drawing so near. Would she be able to handle the new demands and still provide for her husband? Everyone would be required to make some adjustments, but where love is the foundation, anything can be accomplished.

*   *   *

The day before the big party at Cummins & Company, Jim sat before his tilt board stroking his chin in thought. How should the pods be sized? Displacement hulls, standard throughout the shipping industry, relied on length for speed; the longer the waterline length, the greater the potential for higher speeds.

On the contrary, the whole purpose of his designs would be to devise a hull shape that could plane toward the surface, rather than plow through many meters of water. He was projecting that standard speeds would reach fifty knots, so a craft's length would therefore be governed by the design load to be carried. A cargo vessel carrying 10,000 tons of grain would require longer and wider pods than a more compact one designed for 2,500 tons of passengers, crew, plus luggage. The tonnage for fuel oil heating steam boilers would have to be increased proportionately in both cases. He foresaw the future need for lighter fuel, or at least one with higher BTU's so less could be carried; a businessman always wants to cut overhead wherever possible.

What really needed inventing was a way to power the rotation of the turbines without the use of steam, but no one knew how to do that. Using boilers was state of the art in 1906, and even they were still heated with coal. Jim's ideas were far ahead of the existing technology. He would have to be patient, but there was no harm in dreaming. He was good at conceptualizing, but the only thing he had ever had the ingenuity to invent was to place a cup over his toothbrush so it wouldn't collect dust between uses. Except for telling Alice, he'd kept that idea to himself.

He tried configurations of two long, then four or six small, and finally settled on one short pod, probably around thirty feet long, positioned forward at both the port and starboard sides. Each would have an inverted shark fin, as Cooper had called it, protruding downward with a slight swept-backward angle on its leading edge. The length of the fin, or center-board, would be eight feet on the prototype, but it might be stretched out to fifteen feet for a vessel 300 feet long.

Despite this design using four fins, he mused, their total square footage should still be less than that of a standard hull's wetted surface. The truly extraordinary breakthrough these designs suggested was making possible a marked increase in speed; what was more, the faster such a craft steamed, the more she would lift, and thereby actually reduce drag the faster she cruised.

In the past, exactly the opposite had been true as both drag and wind resistance combined to require ever more thrust to generate more speed. Here, the faster a ship went, the easier it would be to maintain that speed.

He'd have to monitor testing under the keen eye of The Man. Together, they'd develop sufficient relationships so that sizing a pod could be reduced to a mathematical formula in the future.

The trailing edge of each forward pod would have a rudder mounted on hinges that was turned by an electric motor mounted inside the pod and controlled from the bridge. Each rudder could be hand-cranked in the event of an electric problem. This required that the bow, or fore-pods, taper toward their stern vertical profile to allow more torque when the rudders were being utilized.

He beamed. These were developing satisfactorily. Moreover, he appeared to be meeting his goal of not using chines on the wetted, buoyant surfaces because these would detract from efficiency. He designed for turns to be effected without significant heeling; thus, incorporating some sort of flat surface would be unnecessary. The fins, protruding downward like the sides of an upside-down cup split in two, would require entirely unique design criteria.

As for the stern pods, these would be vastly more complex as they had to support the screws and propeller shafts as well as provide operating space for the men who ran the turbines powering each shaft. These pods would therefore be sized around ninety or so feet long and at least thirty feet across the beam. He could hardly comprehend the dimensions required for their fins; probably five times as big as those for the fore-pods, he guessed. Then again, the height of the stern pods would probably exceed twelve feet given all the equipment that would be housed inside. Surely they'd have to have an overhead pulley and chain to move equipment around. Once again, trial and error would be his guide.

Aboard ship, these stern pods would have to be able to maintain temperature control and breathable air for the men working therein. Nothing like this could actually be attempted yet because coal was still being used to fire up boilers. But double boilers positioned directly in line with turbines could possibly be made to run on oil. The trick would be sizing the boilers to fit such low overheads, or discovering a source of power to run the turbines that was as yet unknown.

The question remained whether to house such fuel supply aboard each rear pod; such a configuration would require that an empty tank be positioned astride the oil tank and gradually filled with sea water as the fuel was used up. Otherwise, that ship would lose trim and be in danger of capsizing. If the oil was housed above in some sort of centralized superstructure tank, the advantage of forgetting about shifting ballast would be offset by the huge danger of exposing the fuel line. Even if there were no fire, anything puncturing or compromising that line would make the ship inoperable and it would simply spin around in circles operating on one engine, like a fly with only one wing.

As a matter of fact, Jim couldn't budge from his concern that, as fast and economical as these designs could be, there was that one fatal flaw. If an engine failed, could forward-mounted rudders be effective in steering a one-engine ship in a navigable line? The obvious answer—four screws, rather than just two—would vastly add to the weight, fuel consumption, and complexity of design. Some sort of alloyed high strength steel would be required to support such enormous, concentrated weight.

The other headache he didn't even want to address was the total square footage that the pods would represent. Even with large, open spaces separating the platform support legs, he did not want to be the man employed to sand and smooth the exterior seams prior to surface painting. Even briefly imagining the labor required brought small beads of sweat to his forehead. He wiped them away.

"Hmmm," he hummed, musing on the various challenges. Looking into the future, he thought, "Someone must invent a motorized sander to speed up construction. Also, these ships will require a lighter, more compact fuel. We have got to have some mechanism for eliminating the need to generate steam in favor of firing turbine operations directly. I am forced to let future inventions determine the answer." He softly drummed his fingers on the tilt table.

He should have understood that an opportunity, once offered, doesn't necessarily come around again.

Believing he was finished for the day, he took these latest drawings over to the desk of a young planner who had recently been hired.

"Scott," he began innocently enough, "I want you to make a precise copy of each of these plan designs. How long will you need?"

"Good golly, Mr. Stahl, at least three entire days, I would wager," stated the young designer as he leafed through all the sketches.

"Not good enough. Here, let me show you a trick I devised but haven't yet had a chance to try out. Fetch me that large open crate over there, will you."

Setting the box on the floor, he elevated each corner with some large reference books. Next, he placed an electric bulb in the center down low. "That's so the heat will dissipate," he explained, pointing to all the airflow spaces. Then he covered the upper opening where the lid had been with a clear glass pane, and above that one of his finished drafts. Above that he lowered a similar glass pane about thirty inches square. When he turned on the bulb and taped one of his blank drafting papers atop the glass, the image of his black lines came though the fresh paper clearly and distinctly.

Scott Terry was astounded. "Good golly, Mr. Stahl, I can trace your design and have these back to you this afternoon. Your invention makes it a snap. Thank you, sir!"

"Thank you, my boy. Be clean and accurate. Be sure to tape down the corners so the two papers remain aligned. Once the tracing is complete, remove my original drawing and simply free-hand the specifications along the side of the copy you made. Now, there is only one caution, son, but it's a caution you must take."

"What's that, sir?" The lad's eyes were wide and alert, taking it all in. On the spot, he had concluded that his boss was one magnificent fellow.

"You must pay absolute attention to what you are doing. No distractions, once you start. That means take your lunch or go down the hall to urinate or whatever you have to do, but once you begin, complete the entire drawing and then promptly remove the original from beneath the glass. I estimate that you'll have perhaps ten to fifteen minutes to do each copy before the bulb generates dangerous heat. Can you see that if you are careless, the drawings I rendered—and these are my only copies, understand—could ignite from the lamp? Put your hand there; see? That's a lot of heat if focused for any length of time. Do you understand?"

"Aye, aye, sir, loud and clear!" affirmed the junior draftsman.

For a moment, Jim imagined they were on board ship. "Don't rush things," he thought. "My time at sea will come soon enough."

"Good. Now, when you're done, I may not be here, so return the originals to my storage chest in my office; do you know where that is?"

"Not yet, sir. I'd be grateful if you'll take me there and show it to me now. I've been sort of scared anytime I get too near your office; it's kind of sacrosanct ground to us junior draftsmen. Do you know what I mean, sir?"

"Of course, of course. Come with me." The office was not forbidding; rather, Jim considered it welcoming and open. But he could understand a seventeen year-old being timid.

"Right there, put the drawings in that box. Now, this is important. Review your copies, and if you are satisfied with their accuracy, roll them up and have Brewster over at the post office mail them to Peter North, 36 Ludlow Street, down there in Newport News. Be absolutely certain you get them mailed before you leave today. Understand?"

Yes, sir. 36 Ludlow Street, Mr. Peter North."

"Gads! Thank you for reminding me. Good lad! It's 2nd Officer Peter North. I should be more clearheaded."

With that, they shook hands and Stahl returned to his tilt table for further work. The fact that his best friend was advancing in seagoing rank ahead of him was not a cause for jealousy. After all, as a company vice-president, he held an important title as well.

* * *

The next day dawned with a beautifully rose-colored sun, indicating that the temperature would be warm. When everyone had dressed for the company party, Samuel Stahl drove the three of them to the building housing all the executives. Jim's wife had never been to the shipyard or its design support facility; however, the guards at the gate had been prepped to expect them, so the Stahl party entered without delay. Alice directed Sam to park in the designated lot at a slot a bit removed from the festivities. She had been housebound all day, so she wanted the chance for a little exercise before indulging in the anticipated buffet.

Walking toward the office building, she looked up at its four floors, picked out the spacious window that was sure to be her husband's third-floor office, and gave God a small prayer of thanks for having blessed her, and her soon-to-be family, with such good fortune. Her husband held a position at a company that was both challenging and rewarding, she loved her husband, and soon their love was to be rewarded with a baby. It was so good to be alive!

Alice stepped eagerly into the reception area and began introductions of her husband's parents. Samuel and Estelle were made to feel welcome and, together with Jim—who was already in the swing of things—found themselves having a smashingly good time.

After a little while, Clyde Cummins came over to introduce himself. He could see that the members of the Stahl clan were well fortified with spirits and were enjoying the repartee immensely.

Clyde extended his hand to Samuel, saying, "We're mighty proud of your boy, here. He's hard working and an original thinker. He mentioned to me way back that it was his intention to take to the sea and command a ship someday, but we're lucky that he hasn't pushed the matter. His ideas may make us more successful that our founders ever dreamed!"

What could he do with accolades such as these being showered upon his son? He could affirm how he loved his boy, that's what. Samuel Stahl stood there basking in the success and adulation his son was receiving.

After a few moments, he put an arm around Jim's shoulders and affirmed, "I am, indeed, right pleased with you, my boy. I never thought I'd say this, but you were wise to ignore me and find your own way. I couldn't be prouder of you!"

President Cummins thought this might be an appropriate time for James to show everyone what he had been working on so diligently for the last few weeks.

Turning to his newest vice-president, he asked, "What do you think, my boy? Would you go upstairs to your office and fetch some of those wooden models that Frank Jones made for you? I want you to show them to the folks here so they'll know we are a company that is forward-looking rather than tied down to the past."

"Of course, sir, right away." Then, turning to his wife, he warned, "Be patient, honey. I'm up on the third floor and it'll take a few minutes to find a box in which to carry everything down. Upstairs, I have some small wooden prototypes as well as my blueprints. Will you be all right?" he asked as he looked down at her protruding stomach.

The candlelight reflecting off the pale yellow walls of the lounge area flattered Alice's face and made her eyes glow like fresh bluets.

She looked up into James' eyes and said, "I couldn't be happier. Go get your treasures."

He turned and started to ascend the stairs. Pausing, he looked back over his shoulder at the happy conclave of his boss, all four parents, and adoring wife looking his way with expectant expressions on their faces. Then he disappeared up to the next landing, turned the corner, and climbed the next set of stairs that led to the third floor.

He stored the models in a sturdy container that the company's carpenters had built specially for him.

Meantime, President Cummins had moved over to one corner where the party was becoming gleeful. His second-in-charge, Walker, was laughing heartily at some joke Mr. Cummins had related. Leaning back a little to support his guffaws, his glass tipped over, spilling all of its 90 proof liquor down toward the floor. Cummins saw this and watched with drunken bemusement as it splattered over the junction box containing the pilot light for the gas heating unit.

He thought to himself, "Did the utility man remember to shut that off for the summer..."

Upstairs, Stahl was bending over retrieving his prize creations when there was an overpowering noise. An explosion of hot gases traveled throughout the air spaces in the building and sent choking dust rushing over his desk, models, and himself. All the interior lighting instantly went black. Only the faint glow from streaks of sunlight coming through Jim's ash-besmirched window gave any illumination to the work room. He found his footing and groped for the head of the stairs, but he was immediately driven back by the extremes of hot air and orange flames rushing up from below. These were followed by a cloud of dense black smoke which would suffocate all life as the opaque mass enveloped everything in the building.

In desperation, he took his tall-backed wooden chair and hurled it with all his might against his window. The glass, chair, and all the pane supports folded and crashed to the ground. Looking out the gaping hole, James had only a moment to see that people were rushing madly toward the building; then the escaping heat wave pressed him out through the opening. He oddly heard a disconnected wailing as he wildly flailed his arms: a distant alarm was growing louder as a fire wagon approached.

He grabbed at the protruding flagpole proudly displaying the company's insignia as he sailed downward, stretched himself as long as he could from it, then dropped. A two story plummet onto sun-baked ground would ordinarily be enough to crack leg bones, but Jim's adrenalin was pumped too high. He escaped injury by clenching his teeth to prevent biting his tongue in two, cushioning the fall by allowing his knees and elbows to fold as his feet touched down, and exhaling powerfully as he hit. But he didn't jump up and run to anyone's aid.

Crouching low to stay away from the heat, he bore witness to the shattered, flaming framing of the first floor. All he could see were walls of fire engulfing everything, and everyone, inside. It was simply impossible to make entry for rescue. Some happy partygoer had spilled liquor onto the new gas-fired heating apparatus that, despite it being shut off, must have been leaking. When the pilot light ignited the liquor, this reached the enclosed fuel supply, resulting in sudden, explosive catastrophe.

The fire crews arrived amidst scores of frantic employees. The wails of their sirens added counterpoint to the agonized screams coming from the scorched lounge. Someone found buckets and these were loaded with sand and thrown at the flaming mess. The fire men got the pump working and water poured into the first floor spaces, but by then the fire had really taken hold and it reached with hungry tentacles up into the upper floors. Within twenty minutes, the fire fighters had to back away as the entire structure collapsed and sent incandescent, sizzling sparks high into the sky. This made the firemen turn their full attention to neighboring structures to prevent further spread.

With the entire design and executive building tumbling to the ground, nothing identifiable remained. The happy party-goers, and all the plans and designs which the company men had created over the years, were reduced to black, smoldering bits of charred wood. Even the shiny, heavy steel paperweight that had held so many reports and drafting papers on President Cummins' desk was now merely a misshapen slug of metal. Gradually, the flames were reduced, but immediate probing of the debris by rescuers revealed not a living soul. The nightmare had completely destroyed the company as well as the lives of many of its best and finest.

As the firemen and onlookers gradually packed up and dispersed, someone noticed a figure deeply bent over, remaining still as a stone, apparently heedless of the smoke and danger. One of the guards at the gate, who had run over to try and help, recognized James Stahl.

"This is one of the company's executives!" he shouted for all to hear. "Mr. Stahl, sir, excuse me, what do you want us to do? The fire is controlled but I'm afraid we have found no survivors. Someone should notify their next-of-kin, but sir, I don't know how to go about it. Tell me what to do."

His beseeching plea hung like an anguished surrender in the dank, stinking air. Former Vice-President James Stahl looked up at him. His eyes were bleary from tears and his skin as pale as a peeled onion. He opened his mouth but couldn't speak.

The guard called over his shoulder, "Hey, someone bring a doctor over here! This man is hurt!"

Stahl heard the call for help, but thought only: "It won't do me any good. I'm not hurt, I'm finished. I caused the death of my own parents. My beloved wife and soon-to-be-born son have perished before we ever had a moment together. I have no reason, no will to live."

Then a medical man appeared, knelt before him, shined a light in his eyes, and promptly said, "Take this man to a place out of the wind immediately. He's in shock and needs water and quiet. Let me know where he is taken and I'll check on him soon."

With that said, the doctor moved toward the smoldering ruins but, like those before him, found faceless bodies of varying heights that were identifiable due mainly to the jewelry, cuff links, or such that were associated with each charred corpse.

Stahl was removed to a nearby pump house where the plant's supervisor of water operations maintained his control quarters. Two firemen who had suffered burns from the showering embers sat down alongside him as well, awaiting salve or cool compresses from the doctor.

"Who are you?" inquired one of those men, hoping for some conversation to ease the pain from his burns.

James couldn't speak, but he passed over the identification pamphlet he always carried in his breast pocket.

"Geesh, mister, I think you're the only corporate officer who survived. We've identified Cummins, Walker, and a Harry Harley who I've been told was a vice-president, just like you, I suppose. There were several who seemed to be from out of town; we couldn't find any company identification on them…"

Jim's sudden collapse into a globe of groans and tearful moans startled the two firemen, but they quickly deduced that at least some of the unidentified victims must have been related to him. Dealing with their own pain and suffering was all they could manage. His agony was obviously mental, and they simply let him be. To their relief, the doctor returned and administered to their burns immediately. After seeing to their dressings, he released them to find their way to their buddies for a ride home. Then he turned to address the obviously broken hulk now groveling on the cool cement floor.

"Rise up, my man. You'll have to get hold of yourself. You've suffered the greatest heartbreak a human being can be subjected to, but you are still alive. Now listen to me."

He held Jim's ashen face, so distorted with suffering, and spoke clearly, slowly. "You are still young. You have a strong future ahead of you. Now listen to me, James, listen. You have got to find the strength within yourself to go on living for their memory. Do you understand? The death of your bride, and that of your parents, if we identified them correctly, will be in vain if you give in to despair. You have got to pull yourself together and live as good a life as you can to honor their memory. Are you hearing me, lad?"

There was a glimmer of comprehension, but not yet acceptance, in James' eyes. He allowed the doctor to lift him erect and call out, "Is there anyone who can give this man a lift back to his home?"

Out of the murky gloom a voice piped up, "I know his house, Doc. Me and Fred here can take care of him." Thereupon, the doctor handed James Stahl over to meet his destiny.

CHAPTER NINE

UNDERWAY

Since that singularly awful night, James Stahl had found solace serving aboard ships plying the seas for the last 23 years. He was 50 years old in 1929 and, at long last, had his first command. Justifiably proud of the *Reliance,* he surveyed the ongoing loading, as well as crew and passenger embarkation. Everything went according to schedule. The 238 crew and stewards had boarded in the early morning. At 1400 hours, his ship had all the scheduled passengers—445 of them—tallied. That made 683 people aboard; no animals were to be transported on this voyage. The freight was stowed securely in the holds.

Using his megaphone, he hailed the dockworkers and they quickly withdrew the gangplanks, ascertained that the men using barbuckles to load barrels were finished, and gathered in the painter lines thrown ashore by the ship's seamen.

Reliance was inched by several chuffing tugboats into the main course of the Hudson River. Thereupon, the harbor pilot faced her downriver and put her engine telegraph at half-ahead, cruised past the famous White Star Line pier, past the park bordering the southern tip of Manhattan Island, eased past Governor's Island, then the Statue of Liberty, and thereupon put her engines at idle so the Pilot's Launch could run alongside and allow him to disembark.

With his ship freed at last to undertake her voyage, Jim Stahl took his first real breath of command. He pointed the bow toward the Verrazano Narrows and steered *Reliance* into Lower New York Harbor. Then he had a supreme moment: he faced the open ocean with a ship under his command for the first time. The navigation and ship's course would have been plotted out carefully by one of the upper level officers but, during the first few minutes of any cruise, James always felt as though he was being let out of the starting gate, like a strong young race horse, ready to take on whatever challenge the sea might throw at him. For some reason that remained obscure to him, he was enthralled by the unknown; he therefore found himself exhilarated by the realization that he stood ready to take on whatever the Atlantic Ocean might send his way.

The *Reliance* was divided into twelve compartments defined by bulkheads that, following lessons learned from the tragic sinking of the great White Star Line *R.M.S. Titanic* in 1912, extended from the Tank Top—with its engine rooms and fuel storage— all the way up through C Deck. The B and A Decks for passengers, together with the Bridge for command, Pilot's Room for steering, and officers' quarters were all part of the superstructure. Consequently, these were entirely above the highest line of the hull. With the bulkhead hatches closed, the complete area of the hull could be made into a single, watertight structure. This new approach was referred to as watertight compartmentalization; it prevented overflow from adjacent bulkheads.

The reliable electronic switch system, together with its indicator bulbs, controlling these bulkhead hatches was displayed on the aft wall of the Bridge as well as behind the chief engineer in the engine room. The switch system was designed to be within easy reach of the officer then in command of piloting the ship. As an added measure, Captain Stahl had made it policy, when *Reliance* was underway, that all bulkhead hatches were to be closed between sunset and sunrise.

To accommodate ready access for storage, easy use by passengers, and moving cargo from the nets and crane hooks as goods were offloaded from the dock, the hatches had been designed by Otis & Co. for accessibility to and from adjoining compartments. The Otis craftsmen had tested and perfected a grooved design whereby one side of these large openings utilized a triple-hinged hatchway that could be swung open or closed manually when the larger opening was required, but when not in active use was always—by strict regulation—kept dogged down. During normal operations, the adjacent twin entry was generally left open for passenger and crew ease of access from one compartment to the next. This hatch was also securely triple-hinged against the bulkhead and could be closed either by the hand cranks alongside each hatch frame, or by electric signal from the Bridge. These hatches, fitted on every deck and at each bulkhead, were wider and taller than those constructed on the famous *Olympic* class vessels, but they had been tested by the naval architects to withstand even crushing force.

The shipbuilders at Newport News touted these safety-features when selling them to commercial lines, but they were downplayed in their advertisements to the public. "Deemed absolutely watertight" was all the detail needed for prospective passengers.

One of the weaknesses in the *Titanic* had been her bulkhead hatches. Her ability to suffer damage and simply take it in stride without sinking had been dangerously compromised. As coal was used up in a bunker, an empty space was left, reducing the pressure a neighboring bulkhead could withstand. Moreover, a fire had broken out in one of the storage bins about the time the ship had departed Queenstown, Ireland. The coal been removed to quench the fire, but the steel walls had softened and bowed as a result of the heat, so their strength was badly weakened.[2]

Launched to take advantage of the active demand for passenger traffic between the Continent and the States, the *Reliance* had three decks for her travelers. These top decks were not divided into the old Edwardian principle of a person's class. To keep ticket prices as low as was reasonably profitable, there was one class for all passengers; thus, only one dining room was needed which the passengers happily shared with the officers on the ship. The crew required a separate hall furnished with benches rather than chairs. These could both be served by one galley and thus use the same kitchen. There were separate lounges for men and women (since smoking was still generally popular with just men), and far simpler room decorations. Imaginative painting had replaced the finely carved exotic wood of pre-war vessels.

---

2 Testimony by Chief Engineer Bell at the American Senate subcommittee and the Wreck Commissioner's Court (British) hearings in 1912.

The location of one's cabin determined how much a passenger was charged for his or her ticket. The A Deck rooms were more spacious, had larger portholes, and boasted deeper pile carpeting and wall decorations; these hid the ever present piping in a ship of this size. Opting for a B or C Deck room meant accepting smaller portholes that could not open, thinner carpeting, and metal wall partitions, but correspondingly lower ticket prices. The advantage of these decks was that the rooms could be connected through a double-sided locking hatchway, so family members traveling with more than two in their party could be connected together in a suite of rooms during their voyage.

Given the 24 hour operation of *Reliance*, daily shifts for crew members were sandwiched around human endurance: 5 hours on, 5 hours off, 5 hours on, and then 9 hours off. The shifts for kitchen staffs—tasked with preparing and serving three meals a day plus operating a late night café—were responsible for their own scheduling. The three men manning the radio room were now a part of the ship's company, but they set up their own shift rotations in order to operate around the clock.

The lookouts, drawn from the ranks of the seamen aboard, worked only between dusk and dawn on 2 hour stints. Sixth Officer Ron Jenkins was responsible for overseeing their watches in conjunction with the officer in charge of the Bridge during darkness.

Scheduling this array of duty assignments was a major coordination problem. Thank goodness for Officer Jenkins; his well-organized, mathematical sort of mind freed Captain Stahl from having to keep track of them.

There was a polite knock on the metal wall.

"Excuse me, Captain. There are some passengers below who would like to meet you." Chief Steward Steve Spillane waited by the entry way for the captain's response.

"Thank you, Chief Steward. Please inform them I must remain fully occupied here on the Bridge, but I look forward to dining with our passengers come the dinner hour." Thereupon, Stahl turned his back on the steward and resumed the duties of command.

Obviously dismissed, Spillane returned to the glassed-in veranda area where a clutch of passengers had stretched themselves across various folding lounge chairs. This deck was as high as a passenger could go, unless he was invited to the Bridge by an officer, but no one felt deprived. The view through the wide portals was panoramic; they also completely blocked the bothersome wind.

One of the women had a ten year old boy alongside her.

"Gosh, Mr. Chief Steward, did you ask the captain whether I could come up and help steer the ship?" he asked upon spotting Spillane.

"I did just that, Denny, but the captain is very busy right now. We've been at sea for only an hour, so there are a great many things he has to attend to. Did you know our vessel is longer than two football fields?"

Denny shook his head from side to side, though his wide eyes never left Spillane's face.

"No? Well, she is, and she weighs a whole lot, too! Nevertheless, can you feel how steady she is? Just look at all those waves cavorting about out there, but they don't bother us at all."

Chief Steward Spillane liked children. He better: he and his wife Lisa had four of their own back home in Darien, Connecticut. Their son and his three sisters were old enough to attend school now. This meant that when her husband was away on a job, the house would be so quiet that Lisa occasionally flirted with the idea of another baby, but then 3:00 would come and the children would amble back home one by one. The demands for cookies, juice, and sometimes even crunchy apples would keep Lisa busy as she prepared supper for them all, so she'd forget for another night how empty the house could feel.

"Golly gee, that's big. Two football fields! Wow!" Denny was running on all cylinders at the vivid images that Steward Steve had conjured. "No wonder I got real tired trying to walk around the deck. Mother kept saying it was too dangerous, but I just plain got all tuckered out."

"That's all right, Denny. Wait a couple of days; you'll get your sea legs after a bit, and then we can try again." He paused, thinking. Today was Thursday, so he suggested: "Remind me come Saturday, will you?" As an afterthought, he added, "And, since we're going to be friends and all, Denny, try just calling me Steward Steve. Is that okay with you?"

"I sure will, sir!" The boy had an eager smile of acceptance wreathing his face. "I can remember 'Steward Steve.'" A smile of joy at being aboard a big ocean-going liner seemed to have become a permanent feature of the youngster's face.

Turning his attention to the boy's mother, Steward Steve inquired, "Mrs. Collins, have you everything you need to be comfortable? It will probably be several hours before the galley chefs ring the bell for supper. I wouldn't want you to catch a chill sitting for too long out here."

"Well, now, Chief Steward Spillane, how you do go on! I'm just fine right where I am. I've got this warm blanket across me; it might even be Scotch wool, from the feel of its texture. Besides, I've got to keep an eye on Denny; you've already seen how he can get himself into hot water without even trying."

"Ma'am, you've got a point there. I never saw those marbles he rolled my way while he was playing on the veranda. It's good I have nimble feet! But do keep an eye on him for me, will you please. He's a mighty fine, spritely lad, if I do say so."

"Thank you, that's a lovely compliment, considering his mischievous nature. When the supper bell rings, I'm sure he will be ready to respond!"

She looked appealingly demure, all stretched out and warm beneath the red, yellow, and black of the plaid blanket. She was so firmly tucked in that only her pretty face, with her softly sculpted nose and soft mouth, peeped out. But Steve had been a steward for nigh on ten years. Sure as shooting, messing around with a passenger would risk everything he had worked for so long to achieve. "Let well enough alone," he concluded to himself. Still, her company was certainly pleasant enough.

"I'm sure your correct, ma'am. But in the meantime, if there's anything I, or one of my assistants can do for you or your husband, please let me know."

"Oh! Good gracious, I seem to have misled you. Mr. Collins did not accompany us on this voyage. In fact, my son Denny and I are planning on spending two weeks together exploring the north coast of France near Messines Ridge. You see, my brother was killed there during the closing months of the war. It happened just after the British repulsed the major German offensive in early 1918. Some of the townsfolk have written that they are caring for his grave, as well as those of several hundred of his buddies in the memorial site at Dieppe. Have you ever visited any of the battlegrounds yourself, Chief Steward?"

There was a long pause as Steve tried collecting his thoughts. So, her husband was not aboard! Regardless, she had unknowingly hit him in a very sore spot. He had in fact been part of the "early American invasion," as his compatriots liked to call it. That was when several dozen American flyboys sailed to England and offered their skills to the nascent British flying corps long before America had gotten into the war. They had been accepted and thereafter flown sortie after sortie against the Boche, losing an average of a plane, a flyer, or both each time his squadron went up in 1916.

He'd been fortunate. His engine had been shot up, but he broke only his legs when the plane crashed. In the most amazingly lucky break any flyer could experience back then, his plane had not exploded at impact. He'd been able to glide back across the French lines and thus crash on allied soil. He was soon rescued and taken to a field hospital, but spent nearly two years thereafter trying to recover. By the time he was mended and mostly functional once again, the American doughboys were mopping up the last of the German trench resistance and sending the invaders scurrying past Arras on toward some safe German town.

Following the Armistice in 1919, he thanked the Lord above that he'd been given a second chance to live. He had found himself listening with rapt attention as the American President, Woodrow Wilson himself, spoke of healing deep wounds and bringing the peoples of the conflict together in a league of the world's nations. The president's goals failed to be realized but, on the spot, Steve had resolved to devote the rest of his life in the service of others.

Of course, he had to support himself, so the job he found, and now happily held, seemed like an excellent fit. Along the way he'd met Lisa at an A.T.C. corporate Christmas party. He was smitten by her looks and the pleasantly soft lilt of her voice; she had liked how he spoke of service to others and his bravery for having volunteered so early in the war. Their wedding followed shortly thereafter, and the first of their kids even more shortly after that. Lisa was like a natural-born baby mill. At first, he used to josh her about being more rabbit than human, but that soon grew stale. She adored being a mother. Lisa applied herself to the raising of their kids with such one-track zeal that Steve found himself actually enjoying continual ship duty; it permitted him to find some peace and quiet.

He chuckled to himself. He couldn't abide the constant hubbub from the four loud kids he had created, yet he could survive daily questions and demands from several hundred people whom he'd be around for only a week or so.

"The irony of being in love, yet married," he'd occasionally muse.

Further along the deck, he noticed a junior steward, Robin Jackson, in difficulty.

"Hey there, Steward Jackson, what seems to be the trouble?" His voice had carried, causing several passengers to look his way as he approached the young employee. In fact, Robin was interrupted even before making his answer.

"Mr. Spillane! Thank goodness you're here. Would you just look at this bumbling boy! What he has done, sir, is beyond the pale! I cannot fathom why your company ever hired him. When I think on how we have been out of port for a mere two hours, I ask, 'what does the future hold for this idiot?'"

Harold Bottoms was a ruddy checked, heavily rotund passenger who, in a very short time, had established himself as one of the most demanding passengers Steve Spillane had ever served.

"Well, now, let's reason this all out, shall we, Mr. Bottoms? How did we get ourselves in this fix, anyway?"

The passenger, writhing about the deck as though he was an octopus missing a few tentacles, was desperately trying to extricate himself from a pair of canvas and wood deck chairs that had apparently collapsed in a heap when he had lowered his overly ample posterior upon them. Canvas and wood pieces had mixed in total disarray as a result of Bottoms becoming panicked at finding himself ensnared. Unfortunately, every time he would struggle free, the ship would plunge down a trough or pitch up a crest, causing him to spradle on the deck once again and become further entangled.

"Why, this steward was passing by just as I was sitting down, and he heedlessly distracted me by asking whether I should like a pillow. Can you imagine the thoughtlessness, making an inquiry just at the moment requiring maximum concentration on my part? I tell you, sir, I shall bring this stupidity to the captain's attention!"

Bottoms' cheeks were all puffed out like an indignant bullfrog.

"You don't want to do that, Mr. Bottoms. You might just tempt the captain to have you thrown overboard!" Naturally, Steward Spillane did not actually say this; he only thought it. Instead, he addressed young Jackson.

"Robin, would you mind going to fetch the nurse. Tell her to come promptly in order to give one of our passengers a thorough examination. Along the way, would you fetch one of those sturdy wicker chairs, with the solid four feet, and bring it here. Thank you, now get along with you!"

The chief steward figured the fastest solution to the current situation was to get his young protégé out of the picture as quickly as possible.

With a sigh, he bent over the poor, suffering Bottoms and soothed, "Okay, just relax. Here, move that arm over; there you are! We'll have you free and back on your feet in no time. That's it, press down on that while I lift your shoulder. There you go!"

The plump passenger stood erect, but just for a moment. The ship lurched over to port, sending Mr. Bottoms into the railing.

"That's right, hold onto the railing, and you'll navigate your way along just fine. As soon as the nurse arrives, have her help you to the solid chair that Steward Jackson is fetching."

With that, Steward Spillane walked a bit further along and found Henry "Hank" Fallon and his wife Fay leaning over the rail. He couldn't tell whether they were enjoying the experience of being at sea for the first time, or simply leaving their breakfast behind as the bow rose and fell.

"Hello, folks. Is everything to your satisfaction today?" The chief steward smiled confidently their way.

"Why, yes, quite so. Thank you, Chief Steward. We appreciate you're looking after us, given all your other responsibilities." They each smiled warmly his way.

"Well, you know, if you're feeling a bit woozy, there is a tonic I can recommend." His years aboard steamers had given him a few tricks to offer when needed.

As it turned out, these passengers might be new to steamship travel, but they had been sailors aboard competitive yachts for years. They had met each other, in fact, while members of the New Rochelle Yacht Club. They weren't bending over the rail because they were sick; quite the opposite, in fact. They were admiring the school of dolphins which had picked up on the ship's prow wave and were effortlessly keeping pace with her 24 knot speed.

"Aren't they just beautiful? They have such grace!" Fay Fallon was ecstatic in her praise for the sleek, fast mammals. "When they speak to one another, they sound like they are rejoicing in being alive. Their squeals just delight me!"

Steve joined them in looking over the railing. The *Reliance* was making long, slow rises and falls as she ploughed steadily onward. The deck was bathed in warm sunshine; the lounge chairs were all occupied. The occupants dozed or read or talked in desultory fashion as the dreamy hours passed by. However, all of them were missing the beautiful action passing along right below them.

The ocean, dark blue, churned and ruffled into short little waves that glittered with silver where the sunlight touched them. Gusts of wind blew irresponsibly across the surface, blowing the froth from each wave as it rose to a foamy crest that looked like powdery snow. Steadily, the long swells fell away from under the bow. One couldn't help but be fascinated by the smooth undulations of the ocean coloring into streaked mosaics alongside the hull. As these streaks reached the stern, they boiled into swirls that extended beyond the ship to the endless horizon— which all aboard were busily sailing away from—but which never seemed to recede.

"If I'd been able to swim like those porpoises back in prep school, I'd have never taken up yachting!" exclaimed Hank. "I'd have devoted my athletic endeavors to beating all comers in the pool. But with Fay by my side, we make a swell racing team on sailboats!"

"Really, sir? What do you crew on, a schooner, sloop or ketch?" Steward Steve had a fair appreciation for this milieu.

"Either a sloop or a ketch, but generally we prefer the sloop. With its lone foremast, and sails fore and aft, the two of us have all we can handle to rig her and still manage the tiller. Do you compete, as well, Steward Steve?"

"Well, sir, I appreciate your asking. There was a time when I was quite active, but around the age of seventeen I learned to fly aero planes, fought in the war, and then took up my present profession. In my position as Chief Steward, I'm home for no more than a day or two before I have to report for my next assignment. When I sail nowadays, it has to be on a big metal tub like this one. Perhaps one of my girls, or better yet my son, will catch the spirit and want to learn sailing. All four of my children are the right age to be curious about the sea, but not a one has raised even a peep about my teaching them. Anytime you wish to talk about your exploits, I'd sure enjoy listening. I'd have no trouble following the lingo or your discussions on race maneuvering."

"I say! Hank, we have found a compatriot!" his wife exclaimed ecstatically. "And, you know flying as well. We both have always wanted to go up in a plane, soaring and banking freely without fear of capsizing. We'll keep a lookout for you lounging in a deck chair with nothing to do and then corral you into listening to all our boasting."

The chief steward answered with, "Then you'd have to post a mighty sharp lookout. This job does not allow for very much lounging about, I daresay! Perhaps a meal together, if that is not being presumptuous." He made a brief bow as he took his leave.

It was getting close to the evening dinner hour, so Chief Steward Spillane made his way to the galley where he found Chef Pierre lording it over three under, or "sous," chefs. Alec and Guillaume appeared to be managing just fine. The new man on their team, Marion, seemed rather unsure of himself as he scurried between the boiling kettles and the sizzling trout nestled in an array of wide skillets. The galley aboard the *Reliance* had six large ovens, and they all appeared to be going full tilt this wintry day. A cook who is unsure is hesitant and, consequently, slow. Being slow is not a good recipe for surviving shipboard duty where over 500 meals are prepared three times a day.

"How is everything, Chef Pierre? Is there anything you would require of me before our guests begin filling the dining room for supper?"

"Non, non, everything, she is just as I wish. Thank you, my good Chief Steward Stefan. We will ring the gong *vitement* or, how do you say? Shortly! They will all be most pleased, I assure you. Thank you, my good man, or *mon bon homme* as we say."

The head chef accompanied all of his sentences with arms gesticulating and eyebrows twitching and nose wrinkling. Steven Spillane had known him for some eight years; they had served many times on other ships in the past. He'd never reveal it, of course, but Steve often came to the kitchen to check on how things were coming along simply as an excuse to enjoy "the Chef Pierre Coubert" show, as he called it to himself. He enjoyed this man immensely.

He returned to B Deck and spotted one of his assistants, Harold Conklin, racing past carrying a bundle of fresh, white towels.

"Whoa, slow down there, cowboy! You're liable to trip, or worse, run into a passenger at that speed. What is all the rush, anyway? They're about to serve dinner, and you know that means a stampede will form any minute."

The Chief Steward paused, giving the man a chance to explain behavior that was beyond the norm for a steward managed by Steven Spillane. As he'd stated many times in the past, stewards and chambermaids are to move and behave as though he or she was gliding serenely about a ship where everything was calmly and properly managed.

"So sorry, Mr. Spillane, but I've got to get these towels down to Cabin A-14. Mr. Rothschild has had an accident and overflowed his bathtub. Water is all over the floor and if I don't get it mopped up directly, it could leak down to lower levels, sir."

"Good heavens, what on earth was the man doing taking a bath at this hour?"

He knew this Rothschild. The man liked to refer to himself as Richard Rothschild the IVth or some such high toned label. He enjoyed journeying across the Atlantic several times each year and seeing how many pranks he could lay on innocent stewards who hadn't yet been forewarned. Poor Conklin: he'd obviously just been "Rothed" as the experienced stewards liked to refer to the rich man's pranks. When he had been assigned to the *Reliance*, Steve had noticed this steward was 38 years of age and had served on other vessels in the A.T.C. stable. He naturally assumed the man had been "round the horn," as the saying goes. Apparently, the Chief Steward, in regard to his subordinate Conklin, should have been more careful to instruct him regarding passenger care. It had been his experience that when the really rich were bored by being aboard, so to speak, they often found amusement through cruelty to the unsuspecting.

Okay, don't worry, you're doing just fine. Why couldn't you have simply pulled the plug in the tub? The bath is located in Mr. Rothschild's cabin, is it not?"

"But sir, the plug was gone! I couldn't find it anywhere, yet the water just kept coming and was overflowing when Mr. Rothschild called me to help him. The knobs on the spigots were missing, too. I just got frantic, worrying about the ship sinking and all."

"Calm down, get yourself together. Let's you and I go to his cabin and we'll talk to Mr. Rothschild together. First, let me call for the ship's engineer. He may be required to perform some repairs here."

Pausing to clear his throat, Steve continued: "Engineer Hoskins makes more money than all of us except the captain, so if the work is dirty, he's being well paid for it!"

The Chief Steward got on the squawk box and called Chief Engineer Hoskins to send up a plumber for a clogged tub straightaway to A Deck.

"And Henry," he added, "you better tell whomever you send to bring a spare stopper and spigot handles along with him. Thanks!"

Together, the two men strode down the passageway and climbed the ladder to A Deck, preparing to deal with a man who was so wealthy that everything in life bored him; pranks on the unsuspecting seemed to have become his sole source of delight. Along the way, Steve would make sure the young Conklin heard what being "Rothed" was all about so it wouldn't happen again.

CHAPTER TEN

UPSET BY CIRCUMSTANCE

Five hours later, *Reliance* was cruising comfortably through the star-studded black night. The weather was clear and the seas peacefully rolling with a slow swell. Captain Stahl had posted lookouts at each end of the docking bridge in addition to Seamen Busby and Waltham up in the crow's nest. Each man had binoculars and each could reach the telephone to the Bridge simply by stretching out his arm to it. As an added measure of warning, before lifting the phone, the crow's nest lookouts could press a buzzer that sounded in the Bridge without delay. Pressing it once signaled icebergs ahead, while sounding it twice indicated some other ship was steaming close by.

Since the captain had retired for the night, I had remained on the Bridge a bit longer to look out across the peaceful, partially moonlit surface of the sea. The wind was swirling the tips of the swells into momentary froth, like the whipped cream on top of one's coffee, and I felt real joy course through my veins. My longtime friend Jim Stahl had achieved his pinnacle goal—command—and now, aged fifty, he planned to be in charge of a passenger ship for the next ten years. Whether I was at his side, or was promoted and assumed a command of my own, didn't matter; I was happy just to be at sea with a job to do.

Heading east meant the sailors exposed above decks were a bit more comfortable since the wind would be following, rather than chilling them head-on. Nevertheless, the temperature was the most important factor. In fact, it had dropped below 40 degrees Fahrenheit as the sun set, but around 2300 hours it suddenly seemed to plummet, slipping below 0 degrees Celsius. Landlubbers would call this weather "freezing!" The lookouts drank hot coffee or soup from the thermos each had brought along. Even the men piloting the ship in the enclosed Bridge felt the chill.

It was Thursday, April 19th. Around midnight, I called it a day and retired to my quarters. I felt a soothing calmness overtake me. I was aboard a sturdy ship and was crewing with a longtime, dear friend. The conditions were not particularly pleasant, but they were certainly bearable when in one's cabin. If given the chance, I expected to sleep soundly.

The heavens tonight were blessed with a half-moon that occasionally brightened the blackness. However, should it slip behind a cloud, then the sea, horizon, and sky would blend into one opaque void. Perspective, and indeed the very light that might strike an object floating on the surface, would be bent, distorting an object's distance and size. With the ship steaming along, the entire Watch had been instructed to "look sharp" and this admonition was passed along as each man rotated in. All hatches had been dogged down and other sources of stray lighting forward of the Bridge had been extinguished to minimize glare or distracting reflection.

When the moon hid behind a cloud, one could only assume the surface waves were still wildly tossing their frosted tips about, and then subsiding into dark troughs; however, even when the stars were standing out brilliantly from the dark heavens, the surface of the sea was not visible if a sailor was standing behind the glass partitions enclosing the Bridge. Nevertheless, there was a feeling of freedom, of unfettered power, as the humming turbines rotated the churning screws through the water. The frothing luminescence of *Reliance's* wake trailed out behind as far as anyone could see. Hardly rolling, even with the swells, this ship felt impregnable.

About 0200 hours, or about two hours past midnight, the darkness had deepened to pitch black, but that merely permitted the stars to glint all the more spectacularly. If a man stared straight ahead, where they no longer shone suggested the beginning of the all-encompassing, silent waters of the Atlantic. This was a mighty big assumption, given the slow roll and pitch of the ship and the chilled conditions of standing outside. If it was difficult for a man to distinguish the horizon, this made it difficult for him to distinguish where to focus his search for icebergs. He could mistakenly think he was staring ahead at the ocean surface, while in actuality he was looking at the inky sky.

For everyone manning the Bridge or the crow's nest, standing Watch was a lonely, desperately boring, yet absolutely vital assignment.

First Officer Dougherty was Officer of the Watch tonight but, to him and all those on the Bridge, it must have felt like our ship was out for a joyous jaunt rather than taking on a life and death struggle with the elements. Conditions were perfect for an uneventful cruise: they made you glad to be aboard!

The ship's Watch was therefore alert but relaxed as the hours had slipped past midnight on into the initial hours of Friday, April 20. On the Bridge, confidence was high because *Reliance* had charted her eastbound course to take her south of the last reported locations of ice. Bergs and growlers had been sighted sporadically throughout Thursday by various vessels. True, those ships were all of foreign registry; nevertheless, their warnings were accorded full respect. Each message had been duly posted as it was relayed up the speaker tube by one of the wireless men: Pride, Hawkins, or Lawler.

As Chief Officer, it had been my responsibility to plot *Reliance's* navigation to be comfortably south of all these reported threats. Of course, the ocean is overwhelmingly huge when compared to the narrow vision of men aboard ships. Every officer under Captain Stahl's command knew, either from experience or from stories passed around while safely ashore in some pub, that rogue ice could appear without warning. Even the International North Atlantic Iceberg Patrol boats flying the flag of the United States were mere human interventions; these "patrollers of the high sea" couldn't be expected to be everywhere at once in the vast Atlantic shipping lanes.

To the landlubber, perhaps, it would appear sensible to chart a simple longitudinal course straight across the globe from New York to Europe. Such a journey would, presumably, be far enough south to simply ignore ice threats. Two factors obviated such a plan. First, winters varied in temperature; more importantly, summers varied as well, so calving off the Greenland ice sheets, particularly the large Petterman Glacier (which always seemed to produce large flat-topped bergs that floated south on the Labrador current) would actually rise if last year's May to August period had been unusually warm. Such had been the case during the summer of 1928. Moreover, the strength of the Labradorean current influenced, far more than wind, how far beyond Baffin Bay a giant tower of ice would travel into the North Atlantic Ocean before finally succumbing to the warmth of the Gulf Stream curving up from the south.

If there is a lot of summer melting, the currents will be stronger and the bergs will be more numerous. Thus, assuming that lookouts—whether on domestic or foreign liners—had already spotted the furthest extent of floating ice in any particular year could prove to be a very big mistake.

Secondly, one must always remember that ocean-going cruises offered by rival companies are very competitive. Taking a far longer route nearer the circumference of the world could prove exorbitantly more expensive in terms of time, and thus fuel and food required, than sailing nearer the North Pole on a shorter route. Seafarers who served aboard ocean liners or freighters joked that the rule used by ship owners was to multiply propeller revolutions by the time used to reach their port of destination. Revolutions per minute bore different cost depending on the cargo and age of a vessel, but RPM's could raise the cost of operating a route very quickly beyond profitability.

Ice sheets were even more risky. Not only were they low-lying and thus harder to spot at any time, but also they could be broad—up to 4 miles not being unusual—so detouring around them became mandatory; that is, if a ship's lookout saw such a danger in time. That was why, even in the modern era of double-hulled vessels, constant communication between ships at sea had been mandated by international law ever since 1912. If a lookout spotted ice, even if it was only a growler lying 10 feet above waterline and 15 yards or so long, wrenched by moans and groans as its ice cracked and split, the location and estimated size was telegraphed day and night across the water to all ships within the area. Even a bergy bit lying slightly submerged was noted. Ice of small size meant that larger bergs could well be in the area.

The widely-held assumption was that, even if your lookouts had not spotted a threat, some other ship or the Ice Patrol would have, so your navigator could then be informed of a clear path. As a result—ignoring the occasional detritus left over from the Great War—many operating companies believed that problems with ice in the sea lanes had become a subject for the history books. Even in 1929, such arrogance could cause fatal errors in judgment.

In addition to the careful measures his officers and crew were taking now that they had steamed into latitudes with reported obstacles, Stahl's plan was to make a course correction in an east northeast direction once his ship had closed on longitude 40 degrees and latitude 50 degrees. Sailing some 250 miles northeast from that point would put the *Reliance* in position to make a beeline for the northern coast of France. As this course change was effected, the crew aboard *Reliance* would breathe easier because the ship would be heading away from the typical springtime drift of ice fields.

On this night, before First Officer Pete Dougherty had had a chance to make the planned course correction, our lives took a significant twist.

Just past 0300 hours, Lookout Bill Busby couldn't believe his eyes when he made out a vague mass darker yet than the surface of the sea. What really riveted his attention was that it was not simply massive, but that it didn't seem to be moving. He nudged

John Waltham who was huddled beside him; that man was crouched over, trying to shield his face from the cold wind as he looked out over the starboard quarter. He turned to complement Busby's vision. They both looked straight off the bow. Their glasses only magnified the darkness. Using just their eyesight, they both thought there was something that appeared to be almost dead ahead of the ship's prow. Mouths agape, the two lookouts turned to stare at one another for a stunned moment, and then both reached for the phone.

Seaman Busby gave way so Waltham could warn, "Iceberg half-mile dead ahead!" Busby punched the buzzer. Instantly, all eyes on the Bridge peered into the inky-black abyss.

Everyone on deck was now sharply alert. Standing further back in the Wheelhouse, the helmsman still couldn't make out the danger, but Dougherty saw the huge threat poised ominously just a bit to port. The ship was moving at 22 knots, or 36 feet a second. Considering reaction time delays, he quickly estimated a berg lying less than 1000 yards out gave his ship about one minute before impact. Of course, he also knew that estimating distance in haze or in the dark was just that: a guess. Regardless, action was required immediately.

He ordered: "Right full rudder!" Even before the helmsman began turning the wheel clockwise, Officer Dougherty pulled on the engine telegraphs and yelled down the speaking tube: "Full speed astern on starboard engine, all ahead full on port engine!"

In only the previous year, the electronic cables and gearing that controlled a rudder had finally been standardized to be in direct line with the course to which a helmsman wanted the ship to turn. The long-standing, but confusing, practice of turning to starboard (to the right) by rotating the wheel counterclockwise as the Officer of the Watch ordered "hard a port" had—at long last—been corrected. On   today's vessels, if a commander wanted to turn to the right, he heeled the wheel clockwise which caused the rudder to turn counterclockwise, pushing the stern out to the left and thereby pointing the bow to the right. Since many vessels from earlier decades were still plying the oceans, a pilot had to be absolutely certain—naturally—as to the type of steering commands the ship being managed required.

The helmsman, for his part, simply steered as ordered.

CHAPTER ELEVEN

TITANIC LESSON

It was clear to everybody on board that the Titanic was going to create the greatest stir that British shipping circles had ever known. 2nd Officer C. H. Lightoller [3]

First Officer Peter Dougherty personally had confidence in the rudder of this vessel. During construction of *Reliance*, Dougherty had chanced to be in Newport News visiting a girl. This pretty lady consumed his attentions, and energies, for some time after he showed up at her door all ruddy cheeked and virile, but at a certain point he had needed a break.

Kissing her lightly on the cheek and promising not to be too long, he promptly headed down to the construction dry-dock to look the new hull over for himself. It wasn't that he had a premonition that he might one day be assigned to this particular boat. It was more that she carried a reputation for offering the latest in hull dynamics. He wanted to see what gave rise to all the fuss. Ships were often built as classes based on the same layout and specifications, so there was a good chance he might someday be serving on a similar vessel.

When he arrived at the yards, the activity all about the dry dock and support sheds was so constant and frenetic that he had to show his Seaman's Identity Card to guards controlling entrance by anyone. There was no trouble locating his target once he was inside the gates, however. The scaffolding, derricks, and even the plating of the *Reliance* were smothered with workmen, welders, riveters, and craftsman of every sort.

He had timed his visit well: the stern of the ship was being paid scant attention this day. The port and starboard bronze screws as well as the rudder had been mounted, bolted, plated, and even caulked with Portland cement the week before, so other demands occupied the workers. He inspected the stern, and particularly the rudder, closely. It was mounted on a center steering rod, which he knew would provide excellent response without being overwhelmed by the inertia of water piling against the full side of an offset hinged rudder. The *Titanic* had famously suffered from this disadvantage, but its rudder mount had been necessitated by the use of a central screw. On the *Reliance*, one screw straddled each side of the rudder. This design had been proven both as to speed and maneuverability by the famous trio of Cunard Line. Back then, the engines were less powerful, so the *Mauretania* class ships had all employed four rather than two screws.

---

3 Deborah Hopkinson. *Titanic, Voices from the Disaster*. New York: Scholastic Press, 2012.

He was studying this setup with satisfaction when an attribute caught his attention. It was the shape of the rudder. It extended further astern, for a length of 18 feet he judged, as though reaching to be even with the fantail of the hull perched some forty feet above. Most of its bulk was below the painted waterline of the hull to accommodate the rise and fall of swells, but the fulcrum effect on altering direction would be powerful as the steering post would have very little deflection. For an officer in charge of the Bridge, this meant more immediate response plus a tighter turning radius. Sacrificial anodes to deter rust had not yet been applied. Nevertheless, this rig looked fully capable of permitting a ship to execute a solo docking. Ships did that in Great Britain, he knew. Of course, the tugboat union might have something to say about that.

Conversely, the *Titanic*'s rudder had been built with approximately a quarter of its square footage actually above the waterline, rendering that weighty portion effectively useless while simultaneously increasing the effort required to turn it. Ever since he had first perused photographs of the *Titanic*, it had been his personal opinion that the look of symmetry had guided the design of the White Star liner more than functionality and maneuverability. As events were to transpire, the design and outfitting of this ship very likely contributed to its fateful meeting with disaster. Indeed, as it turned out, the slow turn response of the most elegant ship ever to have sailed the seas had doomed her to sideswiping an iceberg on her maiden voyage. The resulting collision distorted her hull plating, caused rivets to pop, and opened a half dozen slits through which water gushed at a rate that overwhelmed her pumps, flooded over the top of her massive, but woefully too short, hull partitions, and gradually filled each "watertight" compartment in turn as her bow pitched inexorably lower into the darkly clutching waters of the Atlantic.

All but a few of those who fell or jumped into the sea after the last lifeboat had been lowered froze to death in waters that were measured at 28 degree Fahrenheit. The total of fatalities was difficult to tally due to discrepancies in passenger lists and the crew rosters, but a figure of just over 1500 lives lost has generally been accepted by the White Star Line and the British Board of Trade. Slightly less than one-third of Titanic's passengers and crew had been saved by boarding lifeboats.

In a severe case of irony and coincidence, a ship within ten miles of the iceberg that sank the *Titanic* had telegraphed that she, the *Californian,* was blocked in by ice for the night. Her radioman had messages from Cape Race waiting to be transmitted to the great White Star liner, but when he keyed over to Jack Phillips, the two ships were so close that the Morse code practically tore the ears off the telegrapher in the wireless room of the *Titanic*. The *Californian's* operator was curtly cut off as Phillips frantically tapped away at his key in order to catch up on messages by passengers aboard his ship. He and his associate Harold Bride had fallen way behind as a result of their transmitter going down the day before, thereby requiring an all-nighter to restore operations by Sunday. In those days, passenger communications were prioritized--since they were paying good money--over mundane messages between ships.

Phillips was not about to be interrupted by anyone for any reason. Thus, the timely warning from *Californian* was cut short and its import ignored.

Regrettably, Phillips was unaware that the man in charge of the very ship on which he was working so feverishly, Captain Edwin J. Smith, was--at that very moment--steaming the *Titanic* full bore into the same ice field within which the *Californian* had dropped anchor for the night.

A stroke of luck amidst that horribly tragic terror came in the form of the *Carpathia*, a smaller one-stack ship cruising some 58 miles to the south. She had a young Morse code telegrapher, Thomas Cottam, aboard. He had shooed Mr. Vaughn, his steward, out of his cabin that very afternoon: he wanted to nap with the expectation of having to stay up late to catch radio transmissions regarding the coal-strike fervor that was gripping Great Britain. Thus, Cottam had remained awake when, ordinarily, he would be in bed fast asleep. Shortly before midnight, after hearing all the news, he was preparing for bed but, like men in his profession, couldn't resist getting the last tidbit that might come over the wires. Besides, he had sent a message to the *Parisian* which had not yet been answered.

Even as he was removing his shoes, he still had his earphones on. Suddenly, he heard Phillips' crackling signal calling for help.

Out of the inky black darkness came the most dreaded of dots and dashes: "We are sinking fast; water is above the boilers. This is a CQD, old man. Save Our Souls!"

Cottam had trouble comprehending that such a message could emanate from *Titanic.* The scuttlebutt was that she was not just the greatest ship afloat, but unsinkable to boot. For confirmation, he asked whether he should involve his captain. The reply was an unequivocal "yes, do so and come at once!" This bit of luck was compounded by the fact that Cottam rushed to the cabin of one Arthur Henry Rostron, a man born to become a hero. His immediate response upon hearing *Titanic's* message was to issue orders and get his ship rushing toward the disaster site. Only after he had gotten all his crew attending to their emergency duties did he ask his radioman to elaborate.

The *Carpathia* reached the scene in a hitherto impossible 17 ½ knots, all the while dodging a half dozen icebergs along the way. This ship was rated at only 14 knots, but Captain Rostron had his engineer cut off cabin heating and other extraneous uses in order to pour all available steam into turning his screws. If it hadn't been for his prompt response, sparked by the chance curiosity of his telegrapher, survivors of the sunken *Titanic* would have begun dying from the cold, despite they're being dry. Many had left the ship under-clothed for the conditions because they initially imagined all the fuss was merely a drill, so they would soon be returning to the warmth of their cozy and still brightly lit ship.

When the ambient air temperature is a mere thirty degrees or less, a person exposed to wind does not last long unless dressed to explore the Arctic. Neither the passengers nor even the crew members were so clothed. The only real warmth was achieved by huddling close together. There was no testimony at either the British or the American hearing that any of the lifeboats rotated seat positions to share exposure from cross winds by those persons positioned next to the gunwales. If not rescued, they would have been the first to die, assuming everyone had normal blood circulation. The irony is that the very calm that allowed those in lifeboats to survive until *Carpathia's* arrival was what had doomed the ship, since ordinarily the phosphorescence from waves lapping against icebergs gave the night watch a chance to spot their danger from afar.

Despite her being the closest vessel around, the *Californian* would not have seen the lifeboats. Worse, she would not even be looking, because the men conducting her Watch around midnight thought they had witnessed the *Titanic* depart after firing some twelve white rockets as a sort of celebration. At first light, that ship would have simply left the ice field without even looking for tiny lifeboats forlornly bobbing about ten miles distant. In fact, her Captain Lord attempted to negotiate the ice floes only after daylight brought messages about what *Carpathia* was doing. By the time of Lord's arrival, Rostron had all survivors on board and was headed to New York, so the late comer was reduced to a mere body tally of those still floating on the surface.

Sadly, the *Frankfurt*, a vessel of German registry, was floating a mere twenty-four miles from *Titanic* during the sinking, but that ship was on the other side of the giant ice field in which the death berg had floated; thus, any rescue effort by *Frankfurt* was out of the question.

* * *

All that is history from almost two decades ago; hopefully, ship captains and owners had learned better safety procedures from its harsh lessons. Back on the *Reliance*, Officer Brian Stanley, Captain Stahl's Third Officer, was the first to reach the Bridge after sensing the ship's veering change of direction. The boss entered soon after and asked Officer Dougherty for his assessment. He repeated back the orders he had given to steer to starboard, based on the shape of the berg and its position to port, and to alter the rotating spin of the screws.

"You reacted well" thought the captain silently. The three of them stood abreast, no doubt with fingers crossed as each man twisted the soles of his shoes as if to make the deck pivot faster. The helmsman stood riveted to his post, gripping the wheel tight in full hard-a-starboard mode as though that could make a difference. It was going to be very close.

As for me, I had settled into such a deep sleep less than three hours earlier that I didn't learn there was a problem until it was too late for me to do anything.

Down in the bowels of the hull the engineers were sweating like mad to undertake what had been ordered from the Bridge—a huge challenge for a ship of ocean-going class. Such vessels were simply too big to change turbine rotation or the direction of hull momentum with any kind of speedy response. That didn't stop the men from trying.

Each of us in our daily lives has experienced the feeling of stupidity when we're walking along, spy a friend, and turn our head to wave, only to walk into the trunk of a tree or, worse, catch our toe on a cracked sidewalk and fall head-first onto our nose. That's embarrassing, even painful. But what was really painful for the officers and sailors and lookouts who saw what was coming that night was the seemingly inexorable way the *Reliance* continued to plow forward without evidencing any desire to veer to the right. Time seemed to stand still as the now formidable looking iceberg came closer and closer until it appeared, in the scary darkness, to loom above them some 20 feet as an immobile, silent, even glowering menace.

Stahl surmised the berg had a bit less than 100 feet above waterline; this meant some 900 feet would be down in the cold depths of the sea, hard as nails and probably with numerous projecting edges. It would not be enough to simply pass by what they saw above the water: they'd have to give the dangerous lower portions a wide berth, too. When she was a mere 300 yards away, *Reliance* finally began to noticeably turn her bow to the right. As each second ticked by and the distance closed, she angled ever more sharply away from the ominous black shadow above the surface.

Each of the men watching this slow-motion rumba knew that the real threat from this iceberg lurked below out of sight, no doubt armed with hard, serrated protrusions that had never been smoothed by wind or sun melt.

Captain Stahl had one last safety valve at his disposal. Turning to face the row of small lights affixed to the wall behind the helmsman, he punched one master switch to be sure that all the bulkhead hatches that were typically left open for ease of passing between compartments were tightly closed. At the same time, he turned a large black button next to the control panel for the bulkhead hatches. It was something just recently added to ships at sea: a sort of telephone that did not require lifting a receiver to be heard. James admitted to himself he couldn't remember what the darned thing was called—squawk box came to mind—but he did know how to use it. In a firm command voice, he spoke into what would become known as an intercom.

With this device, he could reach every single cabin and many of the holds throughout the ship.

"This is your Captain speaking. Brace for collision. If in bed, remain as you are. If not lying prone, do so at once. Hold onto something secure if available. I say again, brace for collision!"

Having given this emergency message a bit late, but certainly earnestly, the captain rejoined his subordinate officers and watched as the demon loomed ever higher. Could it be that the monster seemed to be sliding off to the left?

He found himself noticing that this particular berg was unusually large, perhaps 200 feet wide and some yards higher than the Bridge of his ship. It had a relatively flat top that tapered lower off to its right, but the left side of which seemed to be a sheer, diamond-hard wall that nothing could penetrate. To his surprise, he found himself breathing a little easier: at least they were not headed straight into that! They did indeed seem to be veering off to the right and passing astride the shorter portion.

All the men on the Bridge remained tensely glued to watching the black mass approach, each one dreading the sound of a buzzer from somewhere below indicating that the hull had in fact been breached and was taking on water. This would mean that terrified sailors were experiencing flooding in their compartments. The seconds ticked by, but only the steady whine of the port engine, and the lower throb of the starboard engine as that shaft finally changed direction, penetrated the silence. In fact, *Reliance* appeared to be sliding by without any contact whatsoever.

"She seems to have missed it!"

This jubilant assessment erupted from the lips of First Officer Dougherty. As the towering iceberg began to recede beyond the port fantail and no call for help issued from the bowels of the ship, joy and salvation danced in the eyes of everyone on the Bridge. Each officer hugged the person nearest him as eyes closed in a dance of relief.

Everyone on or near the Bridge seemed to erupt in pent-up emotions of fear that had instantly been supplanted by the assurance of being safe. It looked as though everyone, and everything, had survived intact. Even I, lately arrived on the Bridge, joined in the celebrating.

At this point, Officer Dougherty relayed the captain's command: "Change course to 30 degrees NE. All ahead, full." The captain had over-corrected to allow for our having steered away from the berg.

Everyone was still milling around rejoicing. Soon, he would order a course correction to 70 degrees in order to resume our heading east northeast.

The moon came from behind a broad cloud that had temporarily obscured its light. Suddenly the helmsman, who had turned the rudder hard over to steer to the left after Officer Dougherty gave the order for a heading of 30 degrees, coughed slightly and whimpered, "Sir, sir..." That was all he could muster.

Captain Stahl turned from whomever he was congratulating and stared into the now brightened darkness. It seemed as though a low dark wall had ominously reared up in front of the bow, like a camouflaged rail fence confronting horse and rider during a steeplechase. There was no time to reverse engines.

"I'll be damned!" was all he could utter. What else could a good Christian man say?

Everyone else was stunned into silence. The ship plowed forward, chewing up the few brief seconds left us.

CHAPTER TWELVE

CAPTURE

It happened so fast. No one had ever reported encountering such a condition on the high seas. Textbooks and coast guard manuals themselves had never postulated that a large berg could completely obscure an ice sheet behind it, yet here it was—solid and implacable. At sea, lookouts can use ice blink to detect its flickering luminosity, but this broad sheet provided no such warning.

Even the lookouts were caught by surprise. Busby clutched the phone but couldn't speak as he stared wide-eyed into the jaws of danger. He remained a mere mute witness to the inevitable. The rather low but implacably solid wall of ice that now lay in the path of *Reliance* was too wide: there would be no escape this time.

Threatening to capture and imprison the ship forever, this irregularly undulating wall had been completely hidden behind the towering iceberg. It's height did not seem that daunting: 10 feet or so tall, but in places rising to 30 feet as the pressing forces of floes one upon another had created mounded hummocks of ice separated by flat expanses. The height, breadth, and "sight-shock" of the large iceberg had simply hidden the inescapable danger that now completely blocked the path of *Reliance*. In the dark of the night, distracted by the threat of the towering berg, everyone had missed seeing the lower lying shelf.

It now lay just thirty yards out, or less than three seconds before the orderly and neat functioning of *Reliance* would be forever ended.

The men on the Bridge braced themselves with whatever they could hold onto. The lookouts stationed at the bow scurried further amidships while Busby and Waltham, in the crow's nest, fairly did a submariner's slide down the ladder of the forward mast. The ship's captain made no move to turn the black dial and speak to the ship's company again: he hoped his first warning still had everyone lying down and bracing. They would need to be.

All 38,300 tons of *Reliance*'s loaded weight plowed head on into the massive ice sheet, with great grinding howls as steel plates were twisted and popped from riveted or welded seams and heavy chains were torn from their housings. The prow reared upward onto the wall as though on a roller coaster, but then folded over forward as the bow and forward decks were split open. It looked like some giant had sliced down with a jagged-edged meat cleaver. The first two holds crumpled toward the stern like parts of an accordion bellows.

In a testament to the designers' emphasis on safety, the holds abaft of the bow—including the first through the third bulkhead—had been constructed as cold storage or for cargo that could withstand the rocking of the bow. Nothing alive was supposed to be located in these holds. Quarters were installed aft of the third bulkhead. This design feature proved to be a lifesaving blessing. The forward hatch and all the consumables or cargo stored in Holds 1 and 2 were crushed or spilled out onto the ice through the various openings which the wrenching collision had created. Barrels of kerosene rolled amongst sacks of potatoes and bags of beets. Tubs of flour split open and mixed their contents with gallon tins of sugar and crates of Florida lemons. An inebriated person might mistake the outpouring as a volcanic eruption, except that along with the flow of foodstuffs appeared suitcases, barrels of nails, and shiny new toy wagons, all tumbling and rolling over the slippery surface while spreading hither and yon. The bow had become unrecognizable, being mashed into twisted jumbles intermixed with frozen chunks bigger than a Clydesdale horse.

On the other hand, though the damage was major, it was presumed that no one had been killed.

With most of its forward mooring cables wrenched from their mounts, the foremast teetered, rocked backward ominously, and then groaned as it regained a standing position. Captain Stahl recovered from being mashed against the bow wall of the Bridge, saw the rocking of the mast, and in a flash dashed to the telegrapher's office. All three operators were inside, trying to set up transmitters and their sending keys amid the jumble of chairs, tables, and message drawers.

"Not to worry, Captain. We're all okay and should have the equipment operating in a jiffy," stated Jim Pride.

"Can you assure us of power for the generator?" Chester Hawkins asked while sprawled across the floor beneath the condenser set. Phil Lawler was similarly occupied with various pieces of the apparatus, but no one complained of injuries. More importantly, since now so many lives depended on the equipment in this single room, no equipment appeared to have been damaged despite manuals and papers thudding to the deck.

"I'll check with Chief Engineer Hoskins," Captain Stahl crisply replied.

These three men were under his command. Their presence now represented salvation for those aboard his stricken ship.

He reached the Bridge and looked toward what had been the bow. In the darkness, the damage from the collision seemed to have stopped forward of the third bulkhead for certain; with luck, the hold aft of the second bulkhead would be intact as well. He reached for the ship's speaking tube to the engine room.

"Report!" the captain commanded sharply. This was not a time to mince words.

There were some fumbling noises on the other end of the tube and then Chief Engineer Hoskins began: "Captain, all boilers are intact and from what I can tell, the shafts and electronics of the turbines have not been affected. The bulkheads aft of the third appear to be intact. I have not yet scrambled forward to check ahead of No. 3 bulkhead, however. As you know, no one among the crew is bunked there; they hold only cargo and foodstuffs, so I have no word on their status. Seaman Kent has gone as far forward as the winch motors and reported, on the basis of limited light, that the bow and anchor housings are utterly destroyed. Not that you need them, but he is sure the anchor chains are virtually useless. Give me fifteen minutes to check on the seals which

No. 3 bulkhead should be providing. Perhaps we may be able to back off and continue under our own steam to the side of another ship for offloading the passengers."

The passengers! For Christ's sake, he'd forgotten all about them in the pressure cooker of the collision and his subsequently assessing the condition of the hull.

He seized the black button of the squawk box and turned it sharply: "Now hear this! This is your Captain speaking!" he announced authoritatively. "If you are not already awake, then I am sorry to awake you, but we have collided with an ice sheet which has extensively damaged our bow. We are analyzing the situation but cannot affirmatively report at this time whether our seaworthiness has been compromised. I apologize for the interruption to your trip, but it appears that we must immediately forgo France and attempt to return to New York for repairs.

"I ask that everyone remain calm and, for the present, remain in your cabins. This will ensure your safety and accountability. If you have been injured in any way, please call for your steward and he will have a member of the ship's medical staff come to your cabin as promptly as possible. I say again, stay in your cabins. Any passenger found to be wandering the hallways will be directed by the stewards to return to their assigned cabin at once! Thank you for your cooperation."

Even as he made his statement, Fay Fallon was beseeching her husband to do something about the awful situation they must now be in. When sailing on the Potomac River, or out on the broader waters of Chesapeake Bay, she and Hank had always been within sight of not just one, but perhaps half-a-dozen other craft. If anyone got in trouble, capsizing or punching a hole in the hull, rescue would be both within sight and mere minutes away. Now, in the pitch dark, in a deeply chilled arena, rescue was neither at hand nor in sight. She clung to her husband with a helpless, almost hopeless, feeling of desperation. Was this to be her final night on this earth?

"Fay, Fay! Get a hold of yourself; I'm right here, nothing bad is going to happen to you or to any of our friends either. We have obviously hit something very large, but can you feel that the ship is now settled? The lights and heating are functioning. There's no sound of water leaking in anywhere. Trust me. We're going to emerge from this nightmare alive!"

"I'll never speak to you again if we drown, Henry Fallon. You better be right!" Her eyes were ablaze with unalloyed fear.

"Yes, darling, I understand. Now, try to relax and simply crawl back under these blankets. We'll read a book or something and await the captain's further orders. That's good; just snuggle down deep like that. I'm right here at your side," Hank said soothingly.

A little later, she was dozing peacefully once more, secure in her man's assured, confident embrace. However, he did not tell her that his own heart was racing so fast he feared it would literally pop right out of his chest.

For his part, Captain Stahl was wide awake and all action. He turned to Third Officer Stanley.

"Brian," he began in a crisply assured tone: "Take a group of seamen and use the forward starboard lifeboats to get onto the ice. We've got to know our situation. Is the ship taking water behind bulkhead No. 2? Can we reload the cargo that has spilled out? Are any of the foodstuffs salvageable? Anything not fully packaged and sealed will have to be left, I'm afraid. Post a man toward the bow, without endangering him, so he can relay your findings back as soon as possible. Now go!"

He turned to First Officer Dougherty.

"I thank you for your cool head and elegant piloting around the big berg. None of us could have foreseen the situation we are now facing. I've never read about such a possibility, not even in the guide manuals the Ice Patrol publishes. We've got to deal with the situation in which we find ourselves.

"Train some lamps shining down on Officer Stanley's gang. Do your best to help them see what the hell they're doing in this appalling chill. Turn on all the ship's upper deck lights for her entire length, both sides. Since they're closer to the shelf, use the portside boats to transport your men. If you think it advisable, lower Lifeboat No. 2, or No. 4 if 2 is too close to the damage. Third Officer Stanley's gang in Lifeboat No. 1 will examine our status from the starboard side as well. Be sure each has a dozen or so lifebelts and float buoys, as well as rescue lines aboard. Above all, monitor his bunch: I don't want anyone slipping off the ice shelf or otherwise being injured while we are stuck fast like this."

He paused, but continued facing the First Officer.

"Assign someone to go along to the main galley to make sure its staff members are not hurt. One thing we and everyone else aboard will need early this morning is coffee, soup, and even cocoa for the younger folk. I want the kitchen up and running immediately to help calm everyone's frayed nerves. Understood?"

As Dougherty saluted and turned to carry out the orders, Captain Stahl confronted me. One of the stewards had thought to rouse me, but I had arrived too late to become scared, so here I stood rubbing mere sleep from my eyes. My Captain bore into me. Putting his hand on my shoulder, he looked me squarely in the eye.

"Wallace, I screwed up." At least Stahl was being forthright. "We should have simply stopped and taken stock of the ship's condition after steering around the berg. I could have let the passengers know the iceberg had been avoided. This might have given the lookouts time to spot the sheet of ice laying in front us. My urge to get going once the danger was passed was too impulsive. When you are called upon by management to explain my actions, it will be appropriate to lay the entire blame for this fiasco at my feet. However, that is in the future.

"For now, we must realize that our ship, and all lives aboard, may be in mortal danger. I want to avoid any more mistakes or misjudgments. Therefore, until I dismiss you, I want you to be at my side without fail until daylight. If you have any qualm about my orders or actions, or feel that I am neglecting some area in my control, tap me on the shoulder and let me know. We are not to rely on protocol here—there is too much at stake. We must act correctly: there'll be no second chance! Have you any questions?"

He paused. We both took a deep breath. I said simply, "Aye, aye, sir!"

Just then the voice of Chief Engineer Henry Hoskins came through the intercom: "Captain?"

"Yes, Henry, go ahead."

"Captain, she's held tight, that is, No. 3 Bulkhead, sir. There is no leakage that I can see into the holds behind it or further aft. The two forward compartments are simply a shambles. The upper tip of the bow appears to be with us simply due to the structural steel from which it extends. The bow plating down to the keel and the entire double hull back through Bulkhead No. 2 are rent asunder and buckled beyond identification."

Silently, Jim thanked his lucky stars that the ship had been constructed using modern metal arc-welding. Rivets would have popped in the frenzy of bending steel, which would probably have led to damage much further astern. Riveted joints were still employed on *Reliance*, but for the purpose of stopping fracture propagation, rather than actual jointure, of plates that had been welded. Of course, with over 38,000 tons of momentum crushing against the bow framing, every member would be bent and twisted regardless of the method of construction.

Engineer Hoskins continued: "I could hear Officer Stanley outside yelling his observations to someone up on the foredeck, so he will confirm my report. Therefore, I can give you my estimation that *Reliance* may still be seaworthy, but she would be able to sail only at the most judiciously slow pace. I would strongly recommend that we simply remain in place and do nothing until dawn provides us with sufficient light to make a thoroughly complete examination. This might allow sufficient time for any vessels in the area to come to our position for the purpose of taking off our passengers prior to attempting any sort of extraction.

"Also, sir, several of the engine room workers in the area of the boilers and turbines were thrown around pretty badly. I am sending them up to the medical quarters for examination. Is that all right with you, sir?"

"Yes, yes, quite so. Thank you, Chief!" He turned away from the speaker tube.

"It could have been a lot worse, couldn't it?" he observed to me.

I responded positively. "Quite right, sir, but we need to consider how to extricate ourselves, and even whether that might be possible. When it's light, I'll send the Chief outside with the ship's carpenters and welders to see whether she'll even budge. It may be that the friction of the hull sliding into the ice promptly softened it so that, around the puncture we made, the ice might be refreezing even as we are speaking. We might be locked in tight come morning. That's not to say we should vary from the Chief's recommendations; we should not try to change our position, but rather just sit tight until light enough to see clearly. However, we should alert nearby ships, as well as management, of our situation at this point."

I took a long breath, satisfied that I had covered every possibility that was churning in my brain.

"Absolutely!" confirmed the laconic captain. He headed for the wireless room. Opening the entry way, he was greatly relieved to see one of the operators calmly sitting in the usual chair at the standard console with his headphones on. Clearly, the three men had successfully restored order to their operations room.

"Yes, captain?" Alert and poised, Radioman Lawler was ready to take the captain's instructions.

In his usual way, Captain Stahl came right to the point.

"Send this message: SOS. MSG. To all ships within 100 miles of our position: we are at Lat.40'00" N, Long.49'20" W. We are not taking on water but have breached an ice sheet and are stuck with our bow smashed. It may be that we are captured and frozen in position. No attempt will be made to extricate ourselves. We are awaiting daylight for a more complete assessment. My plan is to off-load all our passengers to supporting rescue vessels prior to undertaking any recovery action. Advise if you are available to help and what would be your ETA at our position. James Stahl, Captain, *S.S. Reliance*. End of message."

Stahl paused, resting his hand on the transmitter housing as he decided on his next course of action.

"Thank you, Captain," stated Lawler. "I will get this off immediately and notify you should I receive replies. Depending on the response, should I repeat this message at intervals, perhaps every fifteen minutes until dawn, until we hear something?"

"Yes. Very good. However, you're well aware that current maritime law directs all ships to provide 24 hour monitoring of their wireless. You'll doubtless be inundated with responses. I'm interested in whatever vessels can respond quickly and have room to take on any of our passengers. Fast response is important."

With that admonition, our Captain returned to the Bridge. "Anything new?" he asked upon spying me.

"Yes, sir," I replied as I nodded toward Third Officer Stanley. This reliable fellow had departed the Bridge with a positive attitude; his demeanor had reminded me of a lantern that was shining forth its light, beckoning all to follow. Yet here he now stood with drooping shoulders, eyes wide with fright, and almost sullen resignation as he prepared himself to address his Captain with an all too realistic assessment.

"So you're back! That was pretty fast, given the dark and cold. I've heard the 3rd bulkhead is intact and no water is getting in beyond that. Do you concur?"

"That I do, sir. Of course, my men couldn't see the full breadth of Bulkhead No. 3, so I can't verify that the ship is seaworthy. Additionally, I could not ascertain whether we would be able to get off the ice at all. The lower bow plates look to be pretty well lodged in the ice surface. The ship must have ridden upwards when she plowed into the wall, like a rearing horse. We could see about four feet below the waterline paint. From the condition of those plates, it wouldn't surprise me that down toward the keel is just as crumpled. We came into the ice too fast, and with too much momentum given the cargo and passengers, to avoid damaging the Orlop and Tank decks.

"Additionally, despite having a double bottom, the bilge may be compromised and filling with seawater even as we are standing here. We should check whether the engineer can work his pumps with effect down in the bilge. As for the cargo and foodstuffs that fell out onto the ice, they are too widespread and difficult to see, or even test their condition given the cold. Of course, I considered their status of secondary importance. I recommend we look the area over again come first light."

"Very good, Brian. Thank you."

"There are a few other things, Captain," continued Officer Stanley morosely. "One of the seaman pointed out that, while we couldn't see it due to reflections from the lights that Pete was providing from up on deck, everyone could hear screeching, possibly even cracking, sounds coming from within the bow framing. We surmised these were steel thwarts rubbing against one another. Since the stern and major portion of the hull is still bobbing about out there in the ocean, parts of the forward section even further back than the 3rd hold may be twisting and deforming as we rest on the ice sheet. That's our opinion, sir, as best as we could figure it."

"Were the sounds low-pitched, as though groaning?"

Captain Stahl wanted to pin the man down to express himself precisely. If so, this would indicate structural supports were being stressed but not to their breaking point.

"Definitely not!" he confidently responded. "I had a team of six men with me out there on the ice, and we got right up close so we could put out ears to the steel. I didn't want the men to actually touch the protruding and jagged edges due to the danger of frostbite sticking our skin to the metal, but all of us listened real careful like, and the sounds were definitely like this."

Having stated his position so affirmatively, he picked up a sextant and a handy screwdriver and rubbed the metal portions. The metals screeched in protest, sounding like angry, discordant coyotes piercing the night with their shrieks.

Captain Stahl responded, "I see. Any ideas as to what could be happening down there, hey?"

"Not yet, sir, but remember that metal, when chilled, can snap rather quickly if bent back and forth. Perhaps, with morning light, we can work someone into an opening in the wreckage and get a first-hand look.

"I also want to report that, while it's real hard to make out when you're way up high on the ship's Bridge, as we are now, there is a very thick wall of ice nearby that sticks up to just below the deck railing. It's only a yard from where we plowed into the shelf. We could have lost all of us on the Bridge if we had plowed directly into that hard, solid wall. Pete, I mean First Officer Dougherty, did some lucky steering. It's way too dark to form any opinion, but I suspect we may have to use dynamite to blow it out of the way if we try to back out of this ice shelf."

"Thank you again, Officer Stanley. It may come to that. I've got the Morse men calling for help. One of the nearby ships may have explosives for such use, though we most definitely do not." Captain Stahl's voice trailed off into a soft whisper.

Third Officer Stanley was not done, as his downcast expression clearly indicated.

"There is one final thing, Captain. I'm sorry to report this because, under the circumstances, my team could not be sure of what we saw. Does anyone have a log entry in the duty roster regarding seamen being assigned to work on the refrigeration units or any other problem in the food storage hold? All of us were pretty sure we saw a human hand wedged beneath all of that twisted steel and bent plating. You might want to take a head count. That's all I have, sir."

At that, 4th Officer Abel Sims clapped his hand to his forehead.

"Christ, Algernon and Hankins were down in the 2nd hold inspecting the chiller compressor. One of the deck hands had gotten up from his bunk while off duty and reported to me that he smelled smoke, like from an electric short, coming from the forward holds. That was about 0100 hours. I'd sent those two on an inspection and repair mission, but they never reported back to me. I don't think the squawk box reaches that area, sir. One of them may be the seaman that Officer Stanley saw."

The Captain was quiet for a moment. Then he cleared his throat and spoke with heartfelt directness.

"Gentlemen, there may well be two of our men down in that hold. From the report Brian just gave, it is probable that we'll never retrieve these sailors. Let me be very clear: our passengers and our seamen come first. Our mission is to get our ship to the planned destination in the allotted time with all cargo intact and accounted for, that's true. But given our present circumstances, we must insure the safe return of everyone who boarded at home port. The passengers put their trust in us, and our crewmen respect our experience and judgment."

Turning to look me in the eye, he said, "Chief Officer Matthews, you'll have to write up a full Incident Report on this matter for management at A.T.C.; they'll have to notify next-of-kin and file the applicable forms.

"For all of us here tonight, I want to stress that every action you officers take must, above all, insure the safety of those on board. This duty may be obvious from our training, even from a common sense standpoint, but clearly it is necessary that I drive it home. Am I understood?"

The chorus of "Yes, sir!" was loud and clear by all of us.

Nevertheless, in the still, quiet gloom now prevailing on the Bridge, with only the soft hum of the illumination generators whirring from down in the bowels of the ship, it was as if we could hear tears of despair dripping from our Captain's brow upon the floorboards. He had steered his vessel through reported ice by simply treading in the footsteps of so many captains before him. It was still customary for a ship to forge affirmatively ahead, even at night, and even in the face of suspected ice dangers lurking beyond anyone's sight. Positioned in a warm, cozily lighted Bridge with companions and seamen nearby, the idea that you could be committing your vessel to harm, even its demise, would have seemed too remote, and so you put your faith in speed and a providential god.

To top the night off, two of his crew had been forgotten in the melee and lost their lives, or at least it certainly looked that way. I had no doubt that Captain Stahl was wishing he could take back these last sixty minutes of his life.

"Officer Sims, may I see you in my cabin for a minute, please?" Jim's voice was flat and drained, as though he was about to perform an execution. The two men left together.

After the hatch closed behind them, the helmsman observed, "Boy, is that guy ever in the hot seat!"

My response was quick and firm. "Seaman Butler, you are not authorized to make such an observation. Apologize to everyone here present at once!"

I knew what the man meant, but I could not stand aside and tolerate any such laxness in discipline. With that forceful action taken and his apology sincerely delivered, the matter was concluded. An alert but quiet calm enveloped those of us remaining on the Bridge.

After a few minutes, Captain Stahl returned, alone, to the Bridge and asked me to accompany him on a personal tour around the entire deck area. Opening the starboard hatch gave little encouragement to anyone on such a mission. The winds were blowing lengthwise along the hull as they swept unencumbered across the frozen expanse of the imprisoning ice sheet.

The half-moon was now exposed, but its glow certainly yielded no warmth. We turned up our high pea coat collars and beetled our way toward the stern while holding tight to the railings. Our goal was the port side of the docking platform glinting in the heavenly light. When we reached the stern and turned right to walk along the flat end of the cabin area, we were momentarily completely out of the chilling wind.

James took advantage of the break and turned to look full on at the recently avoided iceberg floating about 90 yards astern. He voiced his grim conclusion: "Well, you heartless bastard, you're gonna get us after all, aren't you!"

I said nothing, merely being thankful for a moment's warmth.

We rounded the corner and inched forward toward the port bow. Nothing seemed amiss until we reached a point alongside the forecastle. From this point on, all hell seemed to have broken loose with the ship's bow construction and the equipment housed there. The anchor chains had been tossed asunder as the capstans and motors had been dislodged. The mooring bollards were nowhere to be seen. I suggested that the chain housings would be in a jumble and might even snag on the shelf, thereby impeding our extrication. The anchors themselves were lodged somewhere in the twisted confusion of ribs, cross bracing, and plating. I directed the torch beam down into the pretzel-like tangle of our former No. 2 Hold. When I started to step gingerly forward, the captain wisely restrained me.

"Better leave close inspection for daylight conditions, Wallace," cautioned Captain Stahl. I uttered no objection.

We then edged across the open deck while circumventing its yawning black wound. Upon reaching the starboard side, we grabbed the uppermost rail and pulled ourselves hand-over-hand forward, but the intact portion soon ran out. Holding on against the force of a wind that had suddenly increased, we could make out dark piles of cargo that had spilled onto the ice. Directly ahead and below us was a mass of former hull structural supports. These were now reduced to a mad frenzy of metal tentacles reaching in all directions.

I remarked, "This is going to be hard to swallow come daylight, Captain. We lost what looks like some forty feet of the forward holds as well as the prow and the anchor housings."

Stahl made no comment, being lost in thought as to exactly what his best course of action was going to be after dawn made the picture clearer. Much would depend on whether the Ice Patrol ship was close enough to assist as well as the types of vessels that responded to his SOS call for help.

"Let's see if Radioman Lawler has received any replies," he proposed.

Though we now had our backs to the wind, we had to hold tightly to the railing as a guide in order to avoid being blown off the deck altogether. As we came to the hatch providing access to the Bridge, I reached to open it for Jim and our eyes met momentarily.

James Stahl observed: "This is no place in which to have to set up a camp and try to survive. We must get our ship off this shelf!"

I considered his plea to be meant for the heavens above rather than directed to me. However, for the first time during the calamity, I thought I noticed that Jim's voice seemed to waver. We'd been friends for many years. We'd met while serving together on the *Jason*, a medium sized transport back in 1910 when we were junior officers; we had retained a strong bond even when separated later as rising rank dictated diverse postings. When Stahl had been promoted to command, he had complimented me by specifically requesting my being assigned to *Reliance*. Now, I quietly resolved to provide all the support my superior needed, in whatever form such demand might come.

We went inside.

Third Officer Stanley saw us and immediately stated, "Captain, the wireless room has received confirmation that three ships are within 6 hours of our position: the cutter *Tahoe*, which is the U.S. ice patrol vessel for this vicinity, the *Dorchester*, a British freighter bound for Boston and only 45 miles distant, and finally the *Humboldt*, an American passenger liner bound for New York City. This latter is about 60 miles east of us but was already headed this way when we contacted her. Her Captain Highsmith claims to be a friend of yours. There are other ships that know our situation but these three are the closest, so I took the liberty of confirming that they should come with all possible speed."

"Good work! Yes, have the radioman repeat the message with MSG so they know it's from me personally. That will speed them on their way! While you are at it, better inform the American Transatlantic Company of our peril and the actions we are taking."

Captain Stahl began to look relieved as color drained back into his swarthy face. We were not yet safe, but the mere assurance that rescue ships were steaming our way would give everyone aboard an enormous boost.

He went along the passageway, entered the radio room, looked Radioman Lawler over closely, and then asked, "When did you last get some sleep? Get one of your cohorts in here to relieve you and grab some shuteye. No telling when we'll need a good man like you in here, fully alert. Get along, now!"

With that, the Captain of *Reliance* turned and strode over to his First Officer. Shaking hands with Dougherty, he spoke with his trademark smile of reassurance.

"Okay, we're on the road to recovery. Above all, as we perform our extraction, make it an injury-free day. Now, I want every single person here to go and rouse your relief and then get some sleep. All of us on the Bridge have been through a very trying challenge, but there's more to come and I want you fresh and rested. Report back here at 0900 hours. I should have an action plan coordinated for our rescue by then. Tomorrow, Saturday, will determine whether we can recover and steam back to home port.

"It's time for me to hit the Head, and then it's on to the kitchen to motivate the cooks. I'll have the stewards ready a hearty breakfast for everyone beginning at 0700 hours. Be sure you get one yourselves."

As he strode from the Bridge, he asked me to stay behind and oversee the changing of the Watch. Glancing at the chronometer on the wall, he noted it was going on 0400; a hell of a lot sure had happened in the last hour. He'd better grab a few hours sleep himself. Daylight would bring a day of decisions and coordination the like of which no one aboard had yet dealt with. Being the captain, he most of all would want a clear head.

The calm but chilled air of the night enveloped our stranded ship in silence. As my Captain entered his cabin and closed the entryway behind him, he suddenly felt as though he was frozen in time just like the ship that was gripped by the shelf. He entered the Head and stood looking in the mirror. He saw a man middle-aged, bearded, spouseless, and—most biting of all—without a son. It wasn't that he was wealthy and was worried about an heir. All his life he had longed for a lad in whom he could instill the skills of dealing with this world as he had learned them along the way.

With a heavy sigh, he breathed, "Oh Alice! How I yearn for your comforting smile. I miss you so very much!"

Then, having relieved himself, he fell upon his bunk and doused the lamp. A few cabins away, I was doing much the same thing.

CHAPTER THIRTEEN

EBERLY'S RESPONSE

Some 110 nautical miles north, near Long.42'20" N, Lat.48'10" W, the cutter *U.S.S Tahoe* was patrolling the North Atlantic on a southerly heading. Her mission on this Thursday, April 19, 1929 was to monitor the extent of the ice sheet flowing down from Baffin Bay and determine its most southerly reach now that winter was dissolving into spring. Any icebergs sighted were to be recorded as to width, height, location, and speed of drift in order to estimate their life expectancy and consequent threat to shipping.

At 0320 hours on Friday the 20th, the ship's telegrapher caught a distress message that was followed soon after by an MSG call confirming that the call for assistance was from the captain of the *Reliance*. It gave her location and status. Radioman Everson did not have to look her up in *Lloyd's Register*. The message stated she was a passenger vessel carrying cargo and was approximately 95% loaded; her weight was considered to be some 38,000 tons at present. Her coordinates showed she was about six hours sailing time to the south southwest. He immediately reached for the speaker tube and awoke Captain Barnes Eberly from his sleep.

"How far away is she, did you say?" This captain was a man who liked knowing exactly what the facts were before he did anything.

"Sir, she's at Lat. 40' 00" N, Long. 49' 20" W which is 110 miles from our position. She apparently has, and pardon my saying this, run into a large ice shelf such as the one we have been monitoring."

"Navigator, plot us a course to 40' 00" N, 49' 20" W immediately. If we make headway safely, we should get there in some seven hours," the captain conveyed to Second Officer Nathan Greene. By then, the full daylight would be advantageous to everyone involved.

"I plot our course at 205 degrees and we should arrive there just about 1000 hours, sir." Officer Greene liked being direct and crisp when talking with his captain. This trait cut out delays and confusion; in a situation such as this, time should not be frittered away on idle detail.

"Very good." Captain Eberly was proud and pleased with his crew. True, some bore rough edges when he had first come aboard as the captain of *Tahoe*, but his training and counsel had smoothed his men into responsive and skilled sailors. Without exception, he felt that they were dedicated to the fulfillment of their mission: To provide information regarding dangerous ice conditions. The goal was to prevent collision or other accident in the North Atlantic Ocean.

As for his officers Thomas, Greene, and Belden, his confidence was well placed.

They were products of the Coast Guard's training program whereby every candidate spent a year aboard a triple-mast cutter, learning how to climb between stay mouse rigging and buntlines to set a crab claw, spanker, or topgallant sail, depending on the weather. They had learned to overcome personal fears despite having to operate in the midst of overwhelmingly fractious seas.

He'd had a short course of such training himself: there was nothing quite like being 40 or 50 feet above a swaying deck clinging to a wet, slippery mast or a shifting, 12 inch spar while trying to work a knot in a ceaseless wind that was trying to dislodge you from your perch.

Where it became necessary, he and his officers would take charge of the coordination of any rescue mission in their patrol area. Yesterday, headquarters had notified *Tahoe* that *Reliance* would be shipping a load of nitrates and potash to Liverpool after making stops along the French coast. This particular call for help had the potential to be a very big problem if she became involved in some sort of collision that sparked an explosion.

He immediately had his subordinate Everson dispatch the *Tahoe's* change of course and present mission to U.S. Coast Guard headquarters at Fort Trumbull near New London, Connecticut. Vice-Admiral Halsey would want to be kept abreast so further help could be dispatched if needed.

"We want to win the respect of the seagoing public; let's conduct ourselves with discipline!" he was fond of stating.

He uttered a grateful prayer that telegraphers were now part of the crew of any ship to which they were assigned. No longer under the control of the esteemed Guglielmo Marconi's company, a telegrapher owed his loyalty, and paycheck, to the owner of the ship he was servicing. For the coast guard and navy, of course, that meant Uncle Sam, not some commercial concern. He could be certain that any messages that came in would be promptly delivered to whoever was in command of the Bridge at the time and, most importantly, the captain also would receive a copy of every message. Even on ocean liners, frivolous kibitzing by the passengers for their personal affairs had become secondary to the business of running a safe ship.

There was utility in this arrangement. He remembered hearing stories that the wireless aboard the *Titanic* had broken down the night before the disaster, so after it was repaired, the telegraphers were working nonstop transmitting passenger messages all day Sunday to make up for the backlog. This had resulted in several messages, warning of ice trouble directly in the path of the great vessel, getting put aside without ever reaching Captain Smith's attention.

Who can say whether they might have prevented her demise? He knew about the controversy surrounding Edward J. Smith: that captain was so arrogantly confident in his judgment and the *Titanic's* invulnerability that even the Word of Abraham could not have stopped his headlong dash into infamy. It was Captain Eberly's opinion that Smith was bound and determined to ignore all danger flags in his drive to a "glorious final run" befitting his status as Commodore of the White Star Line.

As far as Barnes Eberly was concerned, there should have been a rule of the sea in place requiring that navigation messages take precedence over personal messages.

It is absolutely imperative to prioritize ice warnings or ship distress signals as they are received. Thank the good lord that just such rules guide the communications of ships in the areas he actively patrols. In the case of *Reliance*, her message had come in loud and clear and was heard without distraction. Rescue in this case could proceed without delay.

He decided to check on other vessels that might be closer than his in this blackest of nights. The chilled, still air outside was good for stargazers bundled up in warm gear, but this rescue was going to be a tough run for his lookouts. "Better keep them on single hour shifts; the wind chill is going to be below 0 degrees Celsius," he opined to himself as he returned to the Bridge.

"Order the lookout doubled to include the bow. Keep the men on only one hour shifts. Tell them to stay sharp!"

Officer Greene relayed the captain's order promptly and it seemed to echo as it was passed along to the men on watch. In this blackest of nights, these men would have one hour on and one hour off for coffee until reaching the *Reliance,* but it would be no picnic. Steaming at 18 knots, the *Tahoe* would breach no quarter for failure to spot danger in these icy waters. Doubtless, this rescue required an immediate response. The arrival of *Tahoe* might mean the difference between offloading some 500 to 700 passengers and support staff safely, or hearing about their drowning if the ship suddenly broke apart and sank by the head. That thought was what drove Captain Eberly tonight.

He remained on the Bridge until his craft came to an unexpected massive ice field some twenty miles in length. It had to be charted; however, doing so would delay his arrival for some hours. It would be a while yet before he and his crew would see the dawn begin streaking the eastern horizon with the pale orange of sunrise. At 0930 hours, Captain Eberly would still be exploring some way clear of his own massive ice field.

CHAPTER FOURTEEN

DORCHESTER RESPONDS

Barry Hines took his seat at the Morse wireless set as the midnight hour eased into Friday. He had been a telegrapher since graduating from Marconi's school at the age of eighteen. Even now, some five years later, he took his job seriously. Serving on what his mates called "the graveyard shift" during this trip, he wasn't about to let his superiors down. Besides, he was serving aboard the freighter *Dorchester* out of London, England. Standards of seamanship by everyone aboard a British merchantman were above average. Assignment to a ship with registry in Great Britain was considered both a high accolade as well as a heavy responsibility. That status had been handed down over the last decade or so ever since the infamous night of April 14, 1912. Safety, and respect for the elements, was adhered to by every one of his shipmates, even if they were the sort who gambled their pay away in drunken binges once ashore.

His ship was headed from its home port in London to Boston with lumber and rubber imported from India. She was out from the States about 500 miles, he figured, so this voyage would soon be ending. It would be good to return to his home in Surrey the week after next. One of his children would be turning 12 years old and he really enjoyed being present for birthdays. Such events were fun when you were young--it was only after you reached 45 that such occasions began to tarnish ever more irrevocably with each passing year. In his opinion, reaching an age in which your friends showered you with respect wasn't half as much fun as being a kid and receiving treasured presents like a bicycle or train set or a three-story doll house.

He had been seated for nigh on 3 hours when he got up to stretch. Having done that, his body reminded him that it was time to visit the Head. He was buttoning his trousers up as he strolled back to the telegrapher's nook, feeling much relieved, when his set began to buzz angrily. He rushed to the set and, without even sitting down, jotted the words quickly onto his message pad.

After a short pause, he used the new side-swipe key (the older press-button wore out one's index finger) to respond: "*S.S. Reliance*, your message received regarding ice peril. Our captain will be promptly notified. What is your position and status, over?"

He received the answer in short order and, with this information in hand, he turned to the speaking tube connected to the Bridge and repeated the information to the First Mate, Gaylord Andrews, who was in the wheel house next to Helmsman Bradley.

With evident glee, Gaylord yelled over to his brother Frank: "Hey, bud, go rouse the captain. I think we got us a hot 'un!" Then he nudged Bradley, "Well mate, get ready, I think we're gonna head out for some rescue mission. You may be changing course right soon enough!"

As Second Mate on the *Dorchester*, Frank Andrews had responsibility for crew assignments on all the derricks, cranes, nets, and hoists that this freighter boasted. Hearing Gaylord's usual loud banter, he hesitated and looked across to check whether his brother was speaking seriously. Seeing Gaylord's enlivened face confirmed that his brother was indeed in the possession of—however momentary—some hot piece of news that, when shared with everyone aboard, would make him feel important.

That clinched it: he didn't need to wait for his brother's confirmation. He tore down the passageway and banged aggressively on the captain's portal. Aldus Barnstable grumbled as he rolled over in his bunk.

"What the hell is it? This better be important!" Barnstable was not a man to be trifled with, especially not at 0335 hours in the morning.

"Sir, we've got a passenger liner/transport stuck out there on an ice shelf fairly close to our position. They've sent us an SOS message, sir!"

Frank had worked himself into a lather of excitement.

"All right, all right, hold onto your britches, Frank. I'm coming. Tell Hines I'll be right along." Aldus stood up, his head nearly grazing the overhead pipes in his cabin. He had to duck them every time he went to his writing desk in the corner. The ship felt stable as he lifted one foot, then the other, to wedge into his shoes.

"That means we've got a placid sea; how in the hell did that passenger ship get into such trouble on such an easy night?" he asked himself. "Well, we'll soon get the answer!"

He trundled down the passageway and stepped directly into his telegrapher's room.

"Say, Hines, what's all this I hear about a ship beached up on some ice?"

The thought flashed through the captain's mind that he just might be dreaming and still asleep back in his warm bunk.

"Sir, I know you wanted to be on schedule for our docking in Boston, but I suspect we're going to be delayed. The vessel is the *Reliance* sailing out of New York with some 700 passengers and crew aboard in addition to freight. She says she weighs 38,300 tons including the cargo. She plowed into an ice sheet and beached her bow while avoiding an iceberg. She does not want to take any recovery action with her passengers aboard. She's waiting until daylight when the damage can be assessed further. She asked for assistance from all available vessels in her area. Sir, that's all I have at this point."

"Very good, Barry. I'll get us moving; we're pretty close now, right?"

"Yes Sir. I estimate about 45 nautical miles," responded the telegrapher. "Her signal is real strong."

"Very good. Reassure the *Reliance* that we should arrive at her position close to 0800. Have her send up flares every ten minutes from 0730 on so she can guide us to her location without risk. Keep me posted on any further developments."

He then shuffled the short distance to the Bridge where he found his first mate and helmsman alert and awaiting his instructions.

"Okay, men, we've got a situation. As a freighter, we may not be much use, but just being there will lend support. Frank, the biggest job is going to fall on your shoulders. We can do 12 knots and should be there by 0800, so in the interim get all your men up, dressed, and posted by their winches and so on by that hour. Unwrap and prepare the lifeboats for launch, just in case she needs to disembark her passengers, and have their assigned teams on standby. Gaylord, roust the cook and his galley gang out right now and get breakfast prepared so everyone can eat and be finished prior to 0750. I want men posted while it's still dark watching for anything untoward, be it ship or ice. Got that?"

"Aye, aye, sir!" came their chorus.

"Good. Now get busy! Helmsman, steer a course of 300 degrees." He pushed the engine-telegraph lever to "full ahead" and his boat lumbered to its top speed of 12 knots. Silently, he hoped that Frank Andrews' gang had done a thorough job when loading all the ship's cargo back in Liverpool. The thought crossed his mind that, if they arrived on scene and the *Reliance* was still afloat, his ship might be required to take aboard passengers, perhaps even crew, from a foundering vessel.

Putting such decisions out of his mind for the moment, he concentrated on his boat's safe transit to the site. He'd worry about finding space for passengers once he was on scene and had a better assessment of the emergency. Under his feet, the engines throbbed as the *Dorchester* plodded north by northwest in search of a ship to save.

CHAPTER FIFTEEN

THE HUMBOLDT TAKES ACTION

Captain's Orderly Charles McDonald had stepped out onto the poop deck of the *Humboldt* to enjoy the fresh air. Despite standing toward the rear of the ship, he was surprised to find how cold it was, made all the worse by the wind blowing full into his face as the *Humboldt* surged westward on her return voyage from Europe. Being aboard this vessel was very satisfactory to him. After some 12 months as a management trainee and then 8 as a novitiate deckhand, he had achieved meaningful status; he had been designated as the Captain's Orderly. Perhaps more importantly, he really liked the officer, Reginald Highsmith, who captained the *Humboldt*.

She was a medium-sized passenger liner built in Germany but handed over to the British as part of reparations for the Great War. Pursuant to English respect for the part played by the Americans during that conflict, her registry had been transferred to the United States. The ship would be among the first to serve in the passenger trade as the Atlantic routes resumed.

The Germans had launched an initially successful offensive in early 1918, but their advance had finally been stemmed by the British in the areas near Ypres and Ostend. Thereafter, the war turned in the allies' favor as the late entry by America provided crucial support. The timing was decisive, as the original combatants had exhausted their resources of men and materiel. While the French were the greatest beneficiaries of the victory, that country had been overrun; virtually all crops and settlements east of Paris had been utterly destroyed. As a result, even with the war finally over, she had little to offer to her allies except *merci beaucoup* (thanks a heap!).

England had lost the youth of a generation; nevertheless, her feelings of warm kinship with "those former colonies" were much fortified by the influence and persuasiveness of Winston Churchill, whose mother was American-born. The United States had asked nothing in the way of reparations following the Paris Peace Treaty signed in 1919. England had therefore generously taken it upon herself to share what came her way as a result of the Armistice.

Once she came under American ownership, the *Humboldt* was refitted with modern fuel-oil-powered turbine generators that drove electric motors turning the twin screws. Fuel oil was far easier to manage and store than coal had been. For her owners, managing from their offices in New York City, the refitting would prove a good investment. The cost would be recouped fairly quickly since the number of crew required to run her would be significantly reduced by the elimination of stokers and trimmers. Greasers were retained, but the men who gave the ship power to move were now referred to as "engineers." This added psychologically to their status if not to their paycheck. The resulting improvement in mood during a cruise meant that brawling while at sea had become far less of a disciplinarian problem; rather, keeping the men well fed on a daily basis had become the biggest challenge.

Management at Oceanic Lines had a unique philosophy: all young men joining the company would get experience as seaman, but their first year of training would give them grounding in accounting and office procedures. The presumption was that exposure early on to the financial aspects of running the company would permanently instill in them the importance of keeping operations profitable. If they had proved loyal and were up to grade, they would spend their second year sailing on a steamer in order to learn what it took to be a crew member.

This approach, while unique, had proved of inestimable value because not a single individual hired and exposed to this training had ever been fired from the company. Moreover, every so often one of these trainees found that life on the high seas was in his blood. Any trainee's request for permanent assignment to shipboard duty would be honored and all further training would be focused on that. In the long run, this approach resulted in significantly lowered insurance premiums for their shipping ventures, so management remained vested in its loyalty program. No oaths were ever administered nor written documents required; the arrangement was so serendipitous that, once hired, a man could expect to spend his working life with Oceanic Lines.

Charles McDonald had joined the company in September 1927 after his father had yielded to his entreaties following the boy's completion of 11th grade. His dad had never gone beyond the 7th grade and had it in mind that his son would be a distinguished high school alumnus. His son's fervor for the sea had been unwavering, however, and his father had yielded. The Company required that all management trainees reside on one of its regional campuses so their "commute" time would be minimal and their time for study maximized, not to mention supervised. For the lad, having both a local campus and his parents close by in Providence was, well, providential.

On September 5, Charles McDonald, Senior, found himself shaking hands with his namesake at the very door of the satellite training facility. It was all he could do to square his shoulders and sternly admonish: "Do well, son. This is what you want, so go to it!"

Then he stiffly turned and walked away without looking back. With a time-honored sigh, he poignantly wondered whether he would ever see the boy again. The sea could be a cruelly unforgiving place, or so his buddies down at O'Malley's Tavern had assured him over many a pint. Deep inside his soul, he uttered a fervent prayer: "Good Lord, look after my son, and give him the strength and wisdom to achieve what he seeks. May he be deserving of your blessing! Thank you, oh dear God."

Humanity is fortunate in that future events hide behind veils of secrecy, becoming revealed only with the sure march of time. Even if big heroic plans lay in store for young Charles, Lady Future would not bother to seek approval for such plans from the senior McDonald.

As required by company policy for his second year, young Charles was given a two week course on sailing a skiff, tying knots, maintaining turbines, and swabbing decks among other tasks. With this crash course completed, he was assigned aboard the

Humboldt as a basic-level greaser. Each month he would be exposed to a new job, with a new superior, and thus rotated through the various functions aboard ship. His winning smile and unassuming nature allowed him to win friends easily.

His buddies on board were, of course, far older than he, but that meant they had much from their own experience to teach him. His ease in their company allowed him to remember their likes and interests, so he was a pleasure to be around. He never needed to seek out a compliment. As he rotated from one section of the ship to the next, each mate or officer responsible for him during that prior month would say, "Sorry to be losing you, lad. It's been good shipping with ya!" or words to that effect. Naturally, he would see these new acquaintances at chow, so his new-found friendships could be maintained as he transferred to each new posting.

In some respects, he became better known that year to the crew of *Humboldt* than the captain himself. Despite this, fate was about to cause him to be assigned as an alter-ego for the captain, or at least as his eyes and ears.

Captain Highsmith had asked his First Officer, Peter Porter, to chaperone the lad through all the various rotating assignments. Porter was some twenty years older, but a good choice. He had three younger brothers back home in Charlottesville, Virginia, and he liked to visit the old homestead and his siblings whenever he got leave. Shepherding young McDonald proved to be a pleasurable diversion from the daily routine of his own duties. The pair got along well and Charles came to look upon Porter as an older brother.

A key benefit was Porter's warnings of the hazing Charles would receive anytime he switched departments. Anyone can laugh and shrug off a bucket of fish oil dumped on your head if you've been forewarned that it will soon happen. Finding a crab stuck down at the foot of his sheets was not so appealing, but he had managed to take that in stride, not ever letting on that it had given his toe a good nip. The next morning, when he had made no complaints, and no one inquired how he had slept, he figured he was beginning to be accepted by the crew.

His confidence increased and he stretched his arms around each new duty as he was rotated into it. His Waterloo, so to speak, finally arrived on the first of April.

This was April Fool's Day, so he wasn't sure whether to believe First Officer Porter when he was transferred out of the kitchen galley and assigned to Ralph Stone, the Head Steward. If ever there was a man who could cajole and encourage a passenger into obeying some rule or pursue some amusement, it was Steward Stone. Nevertheless, when young McDonald was assigned to him for the coming month, Stone wasn't at all sure but that the lad would simply be an annoyance. Some fool running about underfoot, doubtless prone to tripping a man who had important duties to attend to: that was how this steward saw him.

"Why should I bother showing the secrets of my trade, laddie, when you're going to end up ashore sitting behind a desk without a care in the world?" He snorted, just to add emphasis.

Charles took it in stride. He wanted to learn how to care for and attend to passengers; after all, they were to be his primary responsibility should he ever become a ship's officer. Even if he didn't, which was probable, these were the very people who would be paying the fares that ended up as a weekly salary check on his desk when he was managing paperwork back ashore.

Anyway, getting along with people was his natural forte, so he welcomed this new challenge. Getting this new boss to come over to his side would, clearly, be a challenge. He tucked in his tie, buttoned his jacket, squared his shoulders, and got on with it.

"Should I volunteer to help or offer advice, or always wait to be asked," he inquired innocently.

"Don't bother me with your silly questions now, boy. Watch, listen, and you'll learn!"

So, with that admonition, Chief Steward Stone handed young McDonald over to Steward Reinhold.

"Roy," he said, "this fellow wants to learn everything there is to handling passengers. I don't know whether he's up to it, but we'll soon see. Would you please take him under your wing for the next month?"

With that directive, the chief steward hoped he had seen the last of that lad. Without waiting for an answer from Roy Reinhold, he stalked off down the passageway to attend to his own important duties.

During the first week of April, young McDonald had thrived under the tutelage of Steward Reinhold. Born of German ancestry, Roy had a natural tendency to be direct and authoritative; on the other hand, his instructions were always accompanied by explanations of "why." It was the first time in the boy's young life that anyone had bothered to underscore the reason things were done as they were. Charles found himself keeping his eyes open, but his ears really wide-open, in order to take in everything that this knowledgeable tutor was imparting.

He had no way of knowing at the time that, in the near future, he would encounter a much older, but higher ranking, man who had shown a similar affinity for calming frayed nerves and assuaging panic among the helpless. That man was named James Stahl and he had gotten his start by helping people while working at his uncle's hardware store. Fate has a way of bringing good people together.

CHAPTER SIXTEEN

CHARLES MCDONALD'S ASSIGNMENT

Steward Reinhold watched from down the hall as his charge, young McDonald, patiently explained to the elderly couple in Cabin 206 that it was time for them to go to the dining room for dinner. Adam Mansfield had served as a general in the American Army during the Great War and he did not like taking instruction from one who was obviously his inferior. In short order, however, the lad had the old couple laughing at his light banter. Even though they were not hungry at this hour, they realized they would miss the convivial companionship of their fellow passengers if they didn't go to dinner now.

Yet another problem solved, Charles turned to go down the hall to the next pressing concern when he spotted Steward Reinhold. The older man motioned for him to come over.

"Son, you seem to be enjoying your stint in my sector. Have you been this happy in your other training, as well?" he inquired politely.

"Golly, Mr. Reinhold, I sure have. But, and I'm not brown-nosing here, working with the passengers has been nothing but fun. Knowing I'm to deal with people gets me out of the sack every day with a smile on my face! It's been great learning how the engines work and what their maintenance calls for as well as the safe storage requirements for different kinds of goods packed down in the holds, and all that, but, geesh, nothing beats being around people who need your help. There are so many age groups and nationalities aboard; questions just seem to crop up everywhere I go. At this point, I've learned so much about the *Humboldt* that I have yet to encounter a query I can't answer."

Pausing with some thought, the lad continued, "I can remember how, back ashore, dating girls was a lot of fun. I just wish doing so was as easy as this job!"

"Right you are, my son. Frankly, you're the first person I've ever taken on who appears to have been born to this sort of job. When you are older and in top management, I want you to hang onto the experiences you've had here. I'm not referring to the machinery and nuts or bolts. In shipping, the passenger comes first, and everything you do must be geared to encapsulating them in a protective shell of safety, comfort, and security. Very few in our company grasp the significance of that, I believe. So whether you're building ships or monitoring their operation for profitability, always hold service to the passenger as the most important objective, understand?"

"That I will, Steward Reinhold!"

"I'm pleased to have served as your instructor, son. Now, I'm going to take a giant leap of faith here and recommend to Captain Highsmith that he carve out a special niche for you for the remainder of April. I assume you have some areas you still haven't been exposed to, right?"

"That's right." Charles idly wondered where Steward Reinhold was going with this.

"I'm going to suggest to the captain that you become his aide-de-camp. That's a military term for a sort of combination messenger boy, trouble shooter, and ambassador. Essentially, you would be the captain's eyes and ears all around the ship, leaving him free to manage the serious navigation of such an important vessel as the *Humboldt* with all her 1,400 passengers aboard. This position would increase your exposure to what it takes to run a passenger ship crossing the Atlantic Ocean; it would, therefore, stand you in good stead! What do you think?"

"Golly, that would really be top drawer, all right! Of course, I will do whatever Captain Highsmith desires. Thank you, Steward Reinhold."

With that, the steward headed for Chief Steward Stone's quarters with the mission of gaining support for this new function which he wanted to propose to the captain. Along the way, McDonald was hailed by Heinrich Oglethorpe, a bombastic, rotund passenger who always seemed to be in need of fawning attention by the stewards.

"The day's work must go on," the lad joked to himself as he responded to yet another imperious German's call and headed back up the hall.

That had been on the 12th of April. Now it was eight days later and he had served as orderly to Captain Reginald Highsmith both day and night. Depending on how one looked at it, one could say he was a round-the-clock assistant. The only stumbling block had been where to bunk him so he would be in easy reach of the captain, but that had been solved when the radiomen came forward and made room for him in their quarters. This couldn't have pleased Charles more. Now he had access to the ears of the ship and could share in their scuttlebutt, as long as he wasn't nosy. Essentially, he felt like a nurse who was on call 24 hours a day, but a nurse who had special access to the entire ship.

Occasionally there'd be some lagging, perhaps four or five hours, where he did little. When he wasn't grabbing some shut-eye, he'd wander the length of the interior passageways, memorizing all their intricacies. He reasoned it should be his business to know, rather than be forced to ask, how to get from point A to point B. If truth be told, so far it had been his experience that only the officers, and the ship's carpenter, seemed to know the complete ship. Everyone else appeared to have what he called "duty vision," being familiar with only their personal orb of responsibility. With healthy strong legs, a curious mind, and the boundless energy of youth, Charles wanted to explore even the nether regions of the holds so that he knew the vessel inside out.

Following his stint with Steward Reinhold, word had spread among the passengers that this kid would make one's voyage happier, and now the same could be said for crew members. As the Captain's Orderly, none of the older, experienced men ever challenged him, so he roamed all over the interior, absorbing the details of the various ladders and passageways with aplomb. Since this boat had intercom throughout the decks, he was merely a call away from responding, should he be needed. He was very grateful to management for making this experience possible: hands-on knowledge was far more useful than theory from manuals.

Even with his helter-skelter hours, Charles was still surprised when one of the radiomen, Fred Newsome, awakened him at 0400 on Friday, April 20.

"Report to the Bridge right away, laddie. The captain needs you directly!" he was told.

Hastily pulling on his trousers and donning a heavy sweater over his seaman's shirt, he scampered up to the Bridge and went in without knocking.

"Captain, you called for me?" He had no inkling what was going on.

"Charles, a few minutes ago our telegrapher received an SOS from an American passenger/freighter headed east to France. We've got a very serious situation here, perhaps a first for the record books. She's some four hours from our location. We're steaming to her aid at about 24 knots but we have no clear idea of what we'll face once we arrive. I strongly suspect that, having run into and getting captured by an ice sheet, her captain is going to try and extricate her and head back to New York for repairs, but he's got to deal with his passenger load prior to trying any recovery. I'm informed she is close to capacity with some 400 tourists aboard. They're clustered on three decks, which is a boon to informing and managing them.

"You are going to be my alter-ego. We'll transfer you to the *Reliance* as soon as we are able. You know how I think. Her captain and I will communicate by megaphone or semaphore, but you'll be right there to correct any misinterpretations by him.

"Son, I want to be very clear with you, so listen close. There is risk here, very grave risk if the *Reliance* falters and starts to sink while coming off the ice. You've been like the son I never had while on board the *Humboldt.* You are important to me, and I daresay to all members of the crew. I do not feel I have the authority to order you to undertake this assignment, but I would be grateful if you would accept. You're being there would make my job far easier. Are you up to this, my boy?"

For once in his life, Charles McDonald was stunned into silence. It was his high regard for Captain Highsmith that led him to open his mouth and stammer: "Aye, aye, sir. I will perform to the best of my ability."

"Good man. Now, find yourself a cap and gloves, and an extra coat, then get together with First Officer Porter. He'll assign someone to teach you in quick order the intricacies of lowering and raising lifeboats. Be sure and chow down some breakfast right quick, too."

Reaching out his hand, Reginald Highsmith prepared to shake Captain's Orderly Charles McDonald's hand. First, the boy saluted, and then he extended his hand as well. Their eyes met and Charles suddenly felt the full import of this assignment. He was going to be standing in for his captain aboard a vessel in trouble. He must be clear-headed and think straight. He would have to rely on his native instincts: no textbook had ever prepared him for this responsibility.

As the portal closed behind the lad, First Officer Porter turned to face Highsmith. "Sir, this is a lot of responsibility to load on just a kid. He'll have no standing in the eyes of those officers who don't know him. He hasn't rank, not even an ensign's rating, yet he's being tasked to manage a captain of a competing company who is probably beside himself with chagrin and embarrassment. The fate of hundreds of people hangs on this kid avoiding a screw-up or rash action. He barely knows how to wash himself behind the ears. Are you sure about this?"

"Sometimes, when life comes at you in the harshest way, you see the path to sane action as though there was no threat at all," Captain Highsmith stated earnestly. "I've never had more confidence in an individual than I do in that twenty-year-old kid. If he lives through this, he is destined to become one of the finest officers our company has ever been lucky enough to employ. Now, let's get on with the business of arriving safely ourselves! Peter, get out there and show him the ropes for freeing the lifeboats from belay."

With that said, the Bridge and wheelhouse became silent as everyone focused on steering a safe course to *Reliance*. After all, Highsmith knew the man who was in command of *Reliance*. He and his crew would be going to the rescue of a longtime friend as well as a stricken vessel.

CHAPTER SEVENTEEN

DRIFTING THREAT

Captain Stahl stopped by the radio room as the sky began to streak with rosy pink. The day would be clear, at least.

"What do you hear, Hawkins? Are any rescue ships near?"

"It's nearly 0730, sir. I recall one of the ships requesting that we send up a signal flare beginning at 0730 and every ten minutes thereafter. That's when they figured they would be closing on our position. The *Tahoe* is the key ship, since she is familiar with ice procedures. She's not very fast, being capable of only18 knots, plus she was some 110 miles distant so she estimated arriving around mid-morning. The *Humboldt* should be hoving into sight any time after 0800. Our other rescue vessel will probably be the *Dorchester.* She was close, less than 30 miles away when contacted but, being a freighter, her top speed is only 12 knots. She may be just over the horizon. Do you want me to call them up?"

"No, no, let them alone. When they think they're getting near, they'll raise us. Thanks, Sparks."

As the captain left for the Bridge, Chester Hawkins couldn't help smiling. No one had ever referred to his sort as "Sparks," but he knew his buddies would appreciate the acronym. He turned back to face the myriad of tuning dials, distortion suppressors, and gain controllers, then he looked over the generator to insure it was humming smoothly. Then he sat waiting. It wasn't long before the set began buzzing.

"MSG. *Reliance,* this is *Dorchester* calling. We are closing on your reported position. Can you see our smoke? Send up a flare to confirm."

Hawkins reached for the speaker tube: "Captain, the freighter *Dorchester* is closing and needs a flare to pinpoint our position right away."

"Got it. Thanks, Hawkins." Stahl thought that freighter had made good time, it being night and all.

Captain Stahl turned to the men on the Bridge.

"Okay, men, stay alert. Things will start to happen pretty quickly now that help is arriving. Officer Jenkins, get a team out on the ice to review the condition of the bow by daylight and inform me immediately if the status has changed from last night. Officer Dougherty, get the signalman to his post ready to semaphore by flags or lamp. Run up the mast flags with our ship's name together with SOS. Get the stewards to wake all the passengers and insist that everybody eat breakfast now. There is to be no, and I emphasize no wandering or curious exploration by anyone. Our passengers will eat and then return directly to their cabins. There's no telling when their next meal might be. Also, ensure that everyone carries their life vest with them regardless of their complaints. Get moving!"

In a flash, Officer Dougherty was attending to his assignments. The Bridge and wheelhouse quieted down as everyone went to the starboard side of the fantail to try and spot the oncoming rescue. Only the faint hum of the generators producing heat and illumination could be heard from way down in the bowels of the ship.

The first to speak was the fresh-faced relief helmsman.

"There's smoke, captain, off the starboard fantail." After reporting for duty at 0600, Helmsman Petrovich had been stunned by the condition of the bow of *Reliance,* so his voice was barely a soft whisper, but he was as relieved as all the others in the Pilot House by the approach of another ship.

Two seamen were milling around the deck forward of the Bridge; they had a cluster of rockets at their feet. Captain Stahl peered in the direction of a thin wisp of black smoke on the southeastern horizon and immediately called on Seaman Fox to send up a rocket with white phosphorous star cluster.

"Keep them coming at ten minute intervals precisely, sailor, until you can read the name on her bow. Got that?"

"Aye, aye, sir!" came the crisp acknowledgment.

James opened the Ship's Logbook and noted that a rescue ship that identified itself as *H.M.S. Dorchester* was steaming toward their position and should arrive before 0900 hours on Friday, April 20, 1929. His ship and its passengers were not safe yet, but one always feels better in the presence of assistance.

Turning to me, he said briskly, "Come on Wallace; let's make another quick walk of the ship."

We left the Bridge together, but this time we turned to the right for a look full on at the bow under daylight conditions. The wind had died to just a whisper, but in this environment of ice and cold sea, the air was nonetheless frigid. If James was to order anyone off his ship today, he'd have to make certain to limit their exposure to as short a time as possible.

When we looked over the port quarterdeck, it appeared that the ice gripped the crushed tangle of bow plating very firmly. Even with ships assisting the withdrawal using lines secured to bollards, neither of us was confident that such a plan could succeed. Even this plan, of course, had no assurance that the ship was still watertight.

"It's a bit nippy, sir," I observed. "We'll want to limit passenger exposure to as short a time as possible if we undertake an offloading. Do you think it would be possible to utilize the cargo exits on Deck E and suspend flexible ladders down to waiting lifeboats? That would eliminate roping such craft down and then back up."

"That's my plan in the event we off-load crew members as groups, Wallace, but passengers could never handle doing that in this cold. Next time, remind me to take charge of a vessel charted for the Mediterranean!"

We were chuckling as we came to the stern on the port side. Here we both paused, staring upward.

The Captain's mouth was agape as he asked, "I'll be a monkey's uncle! Does that berg look bigger to you this morning, Wallace?"

My mouth was wide open as well as I stared wide-eyed at what now seemed to be a much larger berg than the one the ship had avoided in the depths of the night. I gulped.

"Sir, that's the same monster we side-stepped. I hesitate to say this, but I believe it is getting closer to our position and that's why it seems bigger this morning."

Captain Stahl was stunned into momentary silence. The idea that the berg was catching up to his stranded ship did not seem possible. What was happening here? He reflected back to his training as a student at P.M.I. Part of the piloting course was devoted to handling ships in a harbor: docking, departing, use of tugboats, tying up, and so on. One of the dangers the instructor had dwelt substantial time on had been the effect which passing vessels had on ships moored to their slip. A passing ship's propeller wash could dislodge a moored boat. The *Titanic's* departure on her maiden voyage had brought this problem to the forefront when the enormous suction that her props made had caused a docked liner, the *New York*, to tear her hawsers asunder as she was sucked inexorably toward a certain collision with the far bigger ship. Only superb piloting had avoided a damaging blow.

Captain Stahl spoke up, his voice now filled with dread.

"Consider this. Is it possible that our having rammed that ice shelf has slowed its drift down, so that berg is indeed freely moving faster on the current? It sure looks as though it's headed right for our port fantail. I estimate that since midnight, this ice has moved some twenty or even thirty yards closer to us. That would give us approximately 11, maybe 12, hours before she is crushing right up against our hull. By then, of course, it would be bitching nighttime again. Conditions in which to react would be virtually impossible. What do you think?"

The words of my captain seemed to electrify me. "Sir, by god, you could be absolutely correct. We're in a whole different ballgame now; time may be of the essence! I'll direct the engineer to assign three men to monitor this berg. He can set them up with range-finding equipment so we get an accurate fix on this monster."

In frustration, I turned full on toward the floating threat and yelled: "Haven't you had enough of us? Melt, you son-of-a bitch, melt!"

This was no time to be joking but, despite himself, James couldn't prevent a little smile creasing his lips. His demeanor told me that he not only liked, but frankly enjoyed having me as his chief officer.

We were both back on the Bridge when, at 0840, Helmsman Petrovich spotted more smoke off our starboard stern. Captain Stahl made a mental note to retain that seaman in his assigned post: he had very good vision. With this second sighting, Stahl hurried straight to the radio room.

"We've got two sightings. See if you can raise these ships so we can guide them in close." His captain was all business, so Radioman Hawkins responded promptly.

"MSG. *Dorchester, Humboldt*, this is the *Reliance.* Confirm that you have sighted us. We have a signalman stationed on the quarterdeck to communicate by flag or lamp, whichever is better for you."

Both rescue vessels preferred lamp and they were soon guided to within 300 yards of *Reliance.* Here, they dropped anchor. A small motorized launch was lowered from *Humboldt* and a rowboat from *Dorchester.* Each approached the starboard side of our stricken ship until within hailing distance.

"Ahoy there, Captain Stahl. What seems to be the trouble here? Big boats are designed to plow through water, not ice! Haven't ye learned that, after all yer time at sea?" Reginald Highsmith's face was broadened by his wide smile.

The captain of *Humboldt* and Captain James Stahl were old friends, having served (in an exchange program with England for advanced trainees) on the *Lusitania* some months before she was torpedoed and sunk by a German submarine. The riposte was not long in coming.

"Thanks for the advice, Reggie. I'm glad to hear that you've learned at least something during your service aboard *Humboldt!*" James Stahl smiled a big welcome his way. "Do you want to come aboard or go inspect the bow first?"

"Well, Jim, the first thing to do is to introduce you to Captain Barnstable, Aldus Barnstable, who's been kind enough to join us today."

Captain Barnstable tipped his cap James' way and added, "I don't rightly count on meeting people way out here among the icebergs, captain. Today, however, it appears we don't have much choice in the matter. As long as we're down here on the water, we'll go look at your bow first."

"Right you are. Thanks for coming to our aid but, as you said, we don't have much choice."

The two boats inched up toward the shelf, made a quick inspection, and then returned to confer with Captain Stahl.

"She looks to be wedged pretty tight, I'd say," cautioned Barnstable. "I'm not at all certain but that you might have to blast some of that ice sheet before you can go anywhere. Do you have any dynamite aboard?"

Captain Highsmith was more sanguine. "James, now that we've got daylight, I think you ought to disembark your passenger load completely. My crew can make room for a little over 100; we've got that capacity in empty cabins. Another 200 could use mats on the decks, but of course these people would be without heat or facilities. Let's complete that task before we start throwing words such as 'dynamite' around."

Turning to the rowboat, he asked, "What is your situation, Aldus?"

"Well, captain, we were on our way to Boston anyway, so it won't put us out to carry an extra load of passengers to New York. We'll find some blankets and we can feed your men folk but, naturally, we're full up on bunk space. Freighters aren't made for rescue missions, you know. Everything's already assigned. We could make do for a short time carrying up to 100, I'd judge, if we moved some things and crew around. It'd be best if they were all males. If it comes down to it, the mess hall can serve as a holding area."

After pausing and stroking his chin whiskers, his face crinkled with a smile and Aldus Barnstable shouted up to Stahl, "Say Jim, where do we send our bill?"

Captain Stahl laughed. On the high seas, when one outfit is in trouble, everyone simply pitches in and swallows the overhead. After all, it could be your boat that gets in trouble the next time around.

"I'll notify my passengers and the sailors on *Reliance* will start assembling everyone right now. Let's use lifeboats from each ship; my 3rd Officer Brian Stanley will keep a roster of who goes where. If there's enough daylight, we'll see about off-loading their dunnage, but that's a low priority."

He glanced my way, but I kept my mouth shut. We had decided to keep mum about the approaching nemesis until our passengers had safely disembarked.

"Let's get to it!" The two rescuers returned to their respective ships to take charge of lowering their own lifeboats and preparing space for the shivering passengers that would soon be streaming aboard.

CHAPTER EIGHTEEN

THE PROBLEM

Captain Stahl informed his officers on the Bridge of the day's procedures, then turned to the wall and unhooked the fat black button that put him in touch with most every space aboard the *Reliance*.

"Ladies and gentlemen," the captain intoned smoothly, "We've got a rescue underway. We will be placing single male passengers on the freighter *Dorchester* out of England, and I assure you that you will be treated courteously. Women and families will be transferred over to the passenger liner *Humboldt*, an American ship operating out of New York. Both vessels will head for New York City as that was our original departure point. Please enjoy your breakfast, but move right along because the stewards will begin leading you to the lifeboats starting at 0930 this morning. Each person over the age of 10 will be permitted to take one small suitcase with them. Please be sure it is something you can hold on your lap while in the transfer boat.

"Our officers will be supervising the loading and deployment of our lifeboats. Our crewmen will row family members over to the *Humboldt* where Captain Highsmith there will have deployed an accommodation ladder along the hull of his ship. Please hold both handrails as you ascend. Where necessary, his men will have hoists with canvas slings for lifting children and those unable to use the ladder.

"I say again, your cooperation in carrying one small suitcase will be appreciated. Be sure it contains your valuables. Leave your other bags in your cabin where they are accessible by your steward. We will do our best to transfer your other luggage if circumstances permit, but I must emphasize, folks, we are in a serious situation and must have everyone off-loaded by 1600 hours, or 4:00 PM this afternoon. I extend my sincerest apologies to each of you for this unexpected interruption to your various vacations, but your safety during transit, as well as your safe return to New York, must now be paramount for all of us. Thank you."

If he had been down in the dining room, the captain would have heard grumblings of concern and resentment by the passengers. However, the stewards were omnipresent, reassuring, and firm in their instructions to follow the captain's directives: eat, return to the proper cabin, pack one suitcase, dress warmly, and report to A Deck for offloading into a lifeboat. Since it was daylight and the decks were only slightly tilted down toward the stern, no one appeared to be scared. Loading the small rescue craft proceeded relatively smoothly.

The zone plan of loading was forsaken in favor of: whoever shows up is loaded into the next available space. Officers Dougherty on the starboard side and I on the port side oversaw the loading in the stern zones of the ship, while 3rd Officer Stanley oversaw the truncated starboard bow zone loadings. The lifeboats in the port bow zone were ignored; they would be too difficult to maneuver either down, or around the hull before proceeding over to the rescue vessels.

Fortunately, our passengers were good sports. The threat of impending disaster was mutually shared; its proximity bred polite respect for one another's suffering. They each remained calm and respectful as the off-loading proceeded.   Our biggest problem was their natural curiosity; everyone wanted a good look at the condition of the forward holds. In the interest of their safety, all such requests were refused.

The only comment that I heard was made by Cynthia Pickering as she sat astride her good friend, Hunter Orloff.

"Phew!" she had exclaimed as I walked by. "This air reminds me of the strangely clammy odor I smelled when visiting the Eiger in Switzerland. Its ice walls possessed the same overpowering stench."

"It comes from all the vegetation that a future iceberg picks up on its way along the mother glacier," observed Orloff succinctly. I couldn't have explained it any better.

During a quiet interval, I strolled over to where Jim Stahl was smoking a pipe while overseeing the rescue operations.

"You realize, of course, once our passengers get on the *Humboldt*, and various crew together with the male stewards board the *Dorchester*, neither of those vessels will comply with regulations regarding having a lifeboat for every person on board."

"Of course they won't! Don't bring pressure where we don't already have enough."

Captain Stahl was almost livid at my implication.

He quickly added, "The regulations won't be infracted here; this is clearly an emergency situation. Besides, and I'm expressing just my own opinion—but I think upon reflection that you'll agree with me here—the new guidelines may appear to be the most humane approach, but the regulations regarding lifeboats will, in practice, largely be ignored. It may seem reasonable for such rules to apply to every vessel afloat, but when one considers the different types of design and outfitting, not to mention the variety of registry of vessels sailing throughout the world, the stupidity of trying to set forth a single rigid rule becomes laughable. We need an international study to be undertaken to assess the types of mishaps that are most likely to occur, and then to reword the Regs in terms that will protect against the accident types that are most likely to occur."

James puffed on his pipe for a bit more, preparing to express his thoughts succinctly.

"For example, consider our own predicament right here. We are unable to use the forward port boats due to great risk in even lowering them. Back when the *Titanic* began sinking, its captain foolishly squandered almost an hour before seamen and officers began actually calling for people to get in the lifeboats.

"Both situations illustrate this maxim: *The number of people who can disembark is always determined by the circumstances of the incident.*

"The number of rescue craft available may not matter if they cannot be accessed or lowered. The *Titanic* sank in just over two hours, and much less when you consider how soon the forward lifeboats became inaccessible as the bow submerged. If a ship is rammed by another, the danger of fire may be so great that entire sections of rescue boats might be inaccessible. If a ship were to, god forbid, actually capsize or roll onto her side, its crew might not be able to use any of the lifeboats. When the regulations require a seat for everyone on board, it assumes a best-case scenario with the ship upright in calm waters. That rarely happens at sea."

He paused for breath, as did I, but he was absorbed by his argument and forged on.

"Frankly, the new regulations requiring a lifeboat seat for everyone on board are really just a public relations ploy to enable prospective travelers to be reassured. A real-life situation such as happened to the *R.M.S. Titanic*, where no rescue ships came to her aid until hours after she bumped along the iceberg, is so unusual as to never be repeated. At least, I should hope so, given the volume of traffic and round-the-clock manned telegraphy that is now the rule. My solution would be to have sufficient lifeboats for half the total crew and passengers with the expectation, as here, that other ships in the area would be on scene so quickly that the little boats would be used more as ferries to and from such ships, rather than as life islands unto themselves."

After a few puffs, he surmised: "Of course, my thoughts have to be tempered by the fact that I am experienced only in the Atlantic and Mediterranean routes. Protecting passengers in the much larger Pacific theater would be an entirely different ball game."

"There aren't many bergs one has to worry about in the Pacific Ocean, Jim," I parried. "Not many trips are made through the Bering Strait or down to Antarctica. By the way, why did you call it a 'theater'?"

"Hell, Wally, when you confront an iceberg, you're in a war, sure enough!" The Captain shifted his pipe to the opposite corner of his mouth, as though to staunchly emphasize his point. He continued sucking serenely on the pipe stem, watching the orderly transfer of men to the *Dorchester* as well as families and single women to the *Humboldt*.

After some more puffing, a thought occurred to him, so he added, "Of course, by and large, the vessels plying that vast ocean enjoy far more pleasant weather than we do here. Perhaps a ship sinking in those waters would not be as traumatic as foundering amongst Atlantic icebergs."

I thereupon trotted out my own points for my dear friend's inspection.

"Don't forget that the trauma of Atlantic cold is replaced by death from shark bite in the Pacific. I've heard they sense a human's treading water from quite far off, and as they close on the water disturbance, they can sense our being warm blooded. Their sensory ability is better than that of a bear, whose nose can smell prey from several miles."

I paused, letting these gruesome images make us glad to be dry and aboard a ship, albeit a shaky one.

I concluded with, "I doubt you could find anyone in the world who would enjoy being aboard during a typhoon while their ship sank beneath them. However, I must admit, sir, you've raised some interesting points. I would wager that the committees considering the revisions never received any such testimony."

"Quite so, Wally," responded Stahl, "Quite so." He turned on his heels and returned to the Bridge.

I watched his departure with a trace of sadness. This trip had been his inaugural command of a passenger-carrying ship, yet he'd steered her into disaster on the first night out. I would have to find some way to help him climb out of the deep hole he had dug for himself.

My attention was diverted to Lifeboat No. 5 which was returning from its trip over to the *Humboldt*. There was someone standing in it, looking my way. I had never seen him before.

Positioned in the bow and holding onto the painter line stood a young man whose expectant face was wreathed with excitement at this, his first major assignment. His expression also revealed lines of concern etching his forehead. He had been entrusted with the most important task of his young life: to assist a weather-beaten, tried and true master of the helm who probably believed he needed no coaching from anyone, and certainly not from some doe-eyed, teen-aged stripling. Charles McDonald reflected, as the rescue craft closed on the *Reliance*, that this situation would most likely call upon the very best he had in him.

I slung a ladder over the side and he grabbed it. With firm hands and steady tread, he ascended the flat wood steps purposefully. He did not want to slip; it would make a poor impression. While he was climbing, the attention of those aboard the stranded ship was focused on safely lowering the next lifeboat to leave *Reliance*. Following that, a craft returning from *Humboldt* would be tied into the vacant davit and raised for resumption of loading it with passengers. McDonald needn't have been concerned; no one was looking his way.

As he clambered over the sideboard, he saw a tall officer whose face bore finely chiseled lines of service.

"Permission to come aboard, sir," affirmed Charles as he saluted me.

The first thing on this lad's agenda, apparently, was to introduce himself to a Captain James Stahl, but first he had to get past me. He looked reasonably intelligent and quick-witted. Thus, under the circumstances, I demanded that he fully explain why he wanted to come aboard when, so it seemed, everyone else appeared to be leaving.

"My name is Charles McDonald, sir. I am the Captain's Orderly aboard the liner *Humboldt,* and he has directed me to offer my assistance to your captain, James Stahl, during extraction from the ice shelf."

"Let me take you up to the Bridge where you can meet our captain," I responded. "You will pardon me, but I must return here to direct disembarking operations for the afternoon. As our captain will no doubt inform you, we have a rather desperate situation developing that we have not communicated to anyone."

With that said, we stepped into the enclosed room from which operations were directed. Captain Stahl came forward with curiosity framing his expression.

I provided the formal introduction as the young man saluted: "Captain Stahl, this is Captain's Orderly Charles McDonald provided by Reginald Highsmith of the *Humboldt* to assist you during extraction from the ice shelf. Now excuse me, sir, but I must return to the unloading."

Nodding toward the lad, I added, "Very good to have met you, Charles."

Young McDonald saluted as I took my leave. Turning to address Captain Stahl, he stated, "Sir, as you can see from my uniform, I have no rank. In fact, I am technically just on a year of training aboard the *Humboldt* to familiarize myself with the operations of passenger liners. During my eighth month, I was pulled off my training and assigned to our captain as his orderly. It is my job to interface with the passengers and all operational areas of the *Humboldt* in order to free the captain of mundane problems.

"He offers my assistance today because I know how he thinks, what he would consider priority in event of an emergency, and the probable courses of action he would take to solve a problem. I believe he intends to offer me as your right-hand man, given your long mutual friendship. To come directly to the point, Captain, if there is a sacrifice that has to be made, I have been ordered to undertake such task and thereby save officers who are held in high esteem by the seafaring community."

"Jesus Christ Almighty!" exploded James Stahl. "I never thought I'd ever hear such an affirmation of friendship! I can assure you, son, that if Reggie has this sort of faith in you, I will trust you completely as well. Brace yourself. What I'm about to show you may exceed your wildest imagination."

He took the young man by the shoulder and steered him to the starboard bridge wing where they stood for a moment watching passengers being loaded into small boats that would shortly be sent bobbing about the open ocean. This involved slinging them over the side and lowering them to the sea surface as it ebbed and swelled against the flanks of the *Reliance*. Thereafter, they still faced the harrowing journey over to an unfamiliar craft. Without pausing for breath, it seemed, a replacement boat from *Humboldt* would then be raised toward deck level of *Reliance* and filled with still more passengers who were each clutching a valise or satchel close to their chest.

"This operation should be completed by 1500 hours or so; possibly, we can use the stewards to retrieve the remaining suitcases of the passengers for transfer over to *Humboldt* or *Dorchester*. Without promising that these would be returned, I have asked my passengers to leave them in their cabins. My hope is for that task to be completed by 1700 hours; the stewards will, of course, accompany the bags and remain aboard your ship. This would leave my operations crew and kitchen staff aboard, which should total about 95 souls if all the seamen in the lifeboats return to *Reliance*. However, it may be that I order the seamen that have left our ship during this task to board your boat or the *Dorchester*. Let me show you why."

Having stated the plan regarding off-loading, James turned and walked the young orderly to the far stern of his ship. There he turned to face a rather stupendous iceberg that was approximately 50 yards from the stern. Up to this point, Charles had paid the giant monolith little regard, but now that he was squarely faced with its bulk, he felt puny in the presence of this silent, portentous giant.

He could sense the chilling, rather decaying, odor of the ice waft over him.

"Wow, Captain, I've never been up close and personal with an iceberg before. This monster is huge!" Then, looking down at the watery gap between the stern and the cold threat, he observed, "It looks like it might even block our exit path from the shelf, or at least make removal a very tight squeeze."

"It's far worse than that, son. Directed by the current, it's closing on our position. While we are stuck fast to a frozen field that is, by comparison, stationary, we estimate it will be in contact with our hull about 2230, possibly sooner. My engineer has made a rough calculation from its dimensions. With the exit of our passenger load, our weight will soon be in the neighborhood of 30,000 DT while the berg could be as much as half a million tons. It would rent us asunder like a matchstick. It might even shear us clear of the broken bow sections completely, possibly exposing an enormous opening in the forward bulkheads. Come with me, there's something else you need to see."

With that said, the two sailors walked the length of the starboard deck until they could peer over the torn bow section where it was lodged solidly in the ice shelf.

"Do you see that trough about 3 feet wide at the base of that ice wall?"

"Where am I looking?" asked the confused lad. The glare reflecting from the angle of the now fully risen sun was blinding.

James Stahl adjusted the young man's shoulders and pointed to the left of the ice wall.

"You can see the top of the wall is about even with our "A" deck and its base is adjacent to the right side of the trough. There, do you see it now? It's in shadow what with the sun's position behind our ship's superstructure. During this sunny day, heat is reflecting off our hull onto the tower of ice. The resulting melt is forming that depression as water runs down off the shelf into the sea. If that damned iceberg floats into our hull and begins pushing us, it should have little trouble thrusting our ship until the bow section wedges in that trough and separates completely from the hull. That would mean *Reliance* would slide off the shelf with a very uncertain future.

"Henry—that's our engineer—doubts that Number 3 bulkhead, and possibly even Number 4, would be watertight if so completely exposed; as water gets into those holds, we will be rapidly compromised, start down at the head, and quite possibly flip over onto our port side and founder. All would be lost in a matter of moments. The pressure is on us to come up with a solution quickly. If we don't, and simply let Nature take its course, it is very likely all of this will occur during hours of darkness, making our ability to react virtually nil."

The silence that followed this prophecy of doom created an empty space that was devoid of sensibility or comprehension. Charles found himself trying to fathom an event that had never been conjured by the adept imaginations of inspired fiction writers. Even that prescient novel, *Titan,* which had seemed to foretell the fate that befell the White Star liner *Titanic*, had not come close to the situation that *Reliance* and her crew were now facing.

Though he knew it would be inadequate, McDonald said simply, "I see what you mean, sir. Am I correct in thinking you are contemplating trying to back off the shelf as soon as the lifeboats with the stewards aboard have departed? Will an attempt be made to dynamite this ridge next to the hull before attempting extrication? Whatever you plan, where do the seamen who are still aboard fit; are they to be used to operate the ship should she remain floating? That's the stumbling point for me, captain. If she starts to sink or roll, there'll be no rescue for these men. To me, there's little choice. We should skip the dynamiting and simply shoot for a straight-out extraction. It can't hurt the bow sections any further. They're already lost to us. Then we try for extrication with a mere handful aboard; the sooner we go, the more daylight we'll have. That handful could possibly escape if necessary into a lifeboat or two that was launched and standing by prior to any extraction attempt."

Captain Stahl had pulled out his pipe while listening to the young man postulate. When he concluded, Stahl remained silent for a bit, puffing thoughtfully.

He quietly observed to himself, "I couldn't see it when he was introduced, but now I understand why my old pal Highsmith sent this stripling to me. The kid has a hell of a good brain atop that square set of shoulders. All this has obviously floored, but clearly not overwhelmed, him. Along with Mathews, I think the three of us, together with a couple of volunteers operating the turbines, might be able to pull this off. Of course, she's got to float, once we get *Reliance* off the shelf, or all that sacrifice will have been for nothing."

Instead, he said out loud, "Let's go around and discuss this with Officer Matthews. He's a very reliable man."

Captain Stahl led the way to the Bridge and, leaning over the railing, called down, "Officer Matthews, come up to the Bridge, will you?"

I nodded his way but kept on with the work of lowering and then freeing the ropes to launch the lifeboats.

"Give me a few minutes yet, Captain," I responded.

What with the small boats departing from *Reliance* and the alternate raising of the support craft sent over by *Humboldt* and *Dorchester*, the sides of the ship were beehives of activity throughout the lunch hour and on into mid-afternoon. Everyone, however, remained cooperative. Captain Stahl did not hear a single complaint about anyone missing a meal.

The primary sounds as the day slipped into afternoon were: "Step this way, ma'am. Steady on, hold my hand. There you are. Here's your case. There you be! Now, who's next?" and a little later, "This boat is full. Are we ready on the stern lines? Right. Ready on the bow? We're ready. Lower away!"

Dougherty and I were being kept busy, sure enough!

Despite my exemplary control of the proceedings on the port side, it could not be expected to go smoothly, especially not with such a large, risk-fraught operation. One of the passengers, Hank Fallon I think his name was, offered to help based on his extensive experience handling sailboats, but I rebuffed him.

"You say, my good man, that you are very experienced. How much time have you spent pulling an oar, Mr. Fallon?" Ignoring the possibility of embarrassing the man, I had gone straight to the crux of the question.

"Well none, actually. When I was at the helm of our sloop, the "Fair Fay" never got into a spot where the dingy became necessary."

"When you came into port for the night, didn't you have to row ashore?" I probed.

"Oh, good heavens, Officer Matthews! We belong to the Long Island Yacht Club. We always tied up at the dock after the employees gaffed the hull in. I know nothing about rowing."

A voice piped up from the knot of passengers waiting their turn to board this lifeboat.

"Chief Officer, I coached rowing for several years at the Vesper Boat Club in Philadelphia. I'm really quite good at it, if you need an extra oarsman." An athletic-looking man in his early thirties, I judged, stepped forward and gave me a strong, confident handshake.

"What's your name, sir?"

"Officer Matthews, just call me 'Kirk' for simplicity. It's easy to remember: it means 'church' in Scottish. Now, where do you want me? At stroke?"

I realized that this man knew his art. Few landlubbers would know the significance of that word. No sense in letting on that I was impressed by him, however.

"No, just take a thwart opposite an oar. There's no need for a stroke man aboard a lifeboat; the seaman on the tiller gives the count."

"Fine. I'm glad to help. Here, let me just set this bag down. There, I'm ready!"

As Kirk got aboard Lifeboat No. 4, I spotted the infamous Richard Rothschild about to put his foot over the gunwale. Henry Hoskins had told us officers about that passenger having wedged a plug of tobacco down his tub drain after removing the spigots. All to trap the novice steward serving him in yet another prank. It was too late to push the lifeboat out from the side of *Reliance*. Rothschild already had one foot in it, so I simply handed him over to the waiting seamen. To my horror, he sat down right next to that man who had so selflessly offered to help. I couldn't warn him, under the circumstances, so I hailed Steward Conklin.

"Harold, yes, right here, Mr. Conklin. Steward, would you please take a seat here? Thank you."

I sat him down between them to separate the trouble-maker from the innocent volunteer. However, after he had settled himself, I saw the steward looking askance at Rothschild, but there was no time for explanations. I had to attend to other passengers as they came forward. I just kept my fingers crossed that Conklin would be able to handle what Jim Stahl was calling "the nemesis of American Transatlantic Company" before the others in this lifeboat got taken in by one of Rothschild's pranks.

"Ready on the bow? Good. Ready on the stern? Lower away!"

With that, Lifeboat No. 4 was now headed for the surface of the sea and god knows what difficulties thereafter. I turned to ready the next load but was met by an unexpected challenge. Lifeboat No. 6 was beginning to fill after having dropped off young McDonald. On this day, there was no need to shout: "Women and children first!" All our remaining passengers were going to board the *Humboldt*, since the single men sailing on the *Reliance* and those seamen who could be spared had already made their way to the *Dorchester*. Jim had been smart to disembark them from the port stern; they had longer to go, but they were the stronger group and moved rapidly out of the way and over to the British vessel.

This time, the problem presented was merely a small boy of ten years old. Now, this little person was known—even after one day—to us officers. Chief Steward Spillane had thought it wise to prepare us for his personality.

"Hi, there, Denny, I see you've got a small bag with you, but I don't see any lifebelt on you. Where is it?"

"I don't want one."

"Sure you do, Denny. Every passenger has one stored in their cabin locker. Where's your mother? She should have put one on you."

"She's still in our cabin, getting ready. She said something about wanting to look nice for all the men when she boards the new ship. Can you believe that? What a silly notion. Heck, girls are no fun. They don't interest me at all. Why should she be interested in men?" Denny's mouth pouted as he frowned my way.

"Well now, you're right about that, son. But wait a few years; you'll see value in those darn girls when you're older. Right now, however, it's very important that you get a lifebelt on before you enter this little boat. Look, there's Chief Steward Spillane standing right over there. Run over and ask him to suit you up."

"No! I'm too grownup to need a sissy belt."

With that said, he stamped his foot and folded his arms across his chest, looking as formidable as an Indian chief, I'm sure. However, I was not cowed: I'm pretty formidable myself. I picked him up and held him so he could look at everyone in Boat No. 6.

"See, Denny? There's not a person here who is not wearing a lifebelt."

That having been said, I let him look way down at the chilly waves lapping the side of *Reliance.* When he stood on the deck again, he did an about-face and scampered over to Mr. Spillane. Shortly, he reappeared in front of me proudly wearing a red lifebelt; everyone else wore a white one.

"Okay, my wee man, I see you're dressed right smartly, aren't you?"

"Yes! Now I'm one of the ship's fire crew!" and he smiled broadly while saluting me.

Chief Steward Spillane was impressive; he always seemed to have an answer for every passenger foible. I turned and, to my happy surprise, there stood the boy's mother, Carol Coltrane. She had indeed made herself very presentable. "Well, Mrs. Coltrane, you're going to turn a lot of heads when you get to the *Humboldt.*"

"That's the idea! A lady who ignores her appearance usually finds herself ignored," she confirmed gaily, taking my hand and then alighting easily onto one of the remaining seats.

Her son turned toward her and, after handing her the small bag he carried, proudly proclaimed, "Mommy, I'm one of the ship's crew!"

"Yes, dear. I can see that. We're all proud of you!"

Problem solved. Next, I made a quick count: if every seat was taken, 6 times 8 rows = 48, so together with the seaman on the tiller and one at the bow thwart, this boat bore the maximum of 50 occupants. Once again, I affirmed: "ready on the right, ready on the left," and when my calls were answered in the affirmative by the tiller man, I confirmed: "Lower away, No. 6," and another passenger load was headed toward the *Humboldt.*

I only wished that I could have been aboard the one that I'd sent off previously. It wasn't until several days later that I heard the tale about what transpired on Lifeboat No. 4 as it was rowed to the rescue ship.

The trip over to the *Humboldt* was uneventful until Boat No. 4 started to get close. Thereupon, Mr. Rothschild produced a furry kitten from within his overcoat. I was amazed to learn this! That customer had struck us as someone who enjoyed belittling others and enjoying himself at their expense. Yet somehow he had snuck an animal aboard back in New York, and maintained it in his cabin as well, without any of the ship personnel catching wind of his ploy. Due to the close-knit conviviality of a lifeboat, however, he became an instant celebrity with each of the waifs aboard. The adults in particular appreciated him, for now their children had a diversion to take their mind off the fear and anxiety which leaving a large, warm, and familiar vessel had produced in everyone.

When Richard embarked aboard the *Humboldt,* apparently Reggie Highsmith himself saw the kitten. Although he was busy shepherding all the newcomers aboard, that captain made sure that the warm, purring animal got some milk and meat down in the galley. This little kitten provided calming companionship to a dozen or more of the younger children as the ship headed for New York later that evening.

This generosity was quite a turn for the prankster Richard Rothschild. Recalling this event, I had enjoyed a good laugh. That jokester had a golden streak in him after all! It suddenly occurred to me that this rich man, with a good family name and social position, was really very lonely. All his pranks were simply an expression of his need for attention. Sadly, the method he chose—playing jokes on others—tended to rile people rather than make them warm to him. However, the kitten had been a stroke of genius, despite its being contrary to company policy on ocean crossings, and Captain Highsmith had wisely let the matter slide during the journey back to New York.

About two months later, I chanced to remember this former passenger of ours. The reason Rothschild had come to mind was a newspaper article about him in an early July edition of the *New York Times.* The story held that he had attended a fancy dress costume party the night of the Fourth. He had dressed as a pirate, complete with eye patch, boots, goatee, and tri-cornered hat. When the fireworks display began over the nearby lake, he had drawn a toy flintlock pistol and pointed it at his hostess, making some sort of pretend demand for the jewels which she was wearing. In the flickering light of the pyrotechnics and general excitement, a bodyguard of the wealthy hostess had mistaken this act as real and thereupon shot the guest dead where he stood.

It had been yet another of Rothschild's endless jokes, but this time he had made it far too threatening and had paid the maximum price. His executioner had no charges brought against him; in fact, his employer reportedly doubled the bodyguard's salary!

"Poor Mr. Rothschild," I mused. "I doubt I will live to see another man like him."

My thought was a fitting epitaph. The complimentary ticket that Rothschild had opted to reserve following his interrupted voyage was for passage aboard an A.T.C. ship sailing in August. In his memory, the company donated this prepaid ticket to a member of the man's church. That parishioner had received a gift by pure luck, but he would certainly have big shoes to fill.

Once on the surface, the four seamen assigned to an oar posted to each lifeboat released the davit lines and took their positions on the thwarts to row over to the rescue vessels. After each of the round trips brought an empty boat back to *Reliance,* Officer Dougherty and I relieved the sailors with a fresh foursome of rowers. In this manner, the entire ship was emptied of passengers by 1530 hours. This rotation had the additional benefit of keeping everyone occupied and warmed by activity. With the passenger offloading complete, but with the long light of a sub-polar afternoon still to go, Captain Stahl had the crew members assist all the stewards in bringing up the remaining passenger dunnage for transfer to the *Humboldt.* Attention to the trunks and the diverse cargo packed in the holds of the ship would have to be delayed pending future events.

CHAPTER NINETEEN

LEARN FROM PRIOR MISTAKES

Nobody's to Blame, but Don't Do It Again.[4]

As the various transfer operations were completed, the three vessels enjoyed a breather period where further activity awaited arrival of the *Tahoe*. The telegrapher aboard *Reliance* signaled the other ships that the *Tahoe* had encountered a significant delay and would be arriving in the early evening. Captain Highsmith aboard the *Humboldt* now had two, maybe three hours on his hands, so he figured it would be wise to make a tour of the displaced people occupying his upper decks. These were all crowded together as hundreds of unexpected arrivals mingled with stewards unfamiliar with procedures aboard his ship. While he made his rounds, he had Ralph Stone, as Chief Steward, and his First Officer, Peter Porter, circulate among them as well to ensure that everyone was reasonably comfortable, warm, and had proper sleeping arrangements, even if that did not include an actual bunk bed.

With that burden attended to, he began to stroll casually fore and aft, meeting and smiling with these strangers as he went along. He was some ten minutes into this friendly tour when he entered the lounge on the B Deck and found a rather loud group engaged in debating some hot topic or other.

"Good afternoon, Captain," said Stewart Clothier, IV with a gracious bow. "Please come join us. This is Hiram Gold, Natasha Forbes, that's Tony McAdoo, and this, as you know, is my wife Beatrice."

"Yes, hello Beatrice, we chatted for a bit when you exited Lifeboat No. 6, I believe. Mr. Gold and Miss Forbes, how are you? I believe you are both on my passenger roster, are you not? I apologize for any inconvenience to your voyage home from England."

"Not to worry, Captain," replied Natasha. Then, nodding to the other members of this small group, she added, "If it hadn't been for the mishap, we wouldn't have met the Clothiers and Tony here. So there is compensation from misfortune, don't you agree, Captain Highsmith?"

She turned her lovely face with its porcelain skin toward Reggie; he was left with no alternative but to puff out his chest in a manly fashion as he confirmed her observation.

Then he said, "I didn't catch your last name, Tony. McAdoo, is it? Fine. Has everyone ordered something from the bar? Ah, yes, I see you've been taken care of.

---

4 *Engineering News*: August 15, 1912, summarizing the conclusions rendered on the Titanic's sinking at the American and British hearings.

Did I interrupt something? You seemed to be going at it rather hot and heavy when I came in."

"Indeed sir, you're right!" affirmed Stu Clothier. "We were discussing the sinking of the *Titanic*, as a matter of fact. Now that the war is over and transatlantic steamers are plying the oceans so competitively again, the question of why the devil that magnificent vessel went down so quickly has become relevant in light of our own encounter with some Greenland ice!

Continuing to hold the floor, Stu stated, "It is seventeen years on and still, despite protection from the United States supplying regular monitoring by its ice patrol boats, transatlantic voyages remain filled with peril! Perhaps you can shed some light on our various suppositions."

Stu Clothier took a long breath, indicating that he was not finished, and then added this warning.

"Just so you are not caught unawares, Captain Highsmith, let me note the elegant education of our group. As you will recall, Beatrice and I are related to some of the men in First Class who perished on that dreadful night in April 1912. Miss Forbes is an instructor of psychiatry at Smith College while Hiram here is probably the most erudite of us all, being a full professor at Princeton University. History, and particularly naval history of the United States, is that your area of concentration, Hiram?"

"You are correct, my good man." Hiram's voice was succinct, without emotion.

"Then there's Tony. Being a trained naval architect, he has the most experience in the field. Such is the bastion of knowledge that faces you, Reggie, should you join us for a bit. Do stay, if only for ten minutes." Stu's invitation came with a broad smile of welcome.

"Nothing would please me more!" replied Captain Highsmith. Then, turning to address everyone as a whole, he said warmly "Thank you for inviting me! Please do not be offended if the Bridge summons me; I may have to depart suddenly."

"Not at all, Captain, we're delighted to have some intelligent experience brought to bear on our discussion!" Stu sat down, a look of both exultation as well as anticipation edifying his expression.

The feeling Stu had expressed was agreed to by all those present. They relaxed, sitting back in the cushioned easy chairs. Indeed, if the captain had a bit of time on his hands, it would not hurt to hear these "experts" out. He leaned back, making himself comfortable in the stuffed easy chair.

Before anyone else could open, Tony McAdoo seized the floor and stated flatly, "I simply do not agree with the argument that the White Star liner was safe. Let me detail some things that I know from studying at the Naval Academy in Annapolis. I did further work there in 1922 after earning my B.S. in metallurgy. As a graduate student, the science department gave me special study privileges, and more importantly, access to their closed-door files. What I will share with you now is not considered to be secret information since it does not pertain to military defense matters.

"Frankly, as far as I'm concerned, the more people who know these facts, the more determined our legislatures and shippers will be not to allow competitive bidding to weaken our goal to build ships of the best quality. Vessels designed for whatever purpose must be constructed from the highest quality materials using the best technology that we possess at the time. The lessons learned from this event sure came hard, and such stupidity must never be repeated. I've been very wordy, here, I know, but permit me to expound further because some of these facts may be new to you; their revelation may help you understand this tragedy better.

"First, ask yourself who was in fact running the show at Harland & Wolff? Was it Lord Pirrie, a knighted British subject, or the no-holds-barred Morgan? Or was it, as I suggest, Joseph Bruce Ismay? He was following in his father's footsteps, yes, but he was the sort that is driven to assert himself, to carve out a niche for which he alone is lauded. Each of us here has an opinion regarding that man's character entirely apart from shipbuilding. He should have joined Captain Smith and Designer Andrews in going down with his ship. He was not, however, an honorable fellow. Rather, he was considered to be autocratic, even disdainful, around his employees."

Then Tony proceeded to explain how the construction of the great ship had been undermined by Mr. Ismay to "save weight," i.e., money.

"Wow! That was damning, Tony, just beastly if what you say is true. The owners and builders practically doomed this ship to failure before she was even out on the open sea." summed up Stu.

"Well, we've heard from an educated man, but let me weigh in, if I may make a pun, with an argument that seems to have escaped notice, or at least comment, by anyone in either England or America."

Everyone sat back, took a sip of the warming brandy, and waited for Hiram's analysis.

"A lot of stupid decisions, during design, approval, and execution—based no doubt on strong egos and maniacal focus on the lure of the dollar—caused many hundreds to lose their lives without justification. The craft of the shipbuilder was subordinated to the unspoken directive that short-changes to standard construction must be made so as to allow the owners to make the most money. The unusual concatenation of events thereafter set the scene for a tragedy that became inevitable."

"That's it, you've heard my spiel. Hand me a whiskey, there, would you Stu? Thank you!"

Taking a long swig, he relaxed and relinquished the floor to someone else.

"Miss Forbes, do you have any opinions regarding Edward J. Smith as the captain of the *Titanic*, or indeed of any of the other officers she carried?"

Stu Clothier enjoyed being gracious, and inclusive, when surrounded by a group of people. More importantly, he was aware of this lady's reputation for excellence in a field that, officially, still remained the province of men.

"Thank you, Stu. You've hit the nail on the head, insofar as I'm concerned! You men can talk all you want about technical specifications or capabilities, but when it comes right down to the precise cause for negligence, it's usually careless disregard of the very rules that were put in place to circumvent human misjudgment. If you list all the decisions and events that occurred during construction of the ship and its subsequent management on the water, in the final analysis the sinking comes down to Mankind's absurd belief that he has conquered the sea.

"Captain Smith couldn't better exemplify this. Yes, he was beloved by passengers; they often booked passage based on the mere fact that he was scheduled to be in command of that voyage. But this particular Atlantic crossing was to be his crowning achievement as Commodore of the White Star line. He had served his entire tenure with the company without once finding himself floating helplessly in the sea. In 1902, he had been in command of the *Majestic* when he encountered, but avoided, an iceberg. Perhaps that gave him a feeling of invulnerability, but *Majestic* weighed only 10,000 tons and could react far more quickly than a ship more than four times her size.

"He had, in fact, been party to several instances of collision or close calls in the past. All of you know about the *Titanic* leaving on its maiden voyage and having a near miss with the *New York*, but did you know that he commanded the *Olympic* in 1911 when she damaged a tugboat, the *O. L. Hallenbeck*, and later that year when that same ship collided with the Royal Navy cruiser, *H. M. S. Hawke*. You can say it was the pilot who was doing the steering on those occasions, but of course the captain is responsible for everything that happens on his vessel. This trip was Smith's ultimate reward: he was damned if he wasn't going to follow custom and charge at full speed through ice fields.

"There is an instructive, little known story about one of the prospective crew, Joseph Mulholland, who was scheduled to board in Southampton. As he stepped on the gangplank, he watched Jenny, a cat aboard the *Titanic*, carry her litter of new kittens down the gangplank and position them ashore. Disliking what he had witnessed, he promptly turned his back on the prospective job and returned home. He lived, as did Jenny. Then there's the luck of the three seamen who stayed too late in a bar, rushed to the ship but were delayed at the tracks by a passing line of railroad box cars. Finally reporting for duty, all three were barred by the tally officer due to their tardiness. They too lived. Apparently, there were several First Class passengers, including J. P. Morgan himself, who made other arrangements due to last minute changes in their plans, and they of course were spared, too.

"In this regard, the greatest irony for me is the case of William Bull. He was the chief clerk for White Star Lines, so it was his job to assure that the company's provisioning agent, R. & J. Rea, fully furnished the ship with coal. Barges off-loaded the coal from the *Majestic*, *Philadelphia*, and *St. Louis*, thereby inhibiting any travel by their crews. The *New York* and the *Oceanic* gave up their coal, but they were inactive at that time. This bounty was hand shoveled into chutes that led to *Titanic's* transverse coal bins astride her boilers. When the work was completed, Bull was the last man to leave the *Titanic* prior to her departure from Southampton.

"I've often imagined him taking that final step off the gangplank as he stepped ashore. No doubt he watched the great liner's departure wistfully, wishing he were aboard. Oh! If only I could have interviewed him the moment he learned that *Titanic* had gone down mere days later. Imagine the contrasting feelings of sadness, disappointment, but also relief he must have experienced!

"Those 1,500 to 1,523 men and women who did take passage to their death are blameless. Each boarded putting their trust in the White Star Line and its decision to utilize E. J. Smith."

She ended her line of thought and gently reached forward to lift her cup and sip some tea. Quiet enveloped the group. Their various thoughts, as they ruminated on what had been stated, seemed to make the air crackle with the clash of long-held theories that were being dashed.

At this moment, the professor leaned forward and, spreading one hand across each of his knees, cleared his throat as he looked confidently at each person there in turn. Then Hiram spoke.

"I have more to say on this matter. Let's look, for a moment, past the arrogance and construction flaws to consider the means of obtaining assistance. Radio room practices of the time did not help. Telegraphers acted, unfortunately, on the addressee of messages received. If a warning wasn't addressed "MSG" or to "Captain Smith," it was laid aside. Apparently, the Marconi operators were considered to be toys for the passengers' amusement, rather than as an aid to navigation. Nowadays, however, telegraphers are integral to navigation."

"You'll get no argument from me!" affirmed the *Humboldt's* Captain.

Professor Gold continued. "Now I come to the officers under Smith's command. For me, these are the most interesting subjects for analysis.

"The contrast between Murdoch and Lightoller as to whether to allow persons other than women and children aboard, if empty seats were available, is instructive as to Captain Smith's carelessness when training his men to handle emergencies.

"The extraordinary delay Smith caused in telegraphing news of the trouble until almost 50 minutes into the disaster is simply unforgiveable. At the moment he came on the Bridge and received Murdoch's report, he should have issued a "stand-by" warning for the telegrapher to key. Once the order was given to load lifeboats, Captain Smith seems to have fallen into a state of abulia and thereafter acted as though fuddled for the remainder of the crisis.

"At the moment of greatest need, he became the most useless.

"And then there is William Murdoch! You may not know that he had been demoted just prior to the maiden voyage. Captain Smith preferred having his friend Officer Wilde on board to serve as the chief. Who knows what went through the head of the First Officer as the iceberg was sighted? He reacted defensively, like a man putting up both hands to ward off a blow rather than stepping to the side. He should have taken affirmative action by retaining full speed ahead on the starboard engine, as well as the center screw, and then reversing only the port screw. The ship's rudder would thereby have had far more purchase, regardless of the design of its shape and fulcrum which we already had discussed prior to the arrival of our esteemed Captain Highsmith here.

"If Smith had stayed on the bridge for an hour longer before retiring for the night, he might have steered differently. I could probably author a treatise on how First Officer Murdoch must have felt as he loaded people into lifeboats to escape an emergency he had singlehandedly brought about. Of course, he was just following orders as he plowed along at some 22 knots. How often have we heard that lame excuse?"

Thereupon, Reggie horned in.

"I'm floored, Stu and Bea. No wonder your discussion was so heated. Your circle of friends here are very well informed. I hate to think what you're going to say about James Stahl once we get home safely!"

Reggie Highsmith had been surprised at the erudition displayed. It had never occurred to him that civilians could be so attuned to the problems sailors have on the sea.

"Oh, don't fret yourself on that score, Reggie. None of us think Captain Stahl did anything negligent. Stopping and reconnoitering after missing the iceberg might have been wise, but if I'd been on the bridge, my first instinct would have been: 'Hey, let's get the hell out of Dodge!' None of us fault him, though Bea and I will miss our trunk if we lose it. It has treasures from our visit to the Smoky Mountains National Park; we were taking them as presents for our nieces and nephews living in France."

"Well, don't give up. She hasn't shown any sign of sinking just yet." Reggie countered.

He considered it his job to always be buoyant with passengers, whether they were his responsibility or refugees from another ship. When an emergency was so obvious that everyone understood, even without being told, that they were in real danger, then and only then would Captain Highsmith become dictatorial. Should their lives be at stake, he would speak the plain truth.

Stu stated, "We're left with that awful adage voiced by Winston Churchill during the Great War: 'The terrible *ifs* tend to accumulate to our detriment.' There but for those *ifs,* some sort of ensuing tragedy might have been avoided."

"You're right about that!" affirmed Captain Highsmith. "Your debating here has been instructive and, in my opinion, accurately assesses the numerous negatives surrounding the sinking."

Reggie was beginning to get warm to his subject. He looked from one to the other of the intent, sober audience.

"It's interesting the degree to which fate affected this sinking. If *Titanic* had not received coal from ships docked nearby, she would have had to delay her maiden voyage due to the striking mine workers. If *Olympic* had not collided with *Hawke*, requiring *Titanic's* construction berth for repairs, Captain Smith would have undertaken her maiden voyage a month or more earlier. If Mr. Murdoch had steered straight into the iceberg, she would have lost perhaps 40 feet of her bow, crushing two or perhaps three bulkheads, but she would have remained afloat with that damage. He would have killed crewmen and third class passengers sleeping forward, but the human loss would have totaled perhaps 200 rather than 1500. To my mind, I don't know why he didn't do that; even Ismay himself said the officer on duty should have steered straight ahead after reversing engines. Probably professional pride guided his course."

Captain Highsmith then paused for effect, but he was prevented from further expostulation by Stu's wife. She had been politely silent throughout the conversation thus far, but Bea now began to speak on some of the things she had thought about since the Armistice had been concluded in 1919.

"We still grieve over the loss of our relatives. Young Jack survived, but he lost the elder Thayers. She was my sister. Still, one can't grieve forever. Life is simply too short. On the lighter side, there is a saying that I use when a friend makes a poor decision regarding some problem. I refer to their ineffective dawdling as *merely rearranging the deck chairs on the Titanic in response to the collision.*

"The *Titanic* certainly was not a heroic ship, despite the claims by her builders to the contrary. You have detailed many of the cost-savings that led to her having egregious shortcomings. Her demise is the quintessential saga of failed human judgment. Whether we learn from her tragedy remains to be seen. Several comments by her passengers show that even his less capable passengers could have advised Captain Smith to slow down!

"The first three decades of this century have, together with the Great War, closed down forever the Edwardian mores of class distinction. At the start of the last decade, airplanes, automobiles, and the turbine engine were being developed; thus, everyone became fascinated with speed. The snobbishness of keeping up appearances still holds true, but getting somewhere fast has become the rage.

"Even today, safety and acceleration have not yet learned to coexist. Do you know about the first man who was killed by a moving train? It was in England, of course, since that was the birthplace of fast trains with steam power. A brand new engine was pulling into a station where all the dignitaries had assembled to laud its construction. One official saw her coming and, basing his instincts of care on what he had been exposed to all his life, stepped across the tracks to obtain a view from the other side. In his mind, he was accustomed to 6 miles an hour being the fastest conveyance around at the time, but the train came in at 30 mph and crushed him completely.

"This illustrates a very important characteristic of human beings. We can't simply be forewarned; we have to experience a new development firsthand in order to appreciate its dangers.

"In this decade, I think the need to obtain instantaneous satisfaction is running rampant. Our perspectives have changed. 'Immediacy' is our hallmark. We now gauge the quality of an experience by how fast we are satisfied. The faster, the better! We don't want to journey leisurely to Europe or America, watching the sails puffing gracefully as we hear the swish of the dolphins chasing alongside. We want to cross over without delay. Our mindsets require feverish movement. We want to get somewhere, tomorrow if possible, as this will, presumptively, extend the time available to enjoy ourselves while we are there.

"Comfort in the midst of speed has been developed ahead of reliability. The steamship companies are happily profiting from our headlong, impatient rushing around. I have heard that some enterprising young fellows even want to build airplanes not just for mail delivery, but to transport folk around by air. Now you're talking about lightning fast travel! This will require a totally new look at passenger safety.

"I don't want to sound too harsh, but we have begun an exorable slide in how we value life. Regard for one's neighbor will be degraded as we rush pell-mell in pursuit of our own advantage without regard to anyone who gets in the way. You have only to look at the statistics that have begun piling up showing how often people get in a car, after drinking themselves drunk, and run over an innocent pedestrian or wreck a shop owner's livelihood by crashing into their storefront window. Fate is not capricious; those of us who disregard our neighbor will be held to account."

Bea was silent for a moment. It was clear to everyone that she was wrestling with some gruesome mental image. She looked at the floor as she softly resumed.

"I have bared my soul to you this evening. Thank you for allowing me to do so. I only add this. The sadness of this titanic tragedy was starkly brought home by the *Bremen,* a German liner that passed the scene of the sinking 5 days later. Her passengers saw frozen bodies still floating about. One had a baby clasped to her chest; another had her arms tightly around a large shaggy dog the size of a St. Bernard. There was a lot of love lost in the space of a single, cold night. Regrettably, it was all due to human pride causing common sense to desert those men in charge."

Bea couldn't help continuing to look down at the floor. Clearly, she was lost in her memories of that awful night. She reached over to hold her husband's hand. Her observations put a sobering mood over the heretofore voluble gathering. An enjoyable, informative debate had turned into serious introspection of what those who perished might have wanted out of life, as well as what they were willing to give up in order to obtain their goals. They had paid the maximum price.

At this point, Reggie rose, thanked them for allowing him to sit in, and then took to completing his round of inspections. He came across people swathed in whatever warm wraps they could come by and simply huddling quietly, using their luggage as temporary housing.

Their silent message came through to him loud and clear: "Let's get headed for home as quickly as possible!"

He made his way to the Bridge in order to check on how the *Reliance* was faring.

CHAPTER TWENTY

TAHOE'S TROUBLES

As the afternoon waned to a pale azure in the western sky, it suddenly occurred to Captain Stahl that he had not heard Sparks relay any word about the coast guard vessel that was supposed to be on her way. What was her name? *Tahoe*: that was it! Where the hell was she?

He spoke down the tube. "Who is on duty at the wireless now?"

"Sir, its Radioman Pride, James Pride."

"Have you heard anything from *Tahoe*? I thought they'd be on scene some four hours ago. Raise them, will you?"

"Aye, aye, sir, I'm keying now," he responded confidently.

"Thanks, Sparks."

There was that appellation he'd heard about from Chester. His buddy had been right; it felt good to hear the nickname. Better earn his keep. He bent over his side-tap key and spelled out: "*Tahoe*, this is *Reliance* calling. We are awaiting your assistance. Have you an ETA at our position?"

The response was immediate, but not what anyone on the Bridge was prepared for.

"Sorry, old man, but we've had difficulty of our own. We ran across bergs and a substantial ice sheet as we came 40 miles north of your position. It's my error; I should have messaged you but we've been so busy blasting away at this ice that your troubles slipped my mind. Not good; I could lose my rating for this. Let me get my captain right away! Over and out."

At the signoff, Jim Pride sat back in his chair. He'd never heard of such a signoff, but he could adapt to that. What got his goat was being blown off like that. He couldn't imagine what had gone through the mind of Barnes Eberly. His situation must be pretty dire. Why hadn't he notified *Reliance* of the change in its rescue mission? This was uncalled for, and certainly not to be tolerated in times of trouble. He knew what he was thinking would eliminate a position such as he now had, but he immediately saw the need for radio-telephone whereby ships could talk in real time using words. Surely misunderstandings such as this would be avoided with more modern tools of communication.

No point in dwelling on this neglectful error. He better inform his captain right away. Grabbing the tube, he uttered one of the strangest sentences James Stahl was ever to hear.

"Sir, the *Tahoe* reports she has been tied up with ice problems she encountered on the way to us. She has not given me a new ETA; her radioman, Everson, did not say this, but she may not be coming at all. Do you want me to put through an MSG captain to captain?"

James Stahl was direct: "Put through a message from me to her Captain Eberly immediately. I must talk to him now!"

Pride got right to it: "MSG. To *Tahoe*. Captain Stahl on *Reliance* must communicate with Captain Eberly directly, now." Then, to show he was up-to-date, added, "Over."

The answer from Radioman Everson was concise. "Message received." Shortly, he came back on: "MSG. Captain of *Tahoe* is messaging Captain Stahl on *Reliance* directly. Go ahead, Captain Stahl."

Jim had never met Barnes Eberly, so courtesy demanded titles. "Captain Eberly, we've got a very serious threat, unusual as it may be. I have the freighter *Dorchester* and the ocean liner *Humboldt* standing by at my position. We have off-loaded my passengers. Shortly, I will disembark most of my passenger service crew that are not necessary to the operation of this ship. 45 will remain aboard, including officers. Over"

"We read you loud and clear. What is your status?"

Captain Stahl took a deep breath. Even a hardened seaman like Barnes Eberly, which he doubtless was, is going to have a hard time swallowing what is coming.

"Captain Eberly, I'm absolutely certain that an iceberg that we sidestepped some 15 hours ago is drifting on a path that will cause it to crash into our port side sometime before 2300 hours Friday. It could possibly do so much earlier. My chief engineer estimates that we have about five hours before its proximity and consequent pressure on our ship prevents any evasive action by crew members. That will put contact during the hours of darkness. Over."

The telegraph went silent for a long minute. Then a staccato of: "MSG. *Reliance*. Understood. We will speed to your side at once! ETA 1830. Be sure every seaman knows about the risk that remaining aboard *Reliance* entails. Over and out."

Aboard the *Tahoe* the captain was all action. Pushing the engine room telegraph forward, he called for "full speed ahead" and then to the Helmsman, he ordered: "Break off and head south southwest on course 190 degrees." Turning, he said: "Officer Greene, post extra ice watch, and then get all officers to the Bridge at once." Facing the speaking tube, he ordered: "Radioman Everson, get me in touch with headquarters, and affirm it is of the highest priority."

Then he took a full breath and trained his binoculars over the bow. The sky was clear and visibility some 10 miles. As another seafarer would famously say: "Damn the torpedoes. Full speed ahead!" he breathed a soft prayer to himself: "Damn the ice. All ahead full!"

Though her construction in 1928 was well motivated, neither the government nor the shipbuilders at Bethlehem Shipbuilding in Quincy, Massachusetts had given him much to work with. The vessel had only one 4 bladed screw; it was turbine driven using a synchronous electric motor, true, but her power plant allowed her a maximum speed of only 18 knots, depending on the swells and head winds. This was a far cry from what he had enjoyed crewing on during the war. The hull of *Tahoe* included a flared stem and a cruiser style stern. While these would lessen the shock of the constant swells in the North Atlantic, her draft was sixteen feet; this made attaining speed pretty cumbersome.

"No one can call *Tahoe* a fast response vessel," he ruefully lamented.

He soon found himself surrounded by the other three officers aboard: 1st Officer Bryan Thomas, 2nd officer Greene, and 3rd officer Bill Belden.

"Men, we're making maximum speed to see whether we can save *Reliance*, a passenger/freighter that is stuck with her bow on an ice shelf. By the time we reach her, she will have disembarked her passengers and the support staff. About 45 of her crew will then be still aboard. Her captain claims she is confronting a berg about 80 feet high that will drift against her hull less than six hours from now. Such an obstacle may exceed 400,000 tons or more. Compare this to the 30,000 or so tons that *Reliance* now totals with all her passengers and support staff offloaded. It could press the hull off the shelf and then wedge the entire ship between itself and the ice sheet she beached on. Or it could split her hull and cause her to sink; such is my presumption. She lost her bow and two forward compartments in the collision, but her remaining watertight bulkheads are reportedly holding.

"Chow down now because I doubt any of us will have time for food or sleep once we arrive at 1830 hours. Officer Belden, check with the Chief to be sure we have reserve fuel of at least 5,000 gallons once we arrive. That is all."

Even though she sported a fuel capacity well in excess of that required for standard duty, there'd be no sense arriving on scene only to run out of power just as she closed on the stricken vessel.

Tahoe was designed for duty as a vessel for the International North Atlantic Iceberg Patrol. Her mission was to provide notice of dangerous ice to transiting ocean traffic. In coming decades, draftsmen and builders of such boats would learn how to strengthen the hulls so that these ships would become known as "ice breakers" able to forge a lane through ice sheets. In 1929, they were largely an information gathering tool to radio the location of dangerous conditions to vessels plying the Atlantic shipping lanes. No extra passenger room, hoists, or transfer craft had been designed into these patrol boats. Their role would be to supervise rather than participate in actual rescue work. Sadly, their ability to destroy an iceberg was so puny as to be laughable. What good does it do to fire a five inch gun containing an explosive charge into the visible portion of a berg, only to have it turn on its side or simply rise straight up from the depths when its visible cap portion is removed? However, in 1929, no one aboard *Tahoe* understood the risks.

Captain Eberly was fully aware that his ability to help a stricken ship was limited. He had to put the best face he could on the situation. In 1918, he had commanded a warship, the destroyer *U.S.S. Wickes* during the European conflict, but his warship had been relegated to performing escort missions as a screening force. He had never closed with an enemy surface ship. If he'd seen one, he could easily have engaged it; the *Wickes* could raise steam to exceed 30 knots, very fast for surface ships at that time. Here, however, he was dawdling along to combat the largest foe known to any seaman: a monstrous iceberg with the vast majority of its surface hidden from view. The power of such an enemy could only be guessed at.

He had read about the men on Shackleton's expeditions to the Antarctic fifteen years earlier and the terrible ordeal they went through as they watched their ship get crushed by shifting pack ice. That voyage, however, had been voluntarily undertaken for glorious discovery, not as a routine excursion to the ports of France for a vacation.

He understood completely that, even if Captain Stahl was able to transfer all his passengers safely to rescue vessels, the crew of *Reliance* would be completely unprepared to do battle with an iceberg. That reminded him; he better send a message to the *Humboldt* and *Dorchester* to get them moving to the safety of a port in New York.

"Everson!" he called over his shoulder, "Get me the *Humboldt* and *Dorchester* on your set, will you? Have we had a reply from Fort Trumbull, yet?"

"No, not yet, sir. I'll try them again. It'd be about 1500 hours there with the time difference. If you'll pardon the expression, sir, they may have been out to lunch when I tried earlier."

"No doubt! Now, get on with it."

The telegrapher was in the next room down the passageway so it was easy to overhear his set buzzing away. He confirmed to his captain that the *Dorchester* would get steam up and head out for New York City shortly. She had recovered all her own lifeboats and secured the additional load of male passengers; however, no effort had been made to unload the holds of the *Reliance* of private belongings. These would have to suffer whatever fate befell them. On the other hand, regarding the off-loading to the *Humboldt,* the stewards had been able to transfer all the carry-on suitcases belonging to their passengers on *Reliance*; moreover, these employees had left with their own belongings. This meant that Captain Stahl had the hard-bitten, experienced crewmen who actually ran the ship left on board. This might be a total of 50 or so men, if he knew his medium passenger liners correctly. Additionally, the *Humbold*t did not yet appear to be interested in leaving the scene and was standing by as a back-up. Based on his past experiences with passenger liners, these men would execute any commands he gave, on behalf of Captain Stahl, with celerity. He seriously doubted any action on his part would save the *Reliance*, but if there was a way, such men could help him find it.

His musings were interrupted by Radioman Everson.

"Sir, I've got Vice-admiral Halsey coming in loud and clear. What shall I do?"

"Let me stand right here next to you. Tell the admiral about my rescue mission and intention to extricate the *Reliance* from the shelf if she appears seaworthy, and to blow that iceberg the hell out of the way if I have room. Then add that we spent a considerable portion of today dealing with a huge ice shelf up north and provide him the coordinates."

Everson took the slip of paper handed to him and, holding it in his free hand, bent over his key and side-swiped with such rapidity that it all sounded like one continuous high pitched *tiiiing* to the men on the Bridge. "Boy, that man is fast!" was their mutual thought.

Captain Eberly's boss shot back a "message received and approved" and advised that additional vessels close to *Reliance*'s coordinates would be notified to stand by to proceed to the scene. For his part, Vice-Admiral Halsey immediately raised *U.S.S. Hooker*, a navy supply ship steaming about 50 miles south of Long.40'00" to alter course northeast to coordinates Long. 40' 00" N and Lat. 49' 20" W, and to then standby should *Tahoe* need her assistance.

The naval officer then raised the *Tahoe's* backup cutter, *Chelan,* and advised her captain to get steam up and prepare to race to the rescue scene as soon as his ship was ready.

Her captain, Jack Eagleton, smiled to himself when the order came in. "Geez, old Barney's gotten himself in trouble again!" he idly thought. He laughed softly to himself as he reflected on his longtime friend; then he got his own boat ready for its new task.

CHAPTER TWENTY-ONE

THE PENALTIES OF ARROGANCE

The water was coming in fast throughout the ship now. Our steward appeared at our cabin door and urged us to go topside wearing our lifejackets and then to board one of the lifeboats. As we climbed up the ladder, we looked back at our rescuer. He was resigned to his fate; he merely watched our ascent. Since he was a male staff member, there would be no lifeboat seat for him.[5]

Helmsman Petrovich's voice was loud and confident. "Smoke off the starboard bow, I'm almost sure of it, sir!"

The men on the Bridge peered across the ice sheet as its undulating surface caught sparkles of sunlight. In the far northeast, a dark black but mobile puff of smoke seemed to be crawling across the surface of the ice sheet.

"If that is the *Tahoe*, then she's maneuvering around this sheet, and that means it has a discernible boundary. What's your estimate of distance, Wallace?" the captain asked idly.

For his money, how far this damn thing clutching our ship's hull extended didn't matter. Getting off it did, and therefore time was the crucial consideration.

Clearly, I felt likewise. "Sir, let me get the telegrapher to raise them. Her captain may be navigating clear water around that northeast side and could give us a precise ETA."

I left the Bridge and entered the telegrapher's room. Such space was maintained as an insulated, separate facility to eliminate static interference with transmissions. Radioman Lawler was now seated there with headphones on and his back to the entryway, so I stood astride him so as not to startle this dedicated expert.

When Phil looked up, I said, "We've sighted smoke. Raise the *Tahoe* and get her ETA."

Radioman Lawler turned back to his set and pressed out: "MSG. *Tahoe*, we see you. What is your time of arrival? Over."

The response was loud and prompt. "*Reliance*, we'll make it by 1800 hours. That will leave us about an hour of daylight. Over and out."

There was that message termination that had been so new to Hawkins and Pride. Better get used to it. If the U.S. Navy is using it, everyone soon will be.

---

5 Violet Jessup and Ann Turnbull recounting their departure from the *Titanic*. See: John Maxtone-Graham. *Titanic Tragedy*. New York: W.W. Norton & Co, 2011; pp. 137-139.

Lawler turned to Officer Matthews and confirmed, "She'll be here in less than an hour, sir."

"Very good." I then returned to the Bridge and relayed the news.

Captain Stahl asked the signalman to go up on the compass platform and signal by lamp to the *Humboldt* that the *Tahoe* would be arriving within the hour, so Captain Highsmith should be notified. He then turned to his young ally, who by now had been introduced to everyone on the Bridge.

"Charles, go grab a bite from the galley. We may get pretty busy in the next hour. Save me a sandwich, will you? I'll join you there soon."

As the lad left, James turned to the helmsman and officers Dougherty, Stanley, and me. We five were now the only ones left on the Bridge. His expression was dead serious.

"Men, you've met McDonald. I confess this is one outside the manual. His captain has lent him to us to assist in our extraction. Should we need the *Humboldt's* help, he can let us know how Captain Highsmith will react. That's the rationale on the surface. The real reason, I believe, is that this young man is supposed to be the last one on this ship should she begin to founder; in other words, he's here to make sure each of us survives. If we are indeed able to attempt extraction, I will order a skeleton crew to be left aboard. This will include each of you and McDonald. In the event she founders or otherwise breaks up, each of you must be ready to jump without orders from me. McDonald is strong, so I will use him to assist our orderly departure, should that become possible. Understood?"

"Yes sir!" we replied in unison.

For a moment thereafter, we remained silent. While we did so, the sounds of our predicament seeped through the portholes: a banging hatch that couldn't be battened down, the SOS signal flags flapping in the ever present wind, the guy wires sighing as the breezes wailed through them, the low hum of turbines providing heat from deep within the hull, the groan of hull plates forced to remain too long in the chilled waters and, above all these sounds, the constant screeching of steel support members twisting against one another as the stern bobbed about the weakened bow.

Captain Stahl broke our reverie. "I'm going to grab a bite. It must be twenty-one hours since I enjoyed supper. I'll take young McDonald up to the Docking Bridge and eat there. If you need me, or if *Tahoe* shows up, call me over."

He paused, looking each of us on the Bridge in the eye; satisfied that we were as squared away as the circumstances would allow, he headed to the stern.

As Jim would confide to me later, he soon encountered Charles who couldn't speak; his mouth was stuffed with a half-eaten sandwich.

"Well, young man, true to your age, I see you had no trouble finding the mess hall."

The lad wiped the back of his hand across his mouth as he swallowed and then stated, "You keep a tidy ship, sir, but you can't sweep the smell of good cooking under the rug. I simply followed my nose, and of course my ears. There are few places with more colorful language than that which pours forth from a galley!"

McDonald had smiled the captain's way while handing him a sandwich, an apple, and a large cup of steaming coffee. Then Stahl turned and led the way to the Docking Bridge.

As they ascended, the entire dramatic scene spread before them. The encroaching iceberg was so close they could feel the additional chill its bulk engendered, the rescue vessels lay gently swaying at anchor as thin streams of grey smoke escaped from their stacks, clutches of transferred passengers peered over railings pointing and speculating, a couple of white lifeboats bobbed nearby waiting to be used, the broad ice sheet lay quietly like a giant tufted quilt behind them, and the bright evening sun glinted off all these objects with myriad streaks of yellow.

"I've created quite a mess, haven't I?" Stahl professed. "By and large, everybody here is standing around waiting to see what I'm going to do because, as the captain, I'm supposed to know everything. On the other hand, I myself am waiting on the arrival of a man who will proceed to tell me what to do because, to him, I've demonstrated that I know nothing."

"I think everyone is simply glad to be alive, sir. If they're mulling over anything, it's how cold these sea lanes are, so they're very glad to have a warm bunk and hot food. You faced a situation that had never before been encountered in the depths of the night, and no one has yet died. I think your friends would advise you not to beat yourself up over this, despite its serious nature."

Charles paused, obviously lost in thought. Stahl decided to skip mentioning Hankins and Algernon. He simply waited for this extraordinary young sailor to go on.

Suddenly finding the words with which to express himself, Charles added, "Just think what would have happened if you had hit the ice wall, but your ship had promptly slid backward off the shelf, exposing the forward holds and so forth to flooding. If *Reliance* had started to sink in the terrifying blackness of night, you'd have hundreds of terrified and dying people on your hands. Even if you personally had survived, your career would be in ashes.

"Looking on all this makes me hopeful. Everyone, and every available manmade device, stands ready to assist you and your vessel limping back to safety. The repair bill for the bow could be the only cost. Well, maybe something for all the spoiled foodstuffs. Naturally, A.T.C. as purveyors of your cruise will want to compensate their customers with a free trip next season to replace this one, and all the owners of the Bills of Lading for your cargo will suffer delays, but their goods could be reshipped at a later time. These costs should be quite reasonable."

He paused, and then added, "Everything depends on our being able to back *Reliance* off the shelf and move her successfully."

Jim was quiet for a moment, then he succinctly offered: "That's a great deal to ask, I'm afraid. But, we can still hope."

Turning to look Charles full in the face, he stated: "We had no chance to confirm this, but it is very possible that two of my crewmembers died when we struck the shelf initially. We suspect they are still in the damaged hold."

He paused, stroking his beard thoughtfully. Then, with eyes sparkling with curiosity, he asked Charles, "By the way, you were not even four years old when the *Titanic* went down. Have you studied what we know of her demise to any extent?"

"Good Lord, yes! Her construction and outfitting, her décor and furnishings, the amenities offered, and of course the staffing levels are all stuff of legend. Everyone who works for Oceanic Lines has gone through their two year study and training program.

When you're a part of that, you can't help but become imbued with the *Titanic*'s grand achievements, and of course her gigantic failures as well."

Charles raised his eyebrows for confirmation that Jim understood.

"I agree. Her sinking occurred while I was a junior officer with not quite six years of sea duty completed. I was as stunned as even a landlubber who has no experience traveling on the ocean would be. I mean, she was billed as 'unsinkable' but goes down on her maiden voyage. You have only to look at her sister, the *Olympic,* to know she was well designed and constructed. That ship is still sailing even as we speak of this. The *Titanic* was representative of the last of the luxury and style of the Edwardian period, the end of an era: at least that's what the professor types at my former school told me. But her loss was more than that; it also signaled the need to change from blind faith in technological marvels. The lesson offered up was: do not innocently trust in the power of machines. Yet look at the calamity I have engineered here. I'm afraid that Mankind has yet to accept that lesson."

Letting his voice soften, he then opined: "Still, there has to be more than meets the eye for the *Titanic* to have sunk in less than three hours." Stahl left this observation hanging, implying that it might be more a question than a statement of fact.

At this point, Charles weighed in. "Her owners limited the height to which the watertight bulkheads extended in order to accommodate passenger convenience. This goes beyond even the most elementary sound judgment regarding cautious construction. Such a flaw made them merely partially watertight, or safe up to a certain tilt angle should the bow be pointed downward. I don't ascribe to that way of thinking, where economics and return on investment guides the point of the designer's pencil. You can't make money if your vessel goes to the bottom! Even worse, what a sinking does to the reputation, and therefore future bookings, of any steamship line is unfathomable. Excuse the pun. You see my point, don't you, captain?"

"I not only do but, in fact, concur completely. To extend your argument, my confidence in our ship is all the greater because our double bottom extends up to the D Deck, so it's some ten feet or so above the waterline. The bulkheads are solid through C Deck except for the access hatches that can be closed manually or from the Bridge. The upper decks are part of the superstructure, so they're in a different category from the C through F, Orlop, and Tank decks. All of these are at or below hull height.

"My primary concern is whether the integrity of the girders or bulkheads aft of No. 3 has been compromised in ways that we can't see. Think how soaked you get even when dressed in rain slicker and hat and boots; water has ways of finding a way inside that we often simply fail to appreciate."

Stahl paused for a breath. "Going back to our *Titanic* discussion, what really amazes me is the arrogant disregard for dangers that were in fact reported to its captain. I've seen photographs of Ed Smith. He was a magnificent looking seaman. Perhaps a bit overweight, but my dad used to happily refer to such men as 'substantial citizens' and then, patting his own ample stomach, laugh. Nevertheless, you can't be told ice is in front of your course and go plowing ahead at full speed."

"Didn't you do so, sir, last night?"

The captain found himself gagging as he tried clearing his throat.

"Ahem! That was different. We had not received notice of ice being present so far south." Stahl had found his voice, but nevertheless was still on the defensive. "No one has ever reported a large iceberg floating almost adjacent to an ice field that had congealed as a shelf. Everything that happened last night was unexpected. I fault myself, however, for falling into the pilot's trap. Sitting way up there in the Bridge, you're protected from the discomforts of wind and temperature, so you don't appreciate possible dangers as clearly as you would if standing at the prow. Positioning the lookouts up high, as we do, points their vision downward. Objects floating on the dark waters could blend in and be hidden, whereas they might be seen from an attitude more level with the horizon."

The young man remained silent, clearly listening and taking in what his superior said. Stahl paused, reflecting on where he had just been going.

"Good grief, son, you've got to stop being so sharp! You're right. I'm trying to protect my pride by simply mouthing off. It's my fault; we should have been going at a more prudent pace. Our management at American Transatlantic Company is so complacent that their presumptions have trickled into my bones. If I were out alone for a moonlight sail, that'd be one thing, but when I'm entrusted with the lives of crewmen who believe in my skill, and with passengers who expect and pay for a safe transit, there is no room to play fast and loose. At this point, my responsibility now is to get everyone returned safely, and then to start over on another day--but with greater wisdom."

Charles took a quick breath and then responded. "Golly, sir, I can't imagine what it must be like to be entrusted with the level of responsibility a man in your position is saddled with. In wartime, everyone knows that they are at risk night and day. Whether you enlist or get taken by the draft, you're in the fight to protect your country and there's not much choice in the matter. The enemy has forced the danger upon you.

"When you're running a passenger or freighter route, everyone has willingly come aboard or consigned their goods for safe transit because they believe in the captain's skill, judgment, and expertise. I was nominated to be captain of my soccer team back in high school, but I declined because I knew I'd be seeking employment at Oceanic Lines. If I had remained in school, I would have had to encourage, motivate, even buck up my teammates, but there wasn't any life or death decision I would have had to make. If, someday, I am to bear the load of due diligence required of a man in your position, I will have to mature and get many more experiences under my belt. I don't know if I'll ever be ready for such a level of responsibility."

He turned the conversation over to Jim Stahl simply by looking his way.

"Don't worry, my boy. Confidence will come in time, if you take on sufficient variety of assignments, and if you are lucky enough to serve under capable leaders."

He paused for some seconds, letting the silence of the early evening set the stage for his next remark.

"And, if you find yourself a woman whom you love dearly, so you have someone to return home to, who rejoices in your very existence, you will find that she becomes your guide to do the right thing. I had one, long ago, who was pregnant with my son, but she was killed in a tragic accident. As a matter of fact, you and my boy would probably have met; he'd be just about your age now, if he'd been born."

Jim looked off into the distance, where sky and sea blended on the horizon, reflecting on painful memories that no one should ever be required to endure.

Charles remained quiet, so the captain continued. "You know what I like best about sailing on the seas? It's setting a course where dolphins play and then watching them flaunt themselves just ahead of the prow. Can you imagine flipping your tail so fast that you can keep ahead of a vessel plowing along at 22 or more knots? They are so exquisite, yet so very skilled. After a Labrador dog, they are probably my favorite creature."

Charles thought back fondly to the Malamute Husky his father had owned. As a young boy, Charles had loved that dog dearly, frolicking in the back forty, throwing sticks that "Sam" retrieved even if they landed in a pond, and—his favorite—rolling on the grass with the dog pressed against him. The only time he ever saw Sam with his tongue inside his mouth was when he was asleep at the foot of his bed.

His mother would say that her husband was Sam's owner, but Charles knew that Sam was really his dog. That's why he had been utterly crushed when he returned from school one day and his mother tearfully told him that Sam had been shot by a neighbor for chasing the man's cows. To this day, while he enjoys being a "people-person," his primary love is reserved for the dog he will get for himself in the future. In fact, when this second year of his training with Oceanic comes to a close, that's all he has planned for himself.

To change the subject, Charles stated, "You know, sir, I underwent a two week intensive course to prepare me for crewing on an ocean liner, and during that time I met a man named Frank Jones who introduced me to the concepts of roll and pitch and buoyancy. I've never encountered a person more dedicated and knowledgeable. His skill-set regarding a ship remaining afloat is just mind-boggling! You mentioned that you had done design work prior to going to the sea; have you ever heard of him?"

Jim Stahl looked over at the young man and silently stared at him, as though evaluating what to say next. He drained the last sip of his coffee and then stood up.

"Come with me!" he said abruptly.

Charles tagged along in his wake as Jim strutted forward and on into his cabin. Pulling open a wide drawer located beneath his bunk, he removed a sheaf of papers and spread them before the now wide-eyed youngster.

"Son, not only do I know the Frank Jones of whom you speak, but he has tested the design concepts you see laid out before you and, once we find a company or wealthy individual who can bankroll us, will join me in a partnership to build full scale prototypes for testing in real-life conditions.

"You may not have heard that, just last year, President Coolidge directed the Navy Department to initiate a large expansion program. Secretary of the Navy Wilbur wanted a first-class force in case there should ever be another war. So our timing is excellent. Demand for improved performance may be just waiting for us. Think what all that money being thrown around will do for the industry! Benefits to civilian passenger travel should rub off readily. What do you think of that?"

"Wow! I mean, just wow! These are fantastic. Does anyone beside you, and Jones, know about these? Like the U.S. Patent Office, or the president of A.T.C.? They should!"

Charles was all excited; he had never contemplated concepts such as those that were now laid out before him.

"For the present, these must be kept privately. You are correct, the patent office should be informed; along that line, I've sent them preliminaries but have not yet applied formally. I have a best friend named Peter North, who is an ocean-going captain like me, and he has the drawings from which these were copied. Thus, should I be challenged, I can prove the timeline on their development, but I have to demonstrate that these ideas will work before I go touting their worth.

"Peter is living in Newport News currently, so we haven't spoken for some weeks, but he has a daughter who lives near me outside of Providence. The two of us have dinner whenever I'm back in port. She was born eighteen years ago in December, so her mother and father, for fun, decided to christen her "Holly." If you get a chance, you should look her up; I think you two would enjoy each other."

Thereupon, he took a sheet of paper and wrote down her address and how she knew the captain. Folding it, he handed it over and Charles slipped it into his trouser pocket without looking at it. He had eyes only for Jim Stahl's creations.

"You know, sir, I told you about my soccer success, but my real love was ice hockey. I played left forward. Your drawings bring to mind how that puck would zing down the ice with the simplest of wrist flicks. Your pod-boat looks like it could really fly!"

"I agree. The management at my old employer was very excited about the prospects and was ready to move ahead in full mock-up testing, but everyone except Jones and his team, and me, were killed in an accidental fire. Fortunately, I'd sent a copy to that friend, Peter North, I mentioned earlier, so I was able to reconstruct them. By the way, I played left wing at my old high school."

Charles looked over at the man he had been assigned to help. Their eyes met, only for a moment, but in that short time the two of them recognized that they were bonding.

"Captain Stahl, I have only been introduced to the concepts of naval architecture, hydrodynamics, and displacement vs. buoyancy. Nevertheless, I ask permission to keep one of your drawings. My father has a brother, Cyrus, who works in Washington with the Bureau of Naval Affairs. I don't think he has naval architectural training himself, but he's experienced enough that he'd recognize the value of your designs immediately. My uncle would be in a position to help see them realized."

"I'll do you one better, lad. Let's take them all; here, you take these, and I'll handle these. Fold them lengthwise, then half over, and stuff them into your top shirt like this, see?"

Charles watched as Jim demonstrated. "There! See, now they go where we go, rather than to the bottom of the sea should this ship sink!" Captain Stahl beamed at his newfound confederate.

The squawk box buzzed: "Captain, we have sighted the *Tahoe* off the starboard stern. I'll post the signalman, but I'm sure you'll want to talk to her captain directly. That is all, sir."

"Good," Jim affirmed. Turning to shake Charles' hand, he stated, "Okay, the *Tahoe* is arriving. Her captain will take charge from here on, probably. Let's see how Barnes Eberly assesses our situation."

This assessment was not long in coming. As the *Tahoe* carefully slid between the *Humboldt*'s anchorage and the stern of the *Reliance,* everyone out on deck could see her captain on the forward deck eyeing every detail of the scene. He quickly brought his vessel up alongside so Captain Stahl and he could talk easily across the railings.

"Well, *Reliance,* you've got yourself in a pickle, for sure! Captain Stahl, would you consider disembarking all your crew, save a skeleton operating squad down in the engine room, plus the officers of course, and then attempting a full-power reverse for a self-extraction? If you agree, have your men simply keep their lifeboats in this area until *U.S.S. Hooker* arrives to take them on board. I'm sending the *Humboldt* on to New York. I will shortly position my boat at the edge of the shelf to monitor the reaction of the bow and its watertight bulkheads if the hull does start to extract."

As Captain Stahl made a respectful salute of agreement and got busy disembarking most of the remaining 45 crew members, Captain Barnstable got his signalman to lamp the *Humboldt* that it was time for her to sail for New York City and return her extra passengers to safety. As she raised steam and prepared to depart, *Humboldt* gave a bellow from her fog horn and her signalman lamped a "God Speed!" to *Reliance.* She then gracefully moved away until only the smoke stacks could be tracked; then, even these faded from view.

Jim Stahl watched until she disappeared over the horizon, then he breathed with satisfaction. He had provided all of his passengers with a chance for another go. Then he focused his attention on the actions of Captain Eberly.

The captain of the *Tahoe* had meanwhile contacted the supply ship, *U.S.S. Hooker,* and directed her to change course for a location astride the *Reliance.* She would be used to raise lifeboats in order to board the remaining sailors, kitchen staff, and officers still on duty or floating in lifeboats nearby.

Finally, he radioed his compatriot Eagleton: "*Chelan,* make course immediately for coordinates 40'00" N and 49' 20" W to assist in rescue of crew from possible foundering of passenger vessel. Over and out."

"Okay, Bryan, take her up for a close look at that impact site." As Captain Eberly edged his way to the very bow of *Tahoe,* First Officer Thomas gave the order for, "All ahead slow" and then, about 30 yards from the edge of the ice sheet, brought the vessel to a stop with, "All ahead reverse" and then, "Engines stop!" She bobbed on the slow swells for some minutes while experienced eyes combed the ice and the shards of bow steel.

"I don't think she's going to be able to budge," Captain Eberly opined to his officers. "Let's give it a try, though. Officer Greene, what is the status of that monster berg drifting toward her stern?"

"Sir, there's less than thirty yards separation at this point. No telling what its profile below waterline is shaped like, but I judge contact will be made in the next two hours."

"If she doesn't pull off right now, they've got to abandon ship altogether and wait and see what happens. "Officer Thomas, did you spot that high cliff of ice off the port bow as we motored in?"

"That I did sir. I estimate it's not 4 feet from the hull. That large berg could twist the hull so it lodges adjacent to the ice cliff and then quite possibly snap the broken sections of the bow clean off. The *Reliance* might get freed that way, but I doubt her watertight bulkheads forward would remain effective under that kind of strain."

He couldn't be sure, of course, but that was how Bryan figured it.

"I am in complete agreement. We are to remain up close to monitor any movement, but if calamity ensues, we must be ready to promptly pick men out of the water when they jump. There'll be no time for lowering another lifeboat," Captain Eberly stated.

His voice was hard and cold, the edge of fearsome reality all too close.

The captain of *Tahoe* looked over toward the *Reliance*. "Has she cleared all the lifeboats away?"

His First Officer checked with Captain Stahl. "The *Reliance* is down to a skeleton engine room staff, her officers on the bridge, plus the helmsman, sir."

"Tell her to let her rip in reverse at once," Barnes directed.

All eyes on the coast guard cutter peered across the port side to the ice sheet where it imprisoned the *Reliance*. It was a strange experience for the officers and crew of the *Tahoe*: they were in the thick of a dangerous battle, yet were unable to do anything except watch as a great tumbling of black-green sea water appeared off the stern of *Reliance*. The tumult gradually built into seething cascades as the resulting wakes burbled and tumbled over each successive one. The brief period of suspended animation for the onlookers ended. The screws had churned away without there being any movement in the bow whatsoever. After fifteen seconds, Captain Eberly signaled to Stahl and the props came to a halt.

"No progress at all, James." Captain Eberly's voice was noticeably subdued. "Tell your engine room we'll repeat the same tactic one more time, and then if nothing has changed, extricate your entire remaining crew and I'll shoot the damn berg and try to stop that bastard from ramming your ship. Got all that?"

"Received and understood, Captain Eberly."

The second attempt was no better than the first, whereupon Stahl ordered me to state: "Abandon ship!"

He immediately followed my order with, "Let's all disembark on No. 8 lifeboat; she's already in position to load and lower."

The remaining twelve crewmen plus Ship's Engineer Henry Hoskins trooped up from the belly of the ship and donned lifejackets, then swung their feet over into Lifeboat 8. There followed a pause as the four officers that had been on the bridge completed last-minute tours of the interior to ensure no one had been left below. As officers Stanley, Dougherty, and I stood before him, Captain Stahl turned and together we offered a salute to our ship. I promptly strode forward and lowered the Colors as well as our ship's flag. Then James stood to the side and assisted the exit by each of us lower ranking officers. One by one we extended a foot out and into the lifeboat. The other leg followed as each one of us was pulled across by those already in the rescue craft.

By now it was 2040 hours, shadows were growing long, the air was becoming noticeably chilled, and attention spans were growing short. Only two men remained on the *Reliance*. One had become very experienced in handling himself aboard ship after more than two decades of service. The other was new and untried, but strong and quick. Orderly McDonald looked at Captain Stahl; the older man motioned for him to go ahead and enter. Thereupon, Charles put one leg across the gunwale and securely hooked his toes under the nearest floorboard so he could balance his other leg.

As he was preparing to heave himself over, the *Chelan* steamed into view, sounding her fog horn and blinking her forward searchlights to say she had arrived. There was a momentary loss of attention at the distraction. Almost immediately, Charles saw a look of surprised horror cross the faces of those seated nearby as they looked to where the Captain had been perched. There was a sudden brief flash of blue serge flying across the lad's face. Charles heard a startled yell. Without looking or trying to comprehend, he instinctively reached out and grabbed the cloth with both hands. At the same time, he exhaled and tensed all his leg and back muscles for the huge weight he knew was coming. His fingers held firm around the cloth even as his back bent with the momentum of the falling James Stahl.

Horrifyingly, their combined weight now made the gunwale start to splay away from the side of *Reliance.* Charles began to lose any lifting power as his legs gradually spread wide trying to bridge the growing gap. Another moment and the two would be tumbling some 40 feet to the icy waters below, but luck was with them. His arrest of Captain Stahl's slip and resulting fall had been seen by the others. In an instant, two of them lunged forward to grab the arm and on-board leg of McDonald as I and two others reached over the gunwale to collar the captain.

With everyone safely aboard, and heart rates returning to normal, the sailors slackened the pulley lines and rested lifeboat No. 8 gently on the sea. They then disengaged the lines and rowed over to the perimeter of the other small craft patiently bobbing on the swells. Five partially loaded lifeboats had assembled in a tight ring about 30 yards off the stern. They were far enough out that they could quickly row free of any suction from the *Reliance*, should she sink before their rescue. On the other hand, the ominous threat from the huge iceberg that was now drifting only yards from the stern was in full view.

The *U.S.S. Hooker* should be arriving before daylight fades to take all of us aboard, so we were all relaxing as we watched the show that *Tahoe* and *Chelan* were about to put on.

Captain Stahl reached over and gripped both shoulders of McDonald. Their eyes met, glinting in the low lying sunlight.

"That was very brave, my boy," James affirmed. "Probably the fastest reactions I've ever seen, certainly the fastest that I've ever benefitted from! I will be forever grateful. Reginald was wise to send you over to us."

Charles' eyes shone, as though reflecting the praise. He had been needed and he had performed well.

Captain Eberly, for his part, had missed the entire drama aboard *Reliance.* Even as Stahl was falling overboard, Barnes was focusing all his attention on his cohort Eagleton. As the *Chelan* dropped anchor and floated serenely adjacent to *Tahoe,* the two captains hatched a plan whereby they would fire their cannon, mounted on the forward bow decking for just this purpose, from the same distance but separated by about 30 degrees. This was a tricky task because both shells had to land and explode within less than a second of each other. In fact, Eagleton even observed that such a broad berg would probably require multiple strikes, perhaps first to the left and then to the right.

Perceptive and clear-thinking, that's what Jack Eagleton liked to be.

The two cutters maneuvered so they could fire square to the plane of the berg's long dimension and at slightly offset angles to its left hand corner. That appeared to be its weakest defense. This was Captain Eberly's show. Using two short megaphones facing each gunner, he ordered: "Fire!" which sent both shells into the berg simultaneously. There was a fantastic display of splintering ice shards flying into the air, but the berg seemed unfazed. Indeed, now somewhat lightened, it appeared to be rising a bit higher out of the water.

"Again, Jack, but aim for the center of the right side, down a bit on its sloping side." Barnes still sounded hopeful, though perhaps a little less certain.

"Ready, gunners: fire!" Again the cannons thundered, but this time sending the two shells into the broad right flank of the berg. This attempt had far greater impact, sending sharp splinters and shards in all directions. Even the *Reliance* suffered hits, as ice that had been frozen for many thousands of years yielded to the force of exploding steel charges.

Several long icy spears caromed off the ship's stern toward the defenseless, bobbing lifeboats. Captain Stahl saw the threat. Extreme danger has a way of pulling from ordinary men their very best courage. James lunged across the torso of McDonald, knocking him flat against the seaman sitting behind. With a dull thud, an inch-thick shard pierced the back of Stahl's neck, plunging through his windpipe. Blood immediately began dribbling from his mouth.

With a choked moan, he looked up at young McDonald and sibilated, "My son, I'm counting on you. Live your life so it matters!"

With a parting sigh, our captain's eyes closed and he slumped between the thwarts toward the floorboards.

Charles was stunned. He had been assigned to the *Reliance* in order to assist its captain, yet that man had just sacrificed himself to save a young man who possessed real potential but, as yet, had demonstrated little. To an onlooker, perhaps that could be truthfully stated. However, to James himself, this lad represented the son he lost when his dear wife Alice perished.

The officers and crewmen tried but could not revive Captain Stahl. He was undeniably dead. Heaving together, they lifted him across several seat planks, and then they rowed their boat farther from *Reliance*, urging the others to follow in their wake.

While they did this, Charles reached over and unbuttoned the captain's pea coat and then reached below his Irish knit sweater. Pulling out some folded papers, he proceeded to open his own coat. As he did so, he appeared to make sure that I, and several shocked sailors, saw the papers he already had stowed beneath his own shirt.

Responding to our looks of obvious astonishment, he stated: "He would want me to have these." When our faces remained surprised, Charles explained. "Don't be shocked. These are hull drawings which we were going to develop together, if he had lived. Now your captain, indeed my captain, is gone, and I must carry on where he left off."

Before anyone could protest, all the men floating in the little boats looked up in time to watch the berg rear up, reaching perhaps fifty feet higher than A Deck. The wall of ice bobbed for a bit, but then slowly, inexorably, tilted toward the ship and leaned firmly against the stern of the *Reliance*. Apparently, the change in weight on its upper surface had allowed the great hulk to readjust its buoyancy.

As it did so, there was a tumultuous *clang* that reverberated across the calm waters. Everyone immediately looked toward the *Reliance*. The impact and overwhelming weight pressing against the port stern suddenly shoved the hull sideways, dislodging the ship from the ice shelf's grip. There was a loud *crack!* as the ship was pushed aslant to the shelf. We could see gaping holes in the bow section amidst all the twisted struts and ribs. She soon slid backward off and completely free of the ice shelf.

She rested level for a time, as though awaiting praises from those who had crewed on her. A sinister silence lay like a thick tarpaulin over the scene. The ripples from the movement of the iceberg caught up with the men huddled in the little lifeboats and caused them to jerkily bob around like champagne corks. No one had words for this horror; they remained silent and staring vacantly either at the hull, or at McDonald.

Suddenly, the former helmsman Butler, now refreshed after several hours of being off-duty, pointed and exclaimed, "Look, she's down at the bow. She's taking on water. Her keel must have been damaged more than we realized. Holy Christ, we would have all drowned if we'd stayed aboard! Thank the devil our Captain ordered us off."

Everyone could now see that she was going down. The finality with which the dark sea began swallowing their warm bunks and future wages and delicious chow sent shivers of fear among each of the seamen watching. Ever so slowly, the upper plates enclosing the third hold dipped closer and closer to the black surface, and then they slipped beneath while uttering sputters and gurgles as though choking in terror. At the same time, the stern fantail began to rise into the air and kept lifting until the rudder became visible.

Without warning, much of the heavy cargo shifted in a pell-mell crush forward. There was no saving her now: she was going to go sharply by what was left of her head. The stern stood just beyond forty-five degrees, shuddered, and then our ship slipped quietly into the chilled, black depths. An ever-widening ripple spread across the surface and passed beneath the bobbing boats, as if she had extended a final salute to those who had earlier brought her to life.

The ice wall and the berg now took on an orange glow as the setting sun dipped close to the horizon. Bits of debris popped to the surface and floated about like ginger and red Christmas candles. The top ninth of the iceberg reflected shimmering glints of yellow for a few moments, and then the sun retired fully, allowing the deep chill of the still night air to penetrate even the closely-woven wool of standard-issue pea coats.

Actual deliverance from their immediate circumstances awaited the arrival of the *U.S.S. Hooker*. Accordingly, both the *Tahoe* and *Chelan* moved in close where the boats were floating. Their crews came on deck to banter with the men. Brandy was found and passed around from boat to boat. Smokes were shared. If it wasn't for the danger of freezing, these men might have been able to enjoy a party of sorts. Nevertheless, the inert, prone body of Captain Stahl kept a lid on everyone's mood. To our great relief, lights were sighted on the horizon at 2130 hours, and by 2200 hours we sailors were being loaded onto the navy supply ship for the trip back to the port of New York. No one would be celebrating on this return voyage, however.

CHAPTER TWENTY-TWO

SAVING THE DESIGN PLANS

After the sailors, and then the officers, had eaten, everyone followed Commander Irwin's orders regarding where to bed down aboard the *Hooker*. Members of her crew gave up their extra blanket so the men from *Reliance* would each have at least one cover. A fortunate forty or so were assigned to share bunk space with crew members while those sailors were on duty; the men joked they were playing musical beds. For those without a rotation into an empty bunk, snoozing on the cold deck floor of the ship would be uncomfortable, but they would make the port of New York by early Sunday morning, so their discomfort would not last long.

No one complained: each displaced sailor had hot food, was safely out of the chilled air of the ice fields, and could be utilized aboard the rescue ship getting her boxes of supplies prepared for the subsequent offloading in New York. Commander Irwin had no shortage of volunteers; if the rescued men kept working, their pay would not stop with the sinking of *Reliance*. Some 400 miles away in Providence, the management executives in their high-rise office headquarters for American Transatlantic Company would wisely overlook the exact particulars of civilian seamen performing work aboard a military vessel.

Though day and warm, young Charles McDonald did not have an easy time aboard the *U.S.S. Hooker*. As a management trainee of Oceanic Lines, he had held no rank aboard the *Humboldt*. Then he had been assigned to the *Reliance* to assist someone who was now dead. None of the sailors picked off the waters by Irwin's crewmen knew or cared anything about him.

As he stood in front of Commander Dale Irwin a few hours after coming aboard, he fidgeted. Only last year, the U.S. Navy Department had refused several contract proposals that Oceanic Lines had put forth for governmental approval. He didn't know any of the particulars; he'd simply heard the scuttlebutt at the training facility. He presumed this commander would know nothing of such disputes, but he couldn't be sure.

In accordance with protocol, I took a seat on Dale Irwin's left side: he outranked me. Both of us folded our hands on the table, and then Commander Irwin leaned toward the erect figure of McDonald.

"Now, son, we want a precise explanation of what you were doing going through the pockets of Captain James Stahl as he lay dead in the lifeboat you occupied."

"Sir, I clearly showed everyone what I was doing. You were there, Officer Matthews; you had to have seen the papers I already had inside my shirt. What I removed from Captain Stahl only added to that."

"That's exactly why we think you were stealing them off Captain Stahl's body!" I stated flatly.

I was livid with fury, which served to redden my face with emotion. Here was this novice trainee, barely past his pubescence, whom none of us knew, and with whom we had had the most fleeting of contact while he was aboard the *Reliance*, pilfering documents off our captain even as he lay breathing his last.

"Look, son, I'm trying not to let my close friendship with Jim Stahl affect my thinking. Regardless of my revulsion at what you did, no one is permitted to pick a body apart on the high seas prior to a full and complete investigation as to the particulars of the death and notification to the deceased's next-of-kin."

"I know that! My training at Oceanic included conduct in respect of a deceased. That's why I was open with you, and your men, while on the lifeboat."

At this point, the kid was becoming defensive. I immediately pressed my advantage.

"I don't ascribe any import to that. You could very easily have lifted the documents and stuffed them in your shirt when you were alone with Stahl in his cabin. Maybe he turned his back to you while fetching coffee from his cabinet."

I wanted an explanation, and I wanted it fast!

"Begging your pardon, Officer Matthews, but if you saw me go in with him, you know it was by his invitation. Moreover, you watched as I saved his life when he slipped while watching the *Chelan* hove into sight. If I recall properly, you were one of the men who grabbed us before the captain and I plummeted into the water."

I silently admitted that I was now perplexed. Nevertheless, I didn't want to dissipate my momentum.

"Yes, that is correct, but I didn't know then that you were a thieving bastard!"

The color had not yet drained from my face. I looked all the more threatening as a result.

At this point, Commander Irwin adroitly seized the floor.

"Let me interrupt, here, gentlemen. Charles, what are these drawings of which you two are speaking? Were they the property of Captain Stahl, or did they pertain to the operation of the *Reliance*?"

"Commander, they are privately held plans for an entirely new type of hull design that, if successful in testing, would revolutionize modes of sea travel as we have known them for the last 4,000 years, going all the way back before the time of the Greeks. Despite our wide difference in rank and age, Jim Stahl and I had developed a fast friendship in the space of an afternoon. Using my family contacts in Washington, and his skill and imagination in drafting, we were planning a partnership for marketing his ideas during our spare time. Like a hobby that is so successful it grows into a business that dominates your life, we envisioned someday developing Jim's designs as our sole pursuit."

Pausing for breath, Charles continued: "The drawings were created by Jim while working for a company that no longer exists. Jim Stahl didn't want to make them publicly available until they had been proven to his satisfaction. He had made contact with the U.S. Patent Office regarding their existence, but without formal filing and registration by that agency, they would warrant no protection from being purloined should they be discovered."

Thereupon, I interrupted his explanation. "Captain, you and I, and McDonald here, are the only ones present, excepting the scribe. I am now convinced that this young man, whose very presence aboard my ship was extraordinary the moment he came over from *Humboldt*, is truthful and properly motivated. I move that we drop any charges I have brought against him for your consideration. In the meantime, may we caucus privately?"

"So ordered!" stated the commander of *U.S.S. Hooker.* "Signalman Harlan, you are relieved as scribe. Thank you for your services."

Then, turning to Wallace, he asked, "Well, what do you have for me to consider?"

"These."

Having stated the fact so directly, I brought out all the folded papers that my men had forcibly taken from Charles shortly after he boarded the rescue ship. Unfolding each one, I laid them before Commander Irwin, whose eyes thereupon practically popped out of his head.

"Jumpin' fried frogs! What are these, some sort of science fiction flying saucers? Have you set before me plans for an interplanetary attack, like the *War of the Worlds* tale?"

"Not at all, sir." I turned back to face the young man who was beginning to exert real influence on me.

"Here, Charles, you understand these. Explain them to Commander Irwin and myself."

I slid over so Charles could have access to the drawings.

"Sir, a moment ago you referred to yourself as one of Jim Stahl's best friends. If that is true—and I have no reason to doubt it, because Jim himself referred to you as 'very reliable' during one of our conversations—kindly heed my next words."

Charles' tone was obviously sincere. The lad smoothly launched into his explanation.

"These drawings are known to one Peter North, a professional sea captain living in Newport News. He and Jim are lifelong friends from high school. He is not involved in the preparation of these drawings, but he has a copy in safekeeping for his friend Stahl. At New York Shipbuilding Corporation, there is a team under the direction of one Frank Jones; their job is to test and evaluate naval designs. Mr. Jones is a longtime associate of Jim Stahl from the captain's days at Cummins & Company where he worked as a draftsman before seeking shipboard duty. Other than these men, and me, no one has seen these drawings until they were forcibly removed from my person last night as we exited the lifeboats.

"Now you have seen them. Obviously, they are not comprehensible to you. I hold no rank here, but you can contact Reginald Highsmith, Captain of the *Humboldt*, to confirm why I was in such close association with Captain Stahl."

Nodding my way, he continued. "Chief Officer Matthews can affirm that he was the one who allowed me to board *Reliance* during the disembarking, but I have no proof of the agreement. Regrettably, the fact that Jim and I had decided to pursue the testing of these concepts for approval and construction will have to be taken on faith. I give you my word that I speak the truth here."

"Young man, that's all well and good, but you've got my curiosity aroused. You cannot have these drawings back nor leave this ship until you have explained why these black-inked lines are so almighty important. Why do you have to keep them a secret?"

Thereupon, Commander Irwin sat back and folded his arms, as brooding as a Sphinx.

Charles remained silent, considering the chance he knew he had to take, and the possible ramifications if these men understood Jim's ideas.

For a fleeting moment, I had a worrisome twinge. This naval guy had unwittingly exposed his inner character—a tyrant who will grab center stage without acknowledging credit for what his subordinates created. I let my misgivings slide; I needed to focus on McDonald, but I would sure stay wary of this commander from here on.

Charles was the next to speak. He asked forthrightly: "Commander Irwin, I must inquire, considering the position you and Chief Officer Matthews have placed me in, why would you be interested in what appear to be mere drawings representative of battles by outer space vehicles?"

In these rather tense conditions, the captain suddenly started laughing, in fact laughing loud and long. When at last he had subsided, he had created curiosity on the part of both Charles and me.

"What is so dad-blamed funny?" I asked, hoping to break the tension.

"Wallace, Charles, my initial reaction was a cover to see whether you really understood what we have here. Chief Officer Matthews, these are genius! I may be responsible today for only a supply tub, but that's because it's sort of an honorarium. I'm sixty now and past retirement age for the Navy, but I was aboard the Destroyer *Wickes* during the Great War as her captain. Her engagements and missions are still classified, but I can assure you that my ship saw a great deal of action! With my present command, I've been put out to pasture to just graze, so to speak; this way, I don't have to formally retire. But my mind is still keenly receptive to innovation.

"I can see great potential in these drawings. These concepts make every prior hull design reduced to a mere relic of history. These pods would permit designers to position the decks entirely above the water; the resulting freedom from inertia would allow our destroyers to be the fastest interceptor ships in the world! I want to understand these as fully as you will allow because, quite apart from your ideas about adapting these pods for commercial traffic, I think our government would pay you handsomely to keep them out of the civilian world. Why? Because the United States Navy would want them for our own defense forces. There! If that doesn't convince you what you should do, I don't know what will!"

Dale Irwin sat back in his chair, assured that he had made a forceful impression.

Charles was unquestionably caught off guard. The look of surprise on his face melted rather quickly, however, into wide-eyed realization that he might have stumbled onto an even greater purpose than that envisioned by his esteemed friend James Stahl. He decided to explain the drawings to us but without eliciting any sort of secrecy pledge. His mentor was dead and he himself had no training in naval architecture.

Without question, he would badly need assistance from influential people to make these ideas a reality.

"We shall converse as gentlemen. Do you agree? If so, you must swear you will uphold the claim that originality resides in James Stahl, deceased, which of course means his next of kin. I know nothing about his living relatives, as we never got around to that subject. For all I know, they may all be deceased. In other words, I am asking for your pledge as gentlemen, not to purloin these ideas as your own or for your own profit. I ask again, do you agree?"

"Son, since you are not preventing our joining with you in developing these concepts, I will abide by your statement that ownership of these plans belongs to members of the Stahl family, if said survivors can be located." Commander Irwin looked over at me for my approval.

"Mr. Matthews, what say you?"

I sat forward. It was time to take a position.

"I cannot in good conscience agree. I am a longtime close friend and professional associate of James Stahl. He never mentioned, nor even intimated, anything whatsoever about these concepts. I saw Charles here remove the papers from a dead man, and saw him enter Jim's cabin, but neither is sufficient grounds for me to make any kind of pledge regarding their authenticity or what I would do after studying them. Furthermore, nothing that has been said here would permit me to ascribe any form of ownership to Charles."

For emphasis when I was done, I sniffed, lifting my nose in the air just a bit haughtily.

Dale flashed me a sharp look.

"Oh, stash your trash, Wally! Who do you think you are? The King of Siam? Come on, give your pledge not to purloin the stuff and let's get to it."

It was clear to me that Commander Irwin was all ready to wade into these fresh, new ideas for building hulls.

He affirmed further: "Mr. McDonald has already stated that he and Jim Stahl had agreed to go into business together. We'll know whether he is full of hot air if he can't lead us through these drawings knowledgably."

He had been smart to use a term of respect, referring to the lad as "Mister." Dale almost won the boy's allegiance with that appellation, but Charles remained guarded, nevertheless. He was all alone, on an unfamiliar stage, and trying to protect documents about which he knew little.

It was now up to me. "All right, I will agree on one condition. You personally may not have studied drafting, but you better know these drawings inside out or I'll conclude you are trying to swindle us!"

It was time for a smoke, so I drew out my pipe, tamped down some fresh tobacco in the bowl, and then lit up. As I puffed thoughtfully, I made room for Charles to lean over one of the diagrams and begin to elucidate the secrets within these black-inked drawings.

As his fingers moved along the clean, sharp lines, they began to illustrate the advantages of Stahl's ideas. Fairly quickly, Irwin and I exchanged glances. It was apparent that the lad really did understand what my former friend and captain had rendered.

After some twenty years of fiddling with his original concepts, Stahl had reworked the forward pod as a wide, <u>single</u> support having a flat top but complex arched bottom.

By way of explanation, Charles said: "Imagine a man with a well-groomed handlebar moustache. Now, turn the moustache over; the nose points and the tips duplicate the undersurface of the forward pods. The bow will be the narrowest, then it will widen toward the tail to permit room for the outer flanges to begin about halfway back of the front tip. The center fin, or keel if you will, would be dropped in favor of wing fins astride the port and starboard edges. Each would run the entire length of the pod. Stahl's latest thinking provided no rudder; rather, each bow pod will be steerable, both port and starboard turning together. His innovation of using one wide pod would permit the flanges, or fins, to do the steering. Being some six feet deep, or more for large vessels, navigation should be both extremely tight and without any steering delay whatsoever. A ship could find its way through a checkerboard of icebergs without hitting a single one!"

Continuing on, he added: "Sizing the front pods will require substantial tank testing in order to establish the mathematical relationships for different deck configurations. That's where Frank Jones comes in; that is, unless your contacts at the Navy Department can provide better talent. I've met him, and it's easy for me to understand why Jim Stahl had so much faith in him. He's thorough; better yet, he sees beyond what he's been brought. He's a visionary, able to perceive problems that could kill an idea. So, Commander, are we clear thus far?"

"Aye, aye, son. Go on."

"The stern pods are well ahead of our time. In truth, these designs are ahead of Mankind's knowledge. James had to think in terms of using boilers to generate steam to power turbines, but that's way too complex, not to mention weighty. We have to power the turbines that turn the screws either using electricity, or putting an intake in the stern pod that rotates the turbines through the force of pressure from incoming streams of water as the craft moves forward. At this point, obviously, batteries come into play, and there we are sorely lacking as to how to make them sufficiently powerful. These will have to get the craft moving initially in order for the other parts to function. Additionally, component weight is, presently, a huge problem that has no solution; it must be addressed as a priority.

"Jim was a naval architect, not a mechanical or electrical engineer, so that is where the weakness of this project currently lies. If it can be solved, then the rear pods can be downsized considerably from the original 300 by 30 foot size, eliminating not only weight but also bulk that has a high moment of inertia. These would continue to serve as the primary support for a superstructure. The outer fins will mirror those of the forward pods, only on a grander scale, and of course the position of each stern pod would be stationary. Canting the fins outward has been considered but not investigated.

"A feature he had considered, but had not been able to test, was to mount the drive shafts at a slight angle downward in the water. Perhaps two degrees would be sufficient to propel the hulls not merely forward, but a bit upward as well to lessen the amount of friction. Less hull contact lowers the moment of inertia, but that means a higher center of gravity inducing less control.

"The other drawings simply go into finer detail because the rear pod design is much more complex, but I've given you the main gist. If you have further questions, we'll have to save them for Mr. Jones or someone more experienced than me."

Wrapping up, Charles had one final pronouncement. "Jim envisioned speed as the main competitive advantage for these craft. The size of a passenger load for a cruise/vacation type ship, or cargo holds for a merchant ship, would be limited by this type of design. You can't make the holds or superstructure so top heavy that merely executing a turn tips her over. But with speed comes faster round-trips, so trans-ocean shipping becomes very rapid. Moreover, insurance costs would be considerably lower with a smaller load and crew aboard. Therefore, multiple crossings would likely become the norm, rather than large vessels performing all-or-nothing type transits. Scheduling passenger traffic could be done at much more frequent intervals. This would doubtless increase overall bookings as people find scheduled sailings more to their personal convenience."

The lad sat back down, awaiting our decision as to whether we believed him.

"Well, you've got us there, my boy. Neither of us is any more trained in this area than you are," Commander Irwin mused, taking a long draw on his own pipe. "Well, let's roll these up and store them somewhere safe and dry. Have you any objections, Wallace? Are you all squared away on this?"

"I am, indeed! You've done a good job, Charles. I only wish Jim was here with us; we'll make a good team, but his absence will be telling. I'm turning in; the last 30 hours have been very draining. See you in the morning."

With that, I headed for a bunk. I crawled beneath the covers and fell into a deep sleep. In my dreams, I imagined a future that had come unbidden, but which was surely destined to redirect my life.

CHAPTER TWENTY-THREE

GRIEF ON BOARD THE HUMBOLDT

Way ahead of the *U.S.S. Hooker*, Reginald Highsmith was steaming the *Humboldt* toward New York uneventfully. About five hours from port, his wireless operator received a dispatch from American Transatlantic Company, owner of the *Reliance*. Bill Lay spoke into the tube to the Bridge.

"Sir, we have received a rather lengthy message from management at ATC. It's addressed to the passengers who disembarked from *Reliance*. I presume a similar message has been sent to *Dorchester* for the men on board her. Do you want me to send it on up, or do you want to come along and read it here in case you want to reply?"

"No, send it along to the Bridge. That'll be fine. Thanks, Bill."

Reginald braced himself; this was sure to be some sort of condolence to the former passengers who have had their vacations so abruptly interrupted. No doubt the message would politely request him to address these people and read them the contents of the message. This would not please him. He would never hesitate to step forward and come to the rescue of someone, but he did not relish the tearful commiserating that a situation such as this would demand. A disaster at sea should be just that; let it stay there. Don't bring it ashore and into every household with endless news coverage and wailing in the press for some sort of reform—or worse, retribution.

If it came down to him having to announce the message, he'd use the ship's intercom after insuring that everyone aboard could hear him. If his original passengers got an earful, well, that was just the way the cookie would crumble. The message from American Transatlantic Company was soon in his hand. Captain Highsmith paused, "a-hemming" a few times, and steeling himself for the journey into sadness he was about to undertake. He picked up the microphone, cleared his throat, and began.

"Ladies and gentlemen, may I have your attention, please. Our ship has received a message from the owners of the *Reliance*. I believe all the passengers whom we transferred to our ship had passage booked through that company. Please allow me to read it to you in full. I am sorry I cannot meet personally with each of you; this form of address will have to suffice."

"To the ladies, gentlemen, and children of the good ship *Reliance*, we extend our sincere condolences for the trials and inconveniences you have recently experienced in the North Atlantic. We are grateful that each of you survived in good health. We understand that many of you were able to retrieve your personal items, as well. We believe you have all been part of a new phenomenon hitherto unknown during the winter months. Your patience and adherence to guidance from the officers aboard the

Reliance during the crisis is much admired by all of us here at American Transatlantic Company.

"Our board of directors has accordingly empowered me to offer each of you a ticket for passage on any of our three tours planned later this year. If your family schedules will not allow you to take advantage of those sailing dates, we will reserve a cabin for you for next year, should that be your preference. Our ticket agents will be meeting you in New York to welcome everyone home. Should you decide you would prefer a refund of your ticket, please let that person know as you disembark and arrangements will promptly be made to issue same. For those who left baggage or other personal items on board, please furnish us with an itemized list so we may compensate you."

There was a brief break. Then the message concluded with: "It is my sad duty to inform you that, subsequent to your departure aboard *Humboldt*, the *Reliance* sank after being freed from the ice sheet. In the struggle, Captain James Stahl died as he saved the life of another sailor. As truly regrettable as this terrible ordeal has been, we should take a minute and give thanks that we were privileged to serve with, or be cared for, by a truly great man: James Stahl. Please be assured that we at ATC deeply regret this tragic incident. We trust you will honor us with your continuing support as we go forward. Thank you. See you soon back on home shores!"

The message gram was signed: Albert Jason Weinstein, President of American Transatlantic Company.

Reggie's face was ashen. Whether out of forbearance for his heavy responsibility to ferry an overloaded boat safely home, or because the company was unaware of his long standing friendship with Stahl, he did not care. He had not been kept informed. Reading this message was his first alert that the *Reliance* had sunk and worse, that someone had died. He was proud that his friend had stood straight and tall to the very end, but he deeply regretted his loss. James Stahl had been like a standard bearer for all the officers employed by A.T.C. Possibly the same was true over at competing lines, such as Oceanic, but those officers would never admit it. Despite all that, Reggie had deeply admired Jim as a good friend.

Slowly, he turned to face Peter and said simply, "First Officer Porter, take over. I'm going for a walk around the decks. I want to meet and converse with as many of the folk we have on board as I can for the next few hours. If I'm needed, call me over the squawk box."

"Aye, aye sir!" The emotion among the men remaining on the Bridge was thick as the captain left to walk forward along the wood decking.

Reggie noticed that his sailors had done well. Despite the extensive and unusual activity amidst icy cold conditions during the past two days, the parts of his vessel that a passenger could view were spotless and fresh looking. The *Humboldt* would make a good impression as she steamed into the port of New York City tomorrow.

CHAPTER TWENTY-FOUR

WALLACE'S LETTER TO HIS WIFE

21 April, 1929

Dear Mary,

I am writing this while still at sea aboard the *U.S.S. Hooker*. Events are moving with a speed that has my head spinning. I will deliver it to you personally in order that you receive it in a timely manner. It is important for my personal sanity that I write down the events as they have happened to me in the last week.

The first item I must address, my darling, is the funeral of my longtime, dear friend James Stahl. The newspapers may have carried news of his death already, but now you've heard from me that it's official. He died bravely saving the life of a young man not even on our roster. That one act affirms my long-standing respect and admiration for this man. I have lost a dear friend who offered me self-respect by posting me aboard his ship.

The following details the events that have sped by since we were last together:

1.   You showed me Jim's letter offering me a post aboard *Reliance* as her Chief Officer.
2.   I travel to New York and report for duty.
3.   We take on a full cargo load and largely fill the vessel to capacity with passengers.
4.   We leave port and sail eastward, bound for the northern coast of France and then Liverpool.
5.   We steam into an area of ice floes and narrowly bypass a huge iceberg in the dead of night.
6.   Immediately thereafter we are captured by a hidden ice sheet.
7.   We inspect the ship; her bow is lost and perhaps two or three holds. Cargo is spilled.
8.   We telegraph our situation to management and call for rescue by vessels nearby.
9.   We contact the nearest Ice Patrol vessel and explain our predicament.
10. We are ordered to disembark our passengers when rescue ships become available.
11. The captain and I take a walk around the *Reliance* to inspect her condition.

12. We both notice that the berg we had earlier avoided appears to be moving our way.
13. Rescue vessels arrive; the captain of one is a longtime friend of James.
14. We direct our passengers and service staff to transship over to the *Dorchester* and *Humboldt*.
15. During disembarkation, a young man, Charles McDonald, arrives as directed by his captain.
16. Captain's Orderly McDonald and Captain Stahl spend several hours together talking.
17. McDonald intimates that should the *Reliance* exit the ice and founder, he will be last off.
18. Apparently the two men bond and review hull designs which Stahl made some years ago.
19. The two men exit the captain's cabin, taking the drawings with them.
20. The *Tahoe* arrives and her captain takes charge of the scene.
21. Further removal of our seamen is completed; they remain nearby in lifeboats.
22. The rescue ships sail for home.
23. The ice patrol boat is joined by a second one, the *Chelan.*
24. The men in the engine room and all officers still on *Reliance* are ordered into a lifeboat.
25. As Jim starts to offload into the lifeboat, he slips and is saved by me and four other seamen.
26. Destruction of the iceberg is attempted.
27. Damaging the iceberg causes it to bob upward and fall against the stern of the *Reliance.*
28. The *Reliance* is dislodged from the ice shelf and appears to be stable.
29. Suddenly, Jim Stahl knocks McDonald down to protect him from caroming ice shards.
30. A shard penetrates James' neck and he dies.
31. McDonald reaches into my friend's coat and removes various papers from the body.
32. What these papers were, and why McDonald purloined them, was unknown at this time.
33. The *Reliance* is apparently damaged beyond what we had determined and she sinks.
34. The naval supply ship *Hooker* arrives.
35. All of us still afloat on the water board the *Hooker.* Jim Stahl's body is taken aboard.
36. Coastal patrol vessels resume their patrols while *Hooker* departs for New York.
37. I remove the papers from McDonald and bring him before Commander Irwin for a hearing.
38. Charles convinces us that the papers are, due to the death of Captain Stahl, his property.

39. He shows us the drawings and explains the purpose of the designs displayed thereon.
40. I become convinced that improvements to hull design, as set forth in the drawings, are possible.
41. Commander Irwin, Charles, and I agree to protect the drawings while ascertaining their utility.
42. Jim Stahl remains iced in a temporary coffin as I write this letter.
43. We (presumptively) reach New York on Sunday the 22nd.

Mary, dear, I hope you are well. I will need all of your faculties working at their highest level when next we meet. My life is about to take a huge step into areas with which I have no familiarity. Please provide your wise counsel to keep me on the straight and narrow path.

My sweetest love,
Wally

CHAPTER TWENTY-FIVE

THE HOOKER DOCKS

The *U.S.S. Hooker* steamed slowly past Staten Island and on into Upper New York Bay. Even the hardened sailors held their breath as they sailed by the Statue of Liberty gleaming in her long green robes, then past Ellis Island that had strained under the vast hordes of immigrants following the Great Potato Famine, then astride the mouth of the East River, and finally the southernmost point of Manhattan Island that has become all but engulfed by swarms of office buildings.

Today, in an unusual move for naval vessels, she would be nosed by huffing and chuffing tugboats into the pier at 50th Street. These puffed black smoke as they eased *Hooker* between the long wharfs that had been constructed for liners such as the *R.M.S. Olympic.* It would be from here that her civilian passengers would disembark. Once docked astride the mammoth terminal buildings, she looked like a diminutive child's toy, but she carried significant cargo: shipwrecked survivors.

As the sailors from the *Reliance* prepared to disembark from the *Hooker,* a gaggle of reporters waiting at the base of the gangplank made it clear they wanted interviews. There didn't appear to be any way of escaping them. However, my shipmates and I did not want to relive the night of the 19th and 20th with a group of pushy newsmen, so we milled about in a knot of indecision at the top of the gangplank. No one wanted to be the first to make that walk.

Suddenly, a fancy chauffeur-driven car pulled up and parked astride all the reporters. A dynamic man exuding self-importance pushed through the tight knot of newsmen. Casting them aside as though they were bowling pins, he strode purposefully up the walkway.

Without bothering with salutes or other respectful decorum, he stood face-to-face with Commander Irwin and said, "Let me see my employees. I am A. J. Weinstein, President of American Transatlantic Company based in Providence. Now, where are they? Oh, I see them over there. Thank you, Commander. Will you have a few minutes to speak with me when I have seen my people safely off your vessel?"

"Certainly, Mr. Weinstein. I will remain right here while I disembark my own crewmen. Go ahead, they're waiting for you." Clearly, Commander Irwin was impressed by this man.

Stepping quickly over to the small band of sailors in somewhat disheveled uniforms, he queried, "Okay, gents, where's the body?" A.J. was a man of very direct speech, which of course mirrored his thought processes.

I was dressed as neatly as a man who has been saved from a sinking vessel can be; moreover, my stripes identified me as a man of authority. I stepped forward.

"Sir, I am Chief Officer Wallace Matthews. These are Jim Stahl's former officers and engine room crewmen."

We immediately strode along the line of officers and the Chief Engineer, several seamen, and finally Helmsman Butler, then I guided the company president to the casket of Captain Stahl.

So far, Weinstein hadn't spoken a word directly to us, but then he gruffly ordered, "Raise the lid so I can be sure it's him, will you, Chief?"

I complied and then stepped back so the man could take a good look. If I had been on the stand at some trial, I would have sworn that Weinstein said very softly: "You really screwed us here, didn't you, Stahl?" The president was very quick in his assessments as well as his speech.

He soon turned to address the men who were now my responsibility. A.J. Weinstein did not stand on ceremony.

"Hey, what are you standing around for? Let's get your former captain the hell off this ship and placed in a respectable mortuary. He's Episcopalian, isn't he? Right! I've arranged for him to be taken to Redden Funeral Home in Greenwich Village. If you want to view the body and pay your respects, go there. Gents, as of now, you each have a week off with pay. For those of you who can attend the funeral, it will be held on Tuesday at The Church of the Redeemer in Bryn Mawr, a small town west of Philadelphia. It's scheduled for 1:00 o'clock, or 1300 hours in your lingo. We will pay for an entire railroad car to be attached to the New York–Washington Special scheduled to leave here on Tuesday at 9:00 AM, or 0900 hours. It will arrive in Philadelphia at 11:15. From 30th Street Station, take the Main Line local to the town of Bryn Mawr. The church is only a half-mile walk after you alight from the train. The funeral will start at 1:30 PM, or 1330 hours; don't be late! I will expect to see all the officers there, but anyone who wishes to attend is welcome.

"You there, 3rd Officer Stanley, will you kindly take charge of delivering the body of Captain Stahl to the mortuary? Do you see the hearse parked down there? Yes, that's the one. Thank you, Officer Stanley."

Then he directed all of us to look down toward a bespectacled man sporting a bowler hat and an umbrella.

"Do you see my man Bartholomew standing down there behind the newsmen? Go talk to him about your pay and new assignments for next week. By the way, you'll be relieved to know that my Board of Directors places full blame for this disastrous loss on your deceased captain, so none of you will be subjected to disciplinary action. Seamen Petrovich, Busby, and Waltham have already come ashore and I said the same to them. That is all I have."

As we sailors drifted back over to the railing in order to decide how to confront the melee of reporters, Weinstein turned and briefly conversed with Dale Irwin.

"We at American Transatlantic Company are very grateful to you and your crew for accommodating our men in this unfortunate situation. Since you are military, I presume you are not allowed to accept any sort of cash as my thank-you, but I think it is within regulations for me to invite you and your entire crew to The Blue Tavern at 50

Commerce Street tomorrow, starting at 5:00 PM Monday with no curfew. Ask anyone where it is; it's well known in these parts. Is that agreeable to you, Commander?"

"It's very good of you, sir, and yes, thanks very much! You can count on us showing up."

Just to be sure, Irwin repeated, "5:00 PM, is that right, sir? That's 1700 hours to us. And don't worry; me and The Blue are well known to one another. My men will find it all right!"

With that, A.J. descended the gangplank, swept the reporters aside, and affirmed: "There is no story here. You got the details from all our passengers who disembarked yesterday. Let my men go to their homes in peace."

Then Weinstein returned to his chauffeur, spread his ample bottom on the plush velour of the limousine's seats, and was driven away.

Somehow, my men from *Reliance* managed to wangle their way through the throng of reporters; well, that's not accurate. It required some thirty minutes of short answers to some very fast questioning, whereupon the consensus was that this event had been a freak accident that could have been avoided if Captain Stahl had been steaming more slowly or had stopped his ship, rather than continuing on, after sidestepping the big berg.

All of us eventually made our way over to the clerk, Bartholomew, who was waiting to talk with each one of us. He already had checks prepared as he knew we would be needing money, and soon, in our sorry state. He kept the officers a little longer, issuing some of us new assignments and departure dates.

When I approached him as Chief Officer of a now sunken vessel, the clerk could see a look of great sorrow crinkling my face.

He tried consoling me. "Officer Matthews, why are you so long in the face? I have your pay right here. We do not have an immediate assignment for you yet, but be patient, I'm sure we will find one soon."

I couldn't help being blunt.

"Captain Stahl was one of my closest friends. His loss is a severe blow. Thanks for the check. I'll call the office when I'm ready for reassignment. Thanks again."

Then I crossed the pavement, hailed a cab, and said, "Grand Central Station." I would take the train straight home. I had a letter which I wanted to deliver, in person.

There was one sailor whom Commander Irwin had held back.

"Look, Charles, if you go out there, you'll be mobbed by those reporters. You're part of Oceanic Lines, so Weinstein has no interest in you. Just sit tight here, and after my crew has been paid and disembarked, we can escape unnoticed tomorrow amid all the unloading activity."

"Okay," was all Charles said, but he stayed on board as suggested.

The next morning being a Monday, the dock workers reported for work and got busy as soon as the klaxon sounded at 0600. When Dale was ready to depart his ship, he woke McDonald and together they prepared to disembark. No reporters were to be seen as they descended the gangplank.

"See, didn't I steer you right? You can walk about unmolested by reporters today, I wager." Dale Irwin beamed as if he'd won some victory.

Once ashore, however, the young man immediately tugged at Irwin's sleeve and said, "I want to call home right now to let them know I'm okay, and then I have to phone Oceanic Lines to let them know I'm back."

"Right, right. That's most definitely the thing to do!" and Commander Irwin left him alone to make the calls.

"Well, I'll be!" Irwin thought to himself. "The lad is like a little puppy, whimpering at my feet; This fellow should be easy to manipulate."

In the meantime, he made a call himself to The Blue Tavern. He warned them to prepare to put on the dog: he and his crew would be coming their way that very evening!

As soon as McDonald returned, Irwin asked, "Now, what are you going to do with the design drawings?"

"I'm considering taking them to the Providence Maritime Institute up in Rhode Island," stated Charles confidently. "They'll have storage for their safekeeping. After all, those drawings were created by one of their alumni."

This boy has much to learn about the importance of things, Irwin quietly concluded to himself. It was time to maneuver the lad into using a triple-keyed safe deposit box at a local bank catering to seamen. At such an institution, his rank would open doors that those of lesser rank would find locked.

He asked, "Well now, son, what if Wallace or I wanted to show them to one of our contacts. How will we do that when they're locked up at some school? Their personnel wouldn't know us, you understand?"

Charles gulped. He had talked with his father in order to reassure his family that he was safe. Then he had called his proctor at Oceanic Lines, Jacob Thresher. That man had apparently left a message for McDonald: "Report to Company Headquarters immediately because the *Humboldt* has already docked and Captain Highsmith needs to talk to you."

Now that he knew about this directive, he figured he'd be staying here in New York for the day and then going to the funeral on Tuesday. He'd need a place to sleep, but that was unimportant at the moment. He'd report to Captain Highsmith and fill him in on all that had happened since he had been ordered to the *Reliance*, and then see what Reginald wanted him to do. Probably, they'd be going together to Jim's funeral.

On the other hand, insofar as the drawings were concerned, he really hadn't thought the matter of their safekeeping through. However, Dale Irwin's suggestion that they be put in a bank vault with keys being cut for Dale, Charles, and Wallace did not seem wise. Charles still had them beneath his shirt; he tightened his belt a notch.

"Well, sir, we've gotten along agreeably just fine so far. Please don't object, but I'm taking them to my company where I am apprenticing, and that's final. My proctor, Mr. Jacob Thresher, is the chairman of the ship design department; he'll appreciate the originality of these. Even though I have not had any classes with him, he oversees my training so he knows me very well. You can simply call him to find out where I am. I'll contact P.M.I. after I talk with Mr. Thresher."

"Okay, Charles, if you think that's wise. Remember, the more people who are brought in on this project, the greater the chance someone will steal the ideas and leave us hanging. That's why I suggest using the bank vault. What did you say your proctor's name is, 'Thresher,' was it?"

Suddenly, standing there in the bright sunlight amid pedestrians and automobiles whizzing by, amid the sound and bedlam endemic to this large city, Charles realized that this man was trying to dupe him. It would not be the last time. If three men had a key, a vault box would provide no safety at all. The documents could be removed anytime without notice to the other two. Charles would only find out should he try to remove them for a discussion with someone important, like Frank Jones, but the box would be empty.

Very firmly, he looked Irwin in the eye and stated with finality: "I've told you how to contact me. The drawings remain with me. Thank you for transporting me back to the United States. Now, I have to catch a taxi to Oceanic Lines. Good-bye.

Charles turned and strode resolutely up the street until a cab pulled over.

"Where to, mister?"

"Take me to the headquarters for Oceanic Lines."

"You got it, Mac!" The driver engaged the clutch and the taxi smoothly accelerated away from the wharves. Soon it turned onto Second Avenue and headed for the offices of Oceanic Lines at No. 78.

CHAPTER TWENTY-SIX

MCDONALD SHARES SECRETS

The tires squealed in protest as the cab wheeled sharply around a corner, but Charles was impressed with the man's skill nonetheless. When they pulled up in front of the offices for Oceanic Lines, Charles leaned over to pay the man and asked for his medallion identification.

"I want to know someone in the City who is a good driver, should I ever need to get somewhere in a hurry."

The young man's face was so innocently earnest that Rick Rossetti believed his story. After all, fares were all too uncertain, and he had a daily minimum to produce back at the dispatch station.

"Sure, laddie, here you go. You've got our tele number, right? Then I'll be seein' ya!" With a gritty scrunch of rubber, Rick was off to find other passengers.

As the cab drove away, Charles found himself marveling at his adventure during the last nine months. He had rotated through the various posts aboard the *Humboldt*, been selected as captain's orderly, found himself boarding a competing liner to help a friend of his captain, befriended that man himself and, as a result, been entrusted with unpublished construction schematics, had saved that man's life only to be saved himself by the same Jim Stahl, and now was about to enter the corporate offices of his own employer. So far, he'd known only lecture halls and training facilities while with Oceanic Lines, yet here he was standing in front of the very office building where the esteemed Orville Townsend worked. He turned and entered through the revolving door, then took the elevator to the tenth floor.

The receptionist wanted to know who he was and why he was there.

"I'm apprentice Charles McDonald and I'm here to see either Captain Reginald Highsmith, who was my captain when I was aboard the *Humboldt* recently, or to see my proctor, Jacob Thresher."

"I'm sorry, Mr. McDonald, but Mr. Thresher is out in the field monitoring some trainees. He should return Wednesday. I believe Captain Highsmith is due back shortly; he left only twenty minutes ago to attend to an errand. Would you like to wait for him over there?"

The receptionist pointed to some leather covered benches.

"Thank you. That will be just fine. By the way, have you any directories for Providence, Rhode Island? I have someone's number I want to look up."

"I'm so sorry, sir. That is too distant to warrant my retaining telephone directories for it. Just keeping track of the phone exchanges right here in New York City is complex enough!"

She smiled his way. She was very pretty, as well as easy to converse with. He found himself wishing very strongly that she had the wherewithal to ferret out Holly North's telephone number. He had a gut feeling he was going to enjoy meeting the daughter of one of Jim Stahl's oldest friends very much.

Charles wandered over to the benches but he didn't sit down. As he was now on the tenth floor—the highest he had ever been—he decided to look out the window. As he pressed his nose up against the glass, he didn't merely look: he stared, wide-eyed! It was as though he was in heaven and could watch the entire goings-on of little human creatures scurrying to and fro so far below. After some ten minutes marveling at the view of the Hudson River bearing all sorts of vessels coming and going, he moved to the other side of what was probably a plastered-over, major steel support helping to frame the building. The receptionist couldn't see him now; the post was some two feet thick. He had just gotten comfortable leaning against it when he heard the elevator door open and a familiar voice address the young lady at the desk.

"Good morning, miss, I would like to see Mr. Jacob Thresher."

"Yes, sir, and what is your name, please?" she asked politely.

"I am Dale Irwin, an active commander with the United States Navy, and I have some very important information to share with Mr. Thresher. I believe he is the proctor here for one Charles McDonald, am I not correct?"

No doubt she smiled his way but said, "I am so sorry, sir, I cannot divulge internal company information regarding our employees. You will have to speak to Mr. Thresher personally on that matter. He is expected back in the office on Wednesday. May I give him a message from you?"

She was good, thought Charles. Not a hint of surprise in her voice betrayed the fact that she had spoken to the said Charles McDonald only minutes earlier.

"No, no message. I shall call him on Wednesday. Kindly leave my name, with this as my phone number."

Dale Irwin handed her a rectangular piece of cardboard, she took it, smiled a goodbye his way, and then he turned toward the elevators. In that position, Charles realized Irwin would spot him when he entered the conveyance and turned to face forward, so he quietly moved further along and hid behind some curtains.

The elevator doors opened, the conveyance swallowed Mr. Irwin, and Charles heard the sweet voice of the receptionist, Lois, state, "Now that's no way to act when a gentleman comes a-calling! How would you feel if I hid behind a curtain at the mere sight of you?" but she accompanied the question with a cheery laugh as young Charles emerged from behind the drapes.

"You are very easy to be around, Miss. The company was smart to hire you. Unfortunately, I have spent the last three days aboard that man's ship, and I'm afraid that what he professes is not what he thinks and schemes. I only hope my proctor and I speak prior to Mr. Irwin reaching Mr. Thresher."

His demeanor expressed an eager honesty.

Lois thereupon replied, "Of course I cannot be a part of any sort of interoffice scheming, but I can make it very difficult for Mr. Irwin to converse with Mr. Thresher. I don't even need to know the ins-and-outs. Your face reflects such straight-forward honesty that it's easy to root for you, especially since you are actually an employee of ours. I checked Mr. Thresher's files and I see you started with us twenty-one months ago, which means you have already completed the office skills portion and have clearly been at sea during 1929."

"Yes, ma'am, you are correct in every respect. I am very impressed. I'm glad we've met; it doesn't hurt to know someone on the inside, if you know what I mean!"

"I surely do." Her eyes stayed on him as she smiled, but it was a warm smile as though the two had just hatched some sort of plot. Charles had a quick insight: it doesn't hurt to be twenty and handsome. He neglected to add "self-effacing."

Just then, an elevator door opened and out stepped Reginald Highsmith.

"Captain! Am I glad to see you!" exploded Charles with relief.

"And I you, my boy!" Wrapping an arm around the lad, Reggie looked over at Lois as if to ask whether he could use the small conference rom. Lois simply nodded, so the two men hurried down the corridor and opened the door marked "Conference Room B" and entered. Before they relaxed in the leather upholstered chairs, Reggie said "Let's have a drink!" He stood up abruptly and headed to the bar.

"Sir, if there is any root beer in that ice chest, I'll have a glass of that. Otherwise, just water for me, please."

"Right you are. I remember being impressed aboard the *Humboldt* when it became clear that you didn't drink. It's a bad habit, but one which I thoroughly enjoy, so you'll forgive me if I make a drink right now. Way up high like this, it's sinful, but it's such a pleasure to safely be above the law!" He couldn't help smiling at his own heady pun.

Returning to his comfortable chair, Reggie breathed a sigh of relief as he looked his former orderly over. If someone had asked, he would have said he was damned glad to see his young charge back safe and sound.

"Well, after all that has happened to you, you don't appear any the worse for wear, I must say."

"Then in that case, sir, my looks are deceiving you. Jim Stahl was your longtime friend, so I obeyed your command to serve him in any way he needed prior to his death, but you will not believe what I have become embroiled in as a result of being assigned to the *Reliance*."

Reggie put down his drink, leaned in close toward Charles, and whispered softly: "Go on."

CHAPTER TWENTY-SEVEN

CHARLES IS SMITTEN

As we rolled into the driveway, I looked over at my wife and said, "Mary, pull over and stop the engine. I have an important letter that I want to deliver to you in person."

She bore a quizzical look as I handed her the sealed envelope. I had held her more tightly than usual when she picked me up at the train station, but then I had remained rather quiet during the drive to our house. She was simply relieved and thrilled to have me back alive, given all the horrors she had seen depicted in the Sunday paper sketches of icebergs and cannon fire and sinking of the very ship I was on. Moreover, the death of our dear friend was devastating. The entire family would pay our respects by traveling to Pennsylvania tomorrow.

"What could be in this letter that my husband has guarded so carefully?" Mary wondered. If anyone should be writing heartfelt letters in the Matthews household, it should be her, given her condition. Her hands trembled slightly as she tore open the top portion.

The car was as silent as the ancient tombs of the Egyptians as she read the lines of ongoing drama which I had written. Only the gentle rhythm of our breathing could be heard. The window panes began to fog up as she finished. Mary didn't say anything. She simply let the letter fall to her lap as she reached over and hugged me hard and close. Slowly, as emotions took hold, we both began to cry softly.

"You know I love you, completely and without reserve. Whatever you decide, I will support you fully." My wife could not have been more sincere. "So long as what you take on does not threaten the well-being of our children, you will have my whole-hearted support."

"Thank the good lord for you, Mary. As I wrote in the letter, I don't think I could have handled what I lived through this last week without having you in my thoughts."

We sat there in front of our house on 22 Wimpole Street, listening to the cars swish by and the horse-drawn produce wagons plod homeward. What was important was that we were together. My wife and I drew enormous strength from one another. Unbeknownst to me, Mary knew that this might be the very last such close moment for us. The time when she would be forced into her own private physical battle was drawing near but, at this moment, regrettably, I was blissfully unaware of her crisis and was merely thinking about myself.

She turned to me and whispered softly, "Wally, let's go in the house where it's cozy and warm. I want you to undress me and make love to me with all the skill and experience you can muster."

My wife's face was angelic in its sincerity. I needed no further prodding. We had been married for two decades but my Mary was still as fresh and appealing as when we had been wed. I went around to her side and helped her out, placing my arm lovingly around her waist as I guided her toward our house.

Closing the door, I asked, "What about the children?"

"Don't worry; they're over at Sally's for her son's birthday party. I don't expect them to walk home until dinnertime."

I reached across her shoulders, removing her coat and scarf, and then lifted the back of her hair and kissed the sweet-smelling skin of her neck. As she warmed to my touch, I moved to her ear lobe and she tilted her head back. She moaned as her head pressed warmly against my cheek, then I cradled my arm beneath her thighs and, lifting her off the ground, carried her over to the living room sofa. The daylight was ebbing, and its light reflected pale yellow off the pine boards of the walls, giving a gentle highlight to Mary's smooth cheeks. She kissed my mouth fully, sucking in just a bit so she could nip the lower lip. She then reached down and removed my pants with a simple, practiced release of the buttoned fly. The suspenders were next, but she expertly slipped them off my shoulders before I even realized what was happening.

For my part, I held her shoulders slightly elevated and ever so slowly stroked my fingers over her nipples. She became fired with the thrill of desire and easily slid her body beneath me. My fingers traced the "V" joining her thighs, and when I found the right spot, my fingers drifted in light, lazy circles around her clitoris. As her hips began writhing and then to undulate up and down, I took my very rigid cock and slipped inside her. Her long, deep moan told me I was pleasing her. I arched myself backward by holding both arms straight against my flattened palms, and moved with long strokes in and out of her moist pleasure cave. As we became lost in the thrill of rippling pleasure, we moved together, faster and then even faster until Mary started shaking and, with loud shrieks, gave her body over to wave after wave of multiple sensations. My own body soon followed as I looked upon the woman with whom I was utterly enamored.

Wow! I was spent completely. Even my toes felt drained. Breathing heavily, I collapsed against my wife's limp body. We embraced quietly together. In a bit, I rolled astride her in order to look her fully in the face.

"Mary, I have been so blessed to have fallen in love with you. You have been my light of shining hope, and your having borne our two children has made me a complete man. This new project I discussed in that letter may pull me away from home for long hours each evening, but you will ever be with me. I want to make some mark of achievement in this world, something to leave behind to be remembered by, but if I did nothing else for the rest of my life, having loved you will have completed me. My dearest Mary."

I gently stroked her hair as I held her head against my chest. Mary's eyes closed, happy she could share so completely this last moment of love's greatest expression. Our family would go to Jim's funeral, see friends we'd lost contact with, and then be uplifted by the minister's eulogy. Mary would wait for all those events to be over before telling me about her cancer on the way home. If the doctor was right, her time would be all too limited, but she wasn't about to spoil this fabulous moment she and her man had just shared with some doctor's prognosis.

As for myself, I merely figured that she had been relieved to have me back home in one piece, given the dire content of the radio news she had listened to. Our love-making had been an expression of her gratitude in this regard. To my way of thinking, she had made my homecoming as pleasurable as possible. In my mind, surely our shared love would continue for years to come.

* * *

The next morning was a joyful spring day. It was now late April and the air was beginning to warm and fresh buds were bursting from branches. Flowers were peeping from their winter hibernation beds. Birds were on the wing finding mates and making nests, squirrels scampered across the roadways hither and thither in their seemingly endless search for nuts, and of course rabbits starting hopping and frolicking wherever there was tall grass.

Mary and I, together with our two children, Bill and Alice, got into our reliable Ford Model "T" family car. Alice had been named for Jim's deceased wife. Bill, being aged 17, could help with the drive to Philadelphia. Both of them appeared to grasp the depth of our sadness with the coming funeral. They had really enjoyed "Mr. Stalled," as they jokingly liked to call him, every time he had visited my home. As a result of his being at sea so often, he would return bearing small toys he had purchased abroad. Then, as they reached their teenaged years, he shared lurid stories accumulated from his many years in foreign ports.

The trip down to Bryn Mawr would take some six or seven hours, so we had to get started no later than 0630, or "bright and early!" as Mary would say. Hitting the New York area was my main concern: traffic clogs and jams there could be pretty fierce during the morning rush hour. The children were good travelers, but even a good traveler has limited endurance when it comes to having to relieve oneself.

"Batten down the hatches, kids, we're off!" I announced as I put the car in gear. I must say, we motored the full distance in timely fashion, making only two pit stops, as our children called them, along the way. It had been difficult to keep driving while traveling through Short Hills and Princeton, New Jersey. Mary kept pointing out attractive houses and wanting to stop to gander, but of course we couldn't afford the delay.

"Don't fret yourself, honey. From what I hear, where we are headed will knock your socks off even more!"

I knew I was right; Jim had grown up where we were headed and would extol the beauty of the town just about every time we got together. The homes in the Bryn Mawr area, even for so-called middle income families, could rival those of any town in the United States.

Our family arrived at the Church of the Redeemer where its erudite minister, Canon Earp, was scheduled to conduct the service in memory of Jim. The yellow and white jonquils and lilies festooning the altar put a light, pretty face on this sad occasion. They suggested that today's service would be more a celebration of Jim's life rather than a mournful observance of his passing.

Mary wanted to take the children over to the markers of Jim's parents; the captain himself would be set amongst those graves. I ran into young Charles McDonald along the way. The lad reminded me that many of A.T.C.'s seamen would be coming in by train, so someone should go meet them at the station.

"Mary, you tend to the kids while I check whether there are sailors who need a ride from the station. I'll be back before the service starts, so save me a seat."

"Go along, Wally, dear. You've never been one to lose track of your men!"

In this way, Charles and I found ourselves alone together for the first time since being on board the *Hooker*.

Charles jumped right in, saying, "Mr. Matthews, we work for competing carriers, but you were a genuinely close friend of James Stahl. I think you have come to trust me as I do you. Therefore, I must reveal that I do not like that Irwin fella much. He kept me fed and warm while I was on his boat, but my conversations with him subsequent to your leaving have left me very suspicious of him.

"I have placed the drawings we went over in the capable hands of my former captain, Reginald Highsmith, so they're safely stored at Oceanic headquarters. Dale, however, was very upset by that idea; he urged me to place them in a bank vault with keys being made for the three of us. When I refused, he paid a visit to my boss in order, I believe, to lodge a complaint against me. Mr. Thresher, my proctor, wasn't available, but Dale plans to see him tomorrow while I'm still here in Pennsylvania. The idea, I believe, will be to discredit me in the eyes of the company and thereby insist on their turning over the drawings to him. If I'm away, I can't defend myself. His thinking is very devious. You haven't had such negative dealings with him, so I will understand if you want to keep him in the mix, but as for me, I want nothing more to do with Dale Irwin."

My answer clearly surprised the lad.

"You don't say! I'm very glad to hear it. I'm not without contacts myself, you know, having been in the business for some twenty years. I telephoned my neighbor while I was home in Providence. He's with the navy and has been on the peer review board regarding promotions for officers ever since the war ended. He stated that Irwin has his current posting aboard *Hooker* in order to get him out of the way.

"I also learned that the *Wickes* entered service August 1, 1918, but that she was severely damaged by an unknown hit-and-slip-away vessel which put her out of action until after the cease fire on November 11, 1918. That destroyer never engaged the enemy; she served only on convoy duty. As for Irwin, the naval command will not promote him because it considers him to be a kind of swindler, the sort who is always looking for personal gain at the expense of others, and by "others" I mean the navy. I believe he is treating us in the same manner.

"I learned that the captain of the *Wickes* was actually one Barnes Eberly, whom you may recall commanded the *Tahoe* which had tried to blow that iceberg apart. Our esteemed commander Irwin was doubtless aboard the *Wickes*. He may even have been the officer on duty when the hit by the ghost vessel occurred, but I do know he was passed over for promotion due to some other dereliction of duty and has been held in low regard ever since. I would have no trouble if we cut him out of our plans completely."

I paused, cleared away the lump in my throat, and then looked over at Charles. "By the way, from now on, please call me Wally, or Wallace if you prefer. We're about to start working together; Mr. Matthews is far too formal for partners in business, don't you think?"

"Wow, I am so relieved to hear you say that. If only Jim were here and alive, he would be proud of our attention to detail. He's with us in spirit, I'm sure."

Then, turning to look out the car door window, Charles exclaimed, "Oh look! Here we are. And there's a bunch of seamen types from *Reliance,* without a doubt."

Charles rolled down the window and shouted to a group of men sweltering in their pea coats under the April sun. "Come on guys, get in. We can crowd in five or six; it's just a short hop."

With the men loaded, my good old car creaked and groaned until the church was reached. The group of six men and young Charles exited quickly after we pulled up under the porte-cochere sheltering the main entrance.

"Sir, don't ever ask me to sail with you stuffed into some box crate like that!" said one of the burly seaman.

I simply laughed. "I got you here, didn't I? Think how pooped you'd be if you'd had to hike up that long hill?"

"Well, you're right, sir. But it was still very cramped in there."

"Listen, Petrovich, you're the lucky one! Tomorrow, I have to haul two teenage kids all the way back to Providence. You think you have complaints. You should spend six hours with their sort!"

Even as I said that, I had a broad smile on my face.

Our former helmsman smiled himself. "You did get the short end of the stick on that deal, sir."

I closed the door, parked the car, and entered the church as sonorous, transporting music amongs the pews from a huge organ installed within the chancel. Mary and my kids were sitting alongside Peter North's troop. I proudly looked down the pew at my family and then suddenly became rigid; it dawned on me that my wife was astride not children, but teenagers! Where had the time gone? It was obvious to me that neither Bill nor Alice could be thought of as children any longer. However, long-held habits die only after a father comes to grip, kicking and screaming, with reality.

Jim's closest friend, Peter North, was to be a pall bearer, so he had to sit on the aisle seat. Beside him were his wife Anne and the girl whom Jim Stahl had spoken about both often, and admiringly. Holly had long brunette hair, a serene face with dark eyes highlighted by shapely thin eyebrows, and a coquettish mouth.

I found an aisle seat on the opposite end of North's pew. I too was to be a pallbearer. "Woe betides the lad who falls into the trap of that girl's face," I mused. "He'll lose all self-control, for sure!"

Being completely in love myself, I could admire her without being seduced by Holly's appeal.

Someone nudged me from behind. Turning, I saw the welcoming face of Reggie Highsmith, who likewise sat on the aisle seat as a soon-to-be-called upon pallbearer. "I came down with McDonald," he confirmed as he breathed heavily my way.

As I turned around to face the altar, I could have sworn I detected the odor of bourbon in the air. I dismissed the thought; after all, Prohibition was in effect throughout the country. Except for wine taken with Communion, consuming liquor in a church would warrant no exception to the law.

As time for the service drew near, young McDonald was still wandering around the church. As he strode purposefully down the center looking for an aisle seat, he happened to glance over to where my family was. The lad stopped dead in his tracks. He stared at the girl sitting next to Peter North for so long that she finally turned to look his way. Their eyes met and Charles felt a thrill of pleasure ripple through his brain while chills coursed up and down his spine. As I glanced his way, it looked as though he was about to start dancing a jig!

While aboard the *Hooker*, Charles had confided to me how his father had whittled a ship-in-a-bottle with patient skill and dexterity; as he watched, his spine had tingled as he watched his father work so skillfully. The ship was a wondrous creation, so precise in its detail, but then when he had flattened the masts and slipped the ship into a light green bottle, Charles' admiration for his father had set for life. Those chills had been ones of admiration, not fantasy. When he had remarked to Jim how much he appreciated the artistry his father possessed, Stahl had replied that he himself was skilled at making ships-in-a-bottle; he'd even shown Charles the one he kept above his bunk aboard the *Reliance*.

Now, facing this girl as he was, anyone could see that the rippling chills were far more intense. The kid's brain was so addled that he momentarily forgot where he was, but it was clear to everyone near that, at a stroke, his life was about to change. This girl had completely captivated him with a mere glance.

I could see his brain working: "Who was she? Wally had mentioned that he had a daughter who was now 13 years old. This knockout was more like 17 or 18. Could this girl be the one Jim had told him about in his cabin back on *Reliance*?"

Young McDonald was in trouble. He had mentioned to me in passing that he hoped to soon acquire a dog, but from the look on his face today, his getting a dog was about to be replaced by something, or someone, less furry. Stumbling, he looked ahead and found a seat in the next pew. He politely asked everyone to slide over for him. Since he was to be a pallbearer as well, he had to be on the outside seat.

Once ensconced, he tried to listen to the organ music, but the back of his right shoulder kept itching. He tried resisting, but the urge wouldn't go away. In order to scratch it, he had to screw his head around. The itch overpowered his self-control. He just had to scratch that shoulder, and each time he scratched, he turned his head to the right so severely that he appeared to be looking at the pew behind.

The fourth time he turned around, Peter North himself reached his arm forward and, resting it on Charles' shoulder, said, "Son, we're here for a purpose. Pay your respects to the deceased."

Charles didn't turn around after that. He didn't try to look her way even after the minister finished his sincere eulogy to Jim, a man dearly respected by all present, because now the bug-eyed lad had to rise and bear the coffin out of the church to its burial plot.

As they exited the building and entered the cemetery proper, the pall bearer behind him said, "Son, my name is Peter North, and I roomed with James Stahl while we trained at P.M.I. That girl is my daughter, and from the look on your face, I suspect my family will be seeing a lot of you in the future. We'll talk more after Canon Earp finishes the burial ceremony."

Peter North couldn't see it, but as Charles carried the body of his savior Jim Stahl to its final resting place, he had a big smile on his face.

CHAPTER TWENTY-EIGHT

FALLING FOR EACH OTHER

At the conclusion of the internment ceremony, everyone adjourned to the parish house for the reception. Charles met up with Reggie and made sure he had spoken with me, then I introduced both of them to my wife Mary. She proudly showed off our children, Bill and Alice. A tall, rather large man whom none of us knew approached the enclave we had formed.

"Excuse me, but may I interrupt you? I've come to introduce myself. I was one of Jim's roommates back at P.M.I.; I'm Matt Johnson." Upon hearing that name, Peter North spun around from the group with whom he and his wife Anne were conversing.

"Matt! Son of a gun, it's been twenty years! Hey, fellow, how're you doing?" Peter had a hugely wide smile of greeting spread across his pleased face. "I know this is not how we'd like to be meeting, but we've sure got a lot of catching up to do!"

Drinks in hand, the two former roommates started to wander over to a copse of trees for some shaded conversation, but along the way, Peter spotted Charles craning his neck as though searching for someone.

He went over and touched him lightly on the arm, observing, "She's over there, standing under that big beech tree."

Rejoining his old friend, Peter remarked to Matt, "I think that lad has just fallen for my daughter!" They laughed heartily as they found some chairs and dropped into their own world of reminiscences about Jim Stahl as well as each other.

Charles, red as a beet at having been found out, had nevertheless followed Peter's directions. There she was, indeed, tall and slender and absolutely fetching in her svelte black dress. He caught her eye and moved smartly to where she was.

"Hello! You appear to have found a very pleasant spot in which to stand. May I join you?"

"If you like," she replied noncommittally.

"I believe you are Holly, Holly North. Your father mentioned you while we were on the casket together. I wanted very much to meet you because my friend Jim had told me about you when I was aboard the *Reliance* with him. He spoke so highly of you, I imagined you to be an angel sent from heaven above."

"Well, what do you think, now that you have seen me in the flesh?"

She challenged him to answer by arching her eyebrows, and then she pertly rested her eyes on his. Boys were so easy to be coy with. It had been her experience that she could make men drool when they simply looked her way, but it never took long before they got used to her and began talking exclusively about themselves. She didn't know this man from Adam, of course, but he must have been close to her father's best friend, Jim Stahl, since he had been selected as a pallbearer.

It suddenly dawned on Holly that, compared to all the others who had been on the casket, this fellow was very young, perhaps early 20's, whereas all the other codgers like his father must be approaching 50, or worse. The position of pallbearer is the highest honor the dead can bestow on their friends, so for this young man to have been selected signified that he must be important to the family.

"Who is this strapping young man?" she found herself wondering.

And, there was one other thing she had noticed: this particular fellow seemed to have trouble with his right shoulder, as he kept looking around and scratching it during the service. Indeed, her father had found it necessary to reach over and ask him to stop. "I'll have to follow up on that question," she thought. "Maybe he has a dose of poison ivy. For the moment, I may as well see what this man has to offer. He's certainly easy to look at, and tall, like Jim was," she observed silently.

"Well," she repeated, "what do you think now?"

At her question, Charles was thrown totally off his guard. His senses were already reeling, tumbling out of control at being this close to her. Her hair, which was richly brown and shining with health, shimmered slightly as the springtime breezes swirled about the beech tree. Her slim figure, perched on stunning legs, made the appeal of her face all the more desirable. He couldn't believe it was possible, but he was already falling in love with this girl, yet he'd barely spoken a dozen words to her.

He figured it was time to up the ante and say something impressive.

Charles cleared his throat and replied, "It never occurred to me that the look of an angel could be improved upon, but you surely have done it!"

He knew his color was up, probably even reddening his cheeks a bit, but he'd spoken the honest truth as he believed it, and he couldn't stop what his racing heart was doing to his complexion.

She laughed lightly, her head tilting back ever so slightly to reveal the smoothly inviting skin of her neck. "Man, I'd like nothing better than to bury my head against that and nuzzle it all afternoon long!" but Charles didn't say that, he only thought it. Deciding on a diversionary tactic, he offered to get her some food.

"Eating is why people attend funerals, you know. If food was not offered, few would ever attend such a sad occasion." he pronounced solemnly.

She looked up at him and smiled invitingly: "You could be right about that. You have an interesting way of thinking. What other wisdom can you share with me?" This should bait the trap sufficiently to get him to start talking about himself.

His reply caught her completely by surprise.

He stated, "I wanted to meet you very much because Jim Stahl meant so much to me. The captain and I met when I was assigned by one of his friends, Reggie Highsmith, to help out should Stahl's ship begin to sink. Reggie is standing over there by the bar, do you see him? That's right, that's him. Even nowadays, in the midst of Prohibition, he wants his liquor if he can find someone to offer it."

He cleared his throat, and then he forged ahead.

"Your dad might never have told you this, but Jim's wife and unborn child perished in a freak accident three or four years before you were born. As a result, Jim had been yearning for a son for over two decades when I met him. At any rate, Jim and I knew each other, quite literally, for less than a day, but in that very short time we bonded as though we were father and son. He showed me his most closely held plans for hull designs and accepted my pitifully uneducated comments with grace, I saved his life as we disembarked the *Reliance*, and in short order he saved me from being killed by flying ice shards.

"Currently, I am a mere apprentice with the Oceanic Lines outfit. It's headquartered in New York City, but the company maintains satellite branches along the East Coast for training its new employees and shepherding ocean vessel departures from various ports such as Boston and Providence. That's where I'm based, in Providence. I quite literally would not be standing here talking with you, the woman who fulfills my every dream, were it not for your dad's best friend. Yes, I am young. I'll be 21 next week, as a matter of fact, but my reason... no, my very soul requires that I be here to honor the memory of James Stahl."

By this time, they had sat down on one of the stone benches. As Holly regarded the young man critically, she found herself realizing that here was a person unlike all those who had gone before. Yes, true to form, he had brought himself into their conversation, but not in a self-pontificating sort of way. He was truthful, even self-effacing, rather than boastful. She found herself wanting to get to know him really well, because this might be the person with whom she was destined to make a life and home.

And, more importantly, his quick, almost off-the-cuff compliment had not been missed by her. He had stated, "the woman," not "a woman," and that carried significance.

"I think you mentioned something about bringing me some food, didn't you?"

She had changed the subject, but she needed some space in which to mull over the feelings which this man was stirring within her.

"Yes, yes! I'm sorry; I got carried away there for a second. What would you like: a ham or turkey sandwich, some crudités, or a deviled egg, perhaps? I'm getting a cola; would that suit you, too?"

He started to rise, but he was still listening attentively when she affirmed, "I'll enjoy everything you just mentioned. I'm not much for spicy foods, and oysters make me squeamish. I trust you will take good care of me." With a smile and flutter of her eyelashes, she sent him on his mission.

Charles turned and made a beeline for the food displayed atop the white linen tablecloth. "She said she trusts me to take good care of her. Wow! You bet I will!" he confirmed to himself while loading two plates with delicious goodies he hoped she would relish.

Despite his being quite hungry, he found himself feeling dexterous and secure. He was attending the funeral of a man with whom he had instantly bonded, and that very man had brought him to the side of a girl in whose presence he felt sweetly relaxed. Sitting beside her a few minutes ago had made him feel wrapped in warmth, as though he was in a cocoon of well-being. Today, it was as if all his yearnings and uncertainties had signed a treaty that now left him at peace with himself. Even at this time of great sadness, she made him feel at ease and fulfilled.

Meanwhile, back on the bench, Holly's mind, as well as her libido, was racing at lightning speed.

"Good heavens, what is happening to me?" she thought to herself. She readjusted her position on the bench to showcase her legs. "I was so close to Jim Stahl; he not only had been daddy's lifelong best friend, but he was always so endearing and good at conversation when he came to visit me. I adored him. But he has died to save a young man with whom I may well fall deeply in love." Silently, she added: "Thank you so very much, Jim. Your life has not been given up in vain. You have passed along your ideals and spirit into this Charles McDonald, and you have brought the two of us together with your passing. I certainly didn't want you to die, but your life has been a great gift to us both."

With that affirmation, she sat with her hands in her lap and thought about how pleasant the name James Stahl McDonald would sound. With a man such as the stalwart fellow who had just been so pleasant with her, she was sure the first-born of Charles McDonald would be a male. With wide, expectant eyes and a soft crimson rising to tint her cheeks, Holly North adjusted her skirt—yet again—while she awaited the return of the man she would inspire, someday, to ask for her hand in marriage.

CHAPTER TWENTY-NINE

INVITATION IN NEW YORK

It was late afternoon when I bumped into Seaman 1st Class Edmonds, and I mean literally.

"Good thing I had a plate of chicken legs, sir. If it had been a drink, it would have spilled all down your suit!"

"Not to worry, Ben. Black looks good with whiskey dripping down it."

This resulted in a hearty laugh by both of us, whereupon Seaman Edmonds inquired whether I'd heard what occurred during the transshipping of passengers to *Humboldt*. This was obviously a good opportunity to give this seaman some space in order to feel self-important; I indulged him. When I professed innocence, Ben Edmonds launched into his tender tale.

"Well, sir, you see it went like this. You know that Mr. Rothschild was aboard lifeboat No. 4, right?"

I nodded. After all, I had positioned him there, on the middle of a thwart in the center of the small craft. I figured that was a spot that would restrict his imagination, but apparently he had used it to his advantage.

"Well, sir, it happened like this." Thereupon, Seaman Edmonds regaled me with the tale about this passenger producing a kitten for the relaxation of his fellow fearful passengers. Such a smart tactic to ease anxiety was both prescient and generous. Down deep, Mr. Rothschild was just a young boy needing to be loved. This taught me a valuable lesson. Don't judge a person merely by what they show you on the surface: *Probe for deeper motivations hidden beneath their surface veneer.* You might be surprised by the good you find there. All of us aboard the *Reliance* had failed to see the real Mr. Rothschild secreted beneath his prankster facade.

As evening approached, everyone had paid their graveside respects, listened to Canon Earp expostulate on the forgiveness of the Lord until they were blue in the face, and eaten all they could. The gathering began to break up as people drifted away for the return trips home.

Reginald Highsmith collared Charles McDonald to tell him it was time to catch the train back to New York.

Holly and Charles had finished eating some time ago and had spent the last hour simply conversing in low intimate tones. Occasionally, Charles would enjoy a good belly laugh, but for the most part, these two appeared to be in their own world and oblivious to the presence of anyone else. Reggie's question caught Charles by surprise.

"Why? Are you going? Is it time to leave already?" The young man was slowly returning to the real world from the idyllic planet he'd been exploring with Holly.

"Charles, it's going on 1730 hours. The trains run less frequently at this time of the evening. If we're to get back to the City tonight, we've got to get into Philadelphia in order to board the Washington/New York express at 1900 hours. Haul your butt, sailor!"

That was language which he'd been hearing regularly for the last 21 months at Oceanic. Automatically responding, he stood up, held Holly's hand for a moment, squeezed it, and then the two seamen were catching a ride to Bryn Mawr station with one of the returning crew.

The train arrived right on time, of course. Ships could be late arriving, since they had to cope with the vagaries of ocean currents and weather, but railroads were expected to be reliable. As they rode along, the view outside the windows became increasingly unpleasant as their rail car neared the city. Stores and manufacturing facilities always present their rear ends to the tracks, and "out back" would be where refuse and trash was deposited.

For want of a better view, Charles turned to face Reggie and remarked that he hadn't heard anything about the *Humboldt's* arrival in New York last Saturday.

"Well, our own passengers knew our routine well; they had embarked and disembarked several times with our ship by then. Our arrival and unloading went smoothly, in my opinion.

"As for our additional load, what I did was use an entirely separate exit for them to disembark. I was fortunate; A.T.C. had obtained permission for them to gather in a passenger assemblage area that was adjacent to our pier. There, they were processed by the company's clerks regarding lost luggage and the like, given the option of refunds or replacement tickets, and then escorted to whatever ride was waiting to take them home. The bachelors had been processed earlier because the *Dorchester* docked, dumped them off, and immediately headed back to her original destination, Boston, that very night.

"Given the circumstances and opportunity for tempers to be riled, I thought the entire operation went very smoothly. Of course, the cleaning gang that came on board my boat had to work right through Tuesday night preparing her for a new voyage, so Oceanic decided to give me and my crew a few days off to collect ourselves. That did not sit well with our customers booked for our next departure. Their trip would be delayed until this Saturday. That's when we take off again, bound for several towns along the coast of Ireland. You better believe, should we encounter ice fields, we'll be steaming at 'all ahead SLOW' even in daylight!"

By the time the Paoli Local had deposited them at Suburban Station, Charles was turning his mind fully to the subject that had been raised only yesterday. What was he going to do about Dale Irwin, the plans of Jim Stahl, and Jacob Thresher who was being thrust into a situation well beyond his experience? He was mulling these questions over in his mind when the express coming up from Baltimore pulled in.

He and Reggie promptly boarded and had just taken their seats when the conductor called, "All aboard!" and they were away.

Charles followed Reggie's example and they both got comfortable in the reclining, cushioned seats. Tonight's train would carry light traffic; most travelers took the early morning runs. With the quiet that now settled inside the car as the express whooshed along the tracks, Charles found himself being lulled to sleep by the gently swaying of the parlor car. Before he knew it, Reggie was nudging him awake.

"Here we are, my boy. Listen to that honking: Here it is 2115 hours in the evening on a weeknight, yet the City is acting as though she was just awakening. It must be all those movie-goers and people rushing to yet another play that creates so much hubbub. Well, let's get a cab ourselves and turn in for the night. Our trip may have been short-lived, but I'm exhausted!"

"Reggie, you've got to account for all those whiskey sours and bourbons you put away this afternoon. Now that I've had my nap, I'm wide awake. You go along; I'll see you in the morning at the office. Good night!"

As they parted, Charles headed straight for a telephone. If a traveler was still in the station proper, he could call from one of the phones set against a wall and ask the operator for a number in the City. Someone, probably the cab company owner, must have had the bright idea that offering this courtesy would be good for business.

Charles waited patiently as the phone rang on the other end. "Hello, Oceanic Lines. What may I do for you?"

The voice on the other end of the line was most definitely not that of the receptionist Lois, but it was the very person to whom Charles wanted to speak.

"Hello, Mr. Thresher, this is Charles McDonald. I'm just back from the funeral for the ship captain who died last Friday. Sir, may I come by the office and talk with you?"

"Good lord, Charles, it's 9:20. No one is at Oceanic this late. Your call was transferred over to my home. Where are you, in the station?"

"Yes sir."

Okay, go stand by the entrance doors on the south side of the building. I'll drive in and pick you up. Let's see, I should be there by 2145. Is that good for you?"

"Sir, I will be there. I'm wearing a black suit and striped tie. Can you remember what I look like after all these months?"

"Good heavens, Charles. No one here will ever forget your face. You're a hero! After Reginald Highsmith returned to New York and disembarked all, and I mean all of his passengers, he came back to the office and told us about your adventure. As your proctor, I was hanging on his every word. Even Orville Townsend, our president, came down from the executive suite and listened to Reggie's tale. We've been proud, to one degree or another, of all of our hires over the years, but you, Charles, have carved out a singular niche: a man retaining a cool head under real pressure. Okay, let me get started. See you soon."

Charles hung up and headed straight for the south-facing entrance doors. He positioned himself astride a bright street lamp; he didn't want to be missed. It suddenly occurred to him that he didn't have a place reserved in which to sleep tonight. "We'll worry about that later," he thought. "The important thing is to bring Mr. Thresher up-to-date before Irwin talks to him." He leaned against one of the tall Roman columns. The carving on top was festooned with pigeon droppings. "Is that a Doric or Ionic capital?" he idly wondered. But he didn't really care.

He had been standing outside for a few minutes when a svelte woman sidled up to him. The country was in the grip of Prohibition, of course, but he didn't drink liquor except for champagne. He had simply ignored all the controversy surrounding this restriction on one's freedom. Nevertheless, he had no trouble recognizing the strong odor of bourbon on this woman's breath. She was dressed in some sort of fur coat with one of those popular soup-bowl hats, as he called them, which nestled close to the woman's face as though providing a frame for her heavy makeup.

She came real close to him and, in a breathy voice, asked, "Could you be a sailor? You've got that look, as though you were returning from some faraway place. If you'll come back to my room, I'll remind you what's it's like to be a lover in America!" As she said this, she opened the front of her coat to reveal attractive lingerie beneath. No dress, just satin brassiere and lace-fringed panties. Her eyes remained on his, watching him carefully.

Despite his being preoccupied with thoughts about Jim's inventions, he did steal a glance her way, taking in the sights which this woman was providing as a sort of preview.

After looking her up and down, he replied, "I'm so sorry, ma'am, but I'm actually meeting someone. He's my boss, he'll be irritated coming out late like this, and I expect him to arrive shortly. It's business; I can't put him off. But thank you very much for your generous offer."

Rebuffed, the woman's entire demeanor instantly changed. Using strong epithets that would raise the hair on even a sailor's head, she swore at him as she pirouetted and stalked away. Charles couldn't be sure, but he thought he saw a shadowy figure of some large man slip behind the far corner of the building as the woman-of-the-street sashayed in that direction.

Ruefully, Charles thought to himself, "Probably this prostitute was merely a front for that bum up the street. I'll bet I just saved myself from being hit over the head and robbed. What a joke that would have been! I have no more than three dollars on me."

He decided this was not the place to go rummaging through his wallet. He left it resting safely strapped to his inner left leg and out of sight beneath his trousers. This ritual was what he always did when visiting a place such as the Big Apple. His concerns vanished as Jacob Thresher's car pulled into the drop-off lane. Charles opened the door and slammed it shut in one swift move that surprised Jacob.

As they drove away, Jacob looked over at Charles and remarked, "You made kind of a fast exit there, son. Have any trouble?"

"I was propositioned while waiting for you. A minute earlier and you would have seen her for yourself."

"No thanks. That's not for me. I had enough bouts with venereal disease when I was younger and crewing on ships for Oceanic Lines around the turn of the century. If we get to know each other better, I'll sit back, light up my pipe, and regale you with some of my own tales. For now, you'll just have to take my being worldly-wise on faith."

"That's good enough for me," replied Charles, relieved that he was now out of any danger, or temptation. The things he was about to relate to his mentor would be hair-raising enough without adding in adventure along the streets of New York City.

Thresher's car zoomed across the Brooklyn Bridge as the two men, proctor and trainee, headed for the comfort of Jacob's home.

CHAPTER THIRTY

HOLLY'S NEWS

Evening shadows danced among the gravestones at the Church of the Redeemer as twilight eased into the gentle oranges and pinks of a springtime sunset. Cool breezes began to flutter the newly budding leaves.

I shook hands with Matt Johnson even as I apologized for failing to talk with him more fully. "Any friend of Jim Stahl would be a friend of mine as well," I had assured him, but then Mary and I turned our attention to piling the kids into our car. As we headed home to Rhode Island, the usual teenaged bickering and squabbling coming from the rear seat was all the more animated; I had offered to take Miss Holly North back to Providence with us.

Mary turned around to face the rear seat and, with a twinkle in her eye, asked, "Holly, I know this was a day of sad observance; Jim was very close to each of us. I suspect, however, you are very happy that you did not stay home feigning some illness as an excuse."

"I don't know what you mean, Mrs. Matthews. Why would you say that?" Holly could feint and jab with the best of them.

"Because we saw you; you were all over that tall man with the unshaven face. You can't hide it!" Alice was gleeful over the chance to gossip. At 13, she was just beginning to be aware there was more to boys than frogs, freckles, and slingshots. She pressed her probing: "Why did he keep punching your arm? I thought your right one was going to fall off from all his pushing?"

"Alice, honey, don't bother Holly with all your pestering," her mother scolded. "He wasn't punching her; Charles was merely adding tactile communication to their eye contact."

"Mother! What are you talking about? The two of them couldn't keep their hands off one another!"

"Oh Alice, how you do go on," Mary responded. However, she immediately asked her own leading question. "You two sure were flirting! My father used to call what you were doing as 'giving the feelies' to each other. Rather brazen behavior, given that we were attending a funeral, if you ask me."

"She's not pestering, she's simply asking." piped up Bill. At 17, he already knew he was very interested in girls, despite his loud and annoying younger sister. Alice had, nevertheless, roused his curiosity about the "tall dark stranger" who had so focused Holly's attention during the afternoon.

"Now, look everybody. There's nothing to get all excited about. His name is Charles McDonald; he grew up in Providence and joined Oceanic Lines after leaving high school. He's completing his apprenticeship and thus sails around the ocean getting his 'sea legs,' as the saying goes. The reason we were so interested in one another was our mutual friendship with James Stahl. Charles, as a matter of fact, saved the captain's life when he was in danger of falling from the *Reliance* during a lifeboat operation."

Thereupon, I chimed in, "And I saved the lad when the captain slipped and began falling. The two of them were about to go over the side together when me and the boys caught them."

"Fine, so they have something in common. That doesn't explain why he kept touching you, or why you kept touching him back, while sitting on that bench together." Alice was persistent. The youngster wanted the real lowdown.

"Alice! Now dear, control yourself. Let Holly do the talking." admonished her mother. Turning to face Holly full on, she inquired, "Tell us. Are you attracted to him?"

"Oh golly gee, Mrs. Matthews, I'm just bursting! I've got to tell someone!" Holly's face flushed with excitement. Her deep-seated feelings bubbling to the surface were clearly visible to everyone in the car, even me; I could see her happily animated face in the rearview mirror.

"I think I've fallen for him," gushed Holly. "I'm beyond my most colorful imaginings of what love would be like. I can't wait to see him again. He's returning to New York City now. I don't have any idea when he'll come back to Providence, but I just know he is the right one for me!"

The car fell silent for a moment while everyone else digested the full import of this revelation.

Bill put the lid on the exuberance. "Boy, who would have thought you'd have to go to a funeral to find love. That's not my idea of a romantic setting at all."

His mother retorted, "Dear, you'd be surprised at the places, and moments, when love comes a-calling. Cupid has a timetable which we humans cannot discern."

Turning to address Holly again, Mary asked: "How will you arrange to see him? Are you going to travel down to New York?"

"No. I'm going to be right at home and thus available should he call. He's at a point in his life where events will dictate what he does and where he goes. His schedule is not for him to direct. I'm going to be patient and await his return to me."

"Why?" asked Bill, somewhat confused. If he saw a girl he desired, he pursued her right away while brushing aside all obstacles.

"Because he's the man I want." Holly's direct, assured affirmation left us, again, without any retort. This girl was spoken for, and that was that.

As the car sped along close to fifty miles per hour, Mary looked over at me. To her, I looked strongly attractive in my manliness and, at last, self-assurance. True, I was once again adrift without an active ship assignment, but this time there was an inner light that sparkled in my eyes. Unlike my tortured, drunken behavior of a month ago, she perceived that I now possessed an inner confidence that would make me successful. As we journeyed homeward, there was no need for her to say something lachrymose. Mary relaxed; she innately knew that her husband would continue to provide for their children when she was gone. Most importantly to her, I could furnish love, not merely a watertight roof.

When the time came, she would hate having to say good-bye. However, she possessed one certainty which she would carry with her as she passed on: I had made her life all that she could have wished for.

CHAPTER THIRTY-ONE

OWNERSHIP OF THE DRAWINGS

Jacob Thresher sat back in his favorite office chair, drawing on a cigar as he regarded the all too exuberant lad sitting opposite him. On the surface, this stripling was a mere trainee who should be out on the seas wading slowly through the lessons of ship management. Instead, he was the possessor of concepts that, if proven to be workable, could revolutionize shipbuilding for the next century.

After fetching him at the train station, Thresher had offered to put Charles up for the night. In the morning, they'd come into his office at 78 Second Avenue together. While driving in, Charles had related the saga of his training aboard the *Humboldt*, his promotion to captain's orderly, his assignment aboard the *Reliance* to assist its captain, his bonding with Jim Stahl, the subsequent agreement to pursue development of the plans depicted in his drawings, and then the death of Captain Stahl.

"Charles, this is some tale! It's so out-of-this-world that I don't think anybody could even dream up such a wild scenario. You rescue Jim, and then he turns right around and saves your life! To think that, later, you would be picked up by Dale Irwin, of all people! I never met him myself, but some of the escapades he got himself caught in while on board that Navy destroyer were stuff of scuttlebutt throughout the service. You mentioned it, but I forget… That's it, the *Wickes*! By golly, if you'd been old enough to be part of those escapades, you'd have white hair already. I'm surprised that your friend, Wallace Matthews, never heard anything about the man. Wallace would have been what, 35 or so in 1915? Shortly after that, of course, Irwin landed in the brig for a time, so perhaps his reputation had died down when your friend was serving."

"Actually, Mr. Thresher, I don't believe Wallace has been associated with the military, either during the war, or indeed ever. He was telling me about an event some 25 years back, near the beginning of the century, when some seaman in an engine room had been burned following an explosion in a boiler. Sometime during that rescue, Wally suffered a permanent injury that eliminated any chance of him serving in the army. I'm sorry, I don't recall what it was; we had very important matters that we were discussing at the time, and it's slipped my mind. But I do recall his having said that this event led to him befriending Jim Stahl, so in that respect it was very important."

Charles paused for a moment as he reflected on some vivid memories. Then he continued: "Naturally, one of the first things I want to arrange is for you to meet him, as well as Captain Peter North. We can include Reggie if he is not otherwise assigned and commanding a ship on the high seas somewhere. I must say, that captain does love his work."

Even as he expressed this opinion, Charles smiled. He had enjoyed being around the eager enthusiasm of Reginald Highsmith very much.

Mr. Thresher's reply only added to the young man's estimation of his former captain.

"I'm sure he does, and he's very good at it. You probably didn't know this, but he is one of only two men in active command of ships that has never had an accident on the high seas. I don't mean companywide; I mean any captain, throughout the country. That's quite an accomplishment. Even the esteemed Edwin J. Smith had at least three collisions while he was in a command position, if I recall correctly. And he held the title of Commodore of White Star Line! There are people in the industry who regard that as being on the left hand of the Father, since Christ already occupies the right. I bet you can't tell me who holds the other spotless record."

"Come on, Mr. Thresher. If you're going to question me, at least ask me something that's challenging! You're referring to Arthur Harold Rostron, of course. Even at my age, I admire him."

"So you should. His record should serve as an inspiration to all who strive to command a ship of their own."

"Quite so. What I've read about him surely inspires me. Don't mention him to Wallace, however. That poor man was tossed out on his ear, albeit politely, when he applied for a position aboard one of Rostron's commands. Of course, he didn't go into detail with me, but the reason could have been the same that kept him out of the military. I like him a lot, and am coming around to trusting him as well, but never ask me to pry into his personal weaknesses. Those are his private affair."

Charles then placed each hand on a knee, as though doing so would confirm the strength of his opinion.

"Don't worry, I agree," stated Jacob. "Now, let me review again exactly who is familiar with these plans. There's Wallace, and Reggie of course, but he's sailing this coming Saturday and will be at sea through the month of May, certainly. You mentioned your Uncle Cyrus McDonald who, as yet, knows nothing about Stahl's designs, but who could be very helpful obtaining interviews with Department of the Navy admirals. Obviously, we'll want to involve our president, Orville Townsend. Then there's Peter North, who apparently has had the plans for nearly 25 years, yet has never acted on them. Perhaps he hasn't even looked at them, but was simply retaining a safe copy for his best friend. We should ask him what his position would be regarding developing his friend's ideas."

"Let me interrupt you there, sir," Charles said earnestly. "When we were at Jim Stahl's funeral together, Mr. North told me that he had just been detailed to the submarine construction works at Groton, Connecticut. Captain North's new job will entail developing diesel underwater propulsion systems that will take such craft out of the battery dependent arena, give them longer operating range, and permit far better submerged capabilities. The reason for his transfer from Newport News is not secret; you have only to read the newspapers to see that Germany is not living up to the tenets of the Armistice or the Versailles Treaty. Clearly, our government is beginning to think in terms of the possibility of some future conflict; doubtless, Uncle Sam wants us to be in the forefront of technological development rather than left wallowing in the wake of the future.

"There were some German passengers aboard the *Humboldt*. During my stint there, the apprenticeship I was performing—prior to being assigned as Captain Highsmith's Orderly—was serving those very passengers. They occupied cabins on A Deck along with a boisterous group of Hollywood movie stars. The Americans didn't awe them one bit. The foreigners were very boastful of their own superiority. The Germanic people are capable, intellectually advanced, even strong willed; their great weakness may be insecurity, because they seem to want everyone around them to know just how grand they are.

"During our voyage, several of them mentioned the name of one Adolf Schicklgruber, who has taken the surname of 'Hitler' now that his political party has gained some standing with the people over there. Those passengers on the *Humboldt* seemed utterly enamored of that man."

When he finished speaking, Charles sat back, somewhat surprised at his own erudition.

Unfazed, Mr. Thresher replied, "Yes, I have heard his name. President Townsend himself mentioned that man at our last board meeting, pointing out that if he should ever come to rule Germany, he would do so as an autocrat. One of his prime goals would be to stimulate the Prussian economy, so he would surely emphasize ocean-going ships. If I understand that man correctly—and I think I do, having read his book, *Mein Kompf*—what he constructs will be heavily weighted to warships, with very modern armament, speed, and survivability if shelled. With that background, your 'friend,' if I may make a joke, Dale Irwin was correct in seeing the military value of Stahl's ideas.

"Of course, as far as you and I are concerned, civilian applications for faster crossings should be our priority for the moment. Perhaps the Navy, if they see value in draftsman Stahl's projections, will undertake substantial testing for us as a sort of screen to the public, while they are really evaluating the results for development of new types of fast destroyers and such. If these concepts flop, we won't be any the worse off since the Navy would have provided the funding for the tests. If, on the other hand, Stahl's ideas work, his renderings could introduce the world to an entirely different class of ships in whatever capacity.

"Okay, let's review again. There's you, me, possibly Reggie, most likely Townsend, then Matthews, North, probably Cyrus McDonald who has yet to be contacted, and Irwin who of course will have to be contained. Is there anyone else?"

"Good heavens, sir, don't leave out Frank Jones!" Charles stated with affirmation. "He is the only surviving person I know about who understands Jim's ideas, inside and out! All the progress that the captain achieved with those concepts is due to the development testing that Jones performed, albeit his work is now some two decades or more old. We simply have to have him aboard. I think he works at New York Shipbuilding Company located in Camden, New Jersey.

"Then there are two close friends of Stahl, his roommates Matt Dillon and Art Townsend, who attended Providence Maritime Institute with him. Peter North was the fourth roommate. You already know about Peter's possessing the copy which Jim sent to him prior to the explosion at Cummins & Company. However, I don't think the other two ever got involved with this project. Frankly, Mr. Thresher, I don't have any idea what they do for a living, or even where they are now. Matt was at the funeral, but I was too busy to do more than shake hands with him. Do you want me to contact either of them?"

"Let me talk to President Townsend about them, first. He no doubt has contacts that can let him know their whereabouts and occupation. We can always contact the alumni office at P.M.I., if nothing else turns up."

"That's a great idea! Why not let me go see them in person? The school is in my hometown, you know," Charles stated brightly.

"We'll see. Let me talk to the boss first. I want you to focus on your prime mission, which is contacting Cyrus, right?"

"Golly yes! See, sir, I still need your guidance to insure I stay pointed in the required direction."

"I'm pretty certain, Charles McDonald, that you have learned how to stay focused all by yourself at this point."

"Thank you, sir. Now, there's one other individual I have not yet told you about because we've been so focused on the drawings. I simply haven't gotten round to mentioning him. When Mr. Stahl worked in the drafting department of Cummins & Company, he was promoted to a vice-presidency and soon thereafter took under his wing a teenager named Scott Terry. It was this man who traced and then posted a copy of Jim's earliest drawings to Peter North. Subsequently, he became a capable naval architect in his own right. He's the one who drew up the naval designs and fitting out plans for the *Reliance*, in fact. He is currently in Germany visiting some Bremerhaven ship yards this week; it was too difficult for him to return in time for Jim's funeral. I've never met him, but from the little I know, he ought to at least be told where you and I stand. He might well be interested in joining us. My information is that he will return to the States sometime next week. I assume his return would be to Providence because that's where the head office of A.T.C. is located. Perhaps Lois can call up there to check on this."

Taking a long breath in, Charles concluded: "To the best of my knowledge, that's it."

Jacob's eyebrows rose as he looked over at his companion. "Do I detect that you have developed a certain fondness for our gal Lois, Charles?"

"Hey, come now, Mr. Thresher. I bet you yourself have given her a mighty full once-over! She is very comely. But no, I have my eyes completely focused on a woman I met at the funeral. Her name is Holly, and she is, of all coincidences, the daughter of Peter North. Holly was very close to her dad's best friend, Jim Stahl, so we had someone dear to us in common to talk about. We got pretty friendly and frankly, Mr. Thresher, I am now a man smitten with love. If it hadn't been for these documents we're reviewing, I'd have found some reason to delay my return, for certain!"

"You don't say! The world does seem to turn in circles with interconnectedness, doesn't it?" Then, smiling as he winked at Charles, he added, "You certainly do get around, don't you?"

"Sorry, sir, you trained me to keep my eyes and ears open at all times. Now, I'm so accustomed to listening to others that I pick up stuff without being aware I'm doing it."

"Good lad. By the way, that may be the last time I can refer to you like that, do you know?"

"Why do you say that, Mr. Thresher?" Charles was momentarily perplexed and looked over at his proctor.

Jacob Thresher put a hand on his young trainee's shoulder. "Charles," he began soberly, "I think under the circumstances, you won't mind if I certify that, as of today, you have completed your apprenticeship for Oceanic Lines and you are now ready for real work. I will suggest to President Townsend that you should be assigned to my design office; this means you will report directly to me. If we are going to be working closely together, I want you to call me Jake. Does that suit you?"

"Well, certainly sir! Thank you very much!" Charles couldn't keep his face from glowing with pride.

"Now, how shall we get all these diverse personages together, and under what cover?"

"The first step has to be for me to go to Washington and speak with Uncle Cyrus. I'll call my father and get something set up, if you concur."

"Very good. In the meantime, I'm going to send a special secure post to Matthews, North, and Jones introducing myself, updating them as to where you and I stand, and soliciting their cooperation and input. Does that sound appropriate to you?"

"That it does, indeed!" Charles felt the blood coursing through his veins. A new direction for his life was about to begin. His first move would be to ask Lois whether she could help him contact the Bureau of Naval Affairs in Washington, D.C. Standing at her desk while soliciting her assistance would not be an unpleasant prospect; indeed, she did have something to report to him.

When he reached the reception area, she looked his way and Lois smiled as brightly as she could.

"Well, well, look who is back! You do look a little the worse for wear, however. Perhaps a day off would be good?"

"There's not a chance of that happening, Lois, although I do appreciate the idea. Perhaps next year I'll have time for a nap." They both chuckled at this unrealistic fantasy, but then Charles asked, "By the way, has that fellow Dale Irwin come crawling around here again?"

"No, Mr. McDonald, but he sure has been calling. Three times today, already. I kept saying Mr. Thresher was tied up in a meeting, which of course was true enough."

Charles stroked his nascent beard. He'd been away from a shave for nearly four weeks, and looked it. He had stopped shaving once he became a captain's orderly. He had been well pleased with its growth. Even and full, this beard would set off the sculpted features of his cheekbones and complement his full eyebrows. He had even become impatient to see how it would grow if left to its own devices. He suspected that a beard would make him look more mature, and that would make him more authoritative when he spoke. He'd give it another month and see how it made him feel.

"My feeling is that it'd be okay to put him through if he calls again. I'm pretty sure Mr. Thresher will be prepared to handle him at this point." His face radiated confidence.

"Certainly, sir. That would be a pleasure."

Charles started to say something, but Lois held up a finger as she turned her full attention to her console. Pressing the headphone close to her ear, she stayed motionless for a second, then she gave an acknowledgement. "Yes, sir, he's standing right here. Would you like me to send him upstairs?" A pause, then: "Certainly sir, right away!'"

Lois turned to McDonald and said," The president would like you to come up to his office immediately. Do you know your way there?"

Never having been to President Townsend's suite before, Charles asked for the necessary guidance. Lois gave clear instructions, so he soon found himself standing in front of the august presence of Orville Townsend himself. Matching Charles' 6 feet, two inches of height, the president carried the additional authority of some 240 pounds that filled his buttoned vest to bursting. After forty years in the business, his hair was now silver but still full and sleek. He wore it combed backward so it framed his florid face. When he spoke, you listened. He had the kind of personal magnetism which makes a person feel lucky to be in the presence of profound wisdom.

Leaning forward, he offered Charles a chair next to the already seated Jacob Thresher. He proffered a cigar but Charles refused. The young man wanted to keep his head clear.

President Townsend opened with, "Thresher here tells me you have come into possession of some important documents that incorporate concepts far ahead of the industry standards to which we currently subscribe. Do you have them with you?"

"No, Sir. They are sequestered in Reginald Highsmith's office. You may know I was serving as his Orderly at the time of the demise of *Reliance*. If Reggie is in, he could bring them right along."

Townsend leaned his bulk forward and spoke into what looked like some sort of talking box.

"Miss Thorne, please call Reginald Highsmith and ask him to come to my office. Tell him to drop whatever he may be doing at the moment. Also, have him bring up all the documents pertaining to one James Stahl. Thank you."

Turning to look Thresher's way, he suggested, "I think it's time we gave a name to this project. What do you think of calling it: *'Project James?'* No outsider will know what the hell we're referring to, but all of us will instantly know what it entails."

Both his subordinates readily agreed, but then his phone buzzed. "Yes, Miss Thorne," Townsend asked while holding the receiver close to his ear. "I see, I'll take care of it. Keep him on the line for another minute, will you? Thanks."

As he returned the device to its cradle, he said to Jacob: "There's a Mister Dale Irwin on the line asking to speak with you. This is his fourth call today, apparently. Can you handle this one?"

"I sure can. I've been expecting him. I'll take it in my office."

As he left, Reggie Highsmith appeared at the door holding a wad of folded documents. "May I come in, Orville?"

"Certainly! Enter."

Upon spotting Charles, he greeted him with "Hello, young man. Compared to the other day, this is a cause for real excitement!"

"Hi, Reggie. I've brought Jacob up to date, and he was doing the same with President Townsend when the boss suggested that we take a look at Stahl's drawings. By the way, we're referring to them as *Project James* from here on."

"That's fine with me. Well, here they are." And with that, Reggie spread the pod-hull schematics on the floor of Townsend's office. Laid out all together like this, their significance and originality were far more evident than mere words could convey.

The room fell silent as the men in the room pondered what they were seeing. When Thresher retuned, all aglow from having rid himself of the presupposing Commander Irwin, he gasped. He was head of Oceanic's design department as well as its training division, but he'd never conceived anything like what he was seeing laid out in detail on the rug.

President Townsend, stroking his chin in thought, was the first to break the silence. "Why didn't James Stahl pursue development of these, Charles?"

Before he answered, Charles collected himself. This was going to be tough.

"Sir, Jim conceived the idea for these hull shapes while watching his wife ice skating. She showed him the hollowed blade used for figure skates and the upturned nose short of the teeth. Jim experimented with applying similar principles to watercraft but vastly upgrading them to sustain hulls carrying thousands of tons of weight. Someone named Frank Jones helped him with testing the concepts on water with miniature wooden models. Along the way, a freak gas explosion killed his wife and nascent child, the president of his company, both his parents, the management staff at Cummins & Co., and many of his fellow draftsmen. The resulting fire consumed all documents located in the headquarters building.

"Frank Jones, as a technician, had not been invited, but his company now no longer existed, so he took a job elsewhere and has never gone behind Stahl's back to develop these ideas independently. From what I've heard, he'd be a very good man to have on our team, but I haven't yet met him.

"Even though Jim had conceived these ideas, their association with this most crushing of tragedies was simply too much for him to bear. It is my belief that he held on to the hope that someday they could be proven and developed, but he simply couldn't bring himself to personally do it. When he and I met, we found a common ground of mutual trust; in fact, we were going to pursue their testing and development as partners. Straightaway, however, he died while saving my life as we watched the *Reliance* go down.

Pausing, he hung his head and asked, "Gentlemen, will you give me a moment? I need to collect myself."

"Certainly, Charles, take whatever time you need. We'll be right here when you're ready to return."

When Charles left, Townsend closed the door behind him. "Reggie, Jake, have you ever heard such a saga? I see in this employee someone who, while woefully undertrained in the discipline of naval architecture, demonstrates an innate grasp of the concepts and principles. More importantly, he would pursue design and development with a zeal that is fueled by inner empathy. He would make the safety of passengers his foremost priority. I'm accustomed to my people providing me with answers and ideas because they enjoy their job and like working with me. This man, however, would bring a deeply held sense of personal commitment to his work."

"I couldn't agree more, sir. I recognized it aboard the *Humboldt* simply from the stewards' evaluations of him regarding the passengers. As my orderly, he exhibited a drive to be fully prepared and strove daily to increase the breadth of his knowledge. In a crisis situation, there's no one I'd rather have at my side."

Reggie's face was totally relaxed, evoking an air of absolute confidence in what he had just stated. Quickly, Mr. Thresher spoke up.

"There's no sense in my holding back either, sir. I've told him he has completed his apprenticeship and have taken him on as my personal assistant in the design section. He's too young to have encountered such problems as funds allocation or project terminal deadlines, so my plan is to insulate him from all the normal parameters that guide our development processes. His advantage is an instinctive feel for what is important, and that gives him sharp focus and also powers his drive. I trust I have made the right move here, sir."

Once more stroking his chin in thought, the president paced around the drawings for a bit longer, and then he looked up at Thresher.

"Quite so. Good thinking, Jacob! Now, and this is important, kindly dissuade young McDonald from making contact with his uncle or anyone else at the Department of Naval Affairs. The timing is far too premature. Besides, the more people who are brought into this, the greater the likelihood that the plans will leak out or, worse, someone purloins them. Let's keep this *Project James* known only to a small group of ten or fewer until we have something demonstrable that can be patented. Got that?"

His cohorts nodded his way. There was a knock on the door and Orville asked, "Yes?"

"Sir, it's McDonald. May I come in, sir?"

"Absolutely, son, come right on in! We as a group think these drawings represent an entirely new approach to hull design. I have conferred with Mr. Thresher and have approved his taking you on as his aide. We will refer to you as 'Special Design Assistant.' I don't want to let our competition know that we are up to something by associating your title with a specific project, so keep your stationery and correspondence free of any reference to 'Pod Craft' or 'Project James.' Does that suit you, my boy?"

"Thank you, sir. I hope I've not misled you into thinking I can improve on these designs. I'm too technically ignorant at present. I could manage an office or tell you the location of most any type of appliance affixed to a passenger liner, but I don't even know what to call the tools used to make these renderings."

McDonald wanted to be up front with these men; he would need their trust in order to bring the design parameters to life.

"We know, we know. Don't worry; such knowledge will come with time. Now, let's establish a safe-keeping rack for these drawings. We should produce a backup tracing right away. Jacob, have you found space for this young assistant yet?"

"That is my next task as soon as our meeting is ended," replied Mr. Thresher.

"Very good!" Then, picking up the intercom, he directed Miss Thorne to send up a copy boy, shook Charles' hand, and patted Reggie on the back as he showed him the door.

"I understand you're sailing again this Saturday, is that right, Captain?"

"Yes, the *Humboldt* is getting prepared to voyage along the Mediterranean coasts. The weather should be ideal in May. May I bring you back anything from Italy or Africa, Orville?"

"No, no, just make it a safe transit, will you? Thank you, Reggie. You've a sharp eye for talent, and you've done a good job bringing this fellow along. Thank you, again."

President Townsend shook Reggie's hand warmly and then sent him on his way.

"Jacob, stay behind a minute, will you?"

When the two men were alone together, the president inquired, "What is this I hear about some navy commander wanting to horn in on this *Project James*? Dale Irwin, is that his name?"

"Mr. Townsend, I have not yet met him. I told him flatly on the phone that the drawings were the property of Charles McDonald, and by extension as an Oceanic employee, ours since he was on company business at the time Mr. Stahl entrusted them to him. Irwin got very indignant and hung up on me. We ought to notify our lawyers; I doubt very much whether Dale Irwin will let this matter drop."

"Good, good, I agree."

Then, picking up his intercom mouthpiece again, President Townsend said, "Miss Thorne, get me Martin Standish over at the Morris & Drayton law office, please. When you get a chance, come in prepared to take dictation for three telegrams I want to send out immediately. Thank you."

CHAPTER THIRTY-TWO

GROUP OF SEVEN

In early May, two things happened to Charles McDonald. He turned 21 years of age on the 8th, so he was granted the day off to be with his folks. The next day, Thursday the 9th of May, 1929, he was freed from the constraints by which novice seamen are bound. Moreover, he was now to be included in the corporate deliberations process. He found himself seated alongside the august president of Oceanic, Mr. Orville Townsend, together with Peter North, Frank Jones, and myself, Wallace Matthews. A short time after everyone had introduced themselves, Scott Terry entered, apologizing for being late. He had taken the train down from Providence that very morning but there'd been a delay. After introductions, Jacob Thresher entered and passed around cups of coffee.

When everyone quieted down, President Townsend began to speak.

"Gentlemen, thank you for coming. Look around the room; there are seven of us here today. Only Reggie Highsmith is missing. That man will be commanding a voyage through June, so he has asked that we proceed as we see fit during his absence. I apologize for the sudden urgency of holding this meeting, and especially I convey my thanks to those of you who have not met with me prior to today.

"Our link-pin is, of course, James Stahl, and now with his passing, it is Charles McDonald. He is far younger, and much less experienced, than you others, but he's very quick off the mark and we have undertaken to accelerate his acquisition of drafting skills so he can speak on a level equal with the rest of us. After our discussion of the pod-craft drawings, we'll break for lunch so everyone can become acquainted socially.

Orville Townsend now leaned forward in order to speak more intimately with the six of us.

"Here is what I want you gentlemen to test, rework, and finalize for full-scale development."

He then uncovered eight easels. These displayed Stahl's design drawings. Together, they clearly showed the interrelationship of the four support pods as well as the utilization of their interiors. The support structure would be sized according to "X" number of decks riding atop four pods. Design of superstructures would follow only if the concept of using support pods, rather than hulls, was seaworthy.

"And, of course, marketable," he added as an afterthought. Then Mr. Townsend forged ahead.

"I am assuming overall authority for this venture based on our legal counsel affirming that our company has primacy in regard to ownership of the drawings. I won't bore you with the details; we have the documents legally, and unless we are challenged somewhere along the line, why we are the legal holders regarding their use and development is not important to you.

"What should be important is that all of you are skilled, young enough to be vigorous, and possess sufficient experience to make sound technical decisions. Moreover, you are not going to be disadvantaged coming here to work. Each of you will be furnished with funding at your current income and benefit levels. So, except for giving up much of your social life, you should stay even with your current economic status. All except Peter North; he will be a part-time consultant during development and testing due to his position at General Dynamics in Groton. When actual presentation to a sales prospect will become appropriate, Peter will be our key player given his industry contacts within the navy department.

"Why would you want to leave a situation with which you are familiar? The reason is this: each of you will be given the opportunity to sign a contract with Oceanic Lines that guarantees your participation in a distribution of 5% of the revenue, and let me repeat that word, "revenue" as opposed to profit, which Oceanic makes off your final designs. This is intended to encourage you to share amongst yourselves the tremendous challenges this project will entail; the more people you request to be brought in to assist you, the smaller your individual share will be. If the concepts fail to work, you will have the steady income my company is providing to sustain you and your family. Oceanic will be assuming substantial cost risks as development goes forward and increasingly sophisticated test facilities are required. That's in addition to payment of your salaries. We feel this is a high risk, but even higher reward, project that simply cannot be ignored.

"I am no snake oil salesman. I offer no panaceas. If each of you will ponder what I have put forth, I believe that Project James will be successful. Ten years hence, you could all be millionaires. That prospect is certainly enough for me to be fully involved as coordinator and facilitator. This company stands to profit from what remains after expenses and your 30% revenue participation.

"At this point, I would like Frank Jones to come forward to introduce himself, explain his relationship with the late James Stahl, and relate what he observed and discovered while testing these concepts in the past. Mr. Jones, I hope you will allow each of us to pose questions to you as they come to mind. Currently, you are far ahead of us in regard to understanding these projections. I turn the floor over to Mr. Jones."

With that said, Mr. Townsend sat in back of those present. He had enormous affection for Reginald Highsmith, but that ship's captain was in a job for which he was born. Orville suspected that he would never get himself fired up by *Project James* like these men appeared to be right from the start. He would ask Highsmith to voluntarily withdraw. These six were about to lose themselves in a project with mammoth potential benefits, but taking it on would require their total commitment to the exclusion of a normal workaday life.

Frank Jones reviewed the results of his original testing, and then McDonald stood up to explain the improvements made since. All the while, Townsend sat quietly listening. He had to mull over a location for this new project. It needed large, secret, and enclosed test facilities, secure means of communication with his office in New York and, if Project James got that far, actual testing in the ocean. McDonald, Matthews, and Terry were already located in Providence; he decided that would be the site for this project. North would be close by in Connecticut. He'd transfer Thresher there to head up the team, and pay relocation expenses for Mr. Jones. Bringing these new concepts to a state of reliable operation and acceptance in the market place would be challenging, but he'd done so many times before with both the design, and management, of the company's existing ocean liners.

The one unknown with which he'd have to deal was whether these six could go it alone. Were these men sufficiently cohesive that they could motivate each other, when setbacks occurred, to keep on trying? He suddenly sat back, relaxed with his conclusions. He saw it all clearly. Let them do the thinking and testing as a team; he'd do the worrying and bankrolling.

*   *   *

As it turned out, it would take our group four years to finalize the design, specifications, and working prototype of the Pod Skimmer, as it affectionately came to be called. Along the way, the configuration was altered to include two large stern pods, but a single broad one in the bow.

We seven members took as our rallying cry: *Act safe and think hard, but maintain your guard*! I must admit, collectively we found it difficult to adhere to our own maxim.

As we progressed, Dale Irwin filed for an injunction in federal district court to grant him participation rights based on the fact that James Stahl had a living relative. It was claimed that Jim's father, Sam, had a brother named Harry Stahl who was married. A first cousin was put forward as being the child of Harry and his wife Lilly. At the time of suit, that cousin was a woman fifty-two years old who was betrothed to Mr. Irwin. The claim was thrown out when it was proved that the lady in question was the daughter of Lilly and her first husband, a man who was entirely unrelated to the Stahls. When Harry and Lilly had married, this girl had been nineteen and was therefore never adopted by Harry.

As things worked out, Dale and the bogus cousin never went through with nuptials of their own. At the shop, we had a good laugh; clearly, the man had been "grasping at straw skirts," as we liked to say. Martin Standish, Esq., attorney for Oceanic Lines, also moved for and was granted a Restraining Order on Mr. Irwin preventing his interference with any future project sponsored or developed by his client.

Subsequent to his original filing, a further action was instituted by Irwin for design infringement. He partnered with one of Frank Jones' assistants, Cecil Cooper, claiming prior ownership of the design drawings as stemming from original work performed by Cooper prior to 1906. The judge threw the claim out, and added a hefty fine against Dale Irwin for bringing yet another sham suit before his bench.

In 1933, finally freed from legal harassment if not subterfuge, and secure in our efforts by the issuance of patents on the collaborative designs, we created a full-scale prototype in the secretive confines of our Providence workshop. The Holy Grail would be finding a metal that had high strength-to-weight ratios, resisted corrosion, but was not expensive. We didn't ask for much. Nevertheless, even as the Depression grabbed the heartland of the country by the throat, there were new techniques, such as inert-gas arc welding, and the prospect of light, metal alloys, that gave the team real hope that our work would pay off. Our latest all-metal prototype offered propulsion, fuel storage, operations platform, steering mechanisms, and a three-point flotation base. Since a superstructure would be specifically oriented to a future customer's requirements, such design criteria could be put off until a buyer was located.

What direction should the company go? Should the Pod Skimmer be reserved for vessels constructed only by Oceanic's subsidiary, R. I. B. Shipbuilding Company, or should the designs be offered to outside competitors, or even the military? The debate between me and my compatriots regarding Project James was prolonged, detailed, and at times heated.

The decision was finally made by Orville Townsend himself during August: we would make an initial presentation to the U.S. Navy around the middle of September. At this stage, the coffer from which Oceanic had drawn some $400,000 for Project James was emptying. Further development would be severely hampered by the lack of available commercial lending; banks simply had no more capital with which to make loans. Mr. Townsend sensed that trying to initiate sales to corporate shipping firms at this time would be fruitless. Passenger traffic worldwide had fallen off dramatically.

President Townsend therefore opted for a presentation to Admiral Samuel Williston and his design staff at the Department of Naval Affairs as our best bet.

By the fall of 1933, the country was spiraling into an ever deeper depression as bank after bank failed. However, there was one salient beacon of hope: Franklin Delano Roosevelt had entered office some months before, on March 4, and had immediately set about developing programs that would encourage Americans to pull themselves up by their bootstraps. His administration undertook programs designed to restore pride as well as income for families. The government was not about to simply dole out money; it would provide jobs. These jobs provided the opportunity for a man to be a provider, earn his keep, and restore his dignity.

Moreover, at one time President Roosevelt had been Secretary of the Navy. Like Roosevelt, Townsend was all too aware of the threats to world freedom that were nascent in Europe; he judged correctly that the navy, as a military branch, would be most receptive to hearing about the Pod Skimmer. Its capabilities would make their pursuit ships the fastest in the world. Drawings, specification lists, even steel prototypes must be offered. The focus was not on heavily armored protection; speed and maneuverability would be the prime selling points. Turbo electric motors, which were lighter and more compact than prior systems, a backswept, low-profile stack, a fathometer for constant depth readings, and sleek stabilization fins were offered. The primary weakness was the lack of a lightweight, waterproof outer skin.

Representative renderings of the design drawings follow.

Pod fins side view showing the far more massive rear pod since one houses the port and the other houses the starboard propulsion system as well as the seamen manning these engines. The decking is without any superstructure here. The turbine, generator, and electric motor are offered offset from the screw for gearing purposes.

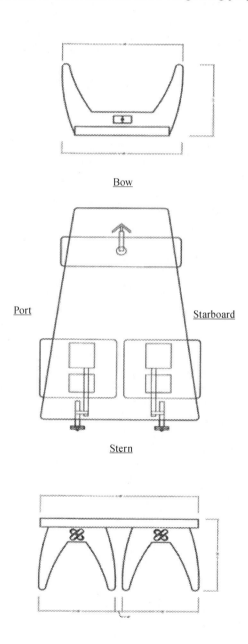

Bow

Port   Starboard

Stern

CHAPTER THIRTY-THREE

AN OLD FRIEND SAVES THE DAY

Behind closed doors at the office of the Secretary of the United States Navy, Admiral Williston leaned forward and said, "These are the documents you asked to see, Mr. President. My office has not communicated with the Group of Seven, as they are calling themselves, since they made their presentation to us. This man over here, Special Agent Art Dillon, is the one whom Vice-Admiral Ramage spoke to you about over the phone yesterday. Agent Dillon knew the person who initially developed these ideas. James Stahl and Agent Dillon were roommates at Providence Maritime Institute.

"As Admiral George Ramage explained to you yesterday, this agent is certain that Joseph Goebbels, and therefore Nazi Germany, is aware of the existence of these plans."

President Franklin Roosevelt removed the cigarette holder from his mouth as he bent forward to peruse the Pod Skimmer drawings. There followed a short silence.

"Let me explain, Mr. President," Rear-Admiral Ramage, a member of the President's Military Advisory Council, interjected. "These are concepts that the company, Oceanic Lines, refers to as 'Project James.' They claim their ideas work, although no actual vessel incorporating a superstructure supported by these pods has yet been built. Nevertheless, since the Group of Seven met with us last week, we have had our technicians and designers pore over these. Everyone is in agreement that these concepts are not just revolutionary, but that they could also completely change the face of conflict as it is currently conducted at sea.

"Troop ships embodying these Pod Skimmers would transport men to a war zone in a fraction of the time now required. It's possible they could be adapted to come right onto a beach and disgorge troops directly. They would have to be towed off, of course, but that would come later after invasion had already secured the area. Possibly, landings could be coordinated with tidal flows where appropriate.

"The speed of moving oil and supplies would be greatly improved. We have not tested the potential for outrunning a torpedo, but the shallow draft of these craft would certainly make sinking a Pod Skimmer more difficult.

"You can immediately see that they would not be suitable as a naval gun platform. The recoil from firing such large caliber guns could wreak havoc with their stability. Perhaps such a vessel could be adapted to carry torpedoes for offense and anti-aircraft guns for defense. We're not sure about depth charges; they may not be suitable for convoy duty, but our destroyers fill that niche already.

"Projected speeds exceed 50 knots. That would be some 50% faster than anything in our fleets. That is why the Germans are so interested. In our war games, we have never posited invasion onto our shores. However, interdicting supplies to Great Britain, France, and even the countries of Norway and Iceland would be high on Germany's list for submarine warfare. Vessels equipped with the Pod Skimmer under-frame could navigate between Denmark and the North Sea area effectively. They would unquestionably alter the conduct of war in the Mediterranean.

"If Congress votes to restrict their oil supplies, Japan will doubtless become aggressive toward the United States. These pod boats would be superior at operating throughout all the shallow water islands in the western Pacific, including our bases in the Philippines."

Admiral Ramage paused to allow Mr. Roosevelt a moment to digest all that he had just predicted. After some time, the overhead lights flashed reflectively off the President's glasses as he leaned back in his rocker chair.

"You know, boys, I think we can use these ideas to advantage. As a peace-abiding nation, we would need these, as well as God, on our side should Germany partner with Benito Mussolini and Emperor Hirohito!"

He moved his cigarette holder back to his mouth, took a deep puff, and then added, "We have two objectives before us. First, we want to get this Pod Skimmer built with an actual superstructure attached and test the heck out of it. I want you to authorize that to happen immediately, Admirals Ramage and Williston.

"Second, and possibly more importantly, we must not let the Germans, or even the Japanese, get their hands on these plans. Scuttlebutt can't be stopped, but these actual drawings, wherever located, must be secured and placed under the protection of a 24 hour guard. If the boys associated with the Group of Seven have to review these in the future, an armed guard must be present in the room to shepherd the documents back to their secure location.

"I am disturbed that Mr. Dillon is under the impression that the very lives of the Group of Seven are at risk. I will contact Mr. Hoover as soon as I return to the White House and confer with him on this matter, but in the meantime, Mr. Dillon, please have your superior contact me. We have got to get notice to those men and figure out some way to protect them without impeding their progress in developing a prototype.

"I should not have to remind you gentlemen about the danger of security leaks. Find out if there is anyone involved in the knowledge stream of these drawings who might be at risk for subterfuge or blackmail. In no uncertain terms, I state to you now that espionage must be eliminated as a threat regarding these concepts. No news coverage whatsoever can be allowed; a complete blackout must be maintained. All launchings must be done in secret at remote sites that can be controlled. Mr. Dillon, when you speak to the members of the Group of Seven, which I assume you will be assigned to do since you are acquainted with some of them, you yourself must take precautions to do so without any fanfare whatsoever.

"Gentlemen, thank you for inviting me in to confer with you. You were wise to do so. From here on, Secretary of War Stimson shall be my go-between. Any message on these matters must be delivered by hand to his office. Use of the telephone must be strictly curtailed to reduce unauthorized eavesdropping. Are we all agreed?"

"Yes, Mr. President!"

"Good. Now, hand me a fresh cigarette. Thank you. It's time for me to get back to the business of getting our countrymen out of the impoverished hole we have dug for ourselves. It is my dearly held hope that it won't require a war to do that. I have a secret weapon at my disposal, as I'm sure you know. The First Lady can be very uplifting. Today is Saturday the 24th and she has a speech scheduled which I must not miss. Thank you again, gentlemen. Good-day."

As F.D.R., as he was affectionately known, left the building, the naval officers turned to the 54 year old Dillon. "Art, can you handle this directly? I really hate to bother Mr. Hoover with the details of your assignment. He has enough on his plate with this damn Chicago internecine fracas."

Admiral Ramage thought it best to be direct. Improperly handled, the gangster situation over prohibited liquor could topple the fragile peace being maintained throughout the world in a heartbeat. Art rose from his seat and spoke directly to the admiral.

"Sir, it would be best if you confer with him first. In this way, he will be properly convinced that I should be given complete authority for handling this matter. I will need to stay in contact with our agents in Germany and France to stay abreast of Hitler's machinations. To be most effective, however, I should remain stateside from here on. The Bureau of Investigation will want to protect the members of the Group of Seven from themselves, as much as from foreign assassins. My first priority will be to keep them operating as they are, together and in one location, so I can monitor their contacts and protect them from harm."

Graying at his temples now that he was moving past middle-age, Art Dillon was no youngster, but he wasn't sure how the brass would receive his next remark. It was peacetime, after all.

"Gentlemen, we have enjoyed an absence of war for more than a dozen years. You are military men and would, therefore, be well aware that despite our being a peaceful nation, skullduggery and spying continue to flourish. If it's not the Germans, then it's the Russians, and apparently now the Japanese. A country doesn't have to have evil goals against us; it may simply want to lift itself to a higher plane of respect among the other nations of the world. Thus, I am extremely concerned that espionage and purloining secrets through clandestine means is possible in this matter.

"A certain navy officer, Dale Irwin, who served dishonorably aboard the destroyer *Wickes* during World War I, has been at odds with the Group of Seven. He has lost two lawsuits against them, so I have no doubt that, even at his age, he harbors ill feeling toward this group and would not hesitate to sell out to the highest bidder should a foreign nation contact him. You should assign someone from Naval Intelligence to keep an eye on him. That is all I have at this time, sirs."

Admiral Ramage was succinct: "Then get to it!"

Art reached over and shook the hands of these famous men. There might not be another chance to do so.

* * *

About a week after he had joined in the Group of Seven's presentation to Admiral Williston, Peter North was sitting in his office in Mystic, Connecticut when his secretary Beth stuck her head in the door.

She announced, "Mr. North, a man calling himself Art Dillon has just shown up and is asking for you. He does not have an appointment. He showed me an identity card that states he is with the Bureau of Investigation. What do you want me to do?"

"Beth, show him right in! He's my old roommate from P.M.I."

Art strode in and was immediately engulfed in a bear hug by Peter. At only five feet tall, it was easy to get lost in such a warm greeting from the six foot North.

"You dog, you! Why didn't you tell me you were in town? It's been just ages. Why the hell weren't you at Jim's funeral?"

"Hold on, hold on. Settle down. Let me explain." Art got up and closed the office door.

Pete had been surprised, all right, but more by his former roommate's manner than by the fact of his unannounced visit. Clearly, this was not to be any sort of reunion celebrated with several rounds of beer steins raised on high.

"Pete, I've come on business that is both highly important and, frankly, if we were in the military, would be classified as 'Most Top Secret.'"

He paused, taking in a long breath and letting it out slowly.

"I'm sorry in the most heartfelt way that I couldn't be at Jim's graveside ceremony. I was in Europe, in Munich, as a matter of fact. Pete, things are getting really skewed over there. This man Hitler has assumed authority like a steamroller, yet his people appear to be utterly wowed by his oratory and apparent ability to get the economy back on its feet. Germans are beginning to earn a living wage again and their children are proud as punch to be strutting around the country as members of the Hitler Youth squads. You should see them marching from one place to another, carrying rakes and pitchforks as though on some summer country harvest. Simply change those implements out for rifles and it will be easy to see how marching to the harvest can be converted to marching in a war.

"The reason I'm here—and this must be kept strictly between us—is that the government there is covertly pouring money into refurbishing their armaments. This includes developing advanced naval combat ships. It's all contrary to the Treaty of Versailles, of course, so they're being very careful to dissimulate these activities. Nonetheless, their design capabilities are dangerously advanced. I wouldn't be surprised if they overtake the British in a decade; that's how good their new ships are!

"Their supreme weakness is the lack of raw materials within the national boundaries of Germany. It is likely that they will eventually reach across borders to obtain what they need, and no doubt that will lead to the future use of force. The victors in the Great War won't stand for that, and we'll be at war all over again. During my stay there, I developed contacts within the German Chancellery, and I can assure you that their naval command has heard about your invention and is planning to do something about the Pod Skimmer."

When Pete's eyebrows rose and he furrowed his brow in a frown, Art pressed his point.

"At both the Bureau of Investigation, and what is left of the O.S.S. from the Great War, we are convinced they have no intention of buying your equipment on the open market. Instead, Nazi spies will travel to America for the purpose of stealing all the drawings and plans for themselves. More to the point, they may possibly try to assassinate anyone who has been associated with these ideas."

He paused, studying Pete closely, then continued.

"Yes, yes, I see the quizzical look on your face, but I am being very straightforward with you here. I've come to you first, rather than President Townsend or Wallace Matthews and so forth, because you already have a 'Secret' clearance for your job. General Dynamics is so conversant with the production of submarines for our navy that many executives here are, doubtless, already worrying about what Herr Hitler may be up to. I thought you would be the most likely to appreciate the serious nature of my visit."

Art paused—more for breath than anything—but he looked over at his former roommate with undeniably serious concern on his face. Pete now spoke up.

"I presume I am not allowed to ask any questions here, but rather simply prepare myself to act on some set of instructions you have been told to deliver."

Pete and Art were like old dogs; they'd been friends for too long to waste time fighting over bones that neither really wanted.

"You never were one for beating about the bush." Art observed.

"I haven't changed," Peter succinctly stated. To himself, he recalled the very first day that he and Jim Stahl as eighteen-year-olds had been allowed aboard a navy ship back at the Philadelphia Navy Yard. His best friend wanted to explore all the inner workings, the "how" of movement as he called it. But Peter wanted to go right to the Bridge. Steering and orders for the helmsman were where everything important happened, so that was where he belonged. He had always preferred to be at the center of the action. In 34 years, he hadn't changed.

CHAPTER THIRTY-FOUR

SPIES IN THE BUSHES

Jacob Thresher heard the telephone ringing. "Hmmm, 10:30 at night. This is unusual." With some foreboding, he picked up the receiver and innocently said, "Hello."

"Jacob, hello. This is Peter North. Sorry to be calling so late, but I've just finished talking with the other five members of our group. We're meeting at the Tank tomorrow at 8:00 AM. Can you make this meeting? It's very important."

"Sure can. What's the rush? Did somebody get pregnant and the bride's father is oiling his shotgun as he prepares to collar the missing groom?"

This late at night, he could afford a little wit.

"I only wish it were that simple. Okay, I'll see you tomorrow." Having stated that, the caller hung up.

"Well, that was certainly mysterious," ruminated Jacob. Now that Project James had been presented to the Navy, the Group of Seven members were more or less sitting around waiting to hear the admirals' decision. Nevertheless, he'd expected a little more formality in their announcement than a curt, late night call.

"Is everything all right?" asked his wife sleepily. She had dozed off an hour earlier while wading through some book by F. Scott Fitzgerald. "Too convoluted and complex for bedtime reading" she had concluded as she laid it aside and promptly fell asleep. The ringing of the phone had awakened her, but she didn't like the tone of her husband's voice as he dealt with the caller.

"Not to worry, my pet. It was just one of the Group of Seven informing me of a meeting tomorrow."

"Oh ricketypoo, Jacob! Did you forget about the picnic we have planned with Betsy and her husband? I know you don't approve of young Appleby, but she loves him and we've got to get used to that. Do you want me to call them in the morning and cancel?"

"Good heavens, no!" exclaimed Jake. "My meeting will probably be very short. It's a Friday, after all. We can't really proceed until we know where we're headed. If the Navy turns us down, we'll probably build a complete ship at one of the local yards, maybe with a scale of one-to-three, just to show potential buyers that it works with a superstructure. You needn't worry your pretty little head, my sweet. I can still be back by noon and make the outing."

He paused in mid-thought, then owned up to his wife: "You know, while I'm not fond of my son-in-law, I'll admit that John Appleby is growing on me. Still, I can't imagine what Betsy sees in the guy. He's just a car mechanic, for heaven's sake!"

"Okay, if you say so." Amy was starting to lie back against her still warm pillow. "Remember, a man who can fix a machine has great value! Just tell me if you change your plans…" and his wife was asleep once more.

Not so for Jacob. His mind leafed back through the frenetic rush of the last few years. In all that time working together, the Group of Seven had maintained a relationship that was consistently collegial and trustworthy. Townsend permitted them pretty free rein, only asking for updates if a new configuration was tried or a recalculation made. He had been true to his word, even when the October 1929 stock market crash had deepened into a "Depression," as the news media was officially referring to it now.

It was a wonder that this unusual arrangement had worked, but they now had a mockup that had proved successful even when heavily loaded. The question was why no one had yet tried to pin any of us down as to what we were doing. He supposed the Pod Skimmer was so outlandish looking that no one could figure out what its purpose was. That made life all the simpler for the Group of Seven. Even when the prototype had been evaluated out on Rhode Island Sound, where fishermen and sailing craft abounded, no one had asked any questions. In fact, the Group had been left quite alone, so testing had proceeded without incident.

However, none of us had counted on persons hidden among the bushes or in the shadows of beach houses along the shoreline. Frequently, there'd be a somewhat grizzled, older man watching the Pod Skimmer team closely through binoculars. Even if Jacob had been sharp-eyed enough to spot a spy, the distance would have been too far to recognize Dale Irwin. After all, he'd only spoken to that man over the phone; he had no idea what that former navy captain looked like. That short conversation had been back in April or May of 1929 when he'd told Irwin, in simple language, to get lost. A lot had happened to Thresher's team since then, and Irwin's name had never once been mentioned. Nonetheless, Dale had thought a lot about us.

CHAPTER THIRTY-FIVE

DEALING WITH DUPLICITY

At 0800 hours on Friday, the 29th of September, all six members of the Group of Seven who resided in or near Providence had assembled at The Man's water test tank. Now that he was nigh on sixty years old, Frank Jones really liked this title. He was so intensely diligent, yet unassuming in his work, that all of us enjoyed deferring to him as "The Man."

During a round-table conversation decades ago, someone had started to compliment Jones about something by saying, "Man, I have to hand it to you..." but the sentence was never finished. One of his other admirers had shouted, "That's it! That's his handle!" He'd been known, both at Cummins & Co. and at New York Shipbuilding, as "The Man" ever since. He saw no reason his 'handle" should change now, even though he was working in a small, tightly-knit team where each member held special value to the others.

He made sure everyone was comfortable, apologized for the absence of Orville Townsend who was back in New York City, and then turned the meeting over to Peter North.

North was the only one who was actively employed by a different outfit—General Dynamics—but that was because his contacts through that company would be valuable should our negotiations with the navy be successful. He visited the Providence facility regularly, driving up from Mystic several times a week, hanging around discussing metallurgy and newly developed materials such as aluminum. No one fully understood the properties of this metal, but it was light, malleable, and--so long as a geologist could locate an area of bauxite deposits--readily available.

At some point in the day, he would drive back to attend to his assignments at the submarine construction firm. Although his specialty was electronics and wiring, he was very current on corrosive effects of sea water, pressure gradients, and propulsion alternatives now that diesel was as accepted as oil as a fuel. Coal had long ago been cast aside regarding ships. Diesel could spark pistons to turn a crankshaft which in turned rotated a propeller shaft, so the bulky equipment used to generate steam had been relegated to history. Diesel absolutely demanded access to an air supply, but while that was a highly technical problem which General Dynamics wrestled with, it was simple for the Pod Skimmer. Vessels utilizing a pod skimmer as a hull would ride on the surface.

Peter, however, was here on a different matter, and he got right down to discussing his conversation with Jim Stahl's former roommate, Art Dillon.

"Mr. Dillon is an agent with the U.S. government, the O.S.S. or something. He quickly became an employee for the Bureau of Investigation after graduating from P.M.I. During the war, he was sent to law school by the Bureau and became a full time agent upon his graduation.

"As the Nationalist Socialist German Workers' Party gained ascendancy during the 1920's, he was assigned to keep track of Adolf Hitler's rise within the German leadership. His contacts revealed to him only last Monday that the extremist Goebbels has discovered our development of the Pod Skimmer. Obviously, none of us are at fault. There must be some American who is desperate for cash and has been seduced by spies in our country into revealing what he has surreptitiously learned. I have been too innocent; I had surmised that our tests out on Rhode Island Sound were so unusual that no one could understand what we had going on. Clearly, if information can get all the way back to Berlin, someone is being highly motivated to track us and is being well compensated for his betrayal.

"Frankly, my focus is on Dale Irwin. You'll recall how he brought those two lawsuits against us some time back. The second is most telling: he conspired with a former associate of Jones here. Although we prevailed, it's clear to me that this man will stoop to any means if it brings him money, even if that requires stealing patented ideas. Let us not be lulled into a false sense of being 'above the fray' here. No world court is going to offer us protection if Herr Hitler gets a hold of our ideas. If that happens, all our work will have gone to waste. An independent aggressor nation could have parity with America with virtually no expenditure of effort. That brings me to why this meeting was held with such urgency.

"The U.S. Navy is, and I say once more emphatically, _is_ very interested in our Pod Skimmer. The office of Admiral Ramage has provided me with these written contracts whereby we are properly compensated for the exclusive development of our invention for the benefit of this country's naval forces. Concomitant with that is the obligation to not reveal any of its mathematical or flotation properties to anyone, least of all a potential aggressor nation.

"Unfortunately, the Nazis do not abide by international law; they play by their own rulebook, and that book is written totally in their own self-interest. They simply make up laws as they push forward, interpreting them through their public information office to justify whatever particular crisis they are then manipulating.

"The long and short of it is that our lives, perhaps even our families, are in danger. Joseph Goebbels has directed his operatives to not merely steal the concepts, but to kill anyone who has been associated with Stahl's ideas in the past. Of course, we ourselves have been circumspect; we have been careful not to discuss our work outside of these walls. Nevertheless, if the German secret police can get to us by intimidating our wives or kidnapping our children, they won't hesitate to do so.

"I'm throwing the floor open to discussion. We've done it: we have sold the Pod Skimmer and here are the contracts to sign. However, there's no sense in losing our lives as a result of our success!

"The Bureau of Investigation has proposed relocating all of us to unknown locations and giving us assumed identities. The fatal flaw with such a proposal is that we could no longer work together on the Pod Skimmer. If you feel as I do, Project James has become the reason I get out of bed in the morning, or even 0200 hours when the occasion demands. Now that the Navy wants it, our project could become a major tool enabling us to win a war, if it should come to that.

"Before any of you make a suggestion, I want to remind you that the smartest man in the world today is a mathematician named Albert Einstein. He is a German. He may actually act intelligently and leave his homeland before he is persecuted for being Jewish, but there's no guarantee. Theoreticians aren't necessarily born with common sense.

"My point is this: Germans are not fools. As a people, they are far average in intelligence and diligence. The take great pride in their inventiveness. Their weakness is that they are easily swayed and led. We are bearing witness to how artfully this man Hitler is distorting the definition of 'leader.' Indeed, when men like Benito Mussolini and that Franco in Spain can rule unfettered, being a rational citizen is fast becoming a treacherous gamble. People who think independently and act on principles of equality have become fair game."

Exhausted from the emotional impact of what he had just delivered, Peter collapsed into a chair. Obviously, the floor was now open to discussion. The shock of what North had revealed required some minutes to process, and then a few more minutes still in order to rationally act. The first to respond was the least experienced, Charlie McDonald.

"As the youngest here, please excuse me if I speak first. We all have more to lose than our own lives. I now have a wife and a new son who is barely a year old. Wally, you still have a teenager living at home as well as a son in college. But even if a child is grown, married, and thus out of the house, like Jacob's daughter Betsy, they're still family. We don't want any of our loved ones to suffer, be kidnapped, tortured, or somehow blackmailed. But we can't scatter to the winds; there's too much to do. Pod Skimmer has become our life's work, and we can't let this marvelous invention slip into the hands of some foreign tyrant or nation. I don't have a solution yet, but I wanted all of you to know how seriously I consider the position we are in."

The sound of me clearing my throat turned everyone's head. I was not merely seated, but quite relaxed as well.

With firm self-assurance, I stated: "As all of you know, I lost my dear wife Mary two and a half years ago to cancer. Her death was a terrible, crushing blow for which I was unprepared. Since then, each day as I wake up, I give thanks to heaven above for the Pod Skimmer. If I didn't have Project James pulling me out of bed each morning, I might well have explored how high a man must be before jumping off a bridge will kill him. Peter's revelations today have reignited my commitment to see this project through to fruition. Jim's inspirations have provided us with a whole new dimension regarding traveling upon the sea. I for one will remain right here, and I will continue working without second thoughts.

"I will undertake to explain to Bill and Alice the element of danger that has now entered our lives. My daughter will be finishing high school in the spring, but she will no longer walk to and from school but rather ride with me or in a friend's car. Moreover, I will cooperate with the Bureau of Investigation in accepting any sort of protective blanket they can provide all of us. But, I will not stop working. If the group decides to transfer operations down to the City where President Townsend has offices, I will resist. Residing in New York would be moving out of the frying pan and into the fire! Staying right here and working on measures for self-protection suits me just fine. What do you others say?"

Everyone agreed that I had stated the group's position clearly. We would remain in Providence and stay dedicated to the success of Project James. After affixing our signatures to the Navy Department's contract, we continued to march, as the army would say. Everyone, however, would become more observant and careful, particularly when on the telephone.

CHAPTER THIRTY-SIX

PROTECTING THE POD SKIMMER

When the telephone rang outside Orville Townsend's office on October 2nd, he could overhear his secretary, Angela Thorne, answering. There was a definite note of concern in her voice. She quickly called to him through the open door; there was no denying the urgency in her tone.

"Mr. Townsend there is a man who says he is from the Bureau of Investigation on the phone, and he's asking to speak with you immediately! Shall I put him through?"

"Certainly!" responded her boss confidently.

Picking up the receiver, he said, "This is Orville Townsend, President of Oceanic Lines. How may I help you?"

"Mr. Townsend, sir, please excuse my calling like this, but I need to stop by your office immediately. My name is Arthur Dillon. I'm a Special Agent with the Bureau. May I come up? I'm right downstairs in the lobby of your building."

Mr. Townsend was taken aback; he'd never been confronted with a visit from law enforcement. The day was about to get very interesting. This was Monday, and Mondays always seemed to be pressure-packed, regardless of who showed up in his office.

"Why yes, that would be fine. Can you find your way? My office is on the top floor."

"Yes, sir, of course. I know where you are located." With that, Agent Dillon hung up the phone.

Well, now. What did he mean by that? Had he been here before without Orville being aware? He was glad he was an above-board businessman; he wasn't built for skulking about in the shadows of criminal dens or safe-houses for spies.

Using his lightest tone, he said, "Miss Thorne, will you please show Mr. Dillon in when he comes up. Thank You!"

It wasn't long before the elevator chimed, its door opened, and out stepped Art Dillon on the tenth floor of the Oceanic Building. He had been on this floor before, but not when anyone working here was present. Members of his agency had penetrated the headquarters of Oceanic only a week ago in order to conduct a sweep of the premises. If they had determined that foreign agents had "bugged" the offices in order to eavesdrop on the financial home of the Pod Skimmer, the team would have highlighted the location of the microphones and then informed the executives affected. His team would then proceed to instruct these victims so disinformation could be conveyed if somebody was listening in. However, nothing had been found; the offices were clean insofar as the Bureau of Investigation could determine.

As a result, the agency had been reduced to maintaining simple 24 hour watches by local operatives. The goal was to monitor the comings and goings in the building. The tough part was the "graveyard shift," as the G-Men referred to those late night hours. It was fairly easy to stay alert during daylight when there were lots of people entering and leaving. As an agent, you only had to trust your partner to split the workload so all the visitors could be accounted for. On the other hand, between 9:00 PM and 6:00 AM, the activity would be light, but so would your attention span.

Staying alert was the least of an agent's problems, however. In the early morning hours, a man pulling surveillance duty had to watch his back in case his car was approached for an ambush. He could drink only so much coffee before his gut got so full he couldn't drink any more, yet those eyelids still had to stay open. Hardest of all, of course, was the fact that it became very difficult to distinguish identities as people moved among the shadows on city streets. Doing so wasn't all that difficult in warm weather, but as soon as the chill of winter made wearing hats and scarves a necessity, monitoring individuals during darkness became very difficult.

The watchful men in the unmarked, unobtrusive cars were not counting totals or anything so simple. Each shift would, in fact, be waging a game of chance. The two man teams would be looking for known foreign agents whom the port authorities had observed but had no legal basis on which to detain them. They would likely have enlarged identity photos of specific individuals lying on the dashboard. Complicating factors included the obvious possibility that a spy had come ashore at some small seaside village not monitored by the Bureau of Investigation and had boarded a train to reach the City.

Fortunately, rail service to this particular building required that a person exit a train or subway car and remain aboveground in order to enter the office building at 111 Eighth Avenue. This had become the new home of Oceanic Lines as the company adjusted to business conditions following the crash of the stock market in 1929. Fortunately for the men monitoring the flow of workers in and out, this building had been constructed without an underground garage.

Then there's the night cleaning crew to consider. These personnel were subject to change at the drop of a mop, so to speak. Cleaning personnel were not known for longevity; their line of work was simply too physically demanding or, worse, tempting. Light-fingered dusting frequently got people in real trouble. To relieve boredom, some of them worked partial hours in order to leave early and go clean entirely separate facilities. The transitory nature of their jobs created real headaches for the agents tracking their identities and intentions.

The only advantage that the agents monitoring this building had going for them was the fact that every single office was devoted to some function at Oceanic Lines. Personnel tracking and records, finance, compensation, ship maintenance, schedule preparation, customer ticketing and public relations, ship design and construction supervision, ordering materials and supplies, testing and evaluation of all kinds, training stewards and shipboard officers, legal, insurance of varied types, advertising and promotion, development of safety procedures and regulations, as well as the executives required to manage these various functions—all these activities occurred right in this one building. If some evil person wanted to listen in on the activities of Oceanic Lines, this would be the place to do it.

That single fact provided the Bureau of Investigation with their simplest and most effective tool: the telephone. If there was a phone in this building, it had to go through the basement exchange. Every routing was hard-wired, and every line could therefore be readily checked regarding nefarious tampering. A telephone couldn't be tapped at the exchange; it would be too obvious. Moreover, whether it was tapped could be determined by a simple readout of signal-strength feedback as the telephone operators worked their consoles. Agent Art Dillon had ordered this to be set up the day after his team had "swept the joint" and found no bugs.

Regardless of all the precautions he and his agency had taken, he now had to explain to the company's president the real dangers that perfection of the Pod Skimmer posed to company personnel. Taking a deep breath, he opened the main door to the reception area and introduced himself to the person posted at the front desk.

"Hello, I'm Agent Arthur Dillon." The woman manning the desk provided him with her sunniest smile, checked his identification, and then dialed over to Angela.

"Angela, this is Lois. There's a Mr. Dillon here to see President Townsend."

"Yes, we're expecting him. Please send him right along." As she hung up the interoffice phone, Angela said, "Mr. Townsend, Mr. Art Dillon is on his way."

Orville gave a perfunctory "thank-you" and lit up a cigar. "May as well provide the place with some collegial atmosphere," he thought to himself.

When Art Dillon was ushered in by Angela, Orville rose to meet him, extended his hand in his usual businesslike manner, and offered Art a seat at the coffee table. He preferred this more relaxed setting for all his negotiations.

"Well, Mr. Dillon, what can I do for you? Your visit certainly has come as a surprise, so let's get right down to it, shall we?"

Art couldn't help himself. In his line of work, it paid to be suspicious. Yet he liked this man instantly. His dear friend Jim Stahl had worked for a competing company, yet this man was effortlessly making him feel comfortable. His way of doing business was precisely the same as Art's: let's get right to it! Art thanked his lucky stars that he was not dealing with an Oriental. Japanese businessmen felt each other out as a sort of preamble to any business discussions; it might require several hours of gracious, polite repartee before such businessmen finally got down to actual negotiations.

However, Art was in America and speaking to an American. Under the circumstances, he waded right in.

"Mr. Townsend, I have met with Peter North up at General Dynamics; I had him convey to the members of Project James everything I am about to relate to you. Please excuse my being forthright. Frankly, in my opinion, even an hour lost could be extremely harmful.

"First, congratulations on your having secured acceptance of the Pod Skimmer by the U.S. Navy. I am not privy to their plans regarding its use or what type of superstructure they will construct atop it, but I can assure you that, regrettably, our navy is not the only military organization that knows about your wonderful work. Your team up in Providence has been warned in no uncertain terms that the designs, drawings, specifications, and test results are all at risk. Even their lives may be in danger and their family members subject to kidnap."

He could see Orville visibly squirming with discomfort despite the thick plush of his chair cushion. Obviously, he was becoming uncomfortable: his normal florid color was beginning to pale. Art knew that what he was about to add would not alleviate the man's discomfiture, but he had to continue.

"We have set up a monitoring system for calls coming into this building, so should any of your staff members be threatened or propositioned, we will soon learn of it. There is a twenty-four-hour surveillance of this building ongoing. We have established protective measures for the men working in Providence but no actions have been taken regarding their families. Those men—McDonald, Thresher, North, Matthews, Jones, and Terry—have decided amongst themselves to remain in place, continue to work on the Pod Skimmer, and cooperate with us as necessary. They refused our offer of protective custody and relocation inasmuch as that would prevent any further development of your intellectual property. That, of course, may be a moot point now that the U.S. Navy has bought development rights regarding warships, but I'm sure your legal beagles could find an opening in the contract by which your company could continue development for civilian uses.

"I am not interested in, nor indeed a part of, your civilian business arrangements. Where my office becomes involved is to thwart, completely, the German government, or for that matter any foreign power, obtaining access to your development plans and test results. At one of their high councils, men within Adolf Hitler's inner circle have expressly stated that the Gestapo will undertake to obtain these specifications and eliminate anyone in America with knowledge of same. This, naturally, includes you and, to a lesser degree, Reginald Highsmith. Have there been any additional file clerks or office personnel involved in the knowledge stream of the Pod Skimmer?"

At this point, Orville was beside himself. Competition, well, that was one thing; he was well prepared to fend off interlopers in that regard. He had done it successfully his entire working life. But foreign governments, agents, spies; good gracious, even assassins! That was a world totally beyond his comprehension. The high color now returned to his face and made his cheeks rosy red as he prepared to do battle with a counterattack. This showed that he was genuinely disturbed about threats against The Group of Seven, himself included.

He hemmed and hawed for a bit, then simply looked at Agent Dillon and said straight out, "God damn it! Where in the hell do you come off scaring the absolute crap out of me like this? Let me see your identification. Who in the world do you think you are to wade in here and start talking to me like this!"

Mr. Townsend was by this point genuinely scared. It had been his experience that the best defense was often a thrusting offense. After forty years in the business, he was not going to be bullied and pushed around by some pipsqueak.

Art was prepared for this. Few people in this country would listen to news that they were in danger of being assassinated and pleasantly respond with, "Is that one sugar lump, or two, in your tea?"

"Mr. Townsend, I apologize sincerely. I have come on rather strong. I had mistakenly assumed that one of your people up in Providence had called you by now to discuss this situation. Now that I have your full attention, let me give you some background. I graduated from Providence Maritime Institute with Jim Stahl. I was one of his roommates, along with your man, Peter North. I have been posted in Germany for the past six months, allegedly as a shipping magnate. My real mission was to cultivate prime sources of information regarding the developing political situation there. The Bureau is convinced that this new leader, Adolf Hitler, is a master propagandist, but also a very dangerous leader who will ignore humane considerations to make Germany a world power. He isn't enlarging the population base with territorial grabs yet, but we believe that will come as he further establishes his sphere of influence.

"The single most striking attribute of the men who swear allegiance to the Nazi Party is their conniving. Secretive, underhanded, two-faced, prevaricating, double-crossing, you name it. Every such acronym will fit. As they consider world domination, they see the Pod Skimmer as a game changer for control of the sea. Even though they have, at this moment, very advanced battle craft under construction in violation of the Versailles Peace Treaty, no one is doing anything to sidetrack or otherwise interdict them. With a wave of his hand, Mr. Hitler seems able to forge ahead by simply eliminating anyone who stands in his way."

Art could see that Mr. Townsend's demeanor had changed from resentful to a man whose attention was riveted. He was becoming resolved that perhaps he as well as his team members faced real threats to their safety. He was listening intently.

Art continued. "As a consequence, we take threats voiced by men close to Hitler very seriously. They have assigned undercover agents to take the Pod Skimmer as their own. How they became so well informed about your plans, tests, and performance, we have not yet established, although my men are working on that problem even as we speak. Additionally, we know from their past campaigns that when they want some information regarding a nation's security, the Nazis do not hesitate to kill to get it. Once they have satisfied their quest, they will then proceed to eliminate anyone who has had access to the same information. Over the course of the coming month, we expect them to try and destroy the entire Pod Skimmer knowledge base in America.

"To be realistic, there are patent protections on your team's work that will protect their rights in this country, but as you proceed with assembly and production, the cat will have left the bag, so to speak. Of course, the Nazi will simply ignore accepted legal protections as they subvert the concepts to their own evil uses. You don't need to claim that your inventions are not intended for battle craft. The Boche are an ingenious people; if an invention can be subverted, they will certainly find a way to do it! That is why I am here in your office today, and why I have already met with the other members of your development team."

At this point, Orville said simply, "Please continue."

Then he leaned forward to be sure he understood exactly what Art Dillon and the Bureau of Investigation were proposing. A chart was required for illustrating the plan. It was produced. After only fifteen minutes of concentrated discussion, Orville leaned back in his comfortable chair, smiled, and folded his hands across his lap.

"This is a good plan," he offered. "I think it will work. If nothing else, it will surely let the Boche know that we are on to them!"

He stood and extended his hand to Art. As the two men shook hands in agreement, their eyes exchanged reassuring looks. They were allied in an audacious plan.

Don't just sit around and let a problem develop beyond your control: *win the day through affirmative action.* This encapsulated their thinking. This plan would protect the Pod Skimmer by throwing the Germans a poisoned bone, so to speak.

The next three weeks would be busy ones for Hoover's G-Men.

When he left Orville's office, Art approached the Manhattan dispatcher for the city's Yellow Cab Company. After producing his credentials, the agent asked to meet with one Rick Rossetti. The dispatcher looked over the scheduling board and told him to come back in an hour.

"No, I'll just wait for him here," affirmed Art as he took a seat. When Rossetti pulled in to park for the evening, Art stood, introduced himself, and then got right to what he had in mind.

"Mr. Rossetti, we have a serious national security threat which you can help us contain. Do you remember a fare named Charles McDonald a few years back? You delivered him to the old Oceanic Lines office building located at 78 Second Avenue."

Rossetti's eyebrows arched in surprise. "Do I ever! A cabbie never gets asked to be a future referral. That young man left a pleasant mark on me that I won't soon forget!" He smiled broadly.

"Well, sir, he remembers you as well, and he asked me personally to pick you for this assignment. I'm going to lay it out fully for you, in strictest confidence, you understand. You can't even gossip with your missus about this job. Our nation's security may depend on your discretion."

Art let the air fill with pregnant import. This admonition was very serious, Rick realized. He remained silent, ruminating on dark memories from his past.

Then he affirmed: "Mr. Dillon, or I guess I should say, 'Agent Dillon,' I accept. This country has been good to me, and if there's something I can do in return, I will do it willingly."

"Very good. Now, it's a simple task that will be easy for you to perform; however, you must execute it precisely as I shall outline. Ready?"

"I sure am!" Rossetti leaned forward, listening intently, and when Art was finished, he recited the assignment back exactly as it had been delivered.

"Excellent! You're ready. Now, remember: you park on the side of the Ellis Island facility opposite the entrance. That's where the mark will exit. I'll have an agent posted in the processing room. Sometime after the *Europa* docks, you must make yourself ready. Somewhere between one-half to two hours later, our mark will get through the admissions process. As he prepares to leave, one of my agents will come out and give you a physical description of what the man is wearing. Stay alert. Good luck! And, thank you."

Agent Dillon got into his black, government-issue sedan and headed out for the next meeting. He had more to do, and the men he needed to prepare were already awaiting his arrival. He pointed the car in the direction of Long Island.

CHAPTER THIRTY-SEVEN

HANS, HURST, AND HAGAN

Hans Ludwig took a deep breath as the passenger liner *S.S. Europa* left the open ocean and entered the harbor waters south of New York City. He relished the sting of salty sea air, but he loved the tang of challenging, dangerous missions even more. Deceiving people was his sport of choice, but snuffing them in fulfillment of a mission was even better. He had to admit it: doing so produced special sexual thrills beyond what even a woman could arouse.

Speaking of women, there she was: the Statue of Liberty, with her glowing torch gleaming and beckoning. Ludwig despised her. *Herr Kimmel!* The green thing had been a gift from the French; in his mind, they were nothing but a sybaritic bunch of frogs. He looked away.

As the skyline became crowded with dozens of tall office buildings towering over the communication masts of the German vessel, he could feel his adrenaline begin coursing through his body.

"It is good, ya! My reactions will be all the quicker if my blood is surging," he thought confidently.

The *Europa* docked and lowered her gangway. It was the beginning of October, so the foreign passengers who needed verification disembarked quickly for Ellis Island. It wouldn't do to stand around in the chilly breezes sweeping across the mouth of the Hudson River.

As soon as Ludwig entered the building designated for processing and inspections, he scanned the line of customs officials working behind a long counter. There was one in particular he had been told to go to. "That's the man," he realized as he looked over at the second-to-last counter window. However, the Customs Clerk standing behind the glass didn't look German at all.

In a flash, Hans realized that the man was Italian. How smart! No one would suspect this clerk of complicity. The German agent presented his passport, the man glanced at the document, then at Hans, and a broad smile widened his lips as he held the admission stamp poised above the blank page.

"It is very good to have you here, Mr. Ludwig. Welcome to New York! Are you here on business or pleasure? Pleasure. I see, very good, sir. Enjoy your stay!"

He brought the stamp down with an authoritative *wham*! Then Antonio smoothly handed the passport and approved entry visa back to the killer.

Everything he had done had been according to the rulebook, except that he had allowed a known foreign agent into the United States. This was the land for which his parents had sacrificed all their possessions in order to reach a country that offered freedom and opportunity. In 1919, he had been fifteen but he never lost his devotion to Italy like his parents had. It was the land of his birth, after all. He had been too young to understand how harshly the German attackers had dealt with his countrymen; if they were allied with the French, they were sure to perish by torture and starvation. Now, he was nearly thirty and living in America without yet having done anything to make El Duce proud of him. He was strong, ambitious, and virile. Antonio had learned that he could survive here, but he owed it no loyalty as far as he was concerned. He simply needed to take advantage of Opportunity whenever she presented herself. In fact, this clerk was rather proud of the assignment he had just completed; he had proceeded exactly as the German Embassy had instructed.

"Next." the customs clerk called out, and the line trundled forward.

A smooth-faced, khaki-suited workman set his broom against the wall and unlocked a side door. Exiting, he strode directly to a cab parked in the shadows astride the building. The Bureau agent spoke in a precise, clipped tone: "He's dressed in a grey suit, open collar, blond hair, brown shoes, carrying a small brown satchel and a tan overcoat. Stick to the plan!"

With that, Rossetti started the engine and pulled around to the front of the building.

Once an immigrant had received the all-important stamp of approved entry, there was no keeping him from New York City. It was the gateway to "the land of equal opportunity!"

People would roll these words on their tongue, as if savoring the taste of freedom at last! They couldn't be blamed for rushing to the exit to catch a ride for this fabled city. Thus, no one paid any attention to the broad-shouldered, blond-haired man carrying only a coat and a small valise. He seemed to be in a hurry, but the same could be said for everyone bearing a stamped pass into America. As he exited the customs building, Hans held up his arm and a taxicab pulled right up alongside.

He observed to himself, "At least public transportation is efficient in America, even if the rest of the country is decadently overdosing on bootleg liquor, parties, and discordant music."

"Where to, bub?" asked the cabbie as he squashed out a cigar in the ashtray.

"Take me to a medium-priced hotel with clean rooms, and be quick about it!"

"Okay, Mac, I'll get you there, but you're in New York now. No one gets anywhere "quick" as you put it. Just sit back and enjoy the sights."

Rick Rossetti put a new cigar in the corner of his mouth as he looked in the rearview mirror at his passenger. This was indeed the man whom the Bureau of Investigation had told him about.

"For a German, he sure speaks good English!" Rossetti thought to himself. "He's been well trained."

The cabbie had already been paid $25 for this hire. For that kind of money, this passenger could go anywhere in the City he wanted, but Rossetti knew just the place to take him.

Once out in the mainstream of the city's traffic, the cab had to deal with pedestrians, horse-drawn as well as electrified trolleys, and hundreds of cars. Each automobile seemed hell-bent on getting to some destination faster than the vehicle next to it. Traffic snarls became unavoidable and tempers short. Rossetti knew how to deal with the congestion.

After about 20 minutes negotiating the tangle of traffic, Rossetti's cab pulled up in front of the Hotel Carter at 250 W. 43rd Street. It was an imposing building that was famous for holding the line on room prices but, as a result, it had begun to be a bit worn out around the edges. Nevertheless, they had arrived safely at the passenger's destination.

"See, nary a scratch!" boasted Rossetti to his fare.

Ludwig took no notice. He did not have time to voice either compliments or complaints. He exited the cab, paid the driver without tipping him, and strode directly into the rotating circular doorway. As he exited, he instantly went from the chill of early winter winds to the edifying comfort of a warm lobby. He realized he was starting to relax, thereby allowing his perceptions to dull, but he couldn't help himself. He was tired from the voyage. In this spacious reception area, people bustled about intent on making some private meeting or going "out on the town." The famed nightclubs of New York City provided opportunity for both in abundance.

Despite the pleasant ambiance, he wanted to sleep this afternoon so he would be highly alert and prepared come the evening hours. He checked in at the desk and then headed straight for the elevator.

His plan called for his first execution to be in the most public of places. He had been informed that Mr. Townsend resided uptown in a plush apartment overlooking Central Park. He planned on killing the mark with a silenced Luger pistol as the head of Oceanic Lines boarded the underground subway for 49th Street. When the shuttle would arrive and open its doors, everyone would be pressing forward intent on getting aboard. Possibly, they might trip over a person who was falling down, but this would only serve to divert everyone's attention. In the confusion, an assassin could simply melt into the crowd of impatient commuters and vanish before anyone started screaming.

Orville Townsend was a wealthy capitalist; his picture frequently appeared in the newspapers showing him big as life smiling to all his admirers. He wa famous for insisting on taking public transportation between his Manhattan office and his plush apartment. He would be easy to identify. Once Hans had made his mark during the evening rush, he figured the entire event would take fewer than ten seconds. He'd get behind Townsend and then press close against his body, thereby shielding the pistol from view as well as being certain of his aim. Three shots, panned from right to left in the lungs and heart, would kill Townsend instantly yet be drowned out by the noise of the subway cars arriving. He would time his pulling the trigger with a sudden tight grab of Townsend's left arm to keep him close.

He calculated that he could get away clean and then take a commuter train up to Providence to execute his subsequent assignments. He doubted anyone would mount any sort of pursuit; the murder of Townsend would be attributed to those awful gangs vying for control of the bootleg liquor business throughout the city. The death of that executive would garner only passing notice.

His musings were interrupted as he ascended the elevator to his room. Two men in business suits had boarded with him, but it was the short lift operator who surprised him. The lad was only about five feet tall and was dressed in the cap and uniform of a bellhop, so Hans had assumed he was some kid earning money for school and had therefore paid him no attention. When the "kid" turned toward Ludwig as the car doors were closing, however, there was no doubt this fellow wasn't about to ask, "What floor, sir?"

The bellhop kicked him hard in the shin; Hans couldn't help opening his mouth to yelp, and immediately the bellhop pressed his fingers together as he formed a "V" with his thumb and threw it like a rock hard wedge into the spy's throat, catching him square on the Adam's Apple protrusion. This laid the German out flat without a sound. The two "businessmen" then handcuffed the limp form, departed the elevator, strapped him to a stretcher leaning against the hallway, and thereupon carried the helpless spy down the stairway and out a side door to a waiting black hearse.

After removing the mauve uniform with its gold braid, Art Dillon gave a warm handshake to the genuine bellhop, Cecil Curry, and placed a ten dollar bill in his hand. Tipping his hat, Cecil turned and resumed his job at the helm of the elevator. It was not his place to make inquiry of these men—after all, they worked for the famous J. Edgar Hoover, the country's premier crime fighter!

For his part, Art and his fellow Bureau of Investigation agents whisked Ludwig away for a very important "interview" with the great Mr. Hoover himself. In time, he would be convicted at court-martial as a proven spy and be remanded to serve six months in Leavenworth before being executed. His defense had objected to the rough handling leading to his arrest, but based on the documentation provided by the French Sûreté, the convening officer had overruled the objection, citing Ludwig's work as a professional assassin as proof that he embodied the highest degree of danger to citizens of this free country. The convening officer observed as an aside that he would have held Agent Dillon blameless if he had shot the spy on the spot.

Back in the headquarters building of the Bureau of Investigation's New York Field Office, the telephone rang at the desk of one of the enclosed offices.

Picking it up, a man said, "Special-Agent-in-Charge Leon Turrou here."

"Chief," said a matter-of-fact voice at the other end, "the Canadian Mounties have picked up and detained two men whom they suspect are German operatives trying to cross the border without papers. Their names are Heinrich Fleischman and Gustav Gruber, both from Aachen. Shall I give the Canadians that directive you suggested?"

Turrou grunted, "Do that!" and then added, "Good work, Andrews. Remind the Mounties, respectfully, that these are very dangerous agents who need to be placed in a high security jail until further notice from the United States Government. Got that?"

"Yes sir! Also, Chief, you may have already heard that Hans Ludwig has been arrested." Then the phone clicked curtly as the line fell silent.

"Well! That part of my day's work is completed," Agent Turrou calmly concluded. It was time for a tasty cigar. As he rolled a good one between his fingers, he wondered, "Now, who else have those sneaky Boche sent?" He wasn't worried. America had shown she was prepared to protect her borders from German penetration.

* * *

During the second week of October, a heavy overcast developed in the New York area which then led to rain prevailing for several days. As night fell on the 12th, a German submarine with a specially designed foredeck quietly surfaced south of Gardiner's Island in Block Island Sound. Max Hurst and Ernst Hagan peered from the conning tower of the black U-23 but saw nothing floating on the featureless waters of the bay. They were old friends, having been raised back in the seafaring town of Bremen. Their alphabetical seating had kept them together throughout their schooling.

When they had been selected to represent Herr Hitler as young pioneers, they had proudly marched in the daily formations astride one another, innocently shouldering their rakes and hoes. They had immediately volunteered to serve their Füehrer when Goebbels had asked for special recruits from their Brown Shirt unit. They each dreamed of being welcomed into the highly trained, secretive fraternity of Black Shirt Storm Troopers.

They dropped over the side and took low crouching positions in a small dinghy which two crewmen rowed toward a spit of land jutting north from Montauk. All but a few of the beach houses were shuttered and dark, so they were confident their arrival had gone unseen. The weather was dreary enough to keep even fishermen indoors. They quietly departed the little rowboat and soon found an empty summer cottage in which to both sleep and monitor the sound for activity. It was imperative that they avoid not merely customs, but also the authorities. Goebbels had specifically directed that neither was to carry any sort of identification on his person. Should they be stopped and questioned, he didn't want the Fatherland being implicated; should they be arrested and tried as spies, they should hold their heads high and die in the name of Aryan supremacy.

They had been assigned to monitor movements of a new American device that skimmed at great speed over water; testing was scheduled for the very next day in the little used, sheltered waters south of Gardiner Island.

Plans divined do not always run as devised. A longtime resident, Hilda Beckwith, swore she heard crunching sounds on the sand and, when she peered into the darkness, she was certain that some tiny transport had beached, but then promptly departed, leaving someone behind. Everyone seemed to be taking great pains to be as silent as possible. All of them were dressed entirely in black, for Heaven's sake! She didn't understand any of this activity.

Even as she was watching through her porch screen, she was certain she heard noises of glass breaking. All the summer houses were closed for the season. No one should be lurking about in the dead of this night; the rain was constant and cold. Perhaps some couples would be flirting during warm, summer nights, but no one should be about on the beaches this late in the year. This was October, for Heaven's sake!

More importantly, from where had that little dinghy come? She simply didn't like what was going on right under her nose, so she reported the incident to the Long Island shore patrol. If anyone would know what to do, for Heaven's sake, it would be the community's local police!

That notification led to the district chief contacting the Bureau of Investigation.

"I think we've got what we've been waiting for," said Agent Dillon when the report of the landing was handed to him. The plan of action that Dillon and Townsend had hatched some two weeks earlier was put in motion.

Around noon the next day, the showers cleared away. Now with a good field of view, both Hurst and Hagan noticed a schooner enter the sound and begin long, lazy tacks as it skittered along the waters between Montauk and the southern tip of Gardiner's Island. In late afternoon, it streaked across their field of view on the west wind quite quickly. Its double masts had gaff and foresails sails set as well as a mainsail; the boat thus presented as a beautiful, lively work of art gracefully sailing before frothy, wind-driven waves.

The daylight faded with the early onset of a chilly, fall evening. The boat anchored about 100 yards off shore as darkness closed over the sound. Mist began to curl up from the waters, shrouding everything bordering the bay in a quiet, opaque peacefulness.

Around 6:00 P.M., the peace of the night was shattered. The sailboat became aglow as stringer lights rigged up to the mainmast were turned on. The strains of jazz music, glasses clinking, and boisterous laughter filled the air and echoed along the shorelines. One would have thought the happy sounds could be heard all the way to Long Island itself. The usual justification for such merriment was the Yale-Harvard crew race, but that wouldn't be held until early June up at New London. These were simply rich folk enjoying their idleness with a bit of fun.

The two Germans lay on mattresses which they had drawn up to the north-facing windows. As they idly listened to the sounds of merriment, they munched on the last of their cold rations. Tonight would be the night, they were certain, but this fool sailboat might be in the way if their plan unfolded as expected.

They needn't have worried. Around 10:00 P.M., the music stopped and the lights were extinguished. Only the red and green running lights remained faintly aglow. In fairly short order, activity on the boat seemed to cease altogether as the party goers apparently bedded down for the night. By midnight, only the occasional clinking of the halyard clips against the steel wire stays could be heard as small waves in the sound rocked the hull to and fro. As far as Max and Ernst were concerned, the sailboat had ceased to exist.

The night air grew cooler as the temperature continued dropping. Then, hidden by the dark, moonless sky and the now thickened mists, a long, low silhouette seemed to materialize from the black waters. It putt-putted along, passed by the tip of Gardiner Island and slowly cruised past where Hurst and Hagan were now fully alert and glued to the window of the empty summer house. It made some turning maneuvers, but then suddenly stopped dead. The two foreigners could clearly hear frustrated, irate cursing. They didn't need to understand English to perceive that someone was very angry about onboard engine failure.

They exited their hideaway and stood on the edge of the bayside beach. Ernst removed a narrow-beam signaling lamp and pointed it toward the eastern end of the sound: "Target vessel stalled and well-positioned for recovery" the Morse message read. A very short response was forthcoming from the darkness: a single, low intensity flash of acknowledgement.

About an hour passed, and then the men noticed a short, squat tower blacker than even the night gradually rise to just above the surface; thereupon, men appeared on this conning bridge, orders were given in German, and the vessel was slowly moved forward toward the Pod Skimmer. Suddenly, there was garbled, terrified shouting from that craft and several men could be heard jumping overboard. They swam away fearfully and disappeared into the black, still night. One of the sailors on the conning tower had raised a rifle and aimed it their way, but a man who must have been her *Capitan* cautioned the man to desist.

"We are stealing, Klaus. We are not killing tonight. We must be quiet or the operation will fail!" The *Capitan* obviously knew his mission.

The sharpshooter lowered his rifle and put the safety on, but he didn't release the clip. It remained fully seated, just in case.

The two German friends marveled at the skill of the submarine's piloting. Her *Capitan* was commanding via a speaking tube from the conning tower; he guided the slightly submerged hull right between the pod supports, and once that was accomplished, he blew his air tanks and became fully surfaced. A smile broadened his usually stern visage; he had captured the Pod Skimmer fully secured atop the redesigned foredeck. Thereupon, he sent the small boat over to pick up Hagan and Hurst. Once they had boarded, the submarine moved east and slowly disappeared into the safety of the shrouding mists. Her screw churned strongly but, running on batteries, the only noise the craft made was the swish of water gliding alng her hull.

There was no celebrating on the submarine. They had their prize, and the crew was reunited, but they were committed to remaining on the surface. Strict silence had to be maintained until they reached the tender vessel *Deutschland* which was moored about ten miles east of the sound. The Pod Skimmer would be loaded onto her and then the two ships would have to regain international waters quickly if they were to elude the all-out pursuit expected by the Americans.

Meanwhile, the three Americans who had piloted the subterfuge craft into the sound had swum over to the now blacked-out sailboat sitting offshore. She was called *Good Times* by her owner, but she was not moored there for fun, as it turned out. Inside her cabin, men from the Navy Department and the Bureau of Investigation had been monitoring the entire deceit. As the submarine motored out of sight, they welcomed the former collegiate swimmers aboard and, after wrapping them in blankets, shook hands all around. Their plan had worked.

Art Dillon's designated man in charge, Jimmy Tafton, looked at his watch and began to count down. After a little more than two hours, there was a muffled explosion and red-orange streaks briefly brightened the eastern horizon some 12 nautical miles to the east.

Agent Tafton turned to address the men involved in the operation.

"We've done a good night's work. Our deception seems to have worked exactly as planned. The men on the sub will have thought they captured the prototype, they will have radioed success in their mission, and the high command will be duped into thinking our development program has been destroyed. Even if it appears that their nabbing operation went askew, the High Command will believe their submarine blowing up took the Pod Skimmer with it. Therefore, it is vital that we move the real prototype out of its secret warehouse near Warwick and relocate it to Annapolis before dawn breaks. Let's get to work!"

CHAPTER THIRTY-EIGHT

OPERATION COUNTERPOINT

Rear Admiral Oscar Skivers had been assigned to the Naval Office of Public Information some six months ago. He enjoyed his new job. He had become adept at fielding the never-ending probing by reporters. After spending that much time in this position, he could even politely field the constant complaints by summer residents living along the Atlantic seashore about the naval war games and firing at practice targets.

His wife had stood faithfully by his side during his entire 22 year naval career; now, at last, she could actually thrive in this posting. Being assigned to Washington, D.C., meant the couple could enjoy access to museums and restaurants which would delight the curiosity or palate of the most discriminating visitor.

Today, however, the admiral's desk was all a-clutter. He detested such conditions. He preferred things to be neat and tidy, and that applied especially to controlling the paperwork with which his office was continually deluged. He'd been in enough engagements during the Great War to last him the rest of his life, but those experiences had only honed his need for an orderly workplace. The truth was, he was not going to get it today. The date was Friday, October 13, 1933.

He'd barely sat down at his desk that morning when the operator rang his phone. It was the German Ambassador loudly complaining that the United States had deliberately blown up one of the German Empire's submarines. Skivers had no information on this matter, so he made his apologies and promised the ambassador he would find out what had happened and return the call as quickly as he could.

No sooner had he replaced the earpiece when the bells chimed again. This time it was a news reporter who wanted to know about the large explosion and flashing lights in the dead of night off Siaconset Point. Now fed up at being left in the dark regarding some overzealous practice maneuver, he called up Admiral Ramage.

"George, what is all this about explosions and German submarines in close proximity to the Long Island Sound? This is peacetime, for Christ's sake! I've never heard of such a bald-ass stunt in my entire career. I suspect you know what's going on?"

Oscar's rising tone implied he was asking a pointed question; consequently, he expected a direct response.

Admiral Ramage couldn't help smiling. Even his immediate subordinate had been fooled by "Operation Counterpoint." He soothingly spoke into the mouthpiece.

"Oscar, we have a submarine that blew itself up while operating illegally in domestic waters. Perhaps an engine malfunction ignited a fuel line. That's our best guess. Simply say that the Navy has ascertained that there was some sort of fuel-line accident suffered by a foreign submarine as she took on fuel from her resupply vessel. Add that my office is aware of the incident, we have teams combing the beaches for wreckage at present, and we would appreciate an apology from the German government regarding their ships accidentally straying into our territorial waters. Be as brief, or closed-lip, as that. Got it?"

"Certainly, sir, although you have still left me in the dark as to what is going on. This accident occurred almost within sight of our largest metropolitan area. When things have calmed down in a few days, I'd sure appreciate being briefed fully on this matter. Thanks, Admiral Ramage, that's all I have."

"Thank you, Admiral Skivers! Good Day. Over and out." That was all the information that Oscar or, indeed, any shore-based reporter, would ever glean.

Reporters from several competing papers had hired motorboats early that morning to cruise out to the still smoldering wreck site. Apparently, some German submarine had gotten lost while patrolling off the eastern coast of America and had suffered a fire during refueling, resulting in her blowing up and taking the accompanying vessel with her as she sank with all hands lost. The navy had sent vessels to help, but the *Reichsmarine* boats had gone down so quickly that no one had escaped alive. The pieces of wreckage were identified only because the German Embassy had called about one of its submersible craft being unaccountably overdue.

The American Government was extending its condolences through diplomatic channels. As far as the Navy was concerned, that was the end of the matter.

However, everyone had forgotten about Dale Irwin.

CHAPTER THIRTY-NINE

ELIMINATING LOOSE ENDS

"But I'm telling you that I saw it secured to the deck of U-23. You've got to believe me!" Dale Irwin was very agitated. He was calling from the corner drugstore. No one would be monitoring this pay phone, he was certain of that.

He had promised the haughty officials at the German Embassy that the craft near Long Island Sound was—without a doubt—the Pod Skimmer. After all, he'd been monitoring its progress for over three years. He ought to know. It was ripe for the taking if only dam the *Reichsmarine* would listen to his revelations. The embassy clerk whom he had reached today by telephone didn't know Irwin; therefore, he was highly skeptical that the call was genuine. He took his time reporting the call to the German Ambassador. Why would such a high-ranking official be curious about some delusional American spouting off about "some big secret" that no one at the embassy was aware of? None of the recent Enigma encoded messages had carried warnings of any new American military threat.

When the staff assistant finally got around to informing the ambassador, that eminent official merely brushed him aside.

"Yes, yes, of course we already know about that. The matter will be attended to shortly."

The conversation with the American had been on the 14th. Now, word was reaching the embassy that an attempt had indeed been made, executed poorly, and everyone involved in the subterfuge had perished. Ambassador Luther himself made a statement to throw the American reporters off the scent of his countrymen's failure. He'd even contacted the navy admiral in charge of public relations to lodge a spurious complaint. As far as he was concerned, Goebbels and his cronies would have to think up some other ploy. The Americans weren't going to be lulled into inaction twice regarding their spectacularly "Swift Ship" as the *Allemandes* agents had nicknamed it.

Nevertheless, the turncoat Irwin was proving to be more like a nagging annoyance than a helpful source of information. His value to the Third Reich was now outweighed by his liability as a loud-mouth complainer. It was time for him to be silenced. Ambassador Joachim Luther decided to assign someone to take care of the matter. If this American blabbed this strongly to a foreign embassy, he would likely spout a book's worth of words to some damned interrogator from the Bureau of Investigation or, worse, some newspaper reporter.

When Ingrid was contacted by her handler, she asked a few pertinent questions regarding subject location, age, capabilities, and habits. She never inquired as to "why."

Simply receiving orders for termination were sufficient for this experienced and skilled *femme de fatale*, as she liked to be known back home in Berlin. She'd never met the Füehrer himself because she had moved to America in 1924. Nevertheless, over the years that man had become her hero: he would be the savior of her homeland, she was sure of it. As for her own capabilities, she was held in high regard by her superiors back in the Third Reich but, without a doubt, she was merely a female. Her orders had directed her to remain in a low-profile, standby status until needed.

She'd become distantly sociable with the Americans living on her street in rural Cherry Hill, New Jersey. Several of the families there had even invited her to dinner. She had always politeily accepted; being a part of her community would further obscure her real identity. Nevertheless, it wouldn't do to become too friendly with people she might someday have to terminate. Her central location on the East Coast, however, made her ideal from the German High Command's point of view: she could be available on short notice for assignment anywhere from Norfolk to Boston.

Her Nazi handlers had passed some low-level assignments her way during the last eight years. "She had to stay in form; it wouldn't do for her to become slow or careless," her superiors had argued when no worthwhile targets seemed to be surfacing in America. Now, however, she had a military man in her sights. She would have to execute brilliantly; the target's demise must appear to have been an accident, her stateside handler had insisted. The Americans must not be allowed to insinuate anything significant from this man's death.

For a week she tailed Dale Irwin. She even obtained his record of service and noted that he'd run into serious dereliction-of-duty charges while aboard an American destroyer during the Great War. She concluded that he'd been put "out to pasture" to get him out of everyone's hair. He was somewhat portly, certainly in poor physical condition, and couldn't, she imagined, hurt a fly physically. Apparently, however, he had a mouth on him and, lacking self-respect or trappings of dignity in terms of service ribbons, there was a high probability that he would blab about his "favors" performed for the Third Reich over the past three years. He had to be silenced. True to her profession, that was all she needed to know.

After observing his habits and haunts herself, and mulling over the reports of other agents who had been tailing him from the moment he had walked into the German Embassy and offered to exchange secrets for money back in 1931, she decided she would make her move as he left his favorite haunt, The Blue Tavern. Since her mark no longer had shipboard assignments, he appeared to drown his sorrows there each evening, emerging around 11:00 PM and proceeding straight back to his apartment. Drinking himself into a stupor appeared to be his sole diversion. She would give him a new one.

Tonight would be an opportune time. Darkness came quickly this time of year and the air would be noticeably chilly. Particularly if the wind was up, one would be expected to wear some sort of raingear, even a hat and gloves, in order to stave off the chill during an evening stroll. What made it perfect, from Ingrid's viewpoint, was that the weather and blustering wind indicated that a chance of rain was imminent. Carrying an umbrella would be a perfectly natural accessory on the evening of Thursday, October 26.

Right on schedule, there he was. Her mark emerged in an obvious state of inebriation, swaying and mumbling incoherently as he stumbled along the street.

Clearly, he was merely focused on reaching his apartment. She waited on the corner under the street lamp; she wanted him to spot her easily and then to lure him to her.

As Irwin swayed unsteadily toward the street crossing, he kept stumbling over his own feet. His hands stretched forward as though he was groping for something but could never find it. As he closed on the intersection, he was just stepping forward with his right leg when, suddenly, a nice-looking, dark-haired woman whirled and poked him just above the knee with the tip of her umbrella. In his stupor, he never felt pain as a small steel ball penetrated the cloth of his trousers and lodged beneath the skin of his thigh. It would take only twenty minutes or so before the wax plug melted from his body heat and allowed lethal toxin to seep into his body.

"Oh, I'm so sorry. I didn't realize you were so close. May I help you across the street, sir?"

Dale peered at the person next to him and perceived a mysteriously attractive angel with a slender figure set off by a belted trench coat. She held her folded umbrella by her side, offering him a hand as he stepped from the curb. How could he be so lucky to find someone attractive out on the streets of New York this late at night? He thanked his lucky stars for such good fortune. He smiled back at his executioner.

"Oh, don't worry none, miss. I probably startled you, and I apologize. Jus' help me cross over. My apartment's right up there." He tried to point to a brownstone building but his arm was unsteady. He started to pitch into the street, but she caught him and helped him across.

"Well, that was a dandy trip! Thank you miss, I hope to see you in this neighborhood during the daylight proper! Good night."

He fumbled with the street access, got the door open, entered, and then took one long look after the departing apparition as she seemed to fade into the opaque mists. He slowly conquered the steps and reached the landing, but as he reached to put his key in the slender opening, he grew very unsteady, his vision blacked out, his head swirled, and then he turned once and fell flat onto the floor. He had made it up the stairs to his apartment door, but that was as far as he got. His last thought was that his drinking tonight might have been overdone.

That was where his neighbor from down the hall, Mildred Hastings, found him the next morning. His hand was stretched forward, with his fingers still curled as though trying to turn a doorknob, but his body was stiff and cold. Apparently, he'd had a heart attack and passed away on the spot. He was, after all, 65 years old and a war veteran. There seemed nothing unusual about his dying in front of his own apartment. The police investigation went no further than to notify a few relatives; the man had simply succumbed to natural causes brought on by heavy drinking.

"Another survivor of the Great War gone to his rest" was what the press noted in the obituary column the next day. This veteran, however, would simply be buried in a plain, wood box; there'd be no honor guard at his funeral.

After reading the *New York Times* obituaries the next day, Art Dillon opened the black appointment book he kept in his head and scratched a name off the list of suspected traitors.

"Sometimes," he thought, "your enemies unknowingly do you a favor."

CHAPTER FORTY

POD SKIMMER II

Charles hung up the phone. He had just been told by Art Dillon that, insofar as the Bureau knew, his family and those of the other members of the Group of Seven were now free of immediate danger. "At least temporarily," Art had added.

Since the myriad colors of fall were now fading into the monochromatic shades of a windy winter, there'd be little chance for evaluating their redesigned prototype other than in Frank Jones' test tank. At least there they'd be able to stay warm while working.

He picked up the earpiece again and, holding the black mouthpiece close, asked the operator for a number in Washington, D.C. The connection took a minute or two: calling someone as important as a navy admiral required several staff levels to clear. However, when he'd given his name, Charles had added the organization he represented. The mere mention of "Group of Seven" seemed to knock down all barriers. When Admiral Ramage came on the line, he confirmed that the Pod Skimmer was safely moored at Norfolk Naval Shipyard. Experienced naval draftsmen were working on her superstructure design for the craft's ultimate use.

"Admiral, this will confirm that we are proceeding with construction of the next generation of Pod Skimmers. If you want to assign men from the Adjutant General's office to look her over, let us know and we'll make accommodations for them available."

"That won't be necessary, son. There are naval architects working alongside your man Peter North at General Dynamics. Just tell him to keep them informed; those men could make the round trip in one day when your team has something to show."

"Certainly, Admiral, as you wish. My fellow members have asked me to convey that we would be receptive to any suggestions, or the discovery of flaws, that your men experience with Pod Skimmer #1. As you know, our prototype has not been tested with any sort of decking or weapons, so we'd be interested to know how she performs. Of course, we would want to be in compliance with any concerns for national security that you have."

"Don't worry, my boy. We'll stay in touch. Thank you." and with that, the navy boss moved on to other concerns. His day would be very busy with matters unrelated to that invention. The verbose and demonstrative leader of what was becoming known as the Nazi Party was beginning to show his true colors in the Deutschland. Admiral Ramage had a date to meet with President Roosevelt that very afternoon on this subject.

As a former secretary of the navy himself, this president liked being kept abreast of developments, whether technical, or political.

As far as Charles was concerned, he had a broad smile as he turned to his cohorts and said, "Well, we've got the go-ahead from the Navy. Let's get to bed for the night so we can start early tomorrow on Pod Skimmer #2."

Everyone's face bore an expression of relief as we turned toward Charles: despite the deepening depression gripping the country, our work would apparently continue into the foreseeable future. At a time when a quarter of the country's work force was on breadlines hoping for a simple handout, it was very good to have any sort of job, especially one that made each of us fulfilled and, more importantly, paid the bills.

The rest of the afternoon was spent toasting and trading tales at the small, quaint restaurant nestled in the safe, comfortable décor of the Mariners Inn located by the docks. When Charles finally broke away from the merriment and headed for the bungalow he had provided for his bride of three years and their two year-old son, he was in fine fettle.

Thanksgiving was less than three weeks away. His parents would be coming round his house to share the holiday which, this time, would be catered by his wife, rather than his mother. He marveled at how far he had come since being an orderly to Captain Highsmith aboard the *Humboldt*. That dear man had died only the year before while on the job doing what he loved best. The captain had given Charles a breadth of training unavailable to most in his profession, so, thankfully, he was now both a father and a respected part of the Group of Seven.

Each member of this cohesive team had his own particular skill to devote to the project. Our work was seriously pursued not just for profit, but also because it could possibly have profound repercussions throughout the naval world. Besides, we were having too much fun to do otherwise than give it our all each and every day.

The latest version would incorporate a nascent metal—streamlined aluminum—and recently developed diesel generators to provide turbo electric rotation to the screws. To keep weight down, the rear pods would have only one screw apiece, but their design would permit much greater propulsive thrust than all four of those used in P.S. #1. Using a single port and a single starboard screw had become desirable only the week before as the light weight of aluminum made significant design changes possible. Thereafter, we spent the entire week before Thanksgiving working on these improvements. We envisioned that Pod Skimmer #2 would surpass the original for speed and stability, although her maximum load capacity would be somewhat reduced.

A major breakthrough occurred when Scott perfected our using one wide pod, rather than two in parallel, for the bow support. Everyone agreed this was an improvement, so the change was quickly adopted.

There was one change that we were now considering that would be a radical departure from the norm. However, testing it would require actual real-life conditions on the open ocean, rather than merely controlling it in a tank. Thus, it had been relegated to a low priority during the winter months. I had first proposed skipping the rudder altogether, but our presentation to the navy brass, together with all the various foreign intrigues, had so occupied us during the prior months that we simply had not gotten around to seriously considering the possibility.

Our initial rudder designs and placements had confounded us from the very start three years ago. Various team members had put forward words such as "unreliable, inadequate, too complex," and even the rather insulting term, "unworkable" before settling on the forward, dual rudder configuration we were proposing for Pod Skimmer #2.

At that point, I said, "Look, we're continuing to use just two engines, but the new ones have larger, more effective blade designs. I bet we could steer her simply by decreasing the rate of revolutions or reversing either engine, and thus rely on screw propagation alone. What do you think?"

Naturally, the others simply laughed. If Peter North had been up visiting with us just then, I'm certain that he too would have joined in their levity.

"What Wally is proposing," the other three had jeered, "is simply ludicrous!"

At this time, a fast-spinning shaft still required something on the order of 20 seconds to come to a stop before it could be reversed. Leaving the ship without any independent steering mechanism under such conditions would be foolish. When one of the others stated this obvious fact, he provided my opening. I pounced on them even before their laughter had subsided.

"What if we had a brake, a sort of sleeve that could clamp around the circumference of a rotating shaft, and thereby bring it to a halt in about three seconds? This would provide us not merely with minute differentials in rotational speed, but could give us a brake by applying full reverse within a few seconds of perceiving a peril."

On the day I proposed this, Peter had not yet appeared, but he was due in. This left the five of us to stew over my addition to Charles' idea. We spent the rest of the day shuffling around the workroom like silent, cogitating monks lost in our own ponderings. A rudderless craft seemed to be far too risky a proposition. Certainly the Navy would demand rudders; they were too set in their hide-bound traditions to accept such a radical idea. However, as it was wintertime, this idea was essentially tabled until the spring thaw would allow mock-up testing under realistic conditions.

In this awkward state of affairs, our group broke up for the day. Peter had called to say he would be by tomorrow, so there was no sense hanging about holding a hammer yet having nothing to pound. We closed up shop but left Frank Jones alone to continue muddling about his tanks. He always liked staying late into the night.

This is what our latest design looks like:

<u>Pod Skimmer #2</u>
Legend: R = rudder
E = engine room
T = turbine
G = generator
M = electric motor
F = fuel tank
Slanted lines = decking

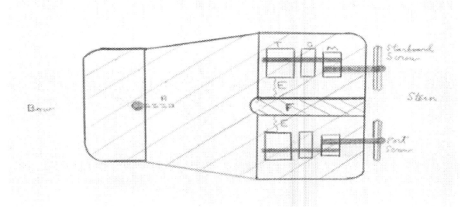

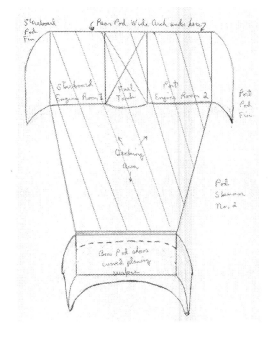

A superstructure would be constructed atop the blunt arrowhead-shaped deck. The support beneath the deck would be gently arched toward its center to allow for passage of waves beneath. The overall length of the support platform is 600 feet. Each stern pod measures 150 by 35 feet, and 12 feet tall in its interior dimension to provide room for the crews running the engines to work. Fuel would be housed conveniently astride each engine room.

*   *   *

As I returned to my own house, I knew it would be silent and empty. My kids were now grown and gone, pursuing their own lives, and my Mary was deceased. So I indulged myself in imagining what young Charles would be experiencing as he opened his front door.

Upon arriving at the doorstep of his bungalow, Charles would fling it open in an exuberant mood, calling, "Holly! I'm home; where are you?"

"Heaven's sake, I'm not in Canada; I'm right here, setting the table for dinner," Holly would trill in her melodious way.

His wife would come around the divider wall and position herself directly in front of him. Her magnificent husband would be left with no alternative. Her scent, the healthy glow flushing her cheeks, and a mouth held in an evocative pout, well, these would be simply too much for the man. He would just have to kiss her, but doing so would prevent his stopping there. Their bodies would fold together with both the tenderness of deeply-held love as well as smoldering lust. The latter could be ignited with a simple soft, warm nuzzle of an ear. The only difficulty was that she had to stand on tiptoe to reach him, and that required that he bend his head down toward her, which in turn provided him with an eyeful of her nubile figure. Even her pregnancy had not diminished the appeal of the slender curves of her rump which Charles would probably cup as he lifted Holly bodily off the ground.

He would state: "I cherish you so completely, Holly. How could a man be lucky enough to fall so utterly in love the very first time he laid eyes on you, yet still be fully enamored after all this time? You are so desirable. I'm consumed by my work, but when I leave for the day, I simply can't wait to rush home and find you here. It's like returning to my mother's womb; you provide such completeness to my life, I have no wish to be anywhere else!"

Holly's facetious retort would be quick in coming: "Oh, come now, you big dolt. I saw you when you returned from your meeting with those navy big shots. Your eyes were all aglow and shining like stars; you were <u>so</u> impressed with yourself!"

"Guilty as charged, you're right. But it was their eagerness to accept our prototype and then pursue its final development that thrilled me. It wasn't the town of Washington at all. Our team pretty much arrived, made our sales pitch, and left. If you want, we could go down and visit that place some day, but everything I need is right here in this house. Where is young James, by the way?"

"Don't fret yourself. He's down and sleeping. Never wake a sleeping baby—you ought to know that by now. Besides, I'm in the mood to do something more interesting, like make another one."

Charles would then look deeply into Holly's shining eyes and find them afire with warm desire. He was not going to say "no" to such an invitation. He would have picked her up bodily and carried her into the bedroom. The blinds would be closed in anticipation of early darkness. The quilted throw looked softly inviting, so he would lay her across the coverlet gently. His attentions were directed to tracing the lines of her legs with his fingers. He'd no doubt slip off her slippers and lightly run his fingers across and over her thighs, gradually ascending ever higher until they were dancing beneath her skirt. She'd begin writhing beneath the incessant stimulation of his fingers, and as he circled her soft mound, she'd moan and raise her hips in slow, circling gyrations.

Slipping off her filmy undergarments, he would nestle his lips in her inviting crescent and breathe warmly. Then his tongue might make light, tender flicks over, around, and across her joy center. She'd become wildly aroused, writhing beneath him. It'd be all he could do to contain himself. As she'd begin to peak, she'd suddenly grab him by the shirt collar and pull his mouth up to hers.

"Take me, deeply, my dear man. Take me now!"

Charles would do as he was bid. After all, this is what he had been thinking about ever since the last toast had been raised back at the Mariner Inn. His legs would part hers as he mounted and allowed her to guide his hot staff inside her. Slowly, gently, just a little bit at first, then more deeply until he was penetrating her as fully as he was capable, causing his wife to writhe and call out his name over and over until, in a frantic series of impatient thrusts, they'd come together. Sheer, inexplicably divine pleasure would doubtless fill them both as they expired in an exhausted, satisfied embrace.

They would relax to let their hearts slow down as he held her close against his chest. With his left hand cradling her shoulders, he would reach across with his right and slowly undo the buttons of her blouse. The clean white fabric would fall away as he undid the pretty ribbons of her camisole. Her breasts would thus be exposed to the air, making her nipples proudly firm in the faint lamplight. Her husband might gently circle first one, then the other, lightly dibbling each nipple so her entire body participated in their lovemaking. The sensations he produced would be deeply satisfying to Holly and she'd snuggle close against Charles. He would then pull the covers up so they could serenely drift off to sleep together.

Shortly Charles would simply have to get up and use the bathroom. Even on a chilled, late fall night, such need could not be ignored. When he returned to the bedroom, his wife's invitingly warm body would form curving mounds beneath the blanket. He'd crawl back in and get toasty almost immediately. Feeling completely whole and proud of his wife, he'd fall instantly asleep once more.

Their son might cry for milk later that night. First Holly, then Charles would hold him as the baby took turns feeding from a bottle kept beneath the sheets; it was a perfect temperature for their love-child, so the boy could drink eagerly and then fall right back to sleep. Peace and comfort would have blanketed the McDonald household that night.

* * *

Yes, I could make up my own rollicking fun, even as an elder statesman in my fifties. I have not yet lost the power to visualize, nor to remember. On the other hand, perhaps the lad's lucky love life was exactly as I imagined it.

CHAPTER FORTY-ONE

NEW AND BRIGHT, BUT STILL UNTESTED

The sun was slow to appear with the dawn on this February day. Overcast clouds filled the seaside air around Providence, parted around 7:00 AM only for a few minutes, and then closed in once more. By the time Charles was leaving his house for the day's work, light snow had just begun trickling down. It was noon before the ground began to become white, but by the end of the day, two inches had fallen. The heck with the groundhog and his shadow: Rhode Island was going to remain in the grip of a frozen countryside.

The weather did not matter to those of us working on the Pod Skimmer #2. We were inside Frank Jones' test facility. The office space had ample drafting tables. The place was heated with fuel from propane tanks adjoining the storage shed out back. True, our team still had to deliver copies of significant improvements to Orville Townsend by posted mail. As our money-man, he had to approve our forecasted expenditures, so this was a necessary step. However, there were days when mail delivery seemed as slow as a snail. The telephone was much faster, but if Orville were to approve any outlay for expenses, he had to be able to justify doing so to the Board of Directors of Oceanic Lines. That required written proof, of course.

Fortunately, we did not have to bother meeting with those gentlemen. They were of a mind that profits had to come through accepted means; they would never have accommodated our new-fangled ideas. After nearly four years, however, the six of us had learned to conceive an idea, mail it down for review, and only thereafter to proceed. Initially, our excitement had caused us to be far too impetuous. We'd spend, we'd design, we'd build and assemble, and only then would we seek approval. Such behavior was quickly tempered by some of our submissions being rejected. We had been required to effect too many tedious removals from a mock-up to ignore those lessons.

Most of us had, at one time or another, spent lengthy hours wrestling with our pride as we attempted to learn the necessary humility and self-control to work with Townsend. As the months stretched into years, we became more in tune with what Orville could handle. Project James meant that much to us. We wanted to bring the Pod Skimmer to life, to make her economical to build yet profitable to sail, as quickly as possible. Our impatience, which earlier had known no bounds, was finally maturing. Making an entirely new concept function properly required daily attention to detail and logical thinking. Trial and error and corrections were the order of our days; all this demanded patience.

As a result of the various bureaucratic permutations, none of us got excited about a new concept anymore; we had become far more business-like. We had left the days of wide-eyed, childlike excitement far behind. We'd also suffered serious threats to our safety. Emotional outbursts would now be reserved only for a successful sale. Besides, with the six of us working as a team, we were able to evaluate an idea pretty thoroughly before ever committing it to the mail and Townsend's veto. At least now, with the sale to the U.S. Navy, Townsend finally had fresh funds with which to finance our pursuit of the successor to Pod Skimmer #1.

That was why everyone else was stumped when I proposed the entire revamping of our steering mechanism. All ships used a rudder of some sort in their stern, so P.S. #1 was unique in mounting it on the stern of the forward pods. Now, here I was suggesting its placement in a new position rather than off the stern of the pods. No one had steered a ship from the front before.

Back when people traveled by wagon, the handler didn't think about steering; the wagon went where the horses went, and that was managed by pulling on one set of reins or the other. A driver thought about what the horses, and later, what the wheels did. In the 1930's, cars had replaced wagons as standard transportation; if you couldn't afford one, you'd go by bus. All these vehicles used front wheel steering. Drivers nowadays thought only about what the front wheels do. The old principle at sea of pushing a rudder right or left in order to thrust the stern outward, thereby repositioning the bow inward, was not applicable to wagon, automobile, or truck traffic.

When I put forward the idea of positioning rudders suspended from the center of the bow pod, everyone sat stunned for a minute. It had never been tried because no one ever thought in those terms before. Turning a ship from the front? Could that be done? Suddenly, as a troop, we all took up our pencils and began scribbling madly across our drafting papers. Thresher came up with the most appealing sketch—embodying a metal strut positioned underwater and joining the bow sections to serve as a base for the steering pinnacle—and we descended on Frank Jones to produce a wooden mockup which could be tested immediately.

That had been a couple of months ago, but now my brain was clicking in high gear. Almost as soon as Charles proposed the forward-positioned rudders, I conceived the idea of leaving out rudders entirely and simply steering by altering the spin of the twin screws. That was too far-fetched, even for my cooperative group, so we had decided to leave that idea alone and address it later come spring. Thus, by agreement on the very day it was conceived, the idea of a rudder-less Pod Skimmer was to be left up to our imaginations. Nothing would be put on paper or calculations attempted until June, if then.

Now, the time to fully consider my new-fangled approach was upon us. Nevertheless, as evening-tide descended, the plan called for Frank to continue testing our by now state-of-the-art twin steered rudders at the tail ends of the forward pod. What would the arc of turn radius be with such a widely-spaced setup? If a superstructure built atop the Skimmer's body was balanced properly, the old dictate that the rudder had to be positioned aft—because that was how the stern would be pushed outward and the bow positioned inward—could be ignored. For my money, having a rudder on both of the downward curving starboard and port skimmers would make turning not only very tight, but also operable on just one screw should there be an engine breakdown. This idea might yield both faster response as well as backup safety. This made me wonder whether a center-mounted rudder could be even half as effective.

We left for the day to put off these concerns while coping with the current demands of shoveling snow off our sidewalks and warming ourselves by the fireplace in the evening. As usual, reliable old Frankie was left to wrestle with his models far into the night. We let him be: he was accustomed to working alone. Moreover, he was now in his early 60's; he could get somewhat short with us if we puttered about his facility bothering him with needless questions. Thus, except for Frank, all of us left for home that night confident that we would soon realize genuine improvements in the Pod Skimmer design.

When the sun came up on February 21, 1934, it should have provided sufficient warmth to melt the fresh snow that had fallen overnight. Sadly, the air remained in the lower 20's; no melting would occur today. The weather would not be the only chilling factor we encountered.

My plan was to rise, do some stretching, and a little later call my daughter Alice to see if she was awake and attending her college classes regularly. I intended to reach the test facility by 9:30, but my plan was shattered when the phone rang at 8:30 and Terry hoarsely lamented that the office was a shambles. He was still in a state of shock at what he'd found that early morning. He wanted me to alert the police while he called the others. All of us should get to the shop as quickly as we were able.

Upon arriving, I found that Scott had not overstated himself. The office area was indeed trashed. All our drawings, specification lists, and the smaller models were missing. Only the large prototypes we had begun framing in wood remained. Each of the drawers, cabinets, and shelves were skewed about, the rug had been lifted to see whether there was some secret chamber below the floorboards, and of course the main entrance had been largely destroyed. The safe was still in place, but that was small consolation. It held only interim funds needed to pay for construction materials as we progressed. We had not yet gotten far enough along on this version to ask for major advances from Townsend. Obviously, these thieves were interested in a prize bigger than mere cash.

Now that our spec sheets and diagrams were gone, we would have two problems: first, resurrecting Pod Skimmer #2 virtually from our combined memories. This was something we not only thought we could do, but indeed set about doing on the spot, with the intention of storing any documents that we produced thereafter in a bank.

The second item was far more serious. Where the hell was Frank Jones? There was no note, no blood, not even a sign of physical struggle. We debated whether to bring in The Bureau of Investigation; however, the arrival of such men would mean this event had taken a very ugly turn. Art Dillon would doubtless head up the team; we could picture the G-Men pondering the situation at their desks, shirt sleeves rolled up, cigars growing short as the hours ticked by without producing any leads, and then their calling it a bust and retiring for the night. What could they do if there were no fingerprints or witnesses? No clues, no ransom notes, no Jones. This was worse than a bad nightmare.

We pictured the men at the Bureau theorizing that Jones had been kidnapped and taken not so much as a hostage, but as someone to grill and torture for information.

That would mean his being kept alive for any length of time would be very much in doubt.

Our minds raced with imaginings. This could not have been the work of mere thugs. It had to have been the work of highly sophisticated and informed operatives. It all pointed to sabotage and espionage by the Germans yet again. Was there another spy in our midst? Good Lord, let the saints deliver us!

With documents in those devious hands, even applying for patent protection would lead to a battle in international court as to who invented the ideas first. The Navy would have to come forward and risk revealing military secrets in public to prove that P.S. #1 had been ours.

This was a major fiasco for which we were totally unprepared psychologically. In typical human fashion, we couldn't believe this destruction and theft had even occurred, but the proof that it had lay all about our drafting office. This terrible, mind-boggling piracy had happened, and it had happened to us, not our competitors, whoever they might be. Blame, guilt, and self-recrimination: we underwent all of those negative feelings. In nautical terms, we were each going off the deep end.

It was useless to point fingers. As a team, we were equally culpable for holding on naively to the idea that we could stay out of the spotlight. Apparently, the Pod Skimmer #2 was now at center stage, either for the Germans or, perhaps, some unknown group of competitors.

As any rational person could surmise, we had become paranoid overnight.

It therefore came as a great relief when Jacob thought he heard a noise in the plumbing apparatus box used to adjust the water levels and flow rates for the tank. He listened more closely; when he was certain he heard something moving therein, he opened the hinged door and there was Frank! The poor man had tried to make himself as small as possible in order to fit inside, and now his legs were cramping and his back was sore. He had to be assisted out of there.

After stretching his limbs and taking a few gulps of water, he started explaining that he had heard sounds of break-in on the exterior of the building around 1:00 AM. Being alone, he had taken refuge in this tiny control box. A short time thereafter, he heard the front door burst in. An average man would not be up and about at such an hour. He had quickly concluded that if he confronted the culprits, he would quickly become a victim rather than a savior, and so he had remained in hiding until we found him.

Even in the midst of our loss, we were now so happy! His conceptual mind, as well as his devoted diligence, were such highly rated assets that we all breathed a welcome sigh of relief when Frank proved to be, give or take a few hours of sleep, hale and hearty. From then on, however, Scott, Jacob, Frank, Charles, and I adopted the following behavior: either we would all leave at the same hour after a day's work, or we would remain in the shop together until the last holdout was ready to call it a night. We also improved the locks on the double doors!

We would leave it up to the police, and the Bureau of Investigation personnel if necessary, to track these thieves down. We neither asked how they would proceed, nor what would happen to the thieves once they were caught. We very much wanted such matters to be out of our minds.

About a week later, a phone call from New York Shipbuilding came as a pleasant surprise. The five of us had really made a mountain out of a molehill. N.Y.S. management had called to notify us that two men in their early 20's had approached their headquarters regarding the sale of hull designs. Their main thrust was that the designs would be unique to the industry. However, one of the draftsmen recognized that they were similar to his mental picture of something that Frank Jones had mentioned while he was still employed there. The police were contacted and the two were immediately arrested and held for theft, transporting stolen property across state lines, false pretense, and breaking and entering a private business.

None of us had seen these men, so there was no point in our testifying as to their identities. The fact that we could prove ownership of the documents in their possession was sufficient to convict them and send them to the penitentiary. Another problem solved. In that short interval, we had used our recollections to reconstruct the plans. It was good to have the originals back so we could compare the accuracy of our memories. Having learned our lesson, these originals were placed in the vault of our local bank, and we quickly returned to the business of development and testing. Once again we had, as they say in the Deep South, a dog in the hunt.

We committed ourselves to rolling out the latest version of Pod Skimmer as quickly as our energies would allow. The renderings for same appear below.

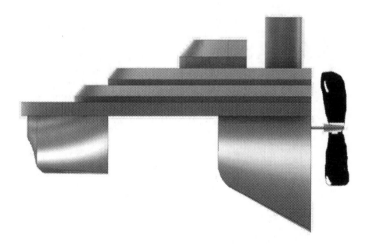

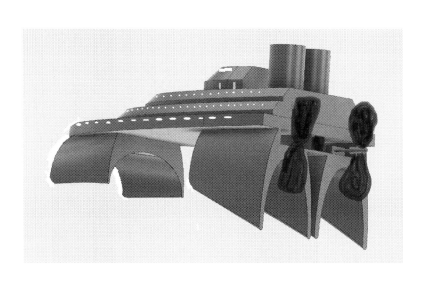

CHAPTER FORTY-TWO

JIM STAHL'S CONCEPTS REALIZED

Pod Skimmer #2 worked better than our expectations. The equipment comprising the engines had been so downsized that the space required to operate them had been dramatically reduced, thereby increasing cargo space. Our initial concept of connecting the forward pods with a connecting span continued to be our preferred method, but now with one broad bow pod, the design became far more complex. A flat deck that eliminated support beams and noticeably simplified the superstructure bracing would be less costly to construct. Moreover, the less weight she carried in the pods themselves, the better we could make the Pod Skimmer perform and the higher she could rise above the surface, thereby lessening the possibility of undercarriage drag.

Now that the weather had warmed, we decided to seriously address testing my idea of twin screws doing all the steering, thereby obviating the need for rudders entirely. When a single hull was constructed with a deep draft, its linear momentum required, absolutely, a separate steering mode. Rudders fitted that need. A great deal of force had to be applied to overcome the inertia of such a large mass continuing in a straight line. But when a vessel was merely skimming the surface with greatly reduced wetted surface, perhaps she could be steered by merely backing off one engine, or even putting that engine into reverse.

The key would be slowing, perhaps even stopping, the rotation of either the port or starboard shaft relatively quickly. One of the major factors that doomed the Titanic was the long delay her engines required before the piston shafts could reverse their stroking. Twenty or so seconds was far too great a lag for my idea to even be considered. Therefore, our idea of fast shaft reversal was given priority when the weather allowed us to experiment on open water. We determined that stopping a shaft completely, and then reversing it in under four seconds, should provide sufficiently fast reaction time to genuinely remove rudders altogether. Theoretically, steering as well as direction change/braking could be effected using the screws alone.

Naturally, if we could prove the feasibility of this idea, the improvement in speed through lowered drag would be noticeable.

The matter of docking had to be considered because the tolerances for mistake in a harbor are very narrow. Most port facilities of the time employed tugs for maneuvering large ships, but the British were famous for approaching a pier, turning the ship around after she had stopped, and then backing into the arms of the quay. This was pretty tricky to execute, especially when navigating some 20,000 or more tons; thus, pilots who knew the currents and wharf dimensions like the backs of their hands were still employed when it came to docking a ship.

Therefore, what we needed to develop immediately was a very efficient brake. One possibility was a sort of sleeve that could clamp down on the shaft as it spun at around 70 and 100 revolutions per minute. Asbestos was becoming available as a heat insulator; perhaps it could be adapted to withstand the high frictional forces that would result from such a brake. The major problem for such a brake was its short life span; jamming was another unwanted possibility. Moreover, I personally objected to the idea of all those worn fibers floating around in the enclosed space of an engine room. We would have to evaluate this material fully.

In this regard, we focused on the diesel generators; if these could be quickly slowed into reverse, so could the shaft, and thus the screw. The solution was so obvious that it nearly went unnoticed: use the transmission. Scott worked closely with Peter for a few weeks; that way, we had expert experience from a submariner to draw on. Submarines were famous for fast turns; they had to be, or they'd be sitting ducks for nimble destroyers on the surface. Our two engineer types came up with a highly accurate mesh for the gear teeth that could make a fast, and smooth, transition from the cog for forward motion across to the one for reverse direction.

It's a truism in naval engineering that nothing new ever comes easily.

As the delights of a moist, fresh spring eased into the more serious bother of summer heat, we were well advanced in our testing. During the first week of June, we took P.S. #2 to the next stage, building a mock superstructure with wide, two story passenger decks. The uppermost third deck would house the command, control, communications, and officer cabins.

The greater the height, the greater is the drag coefficient. This was the dreaded truism that we dealt with every day on this project. All three decks were tapered to reduce air drag by being streamlined; we even designed a sort of "swept-back" look for them, and intended on doing the same for the smokestack cowling in the future. After all, this vessel was expected to achieve a speed of 50 knots. The resistance of wind to forward motion would be substantial even as we were reducing drag from ocean water.

The three decks were to comprise some 36 feet in height. All of that superstructure would be sitting atop a pod bed that itself was some 10 feet above the waterline when the vessel reached cruising speeds. This design might appear to be top-heavy, and therefore easy to roll over, but the broad tri-point placement of the pods was intended to overcome this problem.

It required eight months for us to iron out all the intricacies, as well as several unforeseen snafus, but when we informed Orville Townsend that our mockup had successfully passed her trials, he sent each of us a bonus check for $2,000. This got the year 1935 off to a very good start. The funds would assure future schooling for Charles's young son, James Stahl McDonald, and even ease the burden of repaying my daughter's college education. Peter, as a fairly new grandfather, went right out and bought himself a new pair of red suspenders. Frank simply banked his, and Scott, as usual, invested his money in further night school classes.

I couldn't believe it; my daughter was now nineteen and attending Bryn Mawr College. She had toured its campus briefly while we were in Pennsylvania for Jim's funeral; thereafter, she had written its president, Marion Park, regarding her great desire to study botany there. The long-serving President Park enjoyed Alice's well-composed letter so much that she took an interest in my daughter, checked on her transcript records, and then encouraged her to apply. Mary and I had created a daughter whose future was falling into place.

I was so grateful. Ever since Mary's tragic early death, managing my daughter's development into a young woman had been a challenge for which I was ill-prepared. Growing up had been more difficult for her than I remembered it being for me. I was not equipped to answer her direct, even pointed questions. As she matured, her questioning grew all the more difficult to comprehend, much less answer to her satisfaction. Fortunately, Elizabeth Aston, our next-door neighbor in her mid-forties, would have Alice over frequently for dinner when I was working late. I'm sure their talks solved many of the riddles because, after a few months of taking dinner over at Mrs. Aston's, my daughter stopped plying me with embarrassing questions.

Phew! If truth be told, I was so genuinely relieved that I almost sat down to write a book touting the fact that a person can indeed "dodge a bullet," but as soon as I realized that I would be writing about things of which I knew nothing, I let that project slide.

If truth be told, watching Alice mature into a young woman was a far greater reward than writing some book. She became as pretty as her mother had been. Nevertheless, it occurred to me that I would soon have to prepare myself for the day she would accept some romantic swain's proposal and leave my house forever. That was something I most definitely wanted to put off thinking about.

As for Bill, I couldn't be more pleased with the way my son had grown and developed. He had studied mechanical engineering and then joined the army after graduation in order to become an officer in the Army Corps of Engineers. His head was solidly on his shoulders. I suppose he had timed his leaving home well. No sooner had Mary passed away than he was off to college, so the grief, and utter loss, that I experienced were replaced by his new-found friends and the myriad challenges he found at Yale University in New Haven, Connecticut. I had hinted to him that Providence was not all that far from New Haven, so if he wanted to stop by for a visit, he'd be welcome most any time. Regrettably, as his years progressed from freshman to senior, he stayed away for longer and longer periods. When Alice was still around the house while growing up, I could avoid having to get used to my son being absent. Now that she had left as well, my home had become far too quiet to be relished.

Thank my lucky stars for the Pod Skimmer project; it could consume my attentions completely. In fact, I went to work every day with a broad smile on my face!

CHAPTER FORTY-THREE

TRIALS IN MIAMI

Now that we had a prototype that we could call our own, independent of the navy deal, we needed to show her off. There were plenty of institutions of higher learning around Norfolk as well as businesses needing shipping exporters, but what we really sought was exposure to groups that were interested in travel. Not merely interested, but ones whose members had time on their hands and money in their pockets. The spot on the east coast which offered the best opportunity for the demonstrative marketing that we required was the ocean off the east coast of Florida.

I called up Admiral Hastings. He had replaced Admiral Ramage when that man was assigned to manage the nation's Pacific Fleet based in Pearl Harbor. Hastings and I had become social friends last year when my daughter Alice debuted at the Waldorf-Astoria Hotel with several dozen other young ladies. Our daughters didn't know one another at the time; in fact, the two of them appeared to us fathers to be in competition with one another for the attentions of a certain Mifflin Thomas, a student at the University of Pennsylvania in Philadelphia. Studying at a school that was located midway between Washington and Providence, that lad was well positioned to court either girl as the mood suited him. Therefore, to the girls, this dance meant an all-or-nothing competition for that young man's attentions.

I turned to Hastings and raised my glass. "Here's to the whims of youth!"

"Aye, aye!" he responded, and we laughed heartily together.

Privately, we agreed that Thomas, being a 19 or 20 year-old, would most likely come upon some other girl during his summer vacation and would thus give the slip to both our daughters. No matter; let Nature take her course. For our part, Allen Hastings and I got along famously. We were both mariners at heart. Regarding advances in naval design, we had similar interests: he was the navy's new procurement chief, and I had a new ship to show him.

We agreed to meet in Florida in early September. This would provide some five months for the Navy to finish the combat superstructure atop Pod Skimmer #1 and then to take her out for training exercises. Their vessel would make an interesting contrast to No. 2. We would compare the test specs of each Pod Skimmer as they appeared on paper. Fortified with those theoretical statistics, we could then match the navy's completed armed vessel against our more modern passenger cruise ship with on-the-water performance. What with it now being April, this gave each of our organizations a little over four months in which to complete preparations and training of the crews.

When I brought this idea to the Group of Seven, each of them eagerly embraced the challenge. With proper newspaper coverage, this event would provide free advertising, exhibit the duality of our hull design to advantage and, hopefully, arouse the vacationing public to demand a trip aboard a pod skimmer.

There was no question in our minds that we ourselves would crew the P.S. #2. Only Frank Jones would stay ashore in the dockyards within the town of Miami. That way, he could both help launch P.S. #2 and ensure she was shipshape, and he could also serve as our land-based front man for the numerous interviews which we were sure the convening news organizations would want regarding this entirely new approach to ship design. No one knew the performance characteristics of our Pod Skimmers better than The Man.

For his part, Orville would be left ashore back in New York. He still was managing Oceanic Lines, although his successor as president had been named. As far as his company proper was concerned, our adventure remained a mere sidebar to managing ocean liner cruising. What we were doing with P.S. #1 and P.S. #2 was, in fact, on the balance sheet, but no one in lower management knew anything about these craft. Due to health concerns, Orville would be retiring at the end of 1935. We had not yet formally met with the incoming president-elect. As far as we knew, his replacement had not even been brought into our loop by Orville. Basically, development of pod skimmers still remained rather hush-hush.

Getting together with the navy for head-to-head testing would be an unusual event. It wasn't a competition; rather, it was a chance to show off two separate uses for the same hull design. Normally, the military didn't enter any sort of public competition; whether their men won or lost, competing against civilians could result in bad publicity. In our demonstration project, however, the winner would be the American public. John Q. Public would have a faster pleasure-type conveyance, and the military would be provided with the ultimate in pursuit warships.

The choice of demonstrating off the Miami shoreline was a natural: it offered the presence of large crowds, ample media facilities, and typically reliable sailing conditions. Everything was in place. So long as the fall weather held, nothing should let us down.

By August 30, both pod skimmers were docked in the Miami Marina. The navy's brass and our team sat down for an enjoyable supper and, after fortifying ourselves with glasses of the local "coconut punch," as the bootleg gin was referred to, spent that afternoon poring over the statistics and performance tables that each team had established during the training runs in the prior weeks.

On the morning of the 31st, I awoke feeling somewhat uneasy. Naturally, all of us slept on our boat. In theory, there was room for some three hundred passengers and another 50 crewmen, plus kitchen staff as well as a dozen stewards. Our designs would be competitive not on the basis of large caapcity, but on more frequent voyages that cut transit times in half, making scheduled runs more convenient to a larger customer base. All those cabins and facilities, however, were mere mockups at this point, built solely to provide a silhouette similar to the Navy's Pod Skimmer #1.

The one guiding principle that I had learned under the tutelage of Captain James Stahl was: passengers come first, and their safety comes before their comfort. Until we knew everything there was to learn about operating this type of fast craft, we ourselves would be the guinea pigs.

The equipment was operating well. All the parts fit snugly, the lug nuts were tight, the fuel lines were secure, all the electric systems fused and connected. Regardless, something was bothering me: it was like a hard pit in the pit of my stomach that would not dissolve. It gnawed at me without letup. I had this nagging feeling that I'd forgotten something, left something unchecked, or neglected some list. I couldn't get rid of this concern. It dogged me throughout the day, so much so that by the time we had finished the mutual trials, I was irritating to be around. Charles, concerned, politely made inquiries, but I merely brushed him aside.

Just before we went ashore for a tasty, restaurant-cooked meal, Jacob took me aside, asking, "What the hell's up, Wally? You've been sullen all day. The fact that both vessels performed well doesn't seem to have impressed you at all. What's bothering you?"

"For Christ's sake, leave me alone! I don't know what it is. Something is gnawing at my head: there's something I've forgotten to consider, but I don't know what it is, and the uncertainty is driving me loco!"

I was livid, but with myself, not my friend.

With that retort, Charles looked my way. "You're not thinking about Mary, are you? Perhaps, at this time of our greatest triumph, when there are two versions of what we've been working on for so long, you're concerned that your wife is not here to share in the excitement."

I heard his tone; it was solicitous, almost more a statement than a question, but regardless, I didn't have the answer. Something was telling me that things were not right, that some real danger was brewing, but all I could identify was the foreboding, not the actuality. That was the state of mind I was in as I struggled to get to sleep that night beneath the heavily overcast skies. What the hell was nagging at my brain?

The answer was revealed with the dawn.

CHAPTER FORTY-FOUR

AN ANGRY SURPRISE

The answer to my gnawing concern had nothing to do with acquisitive Germans, theft of ideas, not even competition with standard ocean-going vessels. It was the weather.

On September 1st, I awoke with a start. I'd had a morning dream in which a swift, all-consuming darkness was overtaking me, rousing me from deep slumber to that light stage where you sense things outside the portal or down the passage way, yet you are still ensconced between warm sheets with your head safely resting on a clean pillow. Then either some light crossed my eyes, or the craft rocked a bit further than usual, and instantly I was alert. I looked out the porthole of my cabin and then rushed topside. The other five were already there. Each of them was looking—no, gaping open-mouthed—toward the southeastern sky. The breadth, color, and ferocity of the clouds we saw made each of us gulp with fear. We were transfixed. We may have been brave warriors in the Great War, or performed heroic deeds while upon dangerous seas, but all of that bravado paled in comparison to the roiling, tumbling storm that was blotting out the horizon.

These clouds were not merely dark grey; they were ominously black!

We turned to dress and go off to find some place with a radio. Down here in Miami, ships at sea would relay word on conditions as they experienced them to onshore stations. Although no one could ascertain the height of this approaching storm, they could definitely discern that its breadth was narrow and that its speed of progress across a charted course was unusually fast. The radio warned that the center of this burgeoning dragon was due to hit right on top of us the very next day, September 2.

This would be the worst possible scenario. Everyone would be out and about celebrating the holiday: it would be Labor Day Monday. Even the children would be actively at play since it would be the last day of their summer vacation. School would be in session beginning on Tuesday, and by the first full day, Wednesday, every child would become prisoner to a strict, daily regimen. Freedom to fish, build sand castles, or ride a bike would no longer be within a child's discretion. Arithmetic, spelling bees, and English composition would occupy all their time.

These were paltry concerns. From the look of those clouds, simply surviving until Wednesday looked like it would require all of one's courage and willpower.

As a body, the six of us went ashore; it wasn't breakfast we were after, it was news about the gathering danger. We hadn't long to wait. The very first restaurant we entered had the radio on full blast. The announcer was not his usual urbane, cheerful self; this morning, his voice carried urgency with just a hint of terror thrown in. We listened intently. The weather service was predicting the arrival of unusually strong hurricane force winds on Monday with the center, or eye, passing over the Miami area during the evening. All citizens were being urged to leave and seek housing further inland. If a person lived along the shore, the radio said the local police would be evacuating everyone away from the shoreline throughout Sunday.

It was time for us also to leave.

Such a directive applied to a typical visitor, even a resident. However, how could we go? We had a 70 foot wide, 300 foot long contraption to deal with. If we went, which was quickly becoming a foregone conclusion, we wanted to give P.S. #2 as good a chance of weathering the storm as we could. Already, the waters off the east coast were being churned into such frothy, irresponsible waves that the coast guard was directing all ships actually at sea to seek safe harbor immediately. No option was being extended for anyone to wait until tomorrow. Thus, the authorities were completely cutting off escape by boat.

I walked over to chat with the skipper of P.S. #1 moored nearby. Even the navy men, for all their experience, were ashen-faced. Apparently, they had received more detailed reports from their headquarters than the reporter on the radio had provided. Wondering how anything could be more explicit than the broadcast we had just heard, I innocently inquired about the appearance of their faces. Each hardened veteran looked like a British sailor who had just witnessed his flagship being blown to hell by some shell from an enemy so distant it was over the horizon.

"This storm may be the biggest one any of us have ever experienced. It's come up quite suddenly, and it has an unusually narrow diameter. The forces her winds can apply will be all the greater as a result. Residents of Cuba may only experience severe rain, and people living in Savannah may see just a cloudy day, but people in Miami might not live through it. That's how bad our headquarters assesses the threat to be. I've never known them to overstate themselves. We have been ordered to batten down our Pod Skimmer and depart NLT 1800 hours tonight."

The skipper never blinked as he conveyed this warning of doom to me.

I was so stunned, I actually took two steps backward! My buddies and I had landed into the nest of an angry Mother Nature; apparently, she was now more incensed than any living person had ever witnessed. It was possible that neither us, nor our craft, would survive. Only three days ago, the fall weather had been most balmy and enjoyable. I had to go tell the others. As best we could, we needed to secure P.S. #2, and to do so quickly. After ensuring its survival, we then needed to be like Wild West gunslingers and "get the hell out of Dodge!"

The naval skipper had given me one very important piece of information. There were almost 700 veterans working in Florida to help construct a rail line across the numerous keys that penetrated the dividing line between the Caribbean and the Atlantic Oceans. The Overseas Highway was intended to connect the mainland with Key West. However, during the prior months, there had been heated discussions in Washington as to whether these men were being effective. Stout defenses were raised by the veterans on the job, but strong accusations had been made by Harry Hopkins, Director of the Federal Emergency Relief Administration, that they were merely taking doled-out money.

Regardless of the quality of their work, the fact remained that all of them were now quite possibly in the path of the biggest weather event in American history. They had to be gotten to safety, or the public relations fallout would never be lived down by the government in Washington. No one questioned the directive: if it came from Washington, it essentially came from Roosevelt. That man was held in such high regard that no one wanted to question his judgment. A train carrying these former military men to safety would depart Miami at 4:00 PM, or 1600 hours, Monday and, presumably, outrun the fury of the gale. I made some telephone calls, reached Admiral Hastings, and received permission for my team to be included aboard the Florida Overseas Railroad train departing Miami Monday afternoon.

We would be on that train, come hell or high water, so to speak.

CHAPTER FORTY-FIVE

LAST THOUGHT

The train was due to depart Miami at 1600 hours. As part of a functioning railroad that was scheduled to pick up military veterans, it would most likely be on time. Nevertheless, its cars would most likely be filled to the brim with hundreds of people escaping the fury of the approaching high-velocity winds. We had secured our latest Pod Skimmer as best we could—considering that the harbor facilities were designed for small pleasure craft—and we had helped the navy guys secure Pod Skimmer #1. We had eaten, grabbed some fitful sleep, and then found our way to the train station where we were to board.

While waiting its arrival, I looked around the interior of the station. The palpable fear hanging in the air made a lasting impression on me. Each person's face was lined with a terror that was etching deep furrows in their brow. People were clutching small suitcases as though their lives depended on the contents therein. Simply listening to the dull roar of the stupendous rains pelting the roof was enough to send shivers up one's spine. Human beings are absolutely helpless when Mother Nature has her dander up.

Sitting there with the close companions from the most significant period in my life, I glimpsed what it must have been like when Noah famously loaded all the animals two-by-two on his Ark and floated upon the vast flood waters that had been sent so Mankind could, in effect, start over. Regarding our own souls, we felt reasonably pure of heart. We had sacrificed, or rather devoted—since the last few years had been such fun—ourselves to an honorable task. Of course, all our work was intended to eventually make money for Oceanic Lines, but anyone who took a ship across either of the big oceans would benefit from the quicker voyages that pod skimmers would provide. All our sacrifice would be vindicated by the new age of travel Oceanic would soon make possible.

Meantime, we had to do our best to simply survive to see another day. Together, five of us boarded one of the cars attached to the East Florida "Railway Relief Train" as it was being called. Jones, being Jones, had remained behind to keep an eye on where P.S. #2 was battened down. Like an angel on steel wheels, our train was a special, one-time effort to deliver hundreds of men from a gruesome threat. The resilient Charles had never known military life; however, all of the veterans on this train certainly had known the fear of shelling, the disease that accompanies life in water-logged trenches, horrid cold rations, and terror from nighttime assaults. Nevertheless, the fury of the pelting rain and driving winds was something else altogether. As the train pulled away from the city, it was twenty minutes behind schedule, but we were underway. No one complained.

"Better late than never!" was voiced by all of us aboard that rescue train.
As the newspapers would report the following day, that thought would be their last.

Photographed the next day by airplane flyover, this scene of the wrecked cars shows how impossible it would be for anyone to survive the onslaught of the huge cresting storm surging massively engulfing waters over the innocent rescue cars.

Three days were required before rescue teams could access the torn up railroad cars. In this photograph, laying out the five dead team members on September 5 of 1935 is undertaken prior to sending their bodies back home. Jones' body was never recovered from the harbor.

EPILOGUE

As the fully loaded rescue train traveled north, it was slowed by high winds and then caught in a towering storm surge. All nine of the passenger cars were literally washed from the tracks as twenty-foot-high waves catapulted across the rail line embankments.

Shortly after hearing about the great train wreck on the Florida East Coast Railway that killed everyone aboard save the engineer and coal tender, Orville Townsend suffered a brain embolism that left him unable to form rational sentences or write coherently; within a month, he suffered a severe stroke and passed away.

Frank Jones had bravely stayed behind to oversee the security of P.S. #2, but this action had placed him directly in the path of the storm as it swept across Miami. He had died clinging to the ship, which he had so faithfully helped create, as it was twisted upside down, sunk, and then washed into the sea. The Pod Skimmer purchased by the navy was likewise destroyed in the storm and lost beneath the surface. In this manner, all of the men who had devised and then perfected the Pod Skimmer were lost in one sudden twist of fate. Even the ever-lucky and plucky Charles McDonald was killed in the train wreck.

The nation's Military Secrets Act forbade naval officers who had studied, or merely gone aboard, Pod Skimmer #1 from revealing what they knew about its design or operation. None of the wives or family members of the principals understood what their husbands had been pursuing. The project had been so secretive that nothing could be found in the desks or bureaus of the dead men regarding design concepts. My son found a key in my desk but it was unlabeled. I had known what it opened, so I'd never considered the need to tag it. Bill threw it out with my underwear and other unusable items after my death.

For those who pay attention, there may be a life lesson there: let those with whom you are close know your secrets, or at least tell them how to go about unlocking those secrets should you pass away.

None shall long remember what happened here, but it is hoped that people will learn from it, curb their deadly follies, and live. The story, of course, is really never-ending. All of mankind's ingenuity, and his efforts to insure safe voyages, can be defeated in short order by stupidity and arrogance. In Mankind's ongoing quest for all the answers, Mother Nature's capriciousness will continue to catch us humans off guard. So long as Mankind exists, she will think up some new challenging and heretofore unknown danger so she always stays one step ahead.

No one having a key to the safe deposit box containing the drawings and specifications remained alive. However, you are. The marvelous possibilities inherent in this hull design still reside, unclaimed, in some strongbox in Providence, Rhode Island. That is the key word: "unclaimed." Safe deposit boxes are not drilled unless some authoritative body is seeking stolen property or payment of overdue taxes; in the absence of such directive, these strong boxes remain closed, hiding their contents and simply sitting there until someone comes along to claim them.

What happens if rent for the box falls into arrears and some bank clerk opens it only to see strange, indecipherable drawings? He wouldn't understand what the documents depicted, so he would be directed by the bank's management to turn the contents over to some lawyer who would advertise for ownership. No one would come forward to unravel the documents or their mysterious depictions. A unique chance to improve world travel and commerce would thus be frittered away. Do you want to allow this to happen?

Time is short. The Group of Seven's drawings and schematics must be recovered by some lucky person who is capable of unlocking the secrets of the Pod Skimmers yet again.

How is your luck?

APPENDIX

Following is a summation of the theories as to why *Titanic* perished so quickly. If you have been a part of that debate, perhaps this discussion will provide you with confirmation of your own conclusions.

The answer as to what happened to the *Titanic* is obvious: she scraped against an iceberg and filled with seawater beyond the point of buoyancy. This caused her to sink. When the word "why?" is introduced, then suddenly a simple question acquires broad ramifications. Historians and analysts alike have speculated on the range of "what ifs?" that remain part and parcel of this sad tale of arrogance. Please refer to the Bibliography for veritable book-length discussions.

This exposition is segmented into the following sections:
1. Ownership and authority
2. Construction: materials, tools, and design failures
3. Responsibility for, and failure of, command
4. Training of the crew, their experience, and the equipment available
5. Weather and North Atlantic Ocean conditions before and during April, 1912
6. Conduct leading up to the perception of danger
7. Conduct by officers and crew members thereafter
8. The miracle of rescue

---

1. Ownership and authority

Management is the key link in the chain of irresponsible construction. Recall that the White Star Line was a British company, but it was owned by J. Pierpont Morgan, an individual renowned for getting his way, belittling subordinates, and cutting corners to undercut his competition. Next in line was Lord Pirrie who had been an associate of Mr. Ismay's father; however, he was too old when the keel was laid to responsibly manage the construction of this super ship.

J. Bruce Ismay was thus given huge authority without having developed either sufficient common sense or the ability to regulate his domineering ego. Whether by ignorance, inexperience, or devotion to profitability, he would sweep aside well thought-out design parameters conceived by the superbly capable naval architect, Thomas Andrews.

2.   Construction: materials, tools, and design failures

The prime goal of J. Bruce Ismay was to go beyond the footsteps of his father and make the White Star Line a money-making bastion. This meant that lavish appointments aboard *Titanic*, such as wide promenades and French open air cafes, took precedence over safety features such as lifeboats because those took up money-making space. Far more deadly, as things turned out, was his decision to limit the height of the bulkheads.

The *Great Eastern*, built long before in the 1860's, utilized bulkheads that went all the way up into her superstructure. Admittedly, she proved undesirable as a passenger ship. The owners found great utility in her 700-foot bulk and used her to lay the transatlantic cables across to Europe. When she experienced a significant collision while at sea, she survived due to her watertight bulkheads.

Mr. Ismay was ever conscious of how to make his ship appeal to rich customers. That meant building ships that were convenient to move around in. He ordered the *Titanic* to be constructed with hatches in the bulkheads for ease of passage within the ship's innards. Significantly, he disallowed extension of the bulkheads to be high enough to prevent overflow into adjoining compartments. In actuality, as the ship dipped at the head on April 14, this error didn't merely doom her. It virtually hastened her demise by eliminating any sort of "wallow time." Captain Smith compounded this error by withholding the true state of the crisis from the officers assigned to filling the lifeboats (see #7).

An employee at Harland & Wolff, Tom McCluskie, known around the shop as "Sand Dancer," had the responsibility for safekeeping important records at H&W. These records reveal that the shipyard managers had analyzed the recorded observations of survivors, from Officer Lightoller to ordinary civilian passengers, and concluded that there was a high probability that the stern hull of the ship elevated at least 10 degrees out of the water as the bow sections flooded and were pulled beneath the surface. The rear expansion joint was sited abaft the third funnel. The forces generated on this "V" joint, with the stern in the air and the forward 2/3's grasped underwater, was far beyond design parameters, so the hull readily cracked aft of the third funnel. This being a weak point may have been compounded by construction of the enormous opening for the Second Class staircase.

The *Titanic* should never have sailed with a rudder design that was a holdover from the time ships crossed the Atlantic weighing 5,000 tons or less. At some 880 feet, the momentum for the hull to continue in a straight line and resist the pressure on her stern to swing right or left overwhelmed the small size of the rudder and made her sluggish to respond. Employing a breadth of 17 feet at its broadest point, this rudder did comply with regulations of the time. Ironically, those very rules were updated mere weeks prior to Titanic's launch, but her launch slipped beneath their application. Her sluggish steering forced her demise.

Perhaps appearance and smooth lines were the foremost priority for Mr. Ismay, rather than functionality. Looking closely at photographs taken during the design phase and her actual construction, it can be seen that the trailing, lower edge is rounded; the designers thus cut away the single most leveraged point of the rudder. Striving for symmetry in a device submerged and thus out of the public's view was, at best, a waste of design skill and money.

Recall the illustrations in your high school history books. These depicted Christopher Columbus' boats, and Spanish galleons of the period, with the very high quarterdecks, right? You may never have looked at the stern of those illustrations, but they used the rudder design that Titanic copied. She used a kingpost for a rudder that weighed over 100 tons, so its own inertia resisting any course correction, let alone swinging the stern of the ship out to the right or left, would cause a glacially slow response. The *Titanic's* rudder wastefully stuck fully ¼ of its mass above the water, making that portion useful only as a connection point; unfortunately, this also added to the bulk, and therefore the inertia, of the thing. It was as if the builders wanted to actively hold onto the past while resisting modernity.

The result was very sluggish response to signals from the bridge. Worse, its moment of inertia, that is, the length of time for the prow to move in any direction, was slower than any ship then afloat. This is based on the ratio of rudder square footage to her relevant hull length of 800 feet, as well as Helmsman Robert Hitchens' testimony at the hearings that the ship was slow to respond to his steering. Summarizing his testimony, he opined that both the arc of her turn and speed of execution were deplorable. When that iceberg was sighted, a short liner—such as the *New York*, or even the Cunard liner *Mauretania*—could have turned away from the berg far more quickly and decisively.

The lookout Fred Fleet testified at the hearings to the effect that: "She just kept plowing right ahead forward without giving any sign that she was going to move off her course." No one had a better, or more terrifying, view of the prow heading for the iceberg than that man and his assistant Lee. The rudder was woefully undersized, improperly configured, and poorly powered for a ship boasting some 66,000 Displacement Tonnage.

The most damning design was the stupid use of a central screw. This forced the rudder to be mounted with a fulcrum at a forward swivel point. On the Cunard liners, by contrast, the rudder swiveled on an axle post mounted near its center. With the pinion post centered, moving the stern to the right or left would occur faster since water being pushed forward as it turned was balanced by the force of water rushing away on its other side. Moreover, about 90% of a Cunard liner's surface came into play against water coming directly astride its hull without the kind of swirling and interference that *Titanic's* central screw caused.

There is proof from his records that designer Andrews, during test runs on *Olympia*, had been confounded by shaking, or "panting" as he put it, which indicated dangerous movement in the ship's structure when she was at sea. He strengthened the hull and added steel to the superstructure and ribbing in the bilge area, and he created joints aft of the third stack and forward near the bridge to provide some "give" in the superstructure as the ship maneuvered.

Mr. McCluskie revealed that these joints ended sharply, in a sort of "V," on the *Titanic,* but they were changed to a rounded bulb on *Britannic* in order to distribute stress forces more evenly. That unfortunate vessel was lost when a mine exploded against her hull which caused coal dust to explode and, as she started down at the bow, additional water entered through portholes which had been opened for ventilation in the summertime heat. But that's a different tragedy which did not involve errors in construction.

Ismay himself, in his drive for economy in terms of weight and the amount of coal necessary to move tens of thousands of tons when this ship was fully loaded, issued what may have been a fatal order. He required Andrews to downsize the dimensions of the hardware that had been carefully calculated to make the hull seaworthy. The rivets were to be about 15% smaller than the full inch around specified; additionally, the steel hull plates were downsized to one-inch-thick rather than the one-and-a-quarter-inch originally designed by Andrews. Today, rivets are formed from much more durable steel than what was the norm in 1912. Back then, the impurities of slag could lead the rivets to become very brittle in freezing temperatures, eliminating elasticity and limiting durability. Additionally, modern plates are joined using hydraulic pressure that far exceeds hand-pounding rivets. These modern advances have less influence than the fact that Ismay was responsible for making the frame of the *Titanic* far weaker than the specifications Andrews had originally designed into her hull. 15 to 25% smaller parts may seem insignificant when held in one's hand, but when spread over 880 by 60 or so square feet, for both port and starboard, such a diminution becomes daunting.

3.   Responsibility for, and failure of, command

Once the captain of a ship comes aboard, every decision is deferred to his authority. On the night in question, this may not have been the case.

There is the conversation the owner Ismay had with Captain Smith that was overheard by Mrs. Elizabeth Lyons, as noted in the hearings conducted on the matter, where Ismay is alleged to have said his ship will beat the record of the *Olympic* into New York. She stated that Ismay told Captain Smith words to the effect that, "We'll keep her speed up to get through the ice fields as quickly as possible. Nothing bad will happen to us."

At the trial, Mrs. Arthur Ryerson testified that Captain Smith showed her the ice alert telegraphed by the *Baltic*. As the ship continued steaming along, she had remarked that she supposed the captain would be slowing the *Titanic* down, but Ismay had butted in, replying in a manner similar to his response to Liz Lyons. It is highly probable that he strongly influenced Ed Smith to propel the *Titanic* to its demise by ordering too high a speed for such dark conditions into known ice fields.

Regardless of how he reached his decision, the fact is that the captain had ordered the duty officer to steam at full speed, on a moonless night, when the sea was perfectly calm, all of which limited detection of ice. In the absence of wind, of course, there is no froth or phosphorescence at the base of an iceberg, so no one could observe such telltale giveaways.

On the calm night of April 14, 1912, this drove yet another nail into that titanic coffin.

4.   Training of the crew, their experience, and the equipment available

Why did her designers ever add that middle screw in the first place? To keep this ship abreast of the advantage enjoyed by the Cunard liners, of course, since each of their three liners sported four screws. This caused a fatal gap in the ship's survivability in an emergency. When she was taken out for sea trials, only Captain Smith stood in command. He executed rather perfunctory maneuvers which totaled less than a few hours. As the *Titanic* returned to port, neither Murdoch, Lightoller, or indeed any other officer had taken a turn at commanding the bridge, and the helmsman had performed no unusual steering changes. The engine room had not been asked to suddenly alter the rotational direction of their engines. No one had tested the ship's radius of turn: such knowledge is vital when maneuvering around a collision point.

Upon sighting the iceberg, Murdoch should have kept the central screw running while the starboard blade stayed at full speed; then that fool rudder might have had more purchase to turn the bow in a timely manner. After clearing her amidships, a turn to starboard could have been effected to pass by the icy hulk unscathed.

The lack of binoculars in the crow's nest was not a cause. It has been discovered that the decision to replace 2nd Officer David Blair at the last moment caused all five pairs to be locked in his cabin; when Lightoller came aboard and occupied that cabin, he didn't explore its closets and thus never found the vision aids stored there.

Their unavailability matters little. They are used to identify detail once the human eye has spotted a questionable object; they are of little use to initially spot an iceberg at night, because their limited field of view prevents the perception of gradations of shadow. Human vision at night is deplorable compared to cats and zebras. Best results for sailors are obtained using peripheral vision, rather than looking directly at an object. Binoculars, of course, limit our doing so. The best move would have been to issue the men in the crow's nest plain goggles, without refraction, to prevent their eyes watering in what must have been excruciatingly painful wind chill as the ship plowed forward.

Smith knew the manufacturer of the davits had tested them beyond their rated capacity, yet he never informed his officers of the fact. Sadly, Lightoller testified that he feared loading the lifeboats to capacity, believing doing so would place too great a strain on those strong davits. Moreover, it was the feeling among the officers that the ship was virtually unsinkable; they were not discouraged in believing this falsehood. Captain Smith conducted no passenger drills regarding lifeboat use, and executed only limited training of his crew by practicing unloading and then rowing a lifeboat about while the huge ship was docked!

5.   Weather and North Atlantic Ocean conditions before and during April, 1912

Climatic conditions for the prior year had been unusually warm, resulting in summertime calving from the giant Petterman glacier on Greenland to be more active than usual. The large melt rate allowed the currents to be stronger, thereby pushing ice farther south in mid-April than was typical.

We can only speculate why Captain Smith ordered the Titanic to "turn the corner" below latitude 42 degrees north with only a half hour delay from the usual. This order put his ship a mere 4 miles further south of the Great Circle Route, rather than a safer 20 miles. In his multi-decade tenure at sea, he knew that some 7 ships had struck icebergs in the prior twenty years.[6] Most likely, he acted on the opinion that ice

---

6 These include: *Naronic*(1892); *State of Georgia* (1896); *Allegheny* (1899); *Huronian* (1902); *Lake Champlain* and *Kronprinz Wilhelm* (1907); *Columbia* (1911).

generally melted by that latitude. However, on the 14th, he personally read at least 2 of the 6 ice warnings relayed to his ship. He failed to allow for iceberg drift between receipt of the ice messages and the arrival of *Titanic* on scene. No doubt his ghost is still being lashed down in Hell for his failure to do so.

6.   Conduct leading up to the perception of danger

Named as Captain of this lavishly constructed palace, this trip was Smith's ultimate reward. He would not hesitate to follow custom and charge at full speed through ice fields.

Clearly, his reputation mattered greatly to him. An acquaintance of his, Captain J. C. Barr aboard the *Caronia,* was laughed at derisively by his contemporaries for being sure-footed and slow in the presence of even just fog. Captain Smith's pride would never allow him to be embarrassed like that.

Smith has been described in the newspapers as being arrogantly innocent, but I do not ascribe to that view. Edward J. Smith had come up through the ranks, experienced various assignments, and knew the North Atlantic as well as any man in the industry. Of course, there were major problems with the radio room getting ice warnings to him; a simple speaking tube or telephone could have solved that handicap. On that trip, however, it wouldn't have mattered if fifty warnings had been sent to and posted in the pilot house. Smith was determined to charge ahead and disregard all warning signs. He acted with arrogant indifference to danger, as though his sagacity and good luck insulated him from obvious obstacles. This led to a dangerous overconfidence.

Everyone on board who gave testimony at the formal hearings claimed that the contact with the iceberg was, at most, a glancing blow, more like sliding along some protuberance, but not at all a head-on or smashing kind of collision. Perhaps the ice was powerful enough to cause gashing, but such damage is doubtful. The men working on the tank top and Orlop decks—who experienced the initial flooding into the engine compartments—were unanimous in stating that the water poured in at very high pressure, knocking them off their feet in many cases, and came in streams equivalent to that made by fire hoses.

It is doubtful that the edges of the submerged portion of the iceberg were strong enough to pierce the hull plates like a match burns a hole in paper, curling its edges. Rather, since it was perhaps ten or more times the weight of the vessel, the berg simply remained unmoved and **pressed against the ship with ever increasing force** as the hull widened from the prow to amidships. This irresistible squeezing caused the plates to give and buckle out of alignment, with the consequent popping, or perhaps even shearing, of rivets binding the plates together.

Remember the bunker fire near Boiler Room 5 that occurred as the ship departed Ireland? If the outer hull plates had bulged, or become more brittle, as a result of the sustained heat, an entire plate might have split along one of its riveted edges as the berg increasingly pressed against the hull. Water was allowed to enter through multiple openings. Read the British transcripts of the hearing chaired by Lord Mersey. Edward Wilding—Harland & Wolff's Senior Naval architect—confirmed this analysis. Compare your sieve at home used for straining macaroni. A number of small openings can cumulatively produce a devastatingly large rate of flow. This is particularly apropos to *Titanic* because we know from eyewitness testimony that the water entered five holds, possibly even a sixth, all at once. The overall rate overwhelmed the pumps allocated to manage the flow because that equipment had not been designed with sluice valves to work in unison.

The White Star Line proudly proclaimed the *Titanic* to be the ultimate in luxury and safety. They refrained from touting speed in their promotional material and, presumably, were never going to try to equal the Atlantic crossing record. Who wants to pay the equivalent of $10,000 or more for ocean passage and then rush through the plush, regal-like experience? This attribute for a comfortably luxurious crossing seemed to be forgotten as the ship neared the East Coast; Ismay became ever more gripped by the "need to feel more speed!"

If the captain had ordered a lower speed, just to be cautious, they never would have hit at all. All these 'ifs' belie the fact that *Titanic* was sailing through an enormous ice field. The ice that night extended north to south for some 78 miles. It's a wonder the ship didn't collide with something far earlier; of course, if she had, the telegrapher on *Californian* would have heard her transmission and perhaps the outcome would have been different. There was no reason to speed through the ice infested waters of the North Atlantic other than "that was the way everybody did it" back then.

7. Conduct by officers and crew members thereafter

This topic is the one that makes every analyst, whether amateur or professional, squirm in his seat from discomfort.

Captain Smith was highly experienced, yet he seems to have frozen mentally as the extent of the calamity engulfed his clarity of thinking. After he and the designer had determined the number of holds that were flooding would give the ship around 90 or so minutes to remain afloat, he never conveyed this information to his crew. He simply drifted away to contemplate this stupendous failure that would forever besmirch his exemplary record. He ignored his role as commander of a sinking ship.

The men in charge of loading lifeboats thus operated under an enormous handicap: they did not know that their ship was doomed, and so they undertook their assignments without knowing that they must (1) fully load all lifeboats; (2) do so with all possible dispatch. Consequently, the pace was so slow that the decks became awash before the last two collapsible boats could be properly readied. The equipment to assist doing so was already submerged in the forward area. Quite possibly, some 200 additional passengers died due to the captain's lack of forceful, timely direction.

The very first action he should have taken was to direct the Marconi men to send a stand-by warning order indicating that his ship might need help even **before** he went to check on the damage. If there was nothing amiss, he could countermand the message with a stand-down order. If there was a problem, he could have the radiomen confirm the message and call for help. He would have thereby at least alerted the *Californian,* and possibly additional ships, prior to their operators retiring for the night.

Of course, that is how a string of apparently insignificant factors can lead to catastrophic loss of life, even nowadays.

Arguments have been put forth that the captain should have thought to open all the watertight entries to let the hull flood evenly. She then would have settled with the superstructure still dry, retaining sufficient buoyancy to last another two hours rather than tipping, breaking apart, and then rapidly disappearing down by the head. Think how many more people could have survived if *Carpathia*, and even *Californian*, had been able to quickly pluck them from the chilled waters!

Actually, there is little credence to this scenario. The Titanic started down at the head within a mere twenty minutes of her brush with the iceberg. The pressure from the sea inflow was far too great to regulate the flow evenly throughout the bulkheads. It didn't matter whether, or when, all the bulkhead hatches were opened. As she started down at the head, the vessel became committed to being angled as the fore decks flooded. Her rate of angled sinking would only accelerate as the minutes ticked by.

8. The miracle of rescue

The chance for the *Californian* to help was largely negated when its radioman, Cyril Evans, went to bed without turning on his emergency bell. He was young, with only half a year on the job; he simply didn't know enough to think. That situation was, of course, compounded by the stupidity of Captain Lord. Instead of staying in bed and merely asking his first officer for reports, all he had to do was wake the telegrapher for a simple check-in with the ship in question. In this way, the entire fiasco might have had a better ending. He was complacent because he had safely stopped his ship; someone else's suffering would be their problem, not his.

A stroke of luck that horribly tragic night came in the form of the *Carpathia*, a smaller one-stack ship cruising some 58 miles to the south. She had a young Morse code telegrapher, Thomas Cottam, aboard. Just that afternoon, he had shooed his steward, a Mr. Vaughn, away. He didn't want his cabin cleaned; rather, he wanted to take a nap because he wanted to stay up late and catch radio transmissions regarding the coal-strike fervor that was gripping Great Britain. Thus, he had remained awake later than usual. Shortly before midnight, after hearing all the news, he was preparing for bed but, like men in his profession, couldn't resist getting the last tidbit that might come over the wires. Besides, he had sent a message to the *Parisian* which had not yet been answered. Even as he was removing his shoes, he still had his earphones on; thus, he heard Phillips' plaintive signal cry out from the inky black darkness.

The *Carpathia* reached the scene in a hitherto impossible 17 ½ knots by converting all of the ship's functions to the generation of power for the screws. She dodged half a dozen icebergs herself along the way. If it hadn't been for her captain's prompt response, sparked by the chance eavesdropping by the telegrapher, survivors aboard the lifeboats would have begun dying from the cold. Regardless of whether they had left the stricken *Titanic* in a dry condition, a person exposed to wind does not last long when the ambient air is below freezing.

Slightly less than one-third of those aboard were picked up by the *Carpathia* and thus lived to tell a tale that was all too dreadful.

WITH GRATITUDE

Please refer to the Bibliography. Those authors are well informed, inquisitive, and rational. I owe them all my sincere thanks. This novel has been inspired by the solid foundation of their thorough research regarding the demise of *H.M.S. Titanic*. Many of their conclusions regarding this controversial event have finally been accepted as factual. Nevertheless, Man's continuing contempt for the power of Nature led to my need to write *Ride the Sea*.

Closer to home, my ever steadfast friend, David Linton Watters, urged me to not merely undertake, but also to complete the writing of a book while I recovered from post-operative paralysis. I came up with this historical novel. Much like my prior work, *Europe in Low*, I seem to thrive when immersed in the past.

One of my proofreaders, a former college professor of English, remarked that he was impressed by the paucity of grammar and spelling errors. This was a great compliment because that man watches television while working his internet connections, conversing with friends on the phone, stroking one or both of his dogs, and coping with an active granddaughter. Such is his habit even without my book on his lap! He is a multi-tasker if ever there was one, so I am fortunate that Robert Harrison found the time to help.

Three former naval personnel set my nautical terms straight. Many thanks go to Ken Carpenter and Don Bowen of Franklin's American Legion Post, and Robert Ramage, an officer retired from the United States Marine Corps and now combating hurricanes on Long Island.

A quick way to lose a longtime close friend is to ask her to proofread a book. I am fortunate that Vassar alumna Elise Stokes Meade not only did so, but also suggested valuable organizational improvements. By the way, she is still on speaking terms with me.

You would not be reading this were it not for local friends Tana and Tony Begnaud. They undertook the analysis of my first draft, and their comments turned the story from a ponderous, boring lecture to the vibrantly surprise adventure you have just finished.

Architect Bobby Johns helped me conceptualize the Pod Skimmer into rough form, and then Terri Manoogian, an instructor at Rabun Gap Nacoochee School, Clayton, Georgia, brought this craft to life through AutoCAD so we could all marvel at its sleek design. She can be contacted at terrimanoogian@gmail.com.

If you read *Ride the Sea*, you noted the book's Dedication at the very front. We all have friends: some new, some long-loved, even a few who get on our nerves, but it is rare when a person maintains a camaraderie that furnishes laughter, comfort, and support over the course of decades. Judith Smith, and her husband Tony, are two Philadelphians who make each day worth living simply because our friendship endures.

One last thought, and that is: The purpose of living is the acquisition of memories for, in the end, these are all that we can take with us. I hope *Ride the Sea* has provided good ones.

Thanks for sailing with me!

Samantha Narelle Kirkland

BIBLIOGRAPHY

Adams, Simon. *Titanic*. London: DK Publishing, 2009.

Ballard, Dr. Robert D. *Discovery of the Titanic*. New York: Warner Books, 1987.

_____. *Exploring the Titanic*. New York: Scholastic Press, Inc., 1988.

_____ with Archbold, Rick. *Discovery of the Bismarck*. N.Y.: Warner Books, Inc., 1990.

_____ and Marschall, Kenneth. *Ghost Liners*. Boston, MA: Little Brown & Co., 1998.

Burgin, Michael. *Titanic: Truth and Rumors*. Mankato, MN: Capstone Press, Inc., 1990.

Butler, Dan Allen. *Unsinkable: The Full Story*. Mechanicsburg, PA: Stackpole Books, 1998.

Davenport-Hines, Richard. *Voyagers of the Titanic*. New York: Wm. Morrow, 2012.

Gill, Anton. *Titanic*. Guilford, CN: Lyons Press, 2010.

Green, Rod. *Building the Titanic*. Pleasantville, NY: Reader's Digest, 2005.

Hoskinson, Deborah. *Titanic: Voices from the Disaster*. New York: Scholastic Press, Inc., 2014.

Lord, Walter. A Night to Remember. New York: Holt, Rinehart & Winston, 1955.

N.B.: following *Lassie, Old Yeller*, and *Treasure Island*, this was one of the first books I ever read. Perhaps *Ride the Sea* is my catharsis for carrying around Mr. Lord's vivid tales in my head for six decades.

_____. *The Night Lives On*. New York: Avon Books, 1986.

Lynch, Don. *The Titanic: An Illustrated History*. New York: Hyperion Press, 1992.

_____. Ghosts of the Abyss. Cambridge, MA: Da Capo Press, 2003.

Marschall, Kenneth. *Ken Marschall's Art of the Titanic*. New York: Hyperion Press, 1998.

Matsen, Brad. *Titanic's Last Secrets*. New York: Twelve, 2008.

Maxtone-Graham, John. *Titanic Tragedy*. New York: W. W. Norton & Co., 2011.

Noon, Steve. *The Story of the Titanic*. New York: DK Publishing, 2012.

Price, Sharon S. *Passengers of the Titanic*. Mankato, MN: Capstone Press, 2015.

_____. *Guide to the Kids' Titanic*. Mankato, MN: Capstone Press, 2012.

Ritchie, Dave. *Shipwrecks*. New York: Facts on File, 1996.

Robertson, Morgan. *Futility, or The Wreck of the Titan, 1898*. MN: Filiquarian Publishing, LLC, 2006.

Spignesi, Stephen. The Complete Titanic. Secaucus, NJ: Carol Publishing Group, 1998.

Wells, Susan. *Titanic: Legacy of the World's Greatest Ocean Liners*. New York: Time-Life Books, 1997.

Government Documents containing testimony & statements:

Great Britain, "Parliamentary Debates" (Commons), 5th Series, April 15-Oct. 25, 1912.

U.S. Congress, Senate, "Report of the Senate Committee of Commerce pursuant to S. Res. 283," 62nd Congress, 2nd Session, May 28, 1912, S. Rpt. 806 (#6127).

U.S. Congress, Senate, "Hearings of a Subcommittee of the Senate Commerce Committee pursuant to S. Res. 283, to Investigate the Causes leading to the Wreck of the White Star Line *Titanic*," 62nd Congress, 2nd Session, June 1912, S. Doc. 726 (#6767).

Printed in the United States
By Bookmasters